Huddersfield Drill Hall War Memorial 1914 to 1921

5th Battalion The Duke of Wellington's (West Riding Regiment)

Huddersfield Drill Hall War Memorial 1914 to 1921

5th Battalion The Duke of Wellington's (West Riding Regiment)

compiled by
Scott Flaving and Michael Green

A
VALENCE HOUSE
Publication

First published in Great Britain in 2020
By Valence House Publications
Valence House, Becontree Avenue,
Dagenham, Essex RM8 3HT

www.valencehousecollections.co.uk

The text has been compiled by the authors as an educational, non-profit making publication to inform relatives and researchers of the 'Dukes' soldiers commemorated on the 5th DWR War Memorial in Huddersfield Drill Hall.

Images courtesy of the Trustees of the DWR Museum and Archive, unless otherwise annotated.

Maps © Richard Harvey, DWR Volunteer Archivist.

The publisher is not responsible for the accuracy or continued existence of any websites referenced.

ISBN - 978-1-911391-98-2

All proceeds will be shared between Valence House Volunteers and the Huddersfield Drill Hall and Trust, Charity Number 224671.

Cover Image: Central panel of the 5 DWR War Memorial Boards, 2018.

Back cover image: Essex Farm Cemetery, 1924 and 2019.

5 DWR Synopsis: Extracted from the Huddersfield Examiner, 1919, with kind permission of the Huddersfield Examiner, 2018.

All rights reserved. No part of this publication may be reproduced, stored in a retrieval system, or transmitted, in any form or by any means, electronic, mechanical, photocopying, recording or otherwise, without the prior permission of the copyright owner.

VALENCE HOUSE
a place of discovery

CONTENTS

List of Plates, Illustrations and Maps.	3
Foreword	6
Dedication	7
Introduction	8
Glossary	12
Order of Battle – 49th Division and 62nd Division	14
Roll of Honour	22
Addenda	217
Synopsis of the service of the 5th DWR Battalions in WW1	222
Battles and Campaigns	237
Weapons	243
Heritage and Legacy	244
Acknowledgements	245
Bibliography	246
The Statistics	248

LIST OF PLATES, ILLUSTRATIONS AND MAPS

PLATES:

Front Cover:

Image and design – Richard Harvey, 2019.

Back Cover:

Essex Farm and 49th Division War Memorial – Associated Press, 1924.

Essex Farm and 49th Division War Memorial – Aurel Sercu, 2019.

Other Plates:

J H Lobley painting – by kind permission of Kirklees Art Gallery and Library Service. Displayed in the Drill Hall (Image supplied by Andrew Best and enhanced by Richard Harvey).

War Memorial Board section dividers – Richard Harvey, 2018.

Drill Hall Interior and Farnley Tyas War Memorial – Scott Flaving.

All other images – courtesy of the Trustees of the Museum and Archives of The Duke of Wellington's Regiment or the authors.

MAPS:

Bullecourt, Somme and Ypres sketch maps © Richard Harvey (2018-2019).
Nieuport – extract from Capt P G Bales History.
Bligny – extract from the *Official History of the War*, Capt W Miles (1938) (crown copyright).

1/5th DWR on the front line, Ypres Sector, December, 1915
painting by J H Lobley, 1924

The Drill Hall War Memorial prior to refurbishment, Mr D Alexander providing the scale.

FOREWORD

As Chairman of the Huddersfield Drill Hall Trustees, it is an honour and pleasure to have been asked to write the foreword for this book which adds detail to those named on the 5th DWR War Memorial Boards, which form the front to the south balcony within Huddersfield Drill Hall. Following a decision made at a Trustees' meeting in 2017, work was undertaken to refurbish the 5th DWR honours boards which, after almost 100 years, were looking rather shabby. The refurbished boards now look superb, having had new gold leaf applied, and were unveiled by General Sir Evelyn Webb-Carter KCGO (the last Colonel of the Regiment of The Duke of Wellington's Regiment, before their amalgamation into the Yorkshire Regiment in 2006), on Sunday the 4th November, 2018. This was planned to coincide with the nationwide commemoration of the centenary of the end of the Great War, on 11th November, without clashing with the significant civic ceremonies also taking place during this period.

The refurbished boards are now in pristine condition and all of the 1241 names can now be easily read from the floor of the main hall.

The research undertaken by Mr Flaving and his fellow Archives Volunteer, Mr Green, to compile information about each soldier named on the boards is quite outstanding and represents many hours of hard work over a number of years.

It is interesting to note that, following their research, a small number of names on the boards cannot be traced as DWR soldiers or are not officially listed as having died; whilst some who should be included have, for some reason, been missed. Why these anomalies occurred we do not know and probably never will. The Trustees plan to have another honours board created so that those who were omitted from the original boards can be included in the memorial.

I can wholeheartedly recommend this book to anyone with an interest in the 5th DWR, the Drill Hall in Huddersfield or a more general interest in the Great War and the ultimate price paid by so many local people a century ago.

Major (Ret'd) Stephen Armitage
Chairman of the Drill Hall Trustees
June 2019.

DEDICATION

This book is dedicated to the men recorded on this memorial who suffered so much,
and their families, who grieved so much,
during and after the Great War

May they be ever remembered by future generations

LEST WE FORGET

INTRODUCTION

5th Battalion The Duke of Wellington's (West Riding) Regiment
World War One War Memorial
Huddersfield Drill Hall

The origins of this book.

This book came about as the result of a chance meeting between two of the Trustees of the Huddersfield Drill Hall who had arranged, by coincidence, to host relatives of two of the men listed on the War Memorial Boards and arrange to meet them, at about the same time on the same day, in order to view the Memorial. During this meeting, both Trustees were struck by how badly 'weathered' the lettering had become in places and wondered whether something could be done about this. At the next Trustees' Meeting, those present inspected the War Memorial and agreed to examine the possibility of refurbishing the Boards in some way. Again, by coincidence, a potential source of expertise was discovered during a talk between one of the Trustees and an ex soldier, who knew someone who had worked in the Regimental Pioneers, back in the day. This ex Pioneer was invited to come and examine the scope of the project and asked to supply a quotation. To demonstrate due diligence, the Trustees requested two further quotations from local firms. Not only was the original quotation the best with regard to options and costs, Mr Shipley's empathy with the task of commemorating fellow service personnel was obvious and, once started, his small team fitted in well with the military surroundings and got on extremely well with the Drill Hall staff.

Whilst this work was underway, it was noted that very little was known about those who were commemorated, as only their names and initials had been carved into the panels. At that stage it was not even known exactly how many men were commemorated there. As a result, a small team was set up to start researching each name to discover who they were, and, where possible, what happened to them.

The origins of the War Memorial.

During the First World War, many ideas for locally commemorating those who had fallen were discussed and memorials were even erected in many churches; local firms, working men's clubs and local communities also created their own memorials and rolls of honour. The various local communities in and around Huddersfield also designed and built their own War Memorials and Cenotaphs, in a wave of national commemoration in the months and years following the Armistice. Much of this was described in the pages of the Huddersfield Examiner between 1919 and 1921, and no less than ninety five articles were published between these dates, from the Milnsbridge Library Memorial proposal (9th Jan 1919) to the Oddfellows Memorial in Holmfirth (13th December, 1921).

In September, 1920, the second leaflet of the newly formed 5th Duke of Wellington's Regiment Officers' Dinner Club was published by the first Hon Sec of the Club, Captain Keith Sykes, who had been the Adjutant of the 1/5th and 5th Battalions during the war. In it was the following notice, "It has been decided to erect a War Memorial in the Drill Hall, Huddersfield, containing the names of the Fallen who died whilst serving with the Battalion. Captain Joseph Walker OBE [*brother of the former Commanding Officer, Lieutenant Colonel James Walker DSO*], is the Secretary of the Committee and Captain T Goodall DSO MC, the Treasurer. The Committee will be issuing circulars in due course".

The War Memorial was designed in 1922 and unveiled and dedicated on 30th August, 1924.

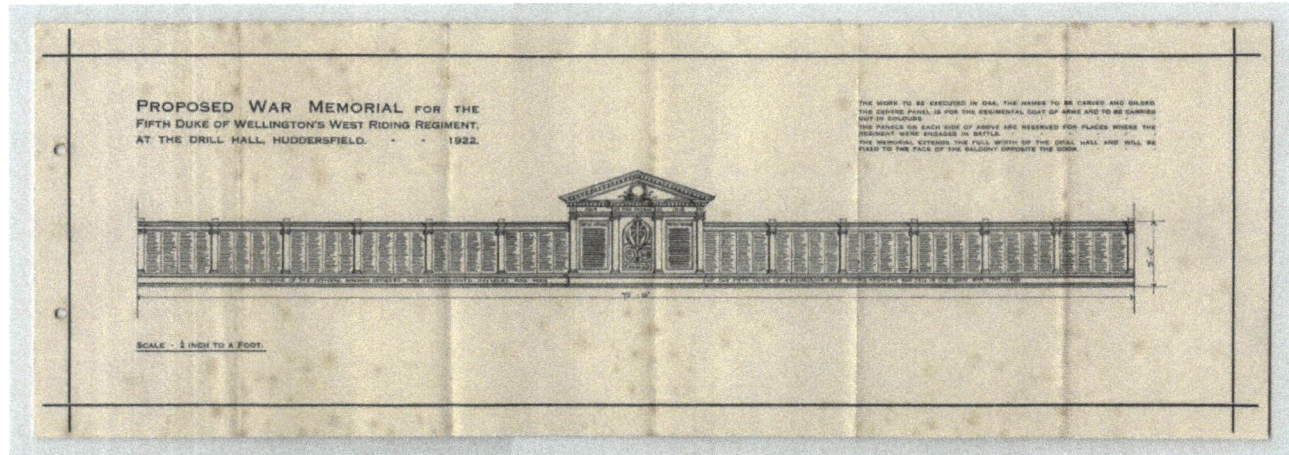

Original diagram of the Drill Hall War Memorial proposal, 1922.

The text on the upper right reads:

The work to be executed in oak, the names to be carved and gilded.
The centre panel is for the Regimental coat of arms and to be carried out in colours.
The panels on each side of above are reserved for places where the Regiment were engaged in battle.
The memorial extends the full width of the Drill Hall and will be fixed to the face of the balcony opposite the door.

The Memorial consists of twelve boards, each of four panels, the first panel contains 98 names, panels 2 to 11 contain 104 names and panel 12 contains 103 names, a total of 1,241 names.

Underneath the boards is inscribed:
IN HONOUR OF THE OFFICERS, WARRANT OFFICERS, NON-COMMISSIONED OFFICERS & MEN OF THE 5th BATT DUKE OF WELLINGTON'S REGIMENT (WEST RIDING)

You will note that the (West Riding) in brackets differs from the title of the book. This is because in January, 1921, the end portion of the Regimental title was changed from ...(West Riding Regiment) to ...Regiment (West Riding).

A note on sources:

Apart from the incredibly detailed and well researched book left to us by the late Margaret Stansfield, we are also indebted to the late Major Tom Goodall for his detailed records concerning D Company of the 2/5th Battalion, from which a great many of the original Regimental Numbers, issued to the men on enlistment, were obtained. These numbers were superseded after the Territorial Force renumbering in April, 1917. Prior to these records being made available, there was only a single Battalion Routine Order, from the 1/6th DWR, which has survived to show how the system of exchanging the old numbers for new ones was achieved. Having both numbers makes researching a little easier, although it is not always helped by the fact that some soldiers killed before 1917 were recorded by the Commonwealth War Graves Commission (CWGC), and often Soldiers Died in the Great War (SDGW), using their new, post-April 1917, numbers. Conversely, some soldiers who were killed in late 1917 and 1918 were buried, or commemorated on memorials, showing the old four and five figure numbers.

For a comprehensive list of other sources, please see the bibliography.

Layout

The layout of each entry follows as closely as possible to the following sequence:

1. Names are listed alphabetically, for ease of reference, although they are not in strict alphabetical order on the War Memorial boards, indeed, Private Doughty appears at the foot of the last panel, for example. Some of the names are incorrectly spelt and corrections or other versions of the spelling are included in parenthesis. Some of the common problems are Hinchcliffe/Hinchliffe; Andsell/Ansdell, Brook/Brooke, Cook/Cooke, etc. Often the sources are at variance, where this cannot be rectified from further research, through census returns, etc, the CWGC version has been taken as the most likely correct version. Some of those named cannot be verified as having been killed during the war, or immediately afterwards, and have left no trace as to why they are included. One identity proved to be quite puzzling, until it was discovered that he had served, briefly, in the Regiment before being discharged for medical reasons. He was, however, listed in Margaret Stansfield's book as having died later, whilst serving in the Royal Navy. In all, some forty two men cannot be traced satisfactorily but we have shown a feasible connection wherever possible, although, in some cases, it would appear that these names may merely be duplications.

2. Numbers. Regimental numbers were originally issued by each battalion of a Regiment, but this proved to be unwieldy during the early part of the war when men were posted between battalions and Regiments. In the short term the Battalion number was used as a prefix, i.e. 3/1234 but this was not effective in the cases of cross Regimental postings. As a result, in April 1917, the Territorial Forces were issued with new six figure numbers, blocks of numbers being allocated to each Battalion of a Regiment. Where known, we have listed both the old four and five figure numbers, as well as the later six figure numbers. Officers were not issued with numbers until after the war.

3. Ranks are abbreviated in the supplementary information sections.

4. Place of birth (family, if known), residence and enlistment; date of embarkation.

5. Battalion, Company (if known); fate of soldier; date(s) of wounding (where known); death; age (where known) and the Battle or Sector in which he fell, where appropriate.
(Please note that the format of the dates is the result of a number of earlier automatic computer updates, which changed the usual date formats from 1901 to 2001, etc, on more than one occasion. This led to the addition of 100 years to all the Boer War dates, for example, on the Regimental Master Index at least twice over a period of two or three years. Many months were spent amending thousands of dates to a format not recognised by the computer during subsequent updates. This has worked so far and so has been adopted).

6. **Burial**, where applicable. A large proportion of them have no known grave. Some of them are undoubtedly buried in unmarked graves – 'known unto God' – and it will be of comfort to relatives to know that work on identifying these men is still ongoing. Two 'Dukes' soldiers buried in unmarked graves in Talana Farm Cemetery, Belgium, have been tentatively identified by a local historian, who is currently working on submitting his findings to the CWGC so that these men can be positively identified and new, named, headstones procured. However, this is a far from simple procedure. There are some images of the headstones in the Archives collection. We have not included them in this book as the quality varies and it is now possible to order high quality images through the Commonwealth War Graves Commission website – cwgc.org.uk.

7. **Commemorations**: we have included as many as can be traced. A large number of national and local War Memorials are yet to be fully transcribed and the names of 'Dukes' can be added to a growing database, which the Regimental Archives Team has been working on for many years. For example, identifying the names and initials of the Mirfield War Memorial is a very large project, yet

to be tackled as far as can be ascertained. It was, however, possible to run a comparison of the 1,241 names on the Drill Hall War Memorial Boards against the 255 names on the Mirfield War Memorial, which yielded 33 names which could then be researched and attributed. Mrs Stanfield's book was instrumental in providing a great number of the local Huddersfield Memorials and Rolls of Honour, where the men are also commemorated. The final commemoration for each entry, also in bold, shows the relevant panel and column on the Drill Hall Memorial in order to aid finding the names, especially those not listed in strict alphabetical order.

8. Details of mentions in other publications are listed, especially the Goodall collection and the Huddersfield Examiner, as well as the Unit War Diaries and a wealth of locally produced publications that we have had access to (please see the bibliography for details of these).

9. The original DWR battalions (i.e. 1/5th and 2/5th Battalions, pre 1918) and former Regiments, where men had been posted into the 'Dukes' from elsewhere, either by commissioning or, more commonly, whilst in transit through the Infantry Base Depots on the French coast, are included to aid research. In particular this is of interest for the period prior to January, 1918, when the original units of the 1/5th (49th Division) and 2/5th (62nd Division) were merged into the 5th Battalion (in 62nd Division).

10. Finally, we have included epitaphs which were submitted by families in the 1920s to be carved at the base of the CWGC headstones. Families were invited to send in their messages to be carved into the Portland stone, at a cost of 3½d per letter.

Example of a full entry:

WALKER Adolphus – 2nd Lieutenant.
Son of Thomas, of Wakefield, possibly resided in Leeds; his next of kin, sister, lived in Rothwell Haigh, Leeds. Embarked for France and Flanders on 21 5 1916. Commissioned into 2/5th DWR in August, 1917.
5th Battalion DWR; killed in action 15 4 1918, German Spring Offensive.
Buried – Gezaincourt Communal Cemetery, 2, L, 20.
Commemorated – Arras Memorial, France; C D Bruce RoH, page 215, and the **Drill Hall WM panel 11, column 4.**
Mentioned in 62nd Division History (wounded) page 198; Unit War Diary (to hospital 14 2 1918 to 22 2 1918) on 28 2 1918; (wounded in action 09 4 1918, died of wounds 15 4 1918) on 30 4 1918. Formerly 15/1818 Sergeant West Yorkshire Regiment (1st Leeds Pals). Originally 2/5th DWR.
IN MEMORY OF OUR DEARLY DEVOTED BROTHER, LOVED BY ALL. WAR'S BITTER COST.

Legacy

It is hoped that this book will help the relatives of those men who are commemorated on the Drill Hall War Memorial to find out more about their forebears who sacrificed their lives for King and Country. It is also intended to reassure readers that these men, and others, from the Regiment are not forgotten by their comrades who have followed them into the ranks of the Duke of Wellington's Regiment, as well as the friends and supporters working to sustain the history and heritage of the Regiment into the future.

GLOSSARY

Common Military terms used:

Cenotaph	Stone monument erected in a local community to commemorate the men from that community who fell in war and whose remains are elsewhere.
DWR	The Duke of Wellington's Regiment. The Regiment was raised as Huntingdon's Regiment in 1702 and numbered 33rd from 1751. Named The Duke of Wellington's Regiment (DWR) on 18th June, 1853. Amalgamated with 76th Regiment in 1881, forming the 1st and 2nd Battalions of the Regiment. Was known as the West Riding Regiment (W Rid R) in the Boer War and Great War. Its soldiers have been proud to bear the nickname 'Dukes' for many years.
First Line	The original Territorial Force battalions, renamed $1/5^{th}$, etc, on the raising of the second line units in August, 1914.
Formation	A grouping of a number of units, a number of Brigades or a number of Divisions.
Great War	The common name for the conflict until WW2. Later WW1, possibly from September 1939, although it had been referred to as a World War towards the end of the conflict.
Ranks	Private (Pte), Lance Corporal (LCpl), Corporal (Cpl), Lance Sergeant (LSgt), Sergeant/Serjeant (Sgt), Company/Regimental Quarter Master Sergeant (CQMS/RQMS), Company/Regimental Sergeant Major (CSM/RSM), 2nd Lieutenant (2Lt), Lieutenant (Lt), Captain (Capt), Major (Maj), Lieutenant Colonel (Lt Col), Brigadier General (Brig Gen), Major General (Maj Gen).
Regiment	Originally raised as a single battalion size unit named after the Colonels who had been commissioned to raise them. From 1751 the regiments were numbered in order of precedence in the Army List; DWR was numbered 33rd. From 1881, as part of the amalgamations of the Cardwell Reforms, Regiments were grouped in two regular battalions, one for home service, and one for overseas service, usually with a Militia Battalion. In 1883, the Volunteer Battalions were formally linked to their local Recruiting District regular units. In 1908 the Volunteers were reorganised into the Territorial Force. In August, 1914, Regiments were ordered to double the number of their Territorial Force battalions as well as raise further Service (Kitchener) battalions. DWR raised 23 battalions during the war, 2 Regular, 1 Militia, 12 TF, 7 Service, 1 Young Soldiers.
Roll of Honour	A list of men who fell, who served, or a combination of these, usually on scrolls, in books or on plaques.
Second Line	The newly raised Territorial Force battalions, named $2/5^{th}$, etc, on the splitting of the first line units in August, 1914, in order to double their strength.
Third Line	The second line battalions were originally used to train and send drafts to the first line units. In 1915 they were ordered to raise third line training battalions to continue this function, in order to carry out collective training for operations. The $3/5^{th}$ Battalion was initially posted to Clipstone Camp, moving to Rugeley in October, 1916.

Unit	A battalion size grouping, approx 1,000 men in the Infantry.
War Memorial	Normally a stone structure, usually carved or bearing a plaque, with the names of the fallen. However, in many places wooden plaques, lychgates, stained glass windows and even village halls have been erected as war memorials.

Farnley Tyas War Memorial, dedicated in 2014. *Scott Flaving*

ABBREVIATIONS

Abbreviations have been kept to the minimum and appear mostly in the Mentions section of each entry:

Bn	Battalion.
CPGW	Craven's Part in the Great War, publication and website.
CWGC	Commonwealth War Graves Commission, publications and website.
Dates	Dates are given in the format dd m yyyy, see introduction.
GOC	General Officer Commanding.
MGC	Machine Gun Corps.
Ranks	See Glossary.
RFC	Royal Flying Corps – until April, 1918, then Royal Air Force (RAF).
RoH	Roll of Honour.
SDGW	Soldiers Died in the Great War publication.
WM	War Memorial.

ORDER OF BATTLE

49th (WEST RIDING) DIVISION
62nd (PELICAN) DIVISION

In September, 1914, each of the original Duke of Wellington's (West Riding Regiment) Territorial Force battalions were ordered to raise a second, mirror image, unit in order to double their strength, using a cadre from each battalion to take in and begin training the crowds of volunteers clamouring to join the army and have a crack at the foe before it was "all over by Christmas".

Thus the 1st West Riding Division (TF) produced the 2nd West Riding Division (TF) in this fashion, and the 2nd West Riding Infantry Brigade, comprising of four first line 'Dukes' battalions, generated the 2/2nd West Riding Infantry Brigade, comprising of the newly created, second line 'Dukes' Battalions.

On 12th May, 1915, the two Divisions were re-designated as **49th (West Riding) Division**, with 147th Infantry Brigade (1/4th, 1/5th, 1/6th & 1/7th Battalions DWR) and **62nd (West Riding) Division**, including the 186th Infantry Brigade (2/4th, 2/5th, 2/6th & 2/7th Battalions DWR).

The various components of the British Army in 1914 were made up of:

Unit/Formation	Number (approx)	Commander
Section	15	Corporal.
Platoon	60	2nd Lieutenant/Lieutenant.
Company	200	Captain.
Battalion	1,000	Lieutenant Colonel.

(Infantry Regiments consisted of various numbers of battalions, each allocated to Brigades in various Divisions).

Brigade	5,000	Brigadier General.
Division	18,000	Major General.
Corps	two or more Divisions	Lieutenant General.
Army	two or more Corps	General.
Expeditionary Force	two Corps (1914) five Armies (1916)	Field Marshal.

An Infantry Battalion was made up of four Rifle Companies; Battalion Headquarters (including the Battalion Orderly Room); Headquarters Company, consisting of the Signals Platoon, Bombers, Machine Gun Platoon, Quartermasters Department, Catering Platoon and Transport Section. Most of these specialist platoons were split between the four Companies when in the Field, according to the tactical situation and operations being undertaken.

The Battalions, Brigades and Divisions were moved frequently between different formations, so a Corps, in particular, could command many Divisions for a particular operation.

The two Divisions in which the men of the 5th Battalion served were the 49th and 62nd Divisions:

49th (WEST RIDING) DIVISION
Symbol: White Rose of Yorkshire.

In 1914, this division was an existing Territorial Force Division, one of many created by the foresight of Lord Haldane in the reforms of 1908, and the establishment of the Territorial Force, which was well trained (by the standards of the day) for the previous war – the Boer War – at annual camps, including Redcar, Marske, the Isle of Man, Ripon, Flamborough and Aberystwyth.

This Division, approximately 15,000 strong, was drawn from the West Riding of Yorkshire, with Divisional Headquarters in York. The three Brigade Headquarters were in York, Skipton and Sheffield and the twelve infantry battalions were located in York, Bradford, Leeds (two), Halifax, Huddersfield, Skipton, Milnsbridge, Wakefield, Doncaster, Sheffield and Rotherham.

Towards the end of July, 1914, the various units of the Division left their Drill Halls for a gloriously hot summer camp at Marske. On the 4th August the Division received orders to return to their Headquarters, with the exception of the 2nd West Riding Brigade, which was ordered to proceed direct from camp for immediate duty. The same day, mobilisation was ordered and what became known as the Great War had begun. Units then proceeded to their allotted war stations as part of the Central Force, Home Defence, and progressive training for war was carried out whilst initially also guarding the east coast in case of the much feared German invasion. The Division was eventually concentrated on Doncaster Race Course for collective training.

On 31st March, 1915, the 1st West Riding Division was informed that it had been selected to proceed to France as a complete Division and embarkation would take place in April.

On 7th April, 1915, a small advance party left Doncaster for Le Havre and, on 12th April, the Division began to entrain to proceed to France and, on 13th April, Divisional Headquarters and the Divisional Artillery left Doncaster and crossed from Folkestone to Boulogne. The infantry also crossed from Folkestone to Boulogne, but the mounted troops, Royal Engineers, Signal Company, Field Ambulances, Sanitary Section, Veterinary Section and the Train, all went from Southampton to Le Havre. By the 19th April the Division completed its concentration behind the River Lys, in the area Estaires – Merville – Neuf Berquin. The infantry began their trench warfare indoctrination in the Fleurbaix Sector.

The Division started out with twelve infantry Battalions, each with two machine guns, by 1916 Machine Gun Companies (MG Coy) and Trench Mortar Batteries (TMB) had been added to each Brigade (Bde) and, in 1918, the number of battalions was reduced to nine per Division. In addition, each Division had under command a Pioneer Battalion (infantry), three Brigades of Field Artillery, one Howitzer Brigade and one Heavy Battery; three Trench Mortar Batteries (from June, 1916); two Field Companies of Royal Engineers, one Cavalry Squadron, one Signals Company; three Field Ambulance units; a Sanitary Section, a Veterinary Section and the Divisional Train (Transport and Supply), as well as the Artillery Ammunition Columns. The Machine Gun Company was added in 1916 (199th MG Coy from June, 1917), later replaced by a Battalion (49th Battalion, MG Corps from March, 1918). The Infantry battalions were from the West Yorkshire Regiment (Depot in York), the West Riding Regiment (Depot in Halifax), the King's Own Yorkshire Light Infantry (Depot in Pontefract) and the York and Lancaster Regiment (Depot in Sheffield):

INFANTRY UNITS	146 Bde	147 Bde	148 Bde
	1/5 W Yorks	1/4 W Rid	1/4 KOYLI
	1/6 W Yorks	**1/5 W Rid**	1/5 KOYLI
	1/7 W Yorks	1/6 W Rid	1/4 Y & L
	1/8 W Yorks	1/7 W Rid	1/5 Y & L
In Jan 1918 Brigades were reorganised on a three battalion basis:-	**146 Bde**	**147 Bde**	**148 Bde**
	1/5 W Yorks	1/4 W Rid	1/4 KOYLI
	1/6 W Yorks	1/6 W Rid	1/4 Y & L
	1/7 W Yorks	1/7 W Rid	1/5 Y & L
Each Bde had a MG Coy and TM Bty attached	146 MG Coy (27 Jan 16)	147 MG Coy (28 Jan 16)	148 MG Coy (6 Feb 16)

146 TMB	147 TMB	148 TMB

Note that in January, 1918, the 1/5th Battalion had been moved to 62nd Brigade to amalgamate with the 2/5th Battalion to form a new 5th Battalion, as it had been titled up until 1914.

The Divisional and Brigade General Officers Commanding (GOC) during the war were:

GOC			From	To	
49 Div	Maj Gen	Baldock	19 9 1911	16 7 1915	(wounded)
(1st W Rid)	Maj Gen	Perceval	17 7 1915	19 10 1917	
	Maj Gen	Cameron	20 10 1917		
146 Bde	Brig Gen	MacFarlane	11 5 1912		
(1st W Rid)	Lt Col	Legge	20 12 1915		(acting)
	Brig Gen	Goring-Jones	17 1 1916		
	Brig Gen	Rennie	18 10 1917		
147 Bde	Brig Gen	Brereton	11 5 1912		
(2nd W Rid)	Brig Gen	Lewes	13 9 1916		
	Brig Gen	Morant	02 9 1918		
148 Bde	Brig Gen	Dawson	01 4 1912		
(3rd W Rid)	Brig Gen	Adlercron	07 6 1916		(DWR)
	Brig Gen	Green-Wilkinson	24 10 1917		

The 49th Division served on the Western Front in France and Belgium throughout the Great War and was engaged in the following operations:

1915
09 5 1915		Battle of Aubers Ridge		4th Corps	1st Army
19 12 1915		First Phosgene Gas Attack		4th Corps	2nd Army

1916
01 7 1916	03 7 1916	Battle of Albert		10th Corps	4th Army
14 7 1916	17 7 1916	Battle of Bazentine Ridge		10th Corps	Res Army
23 7 1916	18 8 1916	Battle of Pozieres Ridge		10th Corps to 24 7	Res Army
27 8 1916	03 9 1916	Battle of Pozieres Ridge		2nd Corps	Res Army
15 9 1916	22 9 1916	Battle of Flers Courcelette		2nd Corps	Res Army

1917
12 7 1917	23 9 1917	Operations on Flanders Coast		15th Corps	4th Army
09 10 1917		Battle of Poelcappelle		2nd Anzac Corps	2nd Army

1918 **Battles of the Lys**
10 4 1918	11 4 1918	Battle of Estaires	147 Bde	15th Corps	1st Army
10 4 1918	11 4 1918	Battle of Messines	148 Bde	9th Corps	2nd Army
13 4 1918	15 4 1918	Battle of Bailleul		9th Corps	2nd Army
13 4 1918	14 4 1918	Defence of Neuve Eglise	148 Bde		
17 4 1918	19 4 1918	First Battle of Kemmel Ridge		9th Corps	2nd Army
		(146 Bde under 22nd Corps)			
25 4 1918	26 4 1918	Second Battle of Kemmel Ridge		22nd Corps	2nd Army
29 4 1918		Battle of Sherperberg		22nd Corps	2nd Army

		Advance to Victory		
10 10 1918	12 10 1918	Pursuit to the Celle	Cdn Corps	1st Army
		The Final Advance in Picardy		
17 10 1918	18 10 1918	Battle of the Celle	22nd Corps	1st Army
01 11 1918	02 11 1918	Battle of Valenciennes	22nd Corps	1st Army

At the end of the Battle of Valenciennes, the 49th Division was relieved in the front line. On 5th November the Division moved back to the north of Douai and was transferred to 8th Corps. It was still resting on the 11th November. The Division remained in the Douai area, where, on 16th December, the Division was inspected on a ceremonial parade by Lieutenant General Sir A J Godley, commanding 22nd Corps.

Demobilisation began in January, 1919, and went steadily on until 30th March, by which date the Division had been reduced to a cadre. The Division was reformed in England in 1920.

62nd (WEST RIDING) DIVISION
Symbol: Pelican, with raised foot
(also 62nd (Pelican) Division)

The 2nd (West Riding) Division was formed at the outbreak of war as a second line Territorial Force Division by the creation of the 2/1st, 2/2nd and 2/3rd (West Riding) Infantry Brigades. The units of these Brigades were formed in their home Drill Halls as the result of an Army Order of 31st August, 1914 and created from a nucleus of the parent Division. Originally, the second line units were designated as Home Service but, later, renamed Reserve and, eventually, 2nd Line, in February, 1915. At this stage they were used to provide drafts of reinforcements to the 1st Line battalions for possible service overseas, the men having volunteered to change their terms of service. In return, the 2nd Line units had soldiers transferred into them who had not volunteered or were considered unfit for active service. Later, these men were transferred to Provisional Battalions used for coastal defence duties, and the newly raised 3rd Line Battalions which then became responsible for training and drafting volunteers, and conscripts from March, 1916.

The Divisional Headquarters assembled at Doncaster on 17th February, 1915. In March the Divisional HQ moved to Matlock and the various Brigades and supporting arms concentrated in the area Matlock, Derby, Belper, Nottingham and Bakewell. From May, 1915, the Division moved to various training areas, including Thoresby Park, Retford, and Newcastle. In early 1916, the Division moved to Salisbury Plain. In June, 1916, the Division moved to Norfolk, based in the Lowestoft area, moving to Bedford in October. In December, 1915, the Division received orders to embark for France and Flanders in January, 1917.

As for the 49th Division, the 62nd Division consisted of four battalions per infantry Brigade until February, 1918, when the number was reduced to three battalions per Brigade. They had the same complement of supporting arms as 49th Division, except that the Pioneer Battalion (1/9th DLI) did not join them until March, 1918):

INFANTRY UNITS	**185 Bde**	**186 Bde**	**187 Bde**
	2/5 W Yorks	2/4 W Rid	2/4 KOYLI
	2/6 W Yorks	**2/5 W Rid**	2/5 KOYLI
	2/7 W Yorks	2/6 W Rid	2/4 Y & L
	2/8 W Yorks	2/7 W Rid	2/5 Y & L

on 03 2 1918 Brigades were reorganised on a three battalion basis:-	**185 Bde**	**186 Bde**		**187 Bde**
	2/5 W Yorks	2/4 W Rid		2/4 KOYLI
	2/7 W Yorks	**5 W Rid**		5 KOYLI
	8 W Yorks	2/7 W Rid	to 18 6 1918	2/4 Y & L
		2/4 Hants	from 14 6 1918	
Each Bde had a MG Coy and TM Bty attached	212 MG Coy (09 3 1917)	213 MG Coy (09 3 1917)		208 MG Coy (04 3 1917)
	185 TMB (1 1917)	186 TMB (1 1917)		187 TMB (1 1917)

Note that the 1/5th Battalion was amalgamated with the 2/5th Battalion, becoming the 5th Battalion in January, 1918.

The General Officers Commanding (GOC) the Division and Brigades were:

GOC			From	To	
62 Div (2nd W Rid)	Maj Gen	Sir K J Trotter	17 2 1915	22 12 1915	
	Maj Gen	W P Braithwaite	23 12 1915	27 8 1918	
	Maj Gen	Sir R D Whigham	28 8 1918		
185 Bde (2nd/1st W Rid)	Col	H W N Guiness	11 2 1915		
	Brig Gen	V W de Falbe	04 1 1916	21 8 1917	(invalided)
	Brig Gen	Viscount Hampden	21 8 1917		
186 Bde (2nd/2nd W Rid)	Col	H G Mainwaring	02 3 1915		
	Brig Gen	F F Hill	09 12 1915		
	Brig Gen	R B Bradford VC	10 11 1917	30 11 1917	(killed)
	Lt Col	H E P Nash	30 11 1917		(acting)
	Brig Gen	J L G Burnett	03 12 1917		
187 Bde (2nd/3rd W Rid)	Col	H B Lasseter	04 3 1915		
	Brig Gen	R O'B Taylor	22 5 1916	08 2 1918	(sick)
	Lt Col	B J Barton	02 2 1918		(DWR, acting)
	Lt Col	W K James	28 3 1918		(acting)
	Brig Gen	A J Reddie	03 4 1918		

The 62nd Division served on the Western Front in France and Belgium throughout the Great War and was engaged in the following operations:

1917

15 2 1917	13 3 1917	Operations on the Ancre		5th Corps	Fifth Army
14 3 1917	19 3 1917	German Retreat to the Hindenburg Line		5th Corps	Fifth Army
11 4 1917		First Attack on Bullecourt		5th Corps	Fifth Army
15 4 1917		German Attack on Lagnicourt	(186 Bde)	5th Corps	Fifth Army
03 5 1917	17 5 1917	Battle of Bullecourt		5th Corps	Fifth Army
20 5 1917	28 5 1917	Actions at the Hindenburg Line		5th Corps	Fifth Army
		Battle of Cambrai			
20 11 1917	21 11 1917	The Tank Attack		4th Corps	Third Army
27 11 1917	28 11 1917	Capture of Bourlon Wood		4th Corps	Third Army

1918   **First Battles of the Somme**

25 3 1918		Battle of Bapaume	4th Corps	Third Army
28 3 1918		Battle of Arras	4th Corps	Third Army

Advance to Victory
Battles of the Marne

20 7 1918	30 7 1918	Battle of Tardenois	22nd Corps	Fifth (Fr) Army

Second Battle of Arras

26 8 1918	30 8 1918	Battle of the Scarpe	6th Corps	Third Army
02 9 1918		Battle of Drocourt-Queant Line	6th Corps	Third Army

Battles of the Hindenberg Line

12 9 1918		Battle of Havringcourt Wood	6th Corps	Third Army
27 9 1918	30 9 1918	Battle o the Canal du Nord	6th Corps	Third Army

The Final Advance in Picardy

17 10 1918	23 10 1918	Battle of the Selle	4th Corps	Third Army
20 10 1918		Capture of Solesmes	4th Corps	Third Army
04 11 1918		Battle of the Sambre	4th Corps	Third Army

After the battle of the Sambre, the Division remained in the front line and fought its way forward toward Maubeuge, advancing past Mecouignies and Neuf Mesnil (8th Nov). On the 9th the southern outskirts of Maubeuge was entered, the River Sambre crossed, Louvroil and St Lazare were captured and the line of the Maubeuge – Avesnes road was reached. On the 11th November, an outpost line was established along the River Soire, with piquets to the east of the river, but no signs of the enemy were encountered by cyclist patrols who pushed on as far as Cerforntaine and Recquignies (3 miles east of Maubeuge). At 11 am the Armistice came into force and hostilities ceased.

With acknowledgements to Ray Westlake, Kitcheners Armies, *(Spellmount, 1998) , Captain Wilfred Miles, compiler of the* Official History of the Great War, Military Operations, *(Macmillan and Co, 1938) and Major Tom Goodall.*

Major Tom Goodall, Seated, centre, OC D Company (Mirfield) 1916.

Huddersfield Drill Hall, 1899.

Huddersfield Drill Hall, 2019.

		ARMITAGE. F.D.	PTE.	BANKS. J.R.	PTE.	BECKETT. E.	PTE.
		ARMITAGE. H.V.	"	BAXTER. C.	"	BECKETT. W.	"
		ARMITAGE. HARRY.	"	BAXTER. J.	"	BELL. W.	SGT.
		ARMITAGE. H.	"	BAXTER. F.	CPL.	BELL. F.W.	PTE.
		ARMSTRONG. S.	"	BAGSHAW. L.	"	BELL. T.H.	"
		ARMISTEAD. D.	"	BARBER. E.	"	BEARDSELL. H.	"
ACKROYD. C.	PTE.	ASTBURY. W.	"	BARNFATHER. G.	L/CPL.	BEARDSELL. F.	"
ADAMS. C.H.	CPL.	ASQUITH. V.	"	BARRACLOUGH. W.	2/LT.	BERRY. W.	L/CPL.
AINLEY. H.M.	PTE.	ASHTON. G.	"	BARKER. S.O.	PTE.	BEAUMONT. G.W.	PTE.
AINLEY. W.	"	ASHBRIDGE. F.	"	BARKER. C.V.	"	BEAUMONT. HARRY.	"
ALLCOCK. G.	"	ATACK. G.	"	BARKER. S.O.	"	BEAUMONT. S.	"
ALDERSON. N.	"	ATKINSON. A.	"	BARRACLOUGH. J.W.	"	BEAUMONT. L.	"
ALLEN. F.	"	ATKINSON. J.W.	"	BARDSLEY. W.	"	BEAUMONT. HERBERT.	"
ALLEN. J.E.	"	ATKINSON. F.A.	"	BAMFORTH. G.	"	BEESLEY. W.	"
ALLISTER. W.C.	"	AYRES. B.R.	"	BAMFORTH. S.	"	BENTLEY. G.	"
ALLFORD. A.E.	"	BAILEY. T.D.	"	BAMFORD. S.	"	BENTLEY. T.	CPT.
ANSDELL. P.	"	BAILEY. J.	"	BARROW. W.H.	"	BENTLEY. I.	PTE.
ANDERSON. W.	"	BAILEY. J.H.	"	BATTYE. D.	"	BENTLEY. C.E.	L/CPL.
ANDERSON. A.	"	BAILEY. W.	"	BATTYE. W.	"	BENNETT. W.	PTE.
ANDERSON. J.	"	BARLOW. E.	"	BATTYE. J.	"	BEDFORD. J.	"
APPLEBY. J.W.	"	BACKHOUSE. C.	"	BARHAM. W.D.	"	BEECHAM. G.	"
APPLEYARD. L. M.M	CPL.	BAIRSTOW. G.	"	BANNISTER. W.H.	"	BEARD. H.	"
ARCHARD. F.J.	PTE.	BATES. N.	"	BARNETT. Q.M.	2/LT.	BEST. T.A.D. D.S.O.	LT/COL.
ARMITAGE. E.	"	BATES. T.	SGT.	BARTON. W.	PTE.	BETTS. W. J.	PTE.
ARMITAGE. A.	"	BALL. A.	PTE.	BAKER. R.	"	BETTS. B.	"
ARMITAGE. F.	"	BANKS. J.	"	BAUMONT. A.	"	BETTS. T.	"

BENNISON. W.	CPL.	BOOTHROYD. P.	PTE.	BROOK. I.	PTE.	BUXTON. F.	PTE.
BENTHAM. H.	2/LT.	BODKER. J.G.	LT.	BROOKE. HORACE.	"	BUTLER. C.	"
BELLAMY. T.	PTE.	BOWER. J.	PTE.	BROOKE. G.	"	BUTLER. R.W.J	"
BIRKS. A.	"	BOWER. C.	"	BROOKE. HENRY.	"	BUSBY. C.E.	"
BICKERDYKE. F.	"	BRADLEY. F.	"	BROOK. C.F.	"	BYRAM. T.R.	L/CPL.
BIRD. H.C.	"	BRADLEY. G.H.	"	BROOKE. J.A.	"	CARTER. A.W.	SGT.
BIRMINGHAM. J.W.	"	BRADLEY. W.	"	BRUNT. F.C.	SGT.	CARTER. H.J.	PTE.
BIRLEY. J.	"	BRADLEY. F.	"	BRACKEN. T.	PTE.	CARTER. E.E.	"
BINNS. S.	"	BRADLEY. N.	"	BRADBURY. C.	"	CASTLE. J.	"
BLACKBURN. W.M.	"	BROADHEAD. A.	"	BRADBURY. H.	"	CASTLE. H.	"
BLACKBURN. B.	"	BROADBENT. W.	"	BRENNEN. M.H.	"	CAINE. T.	CPL.
BLEZARD. A.	"	BROADBENT. S.H.	"	BRAY. W.	"	CAINE. F.	SGT.
BLAKEY. H.	"	BRIDGES. E.E.	L/CPL.	BRAYBROOKS. H.C.	"	CAIRNS. W.	PTE.
BLAKELEY. J.E. M.M	SGT.	BROWN. H.	PTE.	BRUCE. W.J.	"	CAIRNS. J.B.	"
BOYES. F.	PTE.	BROWN. R.H.	2/LT.	BRAND. R.H.	"	CATON. R.	"
BOOTH. P.	"	BROWN. A.	PTE.	BROBBIN. G.	"	CARISS. H.	"
BOOTH. JOHN.	"	BROWN. T.S.	"	BRAZELL. H.A.	SGT.	CARR. J.	"
BOOTH. W.	"	BROWN. W.L.G.	"	BRIGGS. T.	2/LT.	CAREY. A.	CPL.
BOOTH. A.	"	BROWN. G.W.	"	BURKET. T.	L/CPL.	CARRUTHERS. G.	2/LT.
BOOTH. J.	"	BRICK. L.	"	BURNLEY. H.R.	SGT.	CAUSER. J.	PTE.
BOOTH. H.	"	BROOK. W.	"	BURROWS. J.W.	PTE.	CASSIDY. W.	"
BOOTH. P.	"	BROOK. W.H.	"	BURTON. C.F.	"	CALVERT. J.W.	L/CPL.
BOOTH. S.	CPL.	BROOK. HARRY.	SGT.	BUTTERWORTH. E.	"	CALVERT. L.	PTE.
BOOTH. E. DCM. MM	L/CPL.	BROOK. A.	PTE.	BUTTERWORTH. A.S.	"	CALKIN. E.	"
BOTTOMLEY. W.D.A.	PTE.	BROOKE. S.	"	BULL. H.	"	CAWTHORNE. W.	L/CPL.
BOWNESS. W.H.	"	BROOKE. E.	"	BUCKLEY. L.	"	CAWTHRA. W.E.	PTE.

THE WAR MEMORIAL BOARDS

INTRODUCTION:

The entries below are in alphabetical order for ease of looking up the names, which is not actually the case on the War Memorial Boards, for example, the final entry, on Board 12, is for Private Doughty. The panel numbers, 1 – 12, and columns, 1 – 4, printed in bold towards the end of each entry, will identify the position of each soldier's name on the boards. Note that some duplicated names appear on different columns. Some entries cannot be traced in the records that we have access to. There are also a number of spelling errors, which we have tried to correct, using contemporary sources, wherever possible.

ACKROYD Charles - 242805 Private.
Resided in Siddal. Enlisted at Halifax.
1/5th Battalion DWR; died of wounds, 08 10 1917, Battle of Cambrai.
Buried – Oxford Road Cemetery, 1, E, 9.
Commemorated – Halifax Book of Remembrance; Calderdale War Dead, page 38, and the **Drill Hall WM panel 1, column 1.**

ADAMS Cornelius Harry – 5056 (later 241642) Corporal.
Born in Friskney, Lincs. Enlisted at Lincoln.
2/5th Battalion DWR, D Company (Mirfield); killed in action, 27 11 1917, aged 22, Battle of Passchendaele.
Buried – Orival Wood, 2, B, 13.
Commemorated – the **Drill Hall WM panel 1, column 1.**
Mentioned in the Goodall collection.
CHRIST WILL LINK THE BROKEN CHAIN CLOSER WHEN WE MEET AGAIN.

AINLEY Herbert McArthur – 3185 Private.
Born in Outlane and resided in Edgerton. Enlisted at Huddersfield.
1/5th Bn Battalion DWR; killed in action, 17 11 1917, aged 21, Battle of Passchendaele.
Commemorated – Ypres (Menin Gate) WM; M Stansfield, page 3, and the **Drill Hall WM panel 1, column 1.**

AINLEY William – 5279 (later 241832) Private.
Born in Golcar. Enlisted at Halifax, on 22 3 1916, and embarked for France on 10 1 1917.
2/5th Battalion DWR, D Company (Mirfield), later HQ Company; killed in action by shellfire, 27 11 1917, Battle of Cambrai.
Commemorated – Cambrai Memorial (Louverval), France, Golcar (St John's Church) RoH; M Stansfield, page 3; the **Drill Hall WM panel 1, column 1.**
Mentioned in the Goodall Collection (Commanding Officer's Commendation awarded 06 3 1917 for operations between 20 - 28 2 1917). He may also have been listed as wounded in action, according to the Huddersfield Examiner of 07 8 1916, but no Regimental numbers were published on that day, so we cannot verify that this is him.

ALCOCK (ALLCOCK) George – 5829 Private.
Born and enlisted at Bradford, son of George and Sarah Alcock of 170 Bolton Hall Road, Bradford.

1/5th Battalion DWR; killed in action, 17 9 1916, aged 24, Battle of the Somme, age 24.
Buried – Serre Road Cemetery No2, 9, K, 7.
Commemorated – the **Drill Hall WM panel 1, column 1.**
SDGW and the WM Board have his name spelt, incorrectly, as Allcock.

ALDERSON Naylor – 3881 (later 241021) Private.
Was a pre war miner and resided in Liversedge. Enlisted 15 2 1915 at Mirfield.
2/5th Battalion DWR, D Company (Mirfield); killed in action, 03 5 1917, Battle of Bullecourt.
Commemorated – Ypres (Menin Gate) Memorial; Cleckheaton WM; Spenborough WM; C Turpin, page 3, and the **Drill Hall WM panel 1, column 1.**
Mentioned in the Goodall collection (15 Platoon and later a Stokes gunner. Originally reported missing by D Company).

ALLEN Frank – 5226 (later 241785) Private.
Born New Mill and resided in Huddersfield. Enlisted in 1916 at Halifax, embarked for France and Flanders in January, 1917.
2/5th Battalion DWR, D Company (Mirfield); killed in action, 03 5 1917, Battle of Bullecourt.
Commemorated – Arras Memorial; Marsden WM; M Stansfield, page 4; and the **Drill Hall WM panel 1, column 1.**
Mentioned in the Huddersfield Examiner (reported missing in action) on 07 6 1917.

ALLEN James Ernest – 5441 (later 241962) Private.
Born in Walkley, and resided in Sheffield; enlisted at Larkhill.
2/5th Battalion DWR; Killed in action, 03 5 1917, aged 19, Battle of Bullecourt.
Commemorated – Arras Memorial, France; Wellington Cemetery WM; and the **Drill Hall WM panel 1, column 1.**
Mentioned in the Goodall collection.

ALLFORD Albert Edward – 33111 Private.
Enlisted at Sheffield.
2/5th Battalion DWR; killed in action, 20 7 1918, Advance to Victory.
Commemorated – Soissons Memorial and the **Drill Hall WM panel 1, column 1.**

ALLISTER William Clifford – 5547 (later 267409) Private.
Born and enlisted at Todmorden.
5th Battalion DWR; killed in action, 20 7 1918, aged 21, Advance to Victory.
Buried – Courmas British Cemetery, 2, C, 5.
Commemorated – Todmorden WM and the **Drill Hall WM panel 1, column 1.**
Mentioned in the Unit War Diary (reported sick and sent to hospital) on 15 8 1917. Transferred to 5th Battalion some time after renumbering, from 5547, in April, 1917.
Originally B Company, 1/6th Battalion

ANDERSON Albert – 35136 Private.
Born in North Shields. Enlisted at Newcastle.
5th Battalion DWR; died 08 10 1918, aged 18, at home.
Buried – Tynemouth (Preston) Cemetery, C, 12165.
Commemorated – the **Drill Hall WM panel 1, column 1.**
DEATH DIVIDES BUT MEMORY CLINGS.

ANDERSON Walter – 16081 (later 242770) Private.
Enlisted at Beverley.
2/5th Battalion DWR; killed in action, 03 5 1917, aged 19, Battle of Bullecourt.
Commemorated – Arras Memorial and the **Drill Hall WM panel 1, column 1.**
Formerly 33174 East Yorkshire Regiment.

ANSDELL (also ANDSELL) Percy – 242863 (242868?) Private.
Born and enlisted at Halifax, living at 17 Launceston Street, Halifax in 1911.
1/5th Battalion DWR; killed in action, 20 11 1917, Battle of Passchendaele.
Buried – Perth (China Wall) Cemetery, 5, J, 12.
Commemorated – Halifax RoH; Calderdale War Dead, page 41, and the **Drill Hall WM panel 1, column 1.**
NOTE: The spelling of his name, and his number, is at variance between CWGC and SDGW. His headstone bears the name Andsell with the number 242868.

APPLEBY John William – 203155 (303155) Private.
Born and enlisted at Halifax.
5th Battalion DWR; killed in action, 10 4 1918, German Spring Offensive.
Buried – Douchy les Ayette Cemetery, 2, G, 13.
Commemorated – Halifax RoH; Calderdale War Dead appendix, page 41, and the **Drill Hall WM panel 1, column 1.**
SDGW shows his number as 303155. His headstone bears the correct number 203155.

APPLEYARD Lionel – 204703 Corporal. Military Medal.
Resided in Mirfield and enlisted at Huddersfield.
2/5th Battalion DWR; killed in action, 23 7 1918, aged 25, Advance to Victory.
Commemorated – Soissons Memorial, France; Mirfield WM; Upper Hopton WM; R Leedham, page 141; L Magnus, page 295, and the **Drill Hall WM panel 1, column 1.**
MM announced in the London Gazette of 13 3 1918, page 3226, citation not found. Mentioned in the Unit War Diary (MM award was for operations between 20 7 and 27 11 1917, during the Battle of Cambrai. May have been mentioned in the Huddersfield Examiner (wounded in action) on 07 8 1916, but no Regimental numbers were published on that day, so we cannot verify that this is him.

ARCHARD Frederick John – 2798 Private.
Born in Yarmouth and enlisted at Huddersfield.
1/5th Battalion DWR; killed in action, 22 8 1915, Ypres.
Commemorated – Ypres Menin Gate Memorial; M Stansfield, page 7, and the **Drill Hall WM panel 1, column 1.**
Mentioned in the Huddersfield Examiner (killed by a sniper) on 26 8 1915.

ARMISTEAD Richard (Dick) – 5142 (later 241717) Private.
Born in Rochdale. Resided in Huddersfield. Enlisted at Halifax on 16 3 1916.
2/5th Battalion DWR, 14 Platoon, D Company, bomber; reported missing, killed in action, 03 5 1917, Battle of Bullecourt.
Commemorated – Arras Memorial, France, M Stansfield, page 6, and the **Drill Hall WM panel 1, column 1.**
Mentioned in the Goodall collection.

ARMITAGE Albert – 4841 (5/4841) Private.
Born in Dewsbury and enlisted at Bradford. Son of Sam & Susannah Armitage of 14 Rayleigh Street, Paley Road, Bradford.
1/5th Battalion DWR; killed in action, 03 7 1916, aged 27, Battle of the Somme.
Buried – Connaught Cemetery, 13, A, 1.
Commemorated – the **Drill Hall WM panel 1, column 1.**
THOUGH DEATH DIVIDES STILL MEMORY CLINGS.

ARMITAGE Ernest – 3180 Private.
Born in Huddersfield 30 4 1891, and enlisted at Huddersfield in October, 1914, and embarked for France in April 1915.
1/5th Battalion DWR; died of appendicitis at No 13 General Hospital, Boulogne, on 25 11 1915

Buried – Boulogne Eastern Cemetery, 8, C, 60.
Commemorated – All Saints Church, Paddock, RoH (currently in Huddersfield Drill Hall); M Stansfield, page 7; and the **Drill Hall WM panel 1, column 1.**

ARMITAGE Frank – 2390 Private.
Born in Holmfirth to John and Sarah Ann. Resided in Holmbridge, Enlisted at Huddersfield.
1/5th Battalion DWR, B Company (attached 147 MGC); killed in action, 03 9 1916, aged 20, Battle of the Somme (Thiepval).
Commemorated – Thiepval Memorial, France; M Stansfield, page 7, and the **Drill Hall WM panel 1, column 1.**
Mentioned in the Huddersfield Examiner (killed in action) on 13 9 1916.
Originally F Company (Holmfirth)

ARMITAGE Fred – 2459 Private.
Born in Huddersfield to Thomas and Elizabeth, of Holmfirth. Enlisted at Huddersfield.
1/5th Battalion DWR; died of wounds, 25 11 1915, aged 17, Ypres.
Buried – Boulogne Eastern Cemetery, 8, C, 60.
Commemorated – M Stansfield, page 7, the **Drill Hall WM panel 1, column 2.**
Mentioned in the Huddersfield Examiner (died, Doncaster) on 18 6 1915.
NOTE – no trace in SDGW.

ARMITAGE Harry – 203561 (203562?) Private. Military Medal.
Born in Huddersfield on 22 2 1892 to John and Elizabeth of Crosland Moor. Enlisted at Huddersfield in February, 2916.
5th Battalion DWR; died of wounds at 34 Casualty Clearing Station on 02 11 1918, aged 26, Advance to Victory.
Buried – Grevillers British Cemetery, 17, D, 16.
Commemorated – M Stansfield, page 7, and the **Drill Hall WM panel 1, column 2.**
Unit War Diary shows 203562.
Mentioned in the Unit War Diary (award of MM) on 31 10 1918; the Huddersfield Examiner (died of wounds) on 08 11 1918; (in memoriam) on 08 11 1919; L Magnus (MM award) page 296; London Gazette (MM award) on 13 3 1919, page 3429.
Originally 2/5th DWR.

ARMITAGE H
No trace found, possibly a duplication of the above soldier.
Commemorated – the **Drill Hall WM panel 1, column 2.**

ARMITAGE Henry (Harry) Vincent – 3859 (later 241006) Private.
Born in Shelley, Huddersfield, to Willie. Enlisted at Huddersfield.
5th Battalion DWR; reported missing, killed in action 03 5 1917, aged 21, Battle of Bullecourt.
Commemorated - Arras Memorial, France; Mirfield WM; M Stansfield, page 8, and the **Drill Hall WM panel 1, column 2.**
Mentioned in the Goodall collection; the Huddersfield Examiner (reported missing) on 18 9 1917; (previously reported missing, now presumed killed) on 04 10 1917.

ARMSTRONG S
No trace as serving in DWR.
Possibly served in 1/5th Battalion, Northumberland Fusiliers, enlisted at Skipton.
Commemorated - the **Drill Hall WM panel 1, column 2.**

ASHBRIDGE Fred – 235762 Private.
Son of William and Mary, resided in Hull and enlisted at Beverley.
5th Battalion DWR; killed in action 16 9 1918, aged 29, Advance to Victory.

Buried – Sunken Road Cemetery, Boisleux, 2, D, 1.
Commemorated – the **Drill Hall WM panel 1, column 2.**

ASHTON George (initial C on the board) – 25321 Private.
Born in Enderby, Leicestershire. Enlisted at Glen Parva.
5th Battalion DWR; died of wounds 24 4 1918, Advance to Victory.
Buried – St Sever Cemetery Extension, P, 9, N, 6B.
Commemorated – the **Drill Hall WM panel 1, column 2.**
Formerly Private 36937 Leicestershire Regiment. Originally 2/5th DWR.

ASQUITH Vernon – 242279 Private.
Son of Joseph E and Helena. Enlisted at Barnsley.
1/5th Battalion DWR; killed in action 08 8 1917, aged 26, Nieuport Sector.
Commemorated – Nieuport WM, Belgium, and the **Drill Hall WM panel 1, column 2.**

ASTBURY William – 3598 Private.
Resided in Ravensthorpe and enlisted at Mirfield.
1/5th Battalion DWR; killed in action 16 6 1915, Ypres.
Buried – Rue David Military Cemetery, 1, B, 12.
Commemorated – Spenborough (Cleckheaton) WM; D Tattersfield, pp 57 & 381, C Turpin, page 3, and the **Drill Hall WM panel 1, column 2.**
Mentioned in the Unit war Diary (B Company, killed in action) on 16 6 1915.

ATACK George – 266985 Private.
Born in Wetherby to Joseph and Elizabeth. Resided Wetherby. Enlisted at Otley.
2/5th Battalion DWR; killed in action 27 11 1917, aged 19, Battle of Cambrai.
Commemorated – Cambrai Memorial (Louverval), France; Brighouse WM; Wetherby WM and the **Drill Hall WM panel 1, column 2.**

ATKINSON Albert – 3679 Private.
Son of Herbert and Emily. Resided in Holmbridge. Enlisted at Huddersfield and embarked for France and Flanders in April, 1915.
1/5th Battalion DWR; killed in action 14 11 1915, aged 19, Ypres.
Buried – Talana Farm Cemetery, 4, F, 4.
Commemorated – Holme Valley Memorial Hospital WM (plaque 1, Holme and Holmbridge); M Stansfield, page 11, and the **Drill Hall WM panel 1, column 2.**

ATKINSON Frederick Arthur – 26312 Private.
Born in Cranswick, E Yorks, to Jonathan and Annie. Resided in Birmingham. Enlisted at Sherburn in Elmet.
5th Battalion DWR, D Company; killed in action 23 7 1918, aged 25.
Buried - Terlincthun British Cemetery, 17, D, 17.
Commemorated - the **Drill Hall WM panel 1, column 2.**
Mentioned in the Goodall collection.
Formerly 465 Army Service Corps.
R.I.P.

ATKINSON James William – 200844 Private.
Enlisted at Halifax.
2/5th Battalion DWR; killed in action 20 7 1918.
Commemorated – Soissons Memorial, France; Halifax RoH; Calderdale War Dead, page 44, and the **Drill Hall WM panel 1, column 2.**
CWGC shows his number as 20084.

AYRES (AYERS?) Bertie Robert – 267758 Private. Territorial Efficiency Medal.

Born in Dover. Husband of Sarah Ellen of Ingrow, Keighley. Enlisted at Keighley.
1/5th Battalion DWR; killed in action 10 10 1917, aged 40, Battle of Cambrai.
Commemorated – Tyne Cot Memorial; the **Drill Hall WM panel 1, column 2.**
Formerly 1/6th DWR.
SDGW shows date of death as 07 10 1917.
Shown on 5 DWR WM Board as AYRES, other sources show spelling as AYERS.

BACKHOUSE Charles – 2547 Private.
Born in Thurstonland to James Hobson and Sarah of Leeds. Resided in Brockholes. Enlisted at Huddersfield. Embarked for France and Flanders in April, 1915.
1/5th Battalion DWR, B Company; wounded in action on 01 7 1915, died of wounds 11 7 1915, aged 26, Ypres.
Buried – Ferme Olivier Cemetery, 1, J, 8.
Commemorated – Brockholes WM; Thurstonland WM; M Stansfield, page 12, and the **Drill Hall WM panel 1, column 2.**
Mentioned in the Huddersfield Examiner (wounded in action) on 06 7 1915.
AS FOR GOD HIS WAY IS PERFECT.

BAGSHAW Luke – 3916 Corporal.
Enlisted at Doncaster.
1/5th Battalion DWR; killed in action 20 9 1916, Battle of the Somme.
Commemorated – Thiepval Memorial; the **Drill Hall WM panel 1, column 3.**

BAILEY Joseph – 3628 Private.
Born and resided in Dewsbury. Enlisted at Mirfield.
1/5th Battalion DWR; killed in action 11 11 1915, Ypres.
Buried – Talana Farm Cemetery, 4, F, 10.
Commemorated - the **Drill Hall WM panel 1, column 2.**

BAILEY Joseph Henry – 3597 Private.
Born in Dewsbury to Paul, of Hanging Heaton, Batley. Husband of Mary, of Batley. Enlisted at Mirfield.
1/5th Battalion DWR; killed in action 04 7 1916, aged 29, Battle of the Somme.
Buried – Connaught Cemetery, 4, A, 2.
Commemorated - the **Drill Hall WM panel 1, column 2.**
Mentioned in the Unit War Diary (awarded gallantry card by the GOC, killed in action) on 31 7 1916.
HE DIED THAT WE MIGHT LIVE – THY WILL BE DONE.

BAILEY Thomas Dismore – 3189 Private.
Born in March, Huddersfield, 29 12 1895, to William and Selina. Resided in Marske. Enlisted at Huddersfield on 06 10 1914. Embarked for France in April, 1915.
1/5th Battalion DWR, B Company, Stretcher Bearer; killed in action, sniper, 14 6 1915, aged 19, Ypres.
Buried – Rue David Military Cemetery, 1, B, 13.
Commemorated – Holy Trinity Church, Huddersfield, RoH; M Stansfield, page 15, and the **Drill Hall WM panel 1, column 2.**
Mentioned in the Unit war Diary (killed in action) on 14 6 1915; the Huddersfield Examiner (Stretcher Bearer, killed in action) on 17 6 1915; (in memoriam) on 14 6 1917.
JESUS CALLED HIM FROM THE STRIFE.

BAILEY Walter – 5341 (later 241879) Private.
Son of Mary and the late John William of Slaithwaite; Born in Golcar, resided Slaithwaite. Enlisted 24 5 1916 in Halifax. Embarked for France in January, 1917.

2/5th Battalion DWR; reported missing 03 5 1917, aged 37, Battle of Bullecourt.
Commemorated – Arras WM; France; Slaithwaite WM; St John's Church, Golcar, RoH; St James' Church, Slaithwaite, RoH; M Stansfield, page 15, and the **Drill Hall WM panel 1, column 2.**
Mentioned in the Goodall collection; the Colne Valley Almanac (reported missing 03 5 1917, body recovered August, 1917).

BAIRSTOW George – 3026 Private.
Born in Huddersfield on 06 11 1895, to Ernest and Hannah M. Resided in Huddersfield. Enlisted on 04 9 1914 at Huddersfield. Embarked for France and Flanders in April, 1915.
1/5th Battalion DWR, A Company; killed in action (shrapnel to head) on 31 7 1915, aged 19, Ypres.
Buried – Bard Cottage Cemetery, 1, A, 39.
Commemorated – Fartown and Birkby WM; Almondbury Grammar School RoH; St Cuthbert's Church, Birkby, RoH; St John's Church, Birkby, RoH; M Stansfield, page 16, and the **Drill Hall WM panel 1, column 2.**
Mentioned in the Huddersfield Examiner (killed in action) on 05 8 1915; (in memoriam) on 31 7 1917 and on 31 7 1918.

BAKER Richard (Thomas) – 34388 Private.
Born in Aycliffe to John and Martha, of Marske by the Sea. Enlisted at Middlesbrough.
5th Battalion DWR; killed in action 04 11 1918, aged 43, Advance to Victory.
Buried – Ruesnes Communal Cemetery, 1, B, 21.
Commemorated - the **Drill Hall WM panel 1, column 3.**

BALL Arthur – 5830 Private.
Son of Julia and Ernest Midgley (stepfather), born in Bradford. Enlisted at Bradford.
1/5th Battalion DWR; killed in action 25 7 1916, aged 24, Battle of the Somme.
Buried – Forceville Communal Cemetery, 2, D, 8.
Commemorated - the **Drill Hall WM panel 1, column 2.**

BAMFORD Samuel – 242808 Private.
Born Honley. Resided Stoke of Trent. Enlisted at Burslem.
2/5th Battalion DWR; killed in action 03 5 1917, Battle of Bullecourt.
Commemorated – Arras Memorial, the **Drill Hall WM panel 1, column 3.**
Formerly 31432 Private, North Staffs Regt.

BAMFORTH George – 241783 Private.
Born in Marsden to Samuel. Resided in Marsden. Enlisted at Halifax, 1916. Embarked for France and Flanders in January, 1917.
2/5th Battalion DWR; killed in action 03 5 1917, Battle of Bullecourt.
Commemorated – Arras Memorial; Marsden WM, M Stansfield, page 18, and the **Drill Hall WM panel 1, column 3.**
Mentioned in the Huddersfield Examiner (wounded in action, official casualty list) on 11 6 1917.

BAMFORTH Sam – 5509 (later 242002) Private.
Born Stainland to James, of Marsden. Resided in Huddersfield. Enlisted at Halifax in 1915. Embarked for France and Flanders, January, 1917.
2/5th Battalion DWR; killed in action 22 7 1918, Battle of Tardenois.
Commemorated – Soissons Memorial; M Stansfield, page 20, and the **Drill Hall WM panel 1, column 3.**
Mentioned in the Goodall collection; the Huddersfield Examiner (killed in action) on 23 8 1918.

BANKS James – 5836 Private.
Born and resided in Hawes. Enlisted at Keighley.

1/5th Battalion DWR; killed in action 26 7 1916, Battle of the Somme.
Buried – Warloy Baillon Communal Cemetery Extension, 5, B, 7.
Commemorated – Cravens Part in the Great War, page 138, & the cpgw.org.uk website, and the **Drill Hall WM panel 1, column 2.**

BANKS John Robert – 4906 (later 241511) Private.
Born in Sheffield. Enlisted at Huddersfield.
2/5th Battalion DWR; died 12 10 1917 as Prisoner of War.
Buried – Hamburg (Ohlsdorf) Cemetery, Germany, 1, E, 2.
Commemorated – St Stephen's Church, Rashcliffe; J J Fisher, page 139; M Stansfield, page 21, and the **Drill Hall WM panel 1, column 3.**
Mentioned in the Goodall collection.

BANNISTER William Henry – 204711 Private.
Resided in Nelson. Enlisted at Barnoldswick.
2/5th Battalion DWR; killed in action 03 12 1917.
Buried – Lebucquiere Communal Cemetery Extension, 1, B, 14.
Commemorated – Barnoldswick WM; Nelson WM and the **Drill Hall WM panel 1, column 3.**
SDGW shows date of death as 02 12 1917.

BARBER Edgar – 4663 (later 241412) Corporal.
Son of Ruth, of Holmfirth. Enlisted at Huddersfield December, 1915. Embarked for France and Flanders, August, 1916.
1/5th Battalion DWR; reported missing (killed in action) on 03 9 1916, Battle of the Somme (Thiepval).
Buried – Mill Road Cemetery, 1, I, 19.
Commemorated – Holme Valley Memorial Hospital WM (plaques 1 & 2, Holme and Holmbridge); M Stansfield, page 21, and the **Drill Hall WM panel 1, column 3.**

BARDSLEY William – 2831 (later 240450) Private. Territorial Force War Medal.
Born and resided in Lees. Husband of Mrs S A Robinson, formerly Bardsley, of Oldham. Enlisted at Huddersfield.
2/5th Battalion DWR; killed in action 18 4 1917.
Buried – Mory Abbey Military Cemetery, 1, A, 8.
Commemorated - the **Drill Hall WM panel 1, column 3.**
TFWM awarded 20 4 1922, posthumously.

BARHAM William David – 25065 Private.
Born in Barking, Essex to William and Emma. Resided in Barking. Enlisted at Calthorpe Street, London.
2/5th Battalion DWR; killed in action 20 11 1917, aged 24, Battle of Cambrai.
Commemorated – Cambrai Memorial (Louverval), France, and the **Drill Hall WM panel 1, column 3.**

BARKER Charles Victor – 203571 Private.
Born in Seacombe, Cheshire. Resided in Kirkheaton. Enlisted at Huddersfield.
2/5th Battalion DWR; killed in action 20 11 1917, Battle of Cambrai.
Commemorated – Cambrai Memorial (Louverval), France; St John's Church, Kirkheaton RoH; M Stansfield, page 21, and the **Drill Hall WM panel 1, column 3.**

BARKER Sam Oxley – 3424 (later 240744) Private.
Born in Seacombe, Cheshire, the adopted son of Miles and Alice Milner, of Mirfield. Resided in Kirkheaton. Enlisted at Huddersfield on 12 11 1914.

5th Battalion DWR, D Company, 14 Platoon; killed in action 20 5 1918, aged 32, German Spring Offensive.
Buried – Bagneux British Cemetery, 2, C, 6.
Commemorated – M Stansfield, page 22, and the **Drill Hall WM panel 1, column 3.**
Mentioned in the Goodall collection
Originally 2/5th DWR

BARKER Sydney (O) – 26513 Private.
Born and resided in Hunslet. Enlisted at Leeds.
1/5th Battalion DWR; killed in action 20 11 1917, Battle of Passchendaele.
Buried – Perth (China Wall) Cemetery, 5, J, 6.
Commemorated – the **Drill Hall WM panel 1, column 3.**
Probably incorrect initials on RoH Board.

BARLOW Ernest – 3285 Private.
Resided Swinton, Yorks, possibly Thurstonland. Enlisted at Holmfirth on the outbreak of war.
1/5th Battalion DWR; died of wounds 10 7 1915, Ypres.
Buried – Ferme Olivier Cemetery, 1, J, 5.
Commemorated – Thurstonland WM; Holme Valley Memorial Hospital WM (plaques 1 & 2, Holme and Holmbridge); M Stansfield, page 22, and the **Drill Hall WM panel 1, column 2.**
Mentioned in the Huddersfield Examiner (died of wounds) on 27 7 1915.

BARNETT Gilbert Mortimer – 2nd Lieutenant.
Son of Brian and Rebecca, of Leeds, and husband of Emily Barnett, of Leeds.
5th Battalion DWR, killed in action 28 9 1918, aged 39, Advance to Victory.
Buried – Grand Ravine British Cemetery, A, 2.
Commemorated – 62nd Division History, page 207, and the **Drill Hall WM panel 1, column 3.**
Originally 6th DWR, posted to 5th Battalion 03 9 1918.
Mentioned in the Unit War Diary (joined the Bn & killed in action) on 30 9 1918.
HE SLEEPS WITH ENGLAND'S HEROES – FROM LOVING WIFE.

BARNFATHER George – 242270 Lance Corporal.
Son of Jane and late John, of Choppington, Northumberland. Enlisted at Morpeth.
1/5th Battalion DWR; killed in action 07 8 1917, aged 20.
Buried – Ramscapelle Road Military Cemetery, 2, A, 5.
Commemorated – J J Fisher, page 115, and the **Drill Hall WM panel 1, column 3.**
CALLED TO HIGHER SERVICE.

BARRACLOUGH John William – 242384 Private.
Born Norwood Green, Halifax. Enlisted at Bradford.
5th Battalion DWR; killed in action 03 1 1918.
Buried – Dulhallows Advanced Dressing Station Cemetery, 8, C, 28.
Commemorated – the **Drill Hall WM panel 1, column 3.**

BARRACLOUGH W (George Will) – 2nd Lieutenant, Military Cross.
Born in Pontefract. resided in Huddersfield. Enlisted at Dewsbury.
Formerly 2204 (later 203567) Sergeant in the 1/5th Battalion DWR. Commissioned into the 6th Battalion on 28 8 1917, posted to the 2/6th Battalion DWR. Transferred to the 2/7th Battalion DWR on 31 1 1918 on disbandment of 2/6th Battalion (see War Diary entry), then 2/4th Battalion DWR prior to his death.
2/4th Battalion DWR; killed in action 29 9 1918, German Spring Offensive.
Buried – Grand Ravine British Cemetery, Havringcourt, C, 13.

Commemorated – Craven's Part in the Great War, page 77, & the cpgw.org.uk website, L Magnus, page 297; M Stansfield, page 23; 7 DWR War Memorial, panel 3, column 3; and the Drill Hall WM panel 1, column 3.
Mentioned in the London Gazette (award of Military Cross) on 01 2 1919, page 1641; the 62nd Division History (killed in action) page 207; the 2/7th DWR Unit War Diary (OC rear party) on 31 3 1918; the 2/4th DWR Unit War Diary (awarded MC for gallantry in Operations) on 31 10 1918; the Huddersfield Examiner (Sergeant serving in Belgium) on 28 9 1915; (2Lt killed in action) on 10 10 1918.
Name spelt BARMCLOUGH in Officers Died in the Great War (CD ROM).
The citation reads, "For conspicuous gallantry in action at Havringcourt between 12th and 15th September, 1918. With only a handful of men he entered an uncaptured portion of the enemy line and mopped up 100 yards of it, compelling four machine gun teams to surrender. Again, later, in the village, he knocked out a machine gun, which was holding up the advance, and captured it."

BARROW William Henry – 5184 (later 241751) Private.
Born on 16 10 1884 in Huddersfield to George, of Paddock, Huddersfield. Resided in Paddock. Enlisted at Halifax on 17 3 1916.
2/5th Battalion DWR; reported missing (killed in action) 03 5 1917, Battle of Bullecourt.
Commemorated – Arras Memorial, France; All Saints' Church, Paddock, RoH (currently in the Huddersfield Drill Hall); M Stansfield, page, 25, and the **Drill Hall WM panel 1, column 3.**
Mentioned in the Huddersfield Examiner (reported missing, official casualty list) on 27 6 1917; (reported missing, since presumed dead, in memoriam) on 03 5 1920; (in memoriam) on 03 5 1921.

BARTON Walter – 35146 Private.
Born in Hull to John and Emma. Resided in Hull. Enlisted at Hull.
2/5th Battalion DWR; killed in action 13 9 1918, aged 18, Advance to Victory.
Commemorated – Vis en Artois Memorial, France, and the **Drill Hall WM panel 1, column 3.**

BATES Norman -3462 Private.
Born on 21 9 1892 to Ellen, of Newsome. Resided in Newsome. Enlisted at Huddersfield on 13 11 1914.
1/5th Battalion DWR; killed in action (sniper) 17 11 1915, Ypres.
Buried – Talana Farm Cemetery, 4, F, 11.
Commemorated – St John's Church, Newsome, RoH; M Stansfield, page 26, and the **Drill Hall WM panel 1, column 2.**

BATES Tom – 200102 Sergeant.
Born in Leicester. Resided in Ovenden, Halifax. Enlisted Halifax.
2/5th Battalion DWR; killed in action 27 11 1917, Battle of Cambrai.
Commemorated – Cambrai Memorial (Louverval), France; Halifax RoH; Illingworth Moor Churchyard; Calderdale War Dead, Appendix, page 52, and the **Drill Hall WM panel 1, column 2.**

BATTY J – see **BATTYE Joseph.**

BATTYE Dan – 241696 Private.
Born and resided in Marsden. Enlisted at Marsden, March, 1916. Embarked for France January, 1917.
2/5th Battalion DWR; reported missing (killed in action) 03 5 1917, Battle of Bullecourt.
Commemorated – Arras Memorial, France; Marsden WM, Marsden Liberal Club, RoH; M Stansfield, page 27, and the **Drill Hall WM panel 1, column 3.**
Mentioned in the Huddersfield Examiner (reported missing) on 27 6 1917.

BATTYE (Batty?) Joseph – 5270 (later 241823) Private.
Born in Thurlestone to Mr and Mrs Jonas Battye, of Hepworth. Resided and enlisted at Holmfirth.

2/5th Battalion DWR; reported missing (killed in action) 03 5 1917, Battle of Bullecourt.
Commemorated – Arras Memorial, France; Holme Valley Memorial Hospital WM (plaque 6, Hepworth and Scholes); Hepworth Parish Church WM; M Stansfield, page 28, and the **Drill Hall WM panel 1, column 3.**
Mentioned in the Holmfirth Express (request for information by the family) on 23 6 1917.
CWGC records and Arras Memorial spelling was changed from Batty to Battye in 2004.

BATTYE Walter – 5213 (later 241773) Private.
Born in Holme to Mr and Mrs George Battye. Resided Holmbridge. Enlisted at Halifax, 18 3 1916. Embarked for France 17 1 1917.
2/5th Battalion DWR, D Company; reported missing (killed in action) 03 5 1917, Battle of Bullecourt.
Commemorated – Arras Memorial, France; Holme Valley Memorial Hospital WM (plaques 1 & 2, Holme and Holmbridge); M Stansfield, page 28, and the **Drill Hall WM panel 1, column 3.**
Mentioned in the Goodall collection; the Huddersfield Examiner (reported missing, official casualty list) on 27 6 1917.

BAXTER C – Private.
No trace. Possibly 202181 Private Clement Baxter, 2nd Battalion DWR, from Hipperholme, Halifax.
Died 31 10 1917.
Buried - Wancourt British Cemetery, 1, C, 49.
Commemorated – the **Drill Hall WM panel 1, column 3.**

BAXTER Fred – 241360 Corporal.
Resided Slaithwaite. Enlisted at Huddersfield, October 1915. Embarked for France January, 1917.
2/5th Battalion DWR; died of wounds (arm and thigh) 07 5 1917.
Buried – St Sever Cemetery Extension, P, 2, J, 12A.
Commemorated – Slaithwaite WM; St James's Church, Slaithwaite RoH; Colne Valley Almanac; M Stansfield, page 29, and the **Drill Hall WM panel 1, column 3**.

BAXTER J (John William?) – 5/3274 Private.
Born in Mirfield to John of Upper Heaton. Resided in Kirkheaton. Enlisted at Mirfield in August, 1914. Embarked for France and Flanders, April, 1915.
1/5th Battalion DWR; died of wounds 07 9 1916, aged 21, Battle of the Somme (possibly Thiepval).
Commemorated – Achiet le Grand Communal Cemetery Extension, Beaumetz les Cambrai Special Memorial 1; London and North Western Railway Company RoH; M Stansfield page 29, and the **Drill Hall WM panel 1, column 3.**
Mentioned in the Huddersfield Examiner (previously reported missing, now reported as died as POW, official casualty list) on 22 1 1917.
THESE ARE THEY WHO SHALL WALK WITH ME IN WHITE FOR THEY ARE WORTHY.

BEARD Herbert – 241724 Private.
Born and resided in Scunthorpe. Enlisted at Lincoln.
2/5th Battalion DWR; killed in action 03 5 1917, Battle of Bullecourt.
Commemorated – Arras Memorial, France, and the **Drill Hall WM panel 1, column 4.**

BEARDSELL Fred (Freddie?) – 5586 (later 242045) Private.
Born in Holmfirth to Mr and Mrs Dennis Beardsall. Enlisted at Huddersfield. Embarked for France in May, 1916.
1/5th Battalion DWR; reported missing (killed in action) 03 9 1916, Battle of the Somme (Thiepval).
Buried – Mill Road Cemetery, 1, C, 23.
Commemorated – Holme Valley Memorial Hospital WM (plaque 4, Upperthong); M Stansfield, page 30, and the **Drill Hall WM panel 1, column 4.**

BEARDSELL H.
No Trace.
probably BEARDSELL Albert – 240351 Private.
Born in Lockwood on 12 4 1893 to John and Sophia. Resided in Huddersfield. Enlisted at Huddersfield, on 07 8 1914, and embarked for France and Flanders in April, 1915.
1/5th Battalion, DWR; wounded in November, 1915, returned to France in May, 1916, reported wounded and missing on 03 9 1916, aged 23, Battle of the Somme (Thiepval).
Commemorated – Thiepval Memorial, France; St Matthews Church (Primrose Hill); St John's Church (Newsome); M Stansfield, page 30, and the **Drill Hall WM panel 1, column 4.**
Mentioned in the Huddersfield Examiner (reported missing) on 04 10 1916.

BEAUMONT Arthur – 3327 (later 240686) Private.
Born in Honley to George and Ada.
5th Battalion DWR; died at home on 19 2 1919, aged 27.
Buried – Honley Churchyard Cemetery, 36, 3931.
Commemorated – Honley WM; M Stansfield, page 32, C Ford, page 22, and the **Drill Hall WM panel 1, column 3.**
Mentioned in the Goodall collection.
Originally 2/5th DWR.

BEAUMONT George William – 3067 (later 240553) Private.
Born in Holmfirth to Hirst and Harriet Beaumont. Resided in Holmfirth. Enlisted at Huddersfield in August, 1914. Embarked for France in April, 1915.
1/5th Battalion DWR; reported missing (killed in action) 03 9 1916, aged 23, Battle of the Somme (Thiepval).
Buried – Mill Road Cemetery, 9, D, 1.
Commemorated – Holme Valley Memorial Hospital WM (plaque 3, Holmfirth); M Stansfield, page, 33, and the **Drill Hall WM panel 1, column 4.**
Mentioned in the Huddersfield Examiner (reported missing) on 15 9 1916; (family request for information) on 24 11 1916
GONE BUT NOT FORGOTTEN.
Brother of Harry Beaumont, qv.

BEAUMONT Harry – 3552 Private.
Born in Holmfirth to Hirst and Harriet Beaumont. Enlisted at Holmfirth December, 1914
3/5th Battalion DWR; died (pneumonia) Thoresby Camp, Ollerton, Notts, 27 5 1915.
Buried – Upperthong (St John) Cemetery, B, B, 27.
Commemorated – Holme Valley Memorial Hospital WM (plaque 3, Holmfirth); M Stansfield, page 33, and the **Drill Hall WM panel 1, column 4.**
Mentioned in the Huddersfield Examiner (died at home) on 28 5 1915.
Brother of George William Beaumont, qv.

BEAUMONT Herbert – 5536 Private.
Born in Hepworth to Hannah and stepson of George Wibberley, of Holmbridge. Enlisted at Holmfirth in March, 1916. Embarked for France in July, 1916.
1/5th Battalion DWR; wounded 27 9 1916 and died of wounds 10 10 1916, aged 21, Battle of the Somme.
Buried – Abbeville Communal Cemetery Extension, 1, H, 11. Died in 2nd Stationary Hospital or British Red Cross B Hospital (both were in Abbeville at this time).
Commemorated – Holme Valley Memorial Hospital WM (plaques 1 & 2, Holme and Holmbridge); Hade Edge WM; M Stansfield, page 34, and the **Drill Hall WM panel 1, column 4.**
Mentioned in the Huddersfield Examiner (died of wounds, official casualty list) on 09 11 1916.
Attached to 2/10th Battalion King's Own Yorkshire Light Infantry at the time of his death.
THE MEMORY OF THOSE WE LOVED SO DEAR IS OFT RECALLED BY A SILENT TEAR.

BEAUMONT Lewis – 242023 Private.
Born in Thongsbridge to Tom and Annie. Resided Thongsbridge. Enlisted at Halifax
2/5th Battalion DWR; killed in action 03 5 1917, aged 22, Battle of Bullecourt.
Commemorated – Arras Memorial, France; Brockholes WM; Holme Valley Memorial Hospital WM (plaque 5, Netherthong & Thongsbridge); St Andrew's Church, Netherthong, RoH; M Stansfield, page 35, **and the Drill Hall WM panel 1, column 4.**

BEAUMONT Stanley – 241434 Private.
Born in Oakes to Mr and Mrs Lockwood Beaumont. Resided at Lindley. Enlisted at Huddersfield, 08 2 1916.
1/5th Battalion DWR, C Company; killed in action 07 10 1917, aged 24, Battle of Passchendaele (3rd Ypres).
Commemorated – Tyne Cot Memorial, Belgium; Zion Methodist Church, Lindley, RoH; St Stephens's Church, Lindley, RoH; Salendine Nook Baptist Chapel Churchyard, D, 188; Nab Wood Working Men's Club Commemorative Plaque (now held in Mirfield Library, 2018); M Stansfield, page 36, and the **Drill Hall WM panel 1, column 4.**

BECKETT Ernest – 3445 Private.
Born in Dewsbury to William and Sarah, of Ravensthorpe. Resided in Ravensthorpe. Enlisted at Mirfield.
1/5th Battalion DWR; killed in action 14 9 1915, aged 25, Ypres.
Buried – Bard Cottage Cemetery, 1, H, 23.
Commemorated – D Tattersfield, pp 60 & 381, and the **Drill Hall WM panel 1, column 4.**
THY WILL BE DONE – R.I.P.
Brother of Willie, qv.

BECKETT Willie – 3450 Private.
Born to William and Sarah, of Ravensthorpe, Dewsbury. Resided in Ravensthorpe. Enlisted at Mirfield.
1/5th Battalion DWR; killed in action 17 12 1915, aged 24.
Buried – Wimereaux Communal Cemetery, 1, K, 31A.
Commemorated – J J Fisher, page 107; D Tattershall, pp 80 & 381, and the **Drill Hall WM panel 1, column 4.**
TOO DEARLY LOVED TO EVER BE FORGOTTEN BY HIS FAMILY.
Brother of Ernest, qv.

BEDFORD John Edward – 5285 Private.
Born in Linthwaite to Robert on 28 1 1897. Resided in Linthwaite. Enlisted at Huddersfield on 25 2 1916.
2/5th Battalion DWR; killed in action 28 2 1917, Battle of the Somme (Thiepval).
Buried – Mill Road Cemetery, 9, D, 1.
Commemorated – Thiepval Memorial, France; The Rising Sun Public House, Crosland Moor, RoH; St Thomas' Church, Longroyd Bridge; M Stansfield, page 37, and the **Drill Hall WM panel 1, column 4.**

BEECHAM George – 5058 (later 241644) Private.
Born in Thornton le Fen, Lincs, to William and Mary, of New York, Lincoln. Enlisted at Lincoln
2/5th Battalion DWR, D Company; killed in action 03 5 1917, aged 23, Battle of Bullecourt.
Commemorated – Arras Memorial, France, and the **Drill Hall WM panel 1, column 4.**
Mentioned in the Goodall collection.

BEESLEY (BEASLEY?) Walter – 6706 Private.
Born and resided in Greenfield. Enlisted at Upper Mill.
1/5th Battalion DWR; killed in action 13 10 1916, aged 21, Battle of the Somme.

Buried – Foncquevillers Military Cemetery, 1, J, 13.
Commemorated – the **Drill Hall WM panel 1, column 4.**
Mentioned in the Huddersfield Examiner (killed in action) on 20 10 1916; (official notification of death) on 15 11 1916.
Spelt Beasley in SDGW and Fisher, both spellings used in the Huddersfield Examiner.
A PURE LIFE NOBLY SACRIFICED.

BELL Frederick William – 7067 Private.
Resided in Addingham. Enlisted at Skipton.
1/5th Battalion DWR; killed in action 03 9 1916, Battle of the Somme (Thiepval).
Commemorated – Thiepval Memorial, France; Addingham WM; Halifax WM; Addingham Bowling Club WM; St Peter's Church, Addingham, RoH; Calderdale War Dead, page, 55, Craven's Part in the Great War, page 166, & the cpgw.org.uk website, and the **Drill Hall WM panel 1, column 4.**

BELL Thomas Haddon – 26494 Private.
Born in Leadgate, Durham. Resided in Medomsley. Enlisted at Consett.
1/5th Battalion DWR; killed in action 20 11 1917, Battle of Passchendaele.
Buried – Perth (China Wall) Cemetery, 5, J, 2.
Commemorated – the **Drill Hall WM panel 1, column 4.**

BELL William – 1695 Sergeant.
Born in Bradford to Mrs Ada Foster, of Huddersfield, on 06 10 1892. Resided in Huddersfield. Enlisted at Huddersfield in June, 1911.
1/5th Battalion DWR; killed in action 17 11 1915, Ypres.
Buried – Artillery Wood Cemetery, 2, A, 13
Commemorated – St Paul's Church, Huddersfield; London and North Western Railway Company RoH; M Stansfield, page 39, and the **Drill Hall WM panel 1, column 4**.

BELLAMY Thomas – 34386 Private.
Born in Hockley Heath, Warks, to George and Mary. Husband of Mary, of West Bromwich. Enlisted at Warwick.
5th Battalion DWR; killed in action 05 11 1918, aged 27, Advance to Victory.
Buried – Ruesnes Communal Cemetery, 2, A, 1.
Commemorated - the Drill **Hall WM panel 2, column 1.**
Formerly 71075 Royal Berkshire Regiment.
ONLY GOODNIGHT BELOVED, NOT FAREWELL – R.I.P.

BENNETT Wylie – 1201 Private.
Born in Marsden. Resided in Rockferry, Cheshire. Enlisted at Slaithwaite.
7th Battalion DWR; died of wounds 25 9 1915 at Rouen Base Hospital.
Buried – St Sever Cemetery, 11, A, 15.
Commemorated – Marsden WM; M Stansfield, page 39, and the **Drill Hall WM panel 1, column 4.**

BENNISON William – 235588 Corporal.
Resided in Hull. Husband of Annie Lucop (formerly Bennison), of London. Enlisted at Skelton, Yorks.
5th Battalion DWR; killed in action 27 8 1918, aged 21, Advance to Victory.
Buried – Mory Abbey Military Cemetery, 5, A, 6.
Commemorated – the **Drill Hall WM panel 2, column 1.**
Originally 2/5th DWR.

BENTHAM Harley – 2nd Lieutenant.

Son of Thomas and Elizabeth, of Hellifield.
9th Battalion DWR; wounded in action on 12 9 1918, died of wounds 16 9 1918, aged 23, Advance to Victory.
Buried – Sunken Road, Boisleux, Cemetery, 2, B, 28.
Commemorated - the **Drill Hall WM panel 2, column 1.**
Mentioned in the 62nd Divisional History (wounded in action) page 206; the Unit War Diary (died of wounds) on 30 9 1918.
HE LOVED TO DO A KIND ACTION.

BENTLEY Charles Edward – 4107 Lance Corporal.
Resided at Dalton with his wife, Alice Maria. Enlisted at Huddersfield.
2/5th Battalion DWR; accidental drowning near Clipstone Camp, Nottinghamshire, aged 41, 30 1 1916.
Buried – Huddersfield (Kirkheaton) Cemetery, C, 450.
Commemorated – St John's Church, Kirkheaton; J J Fisher, page 110; M Stansfield, page 40, and the **Drill Hall WM panel 1, column 4.**

BENTLEY George – 4419 Private.
Resided in Marsh and enlisted at Huddersfield on 09 8 1915. Embarked for France January 1916.
1/5th Battalion DWR; killed in action, shellfire, 15 11 1916, Battle of the Somme.
Buried - Foncquevillers Military Cemetery, 1, J, 28.
Commemorated – Marsh WM; J J Fisher, page 114; M Stansfield, page 40, and the **Drill Hall WM panel 1, column 4.**
Mentioned in the Huddersfield Examiner (wounded in 1916, shrapnel in right arm) on 14 7 1916. (letter home published) on 31 10 1916; (wounded five times & announcement of death) on 21 11 1916.

BENTLEY Irvin – 5132 (later 241708) Private.
Born in New Mill on 28 9 1890. Married. Resided in Lockwood, enlisted at Huddersfield on 15 3 1916.
2/5th Battalion DWR; reported missing 03 5 1917, Battle of Bullecourt.
Commemorated – Arras Memorial, France; Emmanuel Church, Lockwood, M Stansfield, page 40, and the **Drill Hall WM panel 1, column 4.**
Mentioned in the Goodall collection; the Huddersfield Examiner (reported missing) on 04 6 1917; (reported missing, official casualty list) on 27 6 1917; (in memoriam) on 05 5 1919).

BENTLEY Tom – Captain. Territorial Force War Medal.
Born in Ravensthorpe, Dewsbury, November 1888, to Mr Tom Bentley of Huddersfield. Pre war Volunteer, promoted to Sergeant and later commissioned.
2/5th Battalion DWR; wounded in action 03 5 1917, died of wounds 04 5 1917, Battle of Bullecourt.
Buried – Achiet le Grand Communal Cemetery Extension, 1, A, 15.
Commemorated – Fartown and Birkby WM; T Ashworth, page 76; J J Fisher, page 128; D Tattersfield, page 201; M Stansfield, page 40, and the **Drill Hall WM panel 1, column 4.**
Mentioned in the Goodall collection; the 62nd Div history, page 185; the Unit War Diary (Roll of Officers, Adjt) on 31 1 1917; (killed in action) on 03 5 1917.
War Diary states he was killed in action on 03 5 1917.
Territorial Force War Medal posthumously awarded on 28 6 1923.

BERRY Wilfred – 3257 Lance Corporal.
Born in Lockwood to Harry and Sarah. Resided in Lockwood. Enlisted at Huddersfield on 14 11 1914.
1/5th Battalion DWR; killed in action 03 9 1916, Battle of the Somme (Thiepval).
Commemorated – Thiepval Memorial, France; Emmanuel Church and Mount Pleasant Chapel, , Lockwood; J J Fisher, page 113; M Stansfield, page 42, and the **Drill Hall WM panel 1, column 4.**

Mentioned in the Huddersfield Examiner (reported missing) on 22 9 1916; (previously reported missing, now reported killed in action) on 13 12 1916.

BEST Thomas Andrew Dunlop – Lieutenant Colonel. Distinguished Service Order and Bar, twice Mentioned in Despatches.
Born Clonmel, County Tipperary. Resided in Scotland.
5th Battalion DWR; killed in action 20 11 1917, Battle of Passchendaele.
Buried – Ruyaulcourt Military Cemetery, F, 8.
Commemorated – B Heywood, pp 214-217, and the **Drill Hall WM panel 1, column 4.**
Mentioned in the Goodall collection (CO 2/5th DWR and medal awards); the 62nd Division History (killed in action) pp 78, 87, 191, 239; the Huddersfield Examiner (CO 2/5th DWR) on 24 9 1919, (killed in action) on 25 9 1919; L Magnus (CO, killed in action) pp 79, 292, 153, 160; Unit War Diary entries (awards and actions) on 31 1 1917, 27 2 1917, 25 8 1917, 20 11 1917, 24 11 1917 & 04 1 1918; the London Gazette (award of DSO) on 02 5 1916, page 4428; (award of Bar) on 01 1 1918, page 17; (award of MID) on 05 5 1916, page 4518; (award of MID) on 18 12 1917, page 13235.
Formerly Royal Inniskilling Fusiliers
OF SUCH IS THE KINGDOM OF HEAVEN.

BETTS Benjamin – 16099 (later 242787) Private.
Born in Hull to John and Mary. Resided at Hull. Enlisted at Beverley on 10 10 1916.
5th Battalion DWR, D Company, 14 Platoon; killed in action 29 3 1918, German Spring Offensive.
Buried – Doullens Communal Cemetery Extension, 5, B, 40.
Commemorated – the **Drill Hall WM panel 1, column 4.**
Attached to 186 TMB on 23 9 1917.
Mentioned in the Goodall collection.
ETERNAL REST GIVE UNTO HIM O LORD.

BETTS Talbot – 326420 Private.
Born in Holmfirth to Mr & Mrs J T Betts. Married with one child. Pre war Territorial, probably 1/7th DWR, mobilised 04 8 1914.
After being wounded and returning to France, transferred to Royal Garrison Artillery, 27 7 1917.
Clyde RGA (TF); killed in action, shellfire, 12 8 1917, 3rd Battle of Ypres.
Buried – The Huts Cemetery, 2, D, 1.
Commemorated – Holme Valley Memorial Hospital WM (plaque 6 Hepworth & Scholes); M Stansfield, page 42, and the **Drill Hall WM panel 1, column 4.**
Formerly 38903 Private Northumberland Fusiliers.

BETTS William John –242377 Private.
Born and enlisted at Battersea.
2/5th Battalion DWR; killed in action 28 3 1918, German Spring Offensive.
Commemorated – Arras Memorial, France, and the **Drill Hall WM panel 1, column 4.**

BICKERDIKE Frank – 1800 Private.
Born in Turnbridge, Huddersfield in July, 1891, to Tom Alexander and Martha. Resided Turnbridge. Enlisted Huddersfield.
1/5th Battalion DWR; killed in action 23 8 1915, aged 24, Ypres.
Commemorated – Ypres (Menin Gate Memorial, Belgium; Northumberland Street Primitive Methodist Church; Christchurch, Moldgreen; M Stansfield, page 42, and the **Drill Hall WM panel 2, column 1.**
Mentioned in the Huddersfield Examiner (killed in action) on 31 8 1915 [spelt Bickerdyke].

BINNS Sam – 20665 Private.
Born in Halifax. Husband of Milicent, resided in Luddenden. Enlisted Halifax.

5th Battalion DWR; killed in action 21 7 1918, aged 33, Battle of Tardenois.
Commemorated – Soissons Memorial, France; Luddenden Foot WM and the **Drill Hall WM panel 2, column 1.**
Originally 2/5th Battalion DWR.

BIRD Herbert Cecil – 5820 Private.
Born and enlisted at Bradford
1/5th Battalion DWR; killed in action 05 7 1916, Battle of the Somme.
Buried - Connaught Cemetery, 13, B, 7.
Commemorated – the **Drill Hall WM panel 2, column 1.**

BIRKS Arnold – 2826 Private.
Born in Holmfirth, 09 8 1890 to Mr and Mrs William Brown. Re-enlisted on the outbreak of war, having previously done 5 years with the Territorials, Huddersfield.
1/5th Battalion DWR; killed in action 17 8 1915, Ypres.
Commemorated – Ypres (Menin Gate) Memorial; Belgium; St Stephens Church, Rashcliffe; St Thomas Church, Longroyd Bridge; M Stansfield, page 44, and the **Drill Hall WM panel 2, column 1.**
Mentioned in the Huddersfield Examiner (killed in action at Ypres) on 25 8 1915 & 22 8 1916

BIRLEY John – 5840 Private.
Born in Bradford to Frederick and Agnes. Enlisted Bradford.
1/5th Battalion DWR; killed in action 05 7 1916, aged 21, Battle of the Somme.
Buried – Puchevillers British Cemetery, 1, C, 38.
Commemorated - the **Drill Hall WM panel 2, column 1.**
TRANSPLANTED FROM THE WARFARE OF THE WORLD INTO THE PEACE OF GOD.

BIRMINGHAM John William – 3463 Private.
Born in Huddersfield, 07 8 1895, and fostered by Mrs Firth of Huddersfield. Enlisted 06 11 1914, at Huddersfield.
1/5th Battalion DWR; killed in action 04 7 1916, aged 20, Battle of the Somme.
Buried – Connaught Cemetery, 1, D, 3.
Commemorated – J J Fisher, page 110; M Stansfield, page 44, and the **Drill Hall WM panel 2, column 1.**
Mentioned in the Huddersfield Examiner (killed in action) on 25 7 1916.
HE ANSWERED HIS COUNTRY'S CALL.

BLACKBURN Byron – 201041 Private.
Born in Liversidge to Hannah and the late Abner. Enlisted at Cleckheaton
2/5th Battalion DWR; died of wounds 29 11 1917, Battle of Cambrai.
Buried – Heckmondwike Congregational Church Cemetery, 25.
Commemorated – Cleckheaton WM; Spenborough WM; C Turpin, page 4, and the **Drill Hall WM panel 2, column 1.**

BLACKBURN William Morris – 5298 (later 241846) Private.
Born in New Mill, Huddersfield, 18 12 1878, to John and Elizabeth of Fartown. Resided Huddersfield and enlisted Huddersfield on 23 3 1916.
2/5th Battalion DWR; reported missing (killed in action) 03 5 1917, aged 39, Battle of Bullecourt.
Commemorated – Arras Memorial, France; Fartown and Birkby WM; M Stansfield, page 45, and the **Drill Hall WM panel 2, column 1.**
Mentioned in the Goodall collection; the Huddersfield Examiner (reported missing, official casualty list) on 27 6 1917; (reported missing) on 29 6 1917.

BLAKELEY James Edward – 305907 Sergeant. Military Medal.

Resided Slaithwaite and enlisted August, 1914. Returned with the Bn Cadre from Germany 07 5 1919.
5th Battalion DWR; died, home, pneumonia, 14 5 1919.
Buried – Colne Valley (Slaithwaite) Cemetery, B, 3, 111.
Commemorated – Slaithwaite WM; St James Church, Slaithwaite; M Stansfield, page 45, and the **Drill Hall WM panel 2, column 1.**
Originally 2/5th Battalion DWR.
Mentioned in the Huddersfield Examiner (Colour Party for taking Colours to Germany) on 18 12 1918 & 23 1 1919; (buried at Slaithwaite) on 16 5 1919; (returned with the Cadre and died at home) on 21 5 1919; in L Magnus, (medal roll) page 298; the Unit War Diary (OC billeting party) on 30 9 1918; (Cadre for the Colours Op Order 150) on 31 3 1919; (escort to the Colours) on 02 5 1919; the London Gazette (award of Military Medal) on 16 7 1918, page 8311.

BLAKEY Harold – 204537 Private.
Born in Huddersfield, 10 11 1897, to Joe. Enlisted 15 1 1915 in Huddersfield.
4th Battalion DWR, D Company; killed in action 06 10 1917.
Buried – Tyne Cot Cemetery, 34, G, 22.
Commemorated – Fartown and Birkby WM; St Hilda's Church Cowcliffe; Christchurch, Woodhouse Hill; M Stansfield, page 45, and the **Drill Hall WM panel 2, column 1.**
Mentioned in the 4th DWR Casualty Record, AB 136, (originally buried at grid D.15.b.8.5, Map sheet 28NE) page 34.

BLEZARD Arthur – 269334 Private.
Born in Moldgreen to James. Enlisted 04 8 1917 at Huddersfield.
5th Battalion DWR; killed in action 10 4 1918, German Spring Offensive.
Buried – Douchy les Ayette Cemetery, 2, E, 21.
Commemorated – Christ Church, Moldgreen; M Stansfield, page 46, and the **Drill Hall WM panel 2, column 1.**

BODKER John George – Lieutenant.
Born Folkestone. Married, resided Huddersfield. Commissioned in February, drafted to 1/5th Battalion DWR in November 1915 (from York and Lancaster Regiment) transferred to 2/5th Battalion DWR, 03 5 1917.
2/5th Battalion DWR, killed in action 20 11 1917, Battle of Cambrai.
Buried – Ruyalcourt Military Cemetery, F, 9.
Commemorated – B Haywood, page 214; J J Fisher, page 129; M Stansfield, page 46, the **Drill Hall WM panel 2, column 2.**
Mentioned in the Goodall collection (Intelligence Officer); 62nd Division History (killed in action) page 191; 1/5th DWR War Diary (joined 1/5th DWR) on 28 11 1915; (awarded Gallantry Card) on 31 7 1916; 2/5th DWR War Diary (joined 2/5th DWR) on 05 5 1917; (killed in action) on 18 5 1917; (buried) on 24 11 1917.
Formerly York and Lancaster Regt.

BOOTH Angus – 5851 Private.
Born Bradford, resided in Allerton and enlisted at Bradford.
1/5th Battalion DWR; killed in action 03 9 1916, Battle of the Somme (Thiepval).
Buried – Mill Road Cemetery, 9, B 7.
Commemorated - the **Drill Hall WM panel 2, column 1.**

BOOTH Edgar – 202042 Lance Corporal. Distinguished Conduct Medal, Military Medal.
Born and enlisted at Halifax.
5th Battalion DWR; died of wounds 08 11 1918, Advance to Victory.
Buried – Awoingt British Cemetery, 3, B, 8.

Commemorated – Halifax WM; Calderdale War Dead, Appendix, page 63, and the **Drill Hall WM panel 2, column 1.**
Originally A Company, 1/4th Battalion DWR (MM awarded), then posted to 2/5th Battalion DWR, DCM awarded in 5th Battalion.
Mentioned in the Huddersfield Examiner (award of DCM) on 11 11 1918; P G Bales (medal award) page 309; L Magnus (medal award) page 248; 5th DWR War Diary (award of DCM) on 30 11 1918; London Gazette (award of MM) on 28 1 1918, page 1380; (award of DCM) on 18 2 1918, page 2415.

BOOTH Harry – 26495 (26518?) Private.
Born in September, 1898, in Brocklesby, Lincs, to Thomas and Alice Emma of Kirkby Overblow, Harrogate. Resided at Pannal and enlisted at Keighley on 02 3 1916. Called up for service on 08 2 1917. Embarked for France and Flanders on 11 10 1917.
1/5th Battalion DWR; killed in action 20 11 1917, Battle of Passchendaele.
Buried – Perth (China Wall) Cemetery, 5, J, 8.
Commemorated - the **Drill Hall WM panel 2, column 1.**
SDGW lists him as 26518 Private Booth.

BOOTH John – 4083 (later 241147) Private.
Resided Lepton and enlisted at Huddersfield.
1/5th Battalion DWR; killed in action 03 9 1916, Battle of the Somme (Thiepval).
Buried – Mill Road Cemetery, 1, E, 23.
Commemorated – Lepton Parish Church; M Stansfield, page, 49, and the **Drill Hall WM panel 2, column 1.**

BOOTH Jos – 5837 Private.
Born Daisy Hill, Bradford. Enlisted Bradford.
1/5th Battalion DWR; killed in action 03 9 1916, Battle of the Somme (Thiepval).
Buried – Connaught Cemetery, 12, D, 1.
Commemorated - the **Drill Hall WM panel 2, column 1.**

BOOTH Percy – 2816 Private.
Born in Thongsbridge to James and Eliza. Resided at Thongsbridge and enlisted 05 9 1914 at Huddersfield. Trained at Clipstone Camp and Doncaster. Embarked for France April 1915.
1/5th Battalion DWR; died of wounds, Rouen, 20 7 1916, aged 20, Battle of the Somme.
Buried - St Sever Cemetery, A, 16, 38.
Commemorated – Holme Valley Memorial Hospital WM (panels 4&5, Wooldale); M Stansfield, page 50, and the **Drill Hall WM panel 2, column 1.**

BOOTH Percy – 268829 Private.
Born in Boothtown, Halifax. Husband of Edith. Enlisted at Halifax.
2/5th Battalion DWR; killed in action 20 11 1917, aged 32, Battle of Cambrai.
Commemorated – Cambrai Memorial (Louverval), France, and the **Drill Hall WM panel 2, column 1.**

BOOTH Selwyn – 4616 (later 241401) Corporal.
Born in Bradley, Huddersfield, on 14 5 1896. Enlisted on 02 11 1915 at Huddersfield.
2/5th Battalion DWR; reported missing (killed in action) 27 11 1917, Battle of Cambrai.
Commemorated – Cambrai Memorial (Louverval), France; M Stansfield, page, 50, and the **Drill Hall WM panel 2, column 1.**
Mentioned in the Goodall collection.

BOOTH Walter – 4424 (later 241291) Private.
Resided Dewsbury. Husband of Nancy. Enlisted at Huddersfield.

1/5th Battalion DWR; killed in action 03 9 1916, aged 39, Battle of the Somme (Thiepval).
Buried – Serre Road No 2 Cemetery, 13, M, 4.
Commemorated - the **Drill Hall WM panel 2, column 1.**

BOOTHROYD Percy – 5393 (later 241924) Private.
Born Birkby, 28 5 1893 to T S and E Boothroyd, of Birkby. Resided Huddersfield and enlisted 10 12 1915 in Huddersfield.
2/5th Battalion DWR; killed in action 03 5 1917, Battle of Bullecourt.
Commemorated – Arras Memorial, France; Fartown and Birkby WM; M Stansfield, page 52, and the **Drill Hall WM panel 2, column 2.**
Mentioned in the Goodall collection.

BOTTOMLEY William Dyson Atkinson – 5432 (later 202577) Private.
Resided Stainland, Halifax and enlisted at Halifax.
5th Battalion DWR; killed in action 14 7 1917, Ypres.
Buried – Brandhoek Military Cemetery, 1, M, 18.
Commemorated – the **Drill Hall WM panel 2, column 1.**
Posted in from 1/4th Battalion.

BOWER Charles Frederick – 241714 Private.
Born in Lockwood on 20 12 1893. Resided in Huddersfield. Enlisted in Huddersfield 16 3 1916.
2/5th Battalion DWR, D Company; reported missing (killed in action) 27 11 1917, Battle of Cambrai.
Commemorated – Cambrai Memorial (Louverval), France; M Stansfield, page 54, and the **Drill Hall WM panel 2, column 2.**

BOWER J
No trace of death in 5th Battalion.
Possibly 3024 Private BOWER John Thomas.
Born Huddersfield, resided at Netherton with his wife, Ida. Enlisted at February, 1915.
1/7th Battalion DWR; died of wounds at Royds Hall War Hospital, Huddersfield, 27 4 1918, aged 26.
Buried – Huddersfield (Edgerton) Cemetery, 11, B, 116.
Commemorated – South Crosland and Netherton WM; Huddersfield Corporation Roll of Honour; M Stansfield, page 55, and the **Drill Hall WM panel 2, column 2.**

BOWNESS William Henry – 3370 (later 240708) Sergeant.
Enlisted Mirfield.
2/5th Battalion DWR, D Company, 13 Platoon; killed in action 03 5 1917, Battle of Bullecourt.
Commemorated – Arras Memorial, France; Mirfield WM and the **Drill Hall WM panel 2, column 1.**
Mentioned in the Goodall collection; the Huddersfield Examiner (reported missing, official casualty list) on 27 6 1917.

BOYES Fred – 5843 Private.
Born in Low Moor, Bradford, to Thomas and Annie. Enlisted at Bradford.
1/5th Battalion DWR; killed in action 12 7 1916, aged 21, Battle of the Somme.
Buried – Connaught Cemetery, 3, J, 3.
Commemorated – Mirfield WM, and the **Drill Hall WM panel 2, column 1.**
HE BEING MADE PERFECT IN A SHORT TIME FULFILLED A LONG TIME

BRACKEN Thomas – 241600 Private.
Born, resided and enlisted at Sedbergh.
2/5th Battalion DWR; killed in action 03 5 1917, Battle of Bullecourt.

Commemorated – Arras Memorial, France, and the **Drill Hall WM panel 2, column 3.**

BRADBURY Clifford – 5450 (later 241970) Private.
Born in Holbeck, Leeds. Resided in Walkley, Sheffield, husband of Ellen. Enlisted at Sheffield.
2/5th Battalion DWR; killed in action 03 7 1917, aged 33.
Buried – Achiet Communal Cemetery Extension, 1, N, 8.
Commemorated - the **Drill Hall WM panel 2, column 3.**
CWGC list him as 41970.
Mentioned in the Goodall collection.
AT REST.

BRADBURY Hilton – 241433 Private.
Resided in Delph, enlisted at Upper Mill.
2/5th Battalion DWR; killed in action 04 2 1918, aged 21.
Buried – Roclincourt Military Cemetery, 4, A, 2.
Commemorated - the **Drill Hall WM panel 2, column 3.**
RESTING NOW IN PEACE WITH JESUS – LOVING HEARTS REMEMBER YOU.

BRADLEY Frank – 2087 Private.
Born in Huddersfield to John William and Mary Ann. Resided in Whitehaven, Cumberland.
Embarked for France in April, 1915.
1/5th Battalion DWR; died of wounds, shrapnel, 09 5 1915, aged 32, Fleurbaix Sector.
Buried – Sailly sur la Lys Canadian Cemetery, 2, B, 45.
Commemorated – M Stansfield, page 57, and the **Drill Hall WM panel 2, column 2.**
SDGW shows number as 2807.
AT REST.

OR (either of these two men could be the one listed on the Roll of Honour Board, it is impossible to ascertain the correct one):

BRADLEY Frank – 4717 Private.
Born in Huddersfield, 10 3 1898, to Elizabeth. Resided in Huddersfield. Enlisted at Huddersfield on 08 2 1916.
1/5th Battalion DWR; reported missing (killed in action) 03 9 1916, Battle of the Somme (Thiepval).
Commemorated – Thiepval Memorial, France; Parents' Headstone, Edgerton Cemetery, M Stansfield, page 57, and the **Drill Hall WM panel 2, column 2.**
Mentioned in the Huddersfield Examiner (reported missing) on 02 11 1916; (previously reported missing, now reported killed in action) on 02 7 1917.

BRADLEY George Hubert – 2364 (later 403127) later First Class Air Mechanic, Royal Flying Corps.
Born in Thongsbridge to Fred and Ada. Enlisted 04 8 1914 into 1/5th Battalion (F Company).
Embarked for France, April 1915. Transferred to the RFC in July 1917.
RFC; died of wounds 23 9 1918.
Buried – Terlincthun British Cemetery, 4, C, 26.
Commemorated – Holme Valley Memorial Hospital WM (plaque 5, Netherthong and Thongsbridge); M Stansfield, page 57, and the **Drill Hall WM panel 2, column 2.**

BRADLEY Norman – 241938 Private.
Born on 21 7 1891, in Berry Brow, Huddersfield, to George and Clara. Enlisted 27 3 1916.
2/5th Battalion DWR; accidentally killed 03 4 1917, aged 25.
Buried – Pozieres British Cemetery, 2, D, 26.
Commemorated – Armitage Bridge WM; Parents' Headstone, Newsome Churchyard; M Stansfield page 58, and the **Drill Hall WM panel 2, column 2.**

SON OF GEORGE AND CLARA BRADLEY – BERRY BROW HUDDERSFIELD – LOVED.

BRADLEY William – 5/1683 Private.
Born in Huddersfield on 19 6 1890 to William and Eliza Ann. Resided in Huddersfield. Enlisted at Huddersfield on 04 8 1914.
1/5th Battalion DWR; died of wounds on 15 5 1915, aged 25, Fleurbaix Sector.
Buried – Merville Communal Cemetery, 3, B, 8.
Commemorated – Great Northern Street Congregational Chapel RoH; St Andrew's Church, Leeds Road, RoH (thought to have been destroyed); M Stansfield page 58, and the **Drill Hall WM panel 2, column 2.**
IN LOVING MEMORY OF THE BELOVED SON OF WILLIAM AND E. A. BRADLEY, 14 WILLIAM STREET HUDDERSFIELD.

BRAND Robert Henry – 34755 Private.
Enlisted at Stockton on Tees.
5th Battalion DWR; killed in action 12 9 1918, Advance to Victory.
Buried – Ruyalcourt Military Cemetery, L, 12.
Commemorated - the **Drill Hall WM panel 2, column 3.**

BRAY Willie – 5485 Private.
Born in Lindley, Huddersfield, 12 9 1890, to Fred Bottom and Ann Bray. Enlisted Huddersfield, 20 3 1916.
2/5th Battalion DWR; died of thrombosis, home, Salisbury, 31 5 1916.
Buried – Lindley Zion Methodist Chapel Yard.
Commemorated – Zion Methodist Chapel; St Stephens Church, Lindley; Huddersfield (Edgerton) Cemetery AC screen wall; M Stansfield, page 61, and the **Drill Hall WM panel 2, column 3.**

BRAYBROOKS Herbert Charles – 241666 Private.
Born in Gosberton, Lincs, to Tom and Ida. Resided Spalding. Enlisted at Lincoln.
5th Battalion DWR; killed in action 25 8 1918, aged 24, Advance to Victory.
Buried – Gommecourt South Cemetery, 1, D, 3.
Commemorated - the **Drill Hall WM panel 2, column 3.**

BRAZELL Harry Albert – 242581 Sergeant.
Born and resided in Norwich. Enlisted at Huddersfield.
5th Battalion DWR; killed in action 24 9 1918, Advance to Victory
Buried – Gommecourt South Cemetery, 4, F, 7.
Commemorated - the **Drill Hall WM panel 2, column 3.**

BRENNAN Martin Henry – 4025 (later 241113) Private.
Born Huddersfield, 27 8 1877. Married. Enlisted at Huddersfield on 30 4 1915.
2/5th Battalion DWR; killed in action 07 8 1917, aged 40.
Buried – Queant Road Cemetery, 3, H, 13.
Commemorated – Huddersfield Parish Church; Parents' Headstone Huddersfield (Edgerton) Cemetery; M Stansfield, page 61, and the **Drill Hall WM panel 2, column 3.**
Mentioned in the Goodall collection; the Huddersfield Examiner (killed in action) on 23 8 1917; (killed in action, official casualty list) on 14 9 1917.
THOUGHT DEATH DIVIDES – SWEET MEMORY CLINGS.

BRICK Llewellyn – 240446 Private.
Born in Lindley to Austin and Clara. Resided at Oakes. Enlisted Huddersfield.
1/5th Battalion DWR; killed in action 03 9 1916, aged 23, Battle of the Somme (Thiepval).
Buried – Mill Road Cemetery, 1, E, 19.
Commemorated – the **Drill Hall WM panel 2, column 2.**

Mentioned in the Huddersfield Examiner (previously reported missing, now presumed dead) on 03 7 1917.
AU REVOIR LLEW.

BRIDGES Ernest Edgar – 681 Lance Corporal.
Born in West Newton, King's Lynn, to Frederick James and Louisa Hannah. Enlisted at Sandringham.
1/5th Battalion DWR; killed in action 17 9 1916, Battle of the Somme, aged 20.
Commemorated – Thiepval Memorial, and the **Drill Hall WM panel 2, column 1.**
Formerly 1/5th Battalion, Norfolk Regiment.

BRIGGS Thomas – 2nd Lieutenant. Military Cross.
Posted from 6th Battalion Lancashire Fusiliers to 2/5th Battalion DWR on 06 8 1918, awarded MC with DWR for action in October, 1918, posthumously, in February 1919. Had been posted to 6th Battalion Lancashire Fusiliers prior to death.
Killed in action 18 10 1918, Advance to Victory.
Buried – Quivey Communal Cemetery Extension, D, 30.
Commemorated – the **Drill Hall WM panel 2, column 3.**
Mentioned in the Goodall collection (award of MC); the 62nd Division History (killed in action) page 209; the Huddersfield Examiner (award of MC) on 11 11 1918 & 04 2 1919; the Unit War Diary (joined 2/5th DWR, 06 8 1918) on 30 8 1918; (award of MC) on 30 11 1918; (killed in action) on 31 10 1918.

BROADBENT Stanley Hadfield – 5315 (later 241859) Private.
Born in Diggle to George Edward and Esther Mary. Resided in Diggle. Enlisted at Upper Mill
2/5th Battalion DWR; killed in action 05 5 1917, aged 39, Battle of Bullecourt.
Commemorated – Arras Memorial, France, and the **Drill Hall WM panel 2, column 2.**
Mentioned in the Goodall collection.

BROADBENT Wilfred – 4438 Private.
Born in Huddersfield 12 10 1886. Married. Enlisted 08 8 1915 in Huddersfield.
1/5th Battalion DWR; killed in action by a sniper 09 8 1916, Battle of the Somme.
Buried – Connaught Cemetery, 3, J, 2.
Commemorated – M Stansfield, page 64, and the **Drill Hall WM panel 2, column 2.**
Mentioned in the Huddersfield Examiner (killed in action, sniper) on 15 8 1916.

BROADHEAD Arthur – 2823 Private.
Born in Kirkheaton to Irvy and Alice. Enlisted at Huddersfield.
1/5th Battalion DWR; died of wounds 05 8 1915, aged 24, Ypres.
Buried – Lijssenthoek Military Cemetery, 1, C, 4.
Commemorated – St John's Church, Kirkheaton; M Stansfield, page 64, and the **Drill Hall WM panel 2, column 2.**
Mentioned in the Huddersfield Examiner (died of wounds, hospital) on 13 8 1915.
EVER IN OUR MEMORY.

BROBBIN George – 35059 Private.
Born Ardwick, Manchester. Enlisted at Manchester.
5th Battalion DWR; killed in action 28 9 1918, Advance to Victory.
Buried – Grand Ravine British Cemetery, A, 8.
Commemorated - the **Drill Hall WM panel 2, column 3.**
Formerly 21702 Manchester Regiment.

BROOK Arthur – 5235 (later 241793) Private.
Born in Meltham and resided Meltham. Enlisted at Halifax.

2/5th Battalion DWR; killed in action 03 5 1917, Battle of Bullecourt.
Commemorated – Arras Memorial, France; St Bartholomew's Church, Meltham; Holme Parish Church; M Stansfield, page 65, and the **Drill Hall WM panel 2, column 2.**
Mentioned in the Goodall collection; the Huddersfield Examiner (reported missing, official casualty list) on 27 6 1917.

BROOK Cecil Fred – 35089 Private.
Born in Embsay to John Harling and Margaret Ann. Resided at Silsden, Enlisted at Halifax.
5th Battalion DWR; died of wounds 29 9 1918, aged 18.
Buried – Etaples Military Cemetery, 65, G, 3.
Commemorated – Craven's Part in the Great War, page 361, & the cpgw.org.uk website; and the **Drill Hall WM panel 2, column 3.**
Originally 2/5th Battalion DWR.

BROOK Henry (Harry?) – 240082 Sergeant. Territorial Force War Medal.
Born in Huddersfield to Pearson and Emily. Enlisted July 1911 at Huddersfield.
2/5th Battalion DWR; killed in action 03 5 1917, aged 21, Battle of Bullecourt.
Commemorated – Arras Memorial, France; Fartown and Birkby WM; St Andrew's Church, Leeds Road, Huddersfield; M Stansfield, page 68, and the **Drill Hall WM panel 2, column 2.**
Mentioned in the Huddersfield Examiner (reported missing) on 11 6 1917; (reported missing, official casualty list) on 27 6 1917.
TFWM awarded posthumously on 20 4 1922.

BROOK Irving – 3936 (later 241058) Private.
Born in Thongsbridge. Enlisted at Huddersfield. Severely wounded at Battle of Bullecourt, 03 5 1917 and taken Prisoner of War. He was repatriated to England for further treatment but died.
2/5th Battalion DWR; died of wounds 21 6 1918, home.
Buried – Lydgate Presbyterian Cemetery, SE 427.
Commemorated – Wooldale WM; J J Fisher, page 140; M Stansfield, page 69, and the **Drill Hall WM panel 2, column 3.**
Mentioned in the Huddersfield Examiner (sent postcard from POW camp) on 11 6 1917; (previously POW, died of wounds, London) on 25 6 1918.
SDGW show spelling as Irvin.

BROOK Willie – 242073 Private.
Born in Outlane, 29 12 1894, to Fred and Elizabeth. Attested under the Derby Scheme at Huddersfield, 28 2 1916. Joined the Colours on 01 4 1916.
1/5th Battalion DWR; reported missing (killed in action) 03 9 1916, aged 21, Battle of the Somme (Thiepval).
Commemorated – Thiepval Memorial, France; Outlane Trinity Methodist Church; Bethel United Methodist Church, Outlane; M Stansfield, page 71, and the **Drill Hall WM panel 2, column 2.**
Mentioned in the Huddersfield Examiner (reported missing) on 20 10 1916.

BROOK William Henry – 4791 Private.
Born and enlisted at Mirfield.
1/5th Battalion DWR; died of wounds 28 9 1916, Battle of the Somme.
Buried – Heilly Station Cemetery, 4, I, 22.
Commemorated – Mirfield WM and the **Drill Hall WM panel 2, column 2.**
Mentioned in the Huddersfield Examiner (died of wounds, official casualty list) on 02 11 1916.

BROOKE (BROOK?) Charlie (Charley?) – 240947 Private.
Born in Moldgreen, 16 11 1894, to Thomas and Charlotte, of Dalton. Enlisted 20 1 1915 in Huddersfield.
5th Battalion DWR; died, pneumonia, 15 7 1918, aged 23.

Buried – Marissel French National Cemetery, 663.
Commemorated – Christ Church, Moldgreen; M Stansfield, page 66, and the **Drill Hall WM panel 2, column 3.**
Originally 2/5th Battalion.
CWGC and SDGW show spelling as BROOK. CWGC shows forename as Charley; SDGW shows forename as Charlie.
REST IN PEACE.

BROOKE (BROOK?) Esna? – 5229 (later 241788) Private.
Born in Golcar, 1880, to Joe William of Kirkburton. Enlisted March 1916, in Huddersfield.
2/5th Battalion DWR; died, septic poisoning, 17 6 1916, aged 36, Hamelin Internment Camp, Germany.
Buried – Niederzwehren Cemetery, Germany, 10, F, 17.
Commemorated – All Hallows Parish Church, Kirkburton; M Stansfield, page 66, and the **Drill Hall WM panel 2, column 2.**
Mentioned in the Goodall collection; the Huddersfield Examiner (reported missing, official casualty list) on 27 6 1917; (previously reported missing, now Prisoner of War) on 05 7 1917; (wounded in action, POW, official casualty list) on 27 7 1917; (died of septic poisoning at Hameln) on 10 8 1917.
CWGC and SDGW show spelling as BROOK. CWGC show spelling as Esnor and SGDW shows Emor.
GONE BUT NOT FORGOTTEN.

BROOKE Henry – 241451 Private.
Born in Southport to Ellen and the late Francis. Resided Lockwood Scar. Enlisted at Huddersfield.
5th Battalion DWR; killed in action 29 3 1918, aged 27, German Spring Offensive.
Commemorated – Arras Memorial, France; M Stansfield, page 58, and the **Drill Hall WM panel 2, column 3.**
Mentioned in the Huddersfield Examiner (killed in action, official casualty list) on 04 7 1918.
CWGC show the spelling as BROOK.

BROOKE (BROOKS?) Horace – 241564 Private.
Born in Oakes to John William. Resided in Lindley. Enlisted at Huddersfield.
5th Battalion DWR; died of wounds 13 9 1918, aged 24, Advance to Victory, either at 1, 33 or 38 Casualty Clearing Stations, all were present in the area at this time.
Buried – Sunken Road, Boisleux, Cemetery, 2, A, 5.
Commemorated – Oakes Baptist Church; St Stephen's Church, Lindley; M Stansfield, page 68, and the **Drill Hall WM panel 2, column 3.**
Listed as Brook in SDGW, CWGC and M Stansfield.
GONE BEFORE HIS TIME BUT EVER REMEMBERED,

BROOKE (BROOK?) John Arthur – 305213 Private.
Born in Golcar. Resided at Crimble, Slaithwaite. Embarked for France in January, 1916.
5th Battalion DWR; killed in action 28 9 1918, Advance to Victory.
Buried – Grand Ravine British Cemetery, A, 13.
Commemorated – Slaithwaite WM; St James Church, Slaithwaite; M Stansfield, page 69, and the **Drill Hall WM panel 2, column 3.**
CWGC show spelling as BROOK.
TFWM awarded posthumously on 20 4 1922.

BROOKE Samuel – 200630 Private.
Born, resided and enlisted at Cleckheaton.
2/5th Battalion DWR; died 28 5 1917, aged 35, at either 45 or 49 Casualty Clearing Station, both were present at this time.

Buried – Achiet le Grand Communal Cemetery Extension, 1, I, 15.
Commemorated – Spenborough (Cleckheaton) WM; C Turpin, page 5, and the **Drill Hall WM panel 2, column 2**.
SUDDEN DEATH, SUDDEN GLORY.

BROWN Anthony – 242318 Private.
Resided Spennymoor. Enlisted at Durham.
1/5th Battalion DWR; killed in action 07 8 1917.
Buried – Ramscapelle Road Military Cemetery, 2, B, 15.
Commemorated - the **Drill Hall WM panel 2, column 2**.

BROWN George William – 35621 Private.
Born in Prudhoe, Northumberland, to William and Hannah of Pelton, Co Durham. Enlisted at Newcastle.
5th Battalion DWR; died of wounds 28 9 1918, aged 22, Advance to Victory.
Buried – Lowrie Cemetery, C, 26.
Commemorated - the **Drill Hall WM panel 2, column 2**.
NEARER TO THEE.

BROWN Harry – 5542 Private.
Born in Holmfirth. Resided at Longley, Holmfirth. Enlisted Holmfirth.
1/5th Battalion DWR; reported missing (killed in action) 03 9 1916, Battle of the Somme (Thiepval).
Commemorated – Thiepval Memorial, France; Holme Valley Memorial Hospital WM (plaque 3, Holmfirth); M Stansfield, page 72, and the **Drill Hall WM panel 2, column 2**.

BROWN Robert Henry – 2nd Lieutenant.
Born in Withernsea to Alfred Thomas. Joined the Battalion 29 5 1916, appointed Bombing Officer September, 1916, wounded but remained on duty as Acting Adjutant, 30 9 1916.
1/5th Battalion DWR; died of wounds, bombing accident, 16 1 1917, aged 24.
Buried – Warlincourt Halte British Cemetery, 3, J, 11.
Commemorated – M Stansfield, page 33, and the **Drill Hall WM panel 2, column 2**.
Mentioned in the Huddersfield Examiner (wrote to family of Private G W Beaumont) on 15 9 1916; (wrote to family of Corporal L Lee) on 21 9 1916; the Unit War Diary (joined 1/5th DWR, 29 5 1916) on 31 5 1916; (in action) on 03 9 1916; (OC bombers, wounded in action, remained at duty) on 30 9 1916; (injured in bombing accident) on 02 1 1917; (died of wounds, 16 1 1917) on 31 1 1917.
MEMORIES FRAGRANT AND BEAUTIFUL FROM HIS LOVED ONES AT W'SEA

BROWN Thomas Sydney – 5135 Private.
Resided in North Thoresby, Lincs. Enlisted at Lincoln on 14 3 1916.
2/5th Battalion DWR, D Company, 14 Platoon, sniper; killed in action, shrapnel, 17 2 1917, aged 26.
Commemorated – Thiepval Memorial, France, and the **Drill Hall WM panel 2, column 2**.
Mentioned in the Goodall collection.

BROWN William Lionel Gerald – 35153 Private.
Born in Spennymoor, Co Durham, to Thomas and Susannah. Enlisted at Sunderland.
5th Battalion DWR; killed in action 12 9 1918, aged 18, Advance to Victory.
Buried – Ruyalcourt Military Cemetery, L, 11.
Commemorated - the **Drill Hall WM panel 2, column 2**.

BRUCE William Johnson – 34392 Private.
Born in Hutton Henry, Co Durham. Husband of Mary Edith of Middlesbrough. Enlisted at West Hartlepool.

5th Battalion DWR; killed in action 25 8 1918, aged 37, Advance to Victory.
Buried – Gommecourt South Cemetery, 1, C, 1.
Commemorated - the **Drill Hall WM panel 2, column 3.**
Formerly 16502 Yorkshire Regiment.

BRUNT Frederick Christopher – 3367 (later 240706) Sergeant.
Son of George and Henrietta, of Widnes, husband of Florrie, of Mirfield. Enlisted 07 11 1914 in Mirfield.
2/5th Battalion DWR, D Company, 13 Platoon, gym instructor; killed in action 03 5 1917, aged 27, Battle of Bullecourt.
Commemorated – Arras Memorial, France; Mirfield WM and the **Drill Hall WM panel 2, column 3.**
Mentioned in the Goodall collection; the Huddersfield Examiner (reported missing, official casualty list) on 27 6 1917.

BUCKLEY Leonard – 32008 Private.
Born in Mossley. Enlisted at Huddersfield.
5th Battalion DWR; killed in action 27 3 1918, German Spring Offensive.
Buried – Gommecourt British Cemetery No2, 5, D, 6.
Commemorated – St John the Baptist Church, Mossley, RoH; R Vaughan, page 160, and the **Drill Hall WM panel 2, column 3.**
Mentioned in the Huddersfield Examiner (enlisted in October, 1914) on 19 7 1916.

BULL Harry – 3104 (later 240575) Private.
Born in Dalton, 21 9 1897, to Richard and Georgina. Enlisted at Huddersfield on 29 9 1914.
2/5th Battalion DWR, A Company; reported missing (killed in action) 03 5 1917, Battle of Bullecourt.
Commemorated – Arras Memorial, France; St Andrew's Church, Leeds Road, Huddersfield, M Stansfield, page 75, and the **Drill Hall WM panel 2, column 3.**
Mentioned in the Goodall collection (awarded Commanding Officer's Commendation); the Huddersfield Examiner (reported missing, official casualty list) on 27 6 1917.

BURKITT Tom – 2594 Lance Corporal.
Born in Almondbury on 19 3 1893 to Adah, of Almondbury. Resided Almondbury. Pre war Territorial. Enlisted at Huddersfield, 12 8 1914, and embarked for France and Flanders in April, 1915.
1/5th Battalion DWR, 9 Platoon, C Company; killed in action 25 6 1915, Ypres.
Buried – Rue David Military Cemetery, 1, B, 8.
Commemorated – Almondbury WM; M Stansfield, page 76, and the **Drill Hall WM panel 2, column 3.**
Mentioned in the Huddersfield Examiner (killed in action) on 28 6 1915.

BURNLEY Harry Raymond – 1859 Sergeant.
Born in Boroughbridge to Joseph. Mother resided in Meltham. Enlisted at Huddersfield in August, 1914, and embarked for France and Flanders in April, 1915.
5th Battalion DWR; died of wounds at 17 Casualty Clearing Station, 10 11 1915, aged 20, Ypres.
Buried – Lijssenthoek Military Cemetery, 4, B, 7.
Commemorated – St Bartholomew's Church, Meltham, T Ashworth, page 25; M Stansfield, page 77, and the **Drill Hall WM panel 2, column 3.**
Mentioned in the Huddersfield Examiner (died of wounds, hospital) on 19 11 1915; (in memoriam) on 10 11 1916 & 10 11 1920.

BURROWS Joseph William – 240982 Private.
Resided in Eastwood, Notts. Enlisted at Doncaster.

1/5th Battalion DWR; killed in action 03 9 1916, Battle of the Somme (Thiepval).
Buried – Mill Road Cemetery, 5, A, 9.
Commemorated - the **Drill Hall WM panel 2, column 3.**
SDGW shows date of death as 03 7 1916 and rank as Corporal.

BURTON Charles Forbes – 6698 Private.
Born and resided in Winksley, Yorks. Enlisted at Ripon.
1/5th Battalion DWR; killed in action 19 9 1916, Battle of the Somme.
Commemorated – Thiepval Memorial, France, and the **Drill Hall WM panel 2, column 3.**

BUSBY Charles Edward – 35155 Private.
Born and enlisted at Hull.
5th Battalion DWR; killed in action 12 9 1918, Advance to Victory.
Buried – Hermies Hill British Cemetery, 2, A, 14.
Commemorated - the **Drill Hall WM panel 2, column 4.**

BUTLER Clifford – 34517 Private.
Born in Holbeck, Leeds, to Thomas and Jane. Enlisted at Leeds.
5th Battalion DWR; killed in action 25 8 1918, aged 19, Advance to Victory.
Buried – Gommecourt South Cemetery, 1, B, 4.
Commemorated - the **Drill Hall WM panel 2, column 4.**
INTO THY HANDS O LORD, I COME.

BUTLER Reginald William John – 35129 Private.
Born in Roscombe, Berks. Enlisted at Reading.
5th Battalion DWR; killed in action 15 9 1918, Advance to Victory.
Buried – Hermies Hill British Cemetery, 2, E, 29.
Commemorated - the **Drill Hall WM panel 2, column 4.**

BUTTERWORTH Alfred Spencer – 26496 Private.
Born in Saddleworth to John and Mary, of Greenfield. Enlisted at Uppermill.
1/5th Battalion DWR; killed in action 20 11 1917, aged 19, Battle of Passchendaele.
Buried – Perth (China Wall) Cemetery, 5, J, 4.
Commemorated - the **Drill Hall WM panel 2, column 3.**
HE GAVE US HIS USUAL SMILE AND A WORD OF CHEER AS HE PASSED.

BUTTERWORTH Edgar – 242137 Private.
Born in Bradford to Mary Jane. Enlisted at Bradford.
1/5th Battalion DWR; killed in action 20 5 1917, aged 20..
Buried – La Touret Military Cemetery, 4, C, 26.
Commemorated - the **Drill Hall WM panel 2, column 3.**

BUXTON Frederick – 34731 Private.
Born in Walkley, Sheffield. Parents moved to Australia. Enlisted at Sheffield.
5th Battalion DWR; killed in action 25 8 1918, aged 31, Advance to Victory.
Buried – Mory Abbey Military Cemetery, 4, A, 2.
Commemorated – the **Drill Hall WM panel 2, column 4.**
Formerly 23090 Yorkshire Regiment. Originally 2/5th DWR.

BYRAM Thomas Richard – 5336 (later 241875) Lance Corporal.
Born in Greenfield to James and Mary. Resided and enlisted at Marsden.
5th Battalion DWR; killed in action 20 7 1918, aged 39, Battle of Tardenois.
Buried – Courmas British Cemetery, 2, D, 7.
Commemorated – M Stansfield, page 79, and the **Drill Hall WM panel 2, column 4.**

Originally 2/5th DWR.
THE LOVE OF CHRIST CONSTRAINETH US.

CAINE Frederick – 2380 (later 240244) Sergeant. Military Medal.
Born and enlisted at Huddersfield
1/5th Battalion DWR; killed in action 09 10 1917, Third Battle of Ypres (Passchendaele).
Commemorated - Tyne Cot Memorial, France; M Stansfield, page 79, and the **Drill Hall WM panel 2, column 4.**
Mentioned in the Unit War Diary (award of MM) 30 12 1916; L Magnus (award of MM) page 250; the London Gazette on 09 12 1916, page 12043; the Huddersfield Examiner (killed in action) on 30 10 1917.
Brother of Thomas Caine, qv.

CAINE Thomas – 3321 Corporal.
Born in Huddersfield, resided Turnbridge and enlisted at Huddersfield.
1/5th Battalion DWR; killed in action (shellfire) 20 1 1917 (CWGC shows 30 1 1917).
Buried – Humbercamps Communal Cemetery Extension, 1, C, 14.
Commemorated - M Stansfield, page 80, and the **Drill Hall WM panel 2, column 4.**
Mentioned in the Huddersfield Examiner (killed in action, shellfire) on 31 1 1917; (killed in action, official casualty list) on 15 2 1917.
Brother of Frederick Caine, qv.

CAIRNS John – 242662 Private.
Born in Alnwick, Northumberland, to John and Amy. Husband of Annie, resided at Chathill and enlisted at Alnwick.
5th Battalion DWR; killed in action 25 8 1918, aged 37, Advance to Victory.
Commemorated - Vis en Artois Memorial, France, and the **Drill Hall WM panel 2, column 4.**
Originally 2/5th DWR.
SDGW shows 05 11 1918

CAIRNS William – 33629 Private.
Resided Wellingborough, Northants, enlisted London.
5th Battalion DWR; killed in action 27 3 1918, German Spring Offensive.
Buried – Gommecourt British Cemetery No2, 5, D, 4.
Commemorated - the **Drill Hall WM panel 2, column 4.**
Originally 1/5th DWR.

CALKIN Ellis – 4548 (later 241355) Private.
Resided Aspley, Huddersfield, with wife and four children. Enlisted at Huddersfield.
5th Battalion DWR; died of wounds, accidentally shot, 09 9 1917.
Buried – St Hilaire Cemetery, 3, A, 27.
Commemorated – St Paul's Church, Southgate, Huddersfield; M Stansfield, page 80, and the **Drill Hall WM panel 2, column 4.**
Mentioned in the Goodall collection; the Huddersfield Examiner (wounded in action) on 12 6 1917; (accidentally killed) 20 9 1917; (died, official casualty list) on 12 10 1917.
Originally 2/5th DWR.
SDGW shows number as 241353.

CALVERT John William – 3533 (later 240820) Private.
Born Rashcliffe, 12 12 1881, to William and Eliza Jane. Resided and enlisted, 21 11 1914, at Huddersfield.
2/5th Battalion DWR; killed in action 03 5 1917, Battle of Bullecourt.
Commemorated - Arras Memorial, France; M Stansfield, page 81, and the **Drill Hall WM panel 2, column 4.**

Mentioned in the Goodall collection; the Huddersfield Examiner (reported missing) on 27 6 1917.

CALVERT Lewis – 4349 Private.
Born Huddersfield, 01 8 1879, and enlisted 03 7 1915 at Huddersfield.
1/5th Battalion DWR; reported missing 03 9 1916, Battle of the Somme (Thiepval).
Commemorated – Thiepval Memorial, France; M Stansfield, page 81, and the **Drill Hall WM panel 2, column 4.**

CAMERON Fred – 34249 Private.
Born in Leeds to Mr C N Cameron. Resided and enlisted at Leeds.
5th Battalion DWR; killed in action 25 8 1918, Advance to Victory.
Buried – Gommecourt South Cemetery, 1, C, 6.
Commemorated – the **Drill Hall WM panel 3, column 1.**
Originally 2/5th DWR.

CAREY Alfred – 266463 Corporal. Military Medal.
Born in Guisburn, to Alfred and Elizabeth. Resided in Clitheroe. Enlisted at Skipton
5th Battalion DWR; killed in action 06 11 1918, aged 24, Advance to Victory.
Buried – Fontaine au Bois Communal Cemetery, E, 9.
Commemorated – the **Drill Hall WM panel 2, column 4.**
Mentioned in the Unit War Diary, (award of MM for an action on 20 11 1917, December, 1917; the London Gazette (award of MM) on 13 3 1918, page 3229, L Magnus award of MM) page 279.
Originally from 2/6th DWR to 2/5th DWR.
FOR GOD, HOME, PARENTS, KING AND COUNTRY HE DIED.

CARISS Horace – 242141 Private.
Born to Alfred and Ann, Eccleshill. Resided and enlisted at Bradford.
1/5th Battalion DWR; killed in action 07 8 1917, aged 21.
Buried – Ramscapelle Road Military Cemetery, 2, A, 25.
Commemorated - the **Drill Hall WM panel 2, column 4.**

CARR James – 242940 Private.
Born in Leeds to Peter and Mrs Carr. Resided in Huddersfield with his wife, Elsie May. Enlisted at Huddersfield, 04 8 1914.
1/5th Battalion DWR; killed in action 23 11 1917, aged 21, Battle of Passchendaele.
Buried – Belgian Battery Corner Cemetery, 2, G, 4.
Commemorated – M Stansfield, page 81, and the **Drill Hall WM panel 2, column 4.**
Mentioned in the Northern Roll of the Great War, Volume 7, page 57.
AT REST.

CARRUTHERS Gordon – 2nd Lieutenant.
Born at Skipton
5th Battalion DWR; died of wounds 27 11 1918, Advance to Victory.
Buried – St Sever Cemetery Extension, S, 5, L, 2.
Commemorated – Skipton WM; Cravens Part in the Great War, page 75, & the cpgw.org.uk website; C N Bruce RoH, and the **Drill Hall WM panel 2, column 4.**
Mentioned in the 62nd Divisional History, (wounded in action) page 210.
From 1st Battalion DWR.

CARTER Arthur William – 1713 Sergeant.
Born in Kirkburton to Albert and Sarah, of Highburton. Enlisted Kirkburton, August 1914, and embarked for France in April 1915.
1/5th Battalion DWR, C Company; killed in action 12 7 1916, aged 28, Battle of the Somme.
Buried – Connaught Cemetery, 3, J, 4.

Commemorated – All Hallows Church, Kirkburton; Fisher History, page 110; M Stansfield, page 82, and the **Drill Hall WM panel 2, column 4.**
Mentioned in the Huddersfield Examiner (wrote to family of Private N Spence, qv) on 15 9 1915; (killed by shellfire) on 17 7 1916.
GREATER LOVE HATH NO MAN THAN THIS, THAT A MAN LAY DOWN HIS LIFE FOR HIS COUNTRY.

CARTER Ernest Edwin – 203444 Private.
Resided Royston, son of Sarah Elizabeth and the late Samuel. Enlisted Royston, Herts.
5th Battalion DWR; killed in action 20 10 1918, aged 21, Advance to Victory.
Buried – Quivey Communal Cemetery Extension, C, 64.
Commemorated - the **Drill Hall WM panel 2, column 4.**
Originally 2/5th DWR.
WE LOVED YOU MUCH, BUT JESUS LOVED YOU BEST.

CARTER Horace James - 35099 Private.
Born in Derby, the of Son of James and Annie, of Attercliffe, Sheffield. Enlisted at Sheffield.
5th Battalion DWR; killed in action 12 9 1918, aged 18, Advance to Victory.
Commemorated – Vis en Artois Memorial, France, and the **Drill Hall WM panel 2, column 4.**
Originally 2/5th DWR.

CASSIDY William – 3490 (later 240791) Private.
Resided Halifax and enlisted at Huddersfield.
2/5th Battalion DWR, D Company; killed in action 03 5 1917, Battle of Bullecourt.
Commemorated – Arras Memorial, France, and the **Drill Hall WM panel 2, column 4.**
Mentioned in the Goodall collection.

CASTLE Henry – 2835 Private.
Born 03 2 1893 in Almondbury to Mary. Resided Newsome and enlisted at Huddersfield in 1914.
1/5th Battalion DWR; died of wounds 08 1 1916, aged 23.
Buried – Wimereux Communal Cemetery, 1, L, 2A.
Commemorated – Mirfield WM; St John's Church, Newsome; M Stansfield, page 85, and the **Drill Hall WM panel 2, column 4.**

CASTLE Joe – 2102 Private.
Born Hopton, resided Battyford and enlisted at Mirfield.
1/5th Battalion DWR, D Company; killed in action 03 9 1916, Battle of the Somme (Thiepval).
Commemorated – Thiepval Memorial, France; Mirfield WM; Upper Hopton WM; R Leedham, pp 37-44, and the **Drill Hall WM panel 2, column 4.**
Mentioned in the Huddersfield Examiner (official casualty list) on 19 3 1917.
Originally H (later D) Company 2/5th DWR. Volunteered for foreign service 04 8 1914.

CATHRALL Cyril – 306960 Private.
Born to David of Pitsmoor, Sheffield. Resided and enlisted at Sheffield.
5th Battalion DWR; killed in action 28 9 1918, Advance to Victory.
Buried – Grand Ravine British Cemetery, A, 16.
Commemorated - the **Drill Hall WM panel 3, column 1.**
THOUGH LOST TO SIGHT, TO MEMORY EVER DEAR.

CATON Richard -241376 Private.
Enlisted at Huddersfield.
1/5th Battalion DWR; killed in action 07 8 1917. Nieuport.
Buried – Ramscapelle Road Military Cemetery, 2, A, 7.
Commemorated – J J Fisher History, page 115, and the **Drill Hall WM panel 2, column 4.**

Mentioned in the Huddersfield Examiner (killed in action) on 30 8 1917; (killed in action, official casualty list) on 14 9 1917.

CAUSER Joseph – 268764 Private.
Born Barton under Needwood, Staffs, resided and enlisted at Sheffield.
2th Battalion DWR; killed in action 10 10 1917, Battle of Cambrai.
Buried – Cement House Cemetery, 6, A, 27.
Commemorated – C N Bruce History RoH, page, 220, and the **Drill Hall WM panel 2, column 4.**

CAWTHORNE William – 23348 Lance Corporal.
Born in Wakefield to Stephen and Mrs Cawthorne. Resided Shipley with his wife, Florence Cawthorne (later Welsh). Enlisted at Shipley.
5th Battalion DWR; killed in action 27 3 1918, aged 31, German Spring Offensive.
Commemorated – Arras Memorial, France, and the **Drill Hall WM panel 2, column 4.**
Originally 2/5th DWR.

CAWTHRA Walter Edwin (Teddy) – 241295 Private.
Born 07 9 1897 to Edwin and Mary Elizabeth, of Huddersfield, and enlisted at Huddersfield on 07 8 1915.
5th Battalion DWR, Signals Platoon; killed in action 20 7 1918, aged 20, Battle of Tardenois.
Buried – Courmas British Cemetery, 2, D, 10.
Commemorated - St Stephen's Church, Rashcliffe; Almondbury WM; Huddersfield Corporation RoH; M Stansfield, page 86, and the **Drill Hall WM panel 2, column 4.**
Mentioned in the Huddersfield Examiner (signals platoon, killed in action) on 06 8 1918; (in memoriam) on 20 7 1921.
Originally 2/5th Battalion.
GOD TAKES OUR LOVED ONES FROM OUR HOMES BUT NEVER FROM OUR HEARTS.

War Memorial Boards before refurbishment, 2018

Mr Les Shipley with his brother undertaking the mammoth task of refurbishing the War Memorial, summer 2018.

CAMERON. F.	PTE.	COX. C.	C.S.M.	CROWTHER. H.	CPL.	DAWSON. J.	SGT.
CATHRALL. C.	"	COE. G.B.	PTE.	CRAGG. A.H.	PTE.	DAY. A.	C.S.M.
CHAPPELL. S.	"	COX. G.	"	CRAIG. F.	"	DAWSON. C.	PTE.
CHAPMAN. W.H.	"	COLDWELL. S.	"	CRITCHLEY. P.	"	DAWSON. F.	"
CHIPPINDALE. N	"	COLDWELL. H.	CPL.	CRANE. H.	"	DARRAGH. M.S.	2/LT.
CHAMBERS. C.	SGT.	COLE. H.	PTE.	CROSS. W.	"	DAVIES. D.	PTE.
CHERRY. T.	PTE.	COLEMAN. F.H.	"	CRABTREE. E.	"	DAVIES. W.O.	2/LT.
CHERRY. W.	"	COUPLAND. R.B.	"	CRABTREE. FRANK.	"	DAVIES. W.	SGT.
CHADWICK. T.	"	COWGILL. E.	"	CRABTREE. F.	"	DALE. C.A.	PTE.
CHEETHAM. A.	"	COWGILL. A.	"	CRABTREE. A.	"	DARNBOROUGH. A.	"
CHRISTON. J.W.	"	COWGILL. H.	"	CRABTREE. J.B.	"	DARNBROOK. H.	L/CPL.
CHASE. C.	"	COCKSHOTT. W.	"	CROSLAND. G.	"	DAVIDSON. D.R.	PTE.
CHARLESWORTH.G.V.	2/LT.	COWARD. H.	"	CROSSLAND. T.	CPL.	DENT. W.	"
CHARLTON. W.H.	PTE.	COWLING. F.	"	CROSSLEY. J.	PTE.	DENTON. F.	"
CLIFF. G.E.	"	COUPLAND. R.	"	CROSSLEY. J.	"	DENTON. C.S.	"
CLAYTON. N.	L/CPL.	COLLINGWOOD. J.T.	"	CROSBY. G.	"	DEAN. F.	"
CLEGG. F.	PTE.	COCKER. L.	L/CPL.	CRYER. J.H.	"	DEAN. H.O.	"
CLEMENT. A.J.	"	COCKS. R.	PTE.	CRYER. C.	"	DEARNLEY. E.	"
CLEMENT. H.J.	"	COMPTON. J.L.	"	CREATON. H.E.	L/CPL.	DEARNLEY. G.F.	"
CLARK. ALFRED.	SGT.	COOPER. H.	"	CROWE. F.T.	PTE.	DENNISON. N.	L/CPL.
CLARK. ALFRED.	PTE	CONNOLLY. A.	"	CUNNINGHAM. C.	"	DEANS. J.W.	PTE.
CLARK. ARCHIBALD.	"	CONNELL. H.	"	CUTTS. K.E.	"	DENBY. J.	"
CLAY. L.	"	COATES. O.M.	"	CURTOIS. H.	"	DEWHIRST. G.D.	"
CLOUGH. E.	"	CONWAY. W.B.	"	CULPAN. A.R.	"	DEIONE. A.	"
CLARIDGE. H.	"	CROWTHER. E.	"	CURTIS. P.A.	"	DEMPSTER. G.	"
CLAPHAM. E.	LT.	CROWTHER. L.T.	2/LT.	DAWSON. C.	"	DITCHBURN. J.B.	"

DIXON. W.R.	PTE.	DYSON. H.F.	C.S.M.	EMMOTT. T.O.	PTE.	FOGG. W.	PTE.
DINSDALE. R.	"	DYSON. R.	SGT.	ENGLISH. T.	"	FORSHAW. A.E.	"
DODSON. P.	"	DYSON. J.R.	PTE.	ERRINGTON. W.S.	"	FORREST. H.D.	2/LT.
DOVE. J.	"	DYSON. T.	"	EVANS. E.	"	FORSTER. J.T.	PTE.
DONKERSLEY. W.	"	DYSON. H.	"	FAHY. M.	"	FRANCIS. H.	"
DONNELLAN. W.	"	DYSON. F.C.	SGT.	FARRAR. J.E.	"	FRASER. W. M.M.	SGT.
DOOLEN. E.	"	DYCHE. W.	PTE.	FAIRLESS. W.	"	FROGGATT. G.	PTE.
DOOLAN. E.	"	EASTWOOD. B.	"	FARREL. R. M.M.	A/L/CPL.	FRAINE. J.	"
DOBSON. H.C.	"	EASTWOOD. G.H.	CPL.	FERGUSON. A. M.M.	CPL.	FREEMAN. W.L.	"
DONALD. A.	"	EASTWOOD. F.E.	PTE.	FEATHER. E.A.	PTE	FRANKLIN. H.	"
DODD. D.L.	SGT.	EASTWOOD. H.R. M.M.	SGT.	FETCHETT. E.	"	FRANKLIN. E.	"
DOOK. C.	PTE.	EARNSHAW. A.	PTE.	FEATHER. T. M.M.	"	GARFITT. W.	"
DOVER. L.W.	"	EARNSHAW. H.	"	FISHER. D.A.	"	GAWTHORPE. S.	CPL.
DORLING. B.	"	EARNSHAW. W.	"	FISHER. J.H.	2/LT.	GALLAGHER. W.G.	PTE
DRYDEN. T.	"	EATON. H.	"	FISHER. H.	PTE.	GALLAGHER. J.W.	"
DRINKWATER. W.	"	EDWARDS. W.E.	"	FISHER. A.	"	GARWOOD. J.W.	"
DREW. G.	"	EGLINTON. C. M.M.	CPL.	FISHER. W.	"	GARSIDE. T.H.	"
DRANSFIELD. E.	"	ELSTON. G.W.	PTE.	FIDLER. C.	"	GARSIDE. J.	"
DRUMMOND. T.M.	L/CPL.	ELY. G.W.	"	FIRTH. L.	"	GARFORTH. F.	"
DRAPER. A.J.	PTE.	ELLIS. HARRY.	"	FIRTH. R.	"	GANNON. J.	"
DURRANS. F.	CPL.	ELLIS. G.	"	FITZJOHN. A.T.	L/CPL.	GARROD. F.	"
DURKIN. J.	"	ELLIS. HERBERT.	"	FIRN. A.	"	GEE. B.	"
DUNSHEE. E.R.	2/LT.	ELLIS. W.	"	FLETCHER. D.	PTE.	GIBSON. G.	L/CPL.
DUXBURY. C.	PTE.	ELLIS. R.	LT.	FLINTON. T.	"	GIBSON. W.H.	PTE.
DYER. F.M.	CPL.	ELLIOTT. J.G.	PTE.	FLETT. T.W.	"	GILLING. G.	"
DYSON. A.	PTE.	EMSLEY. J.	"	FOX. J.	"	GILL. W.	"

CHADWICK Thomas – 305836 Private.
Resided and enlisted at Mossley.
8th Battalion DWR; killed in action 27 8 1917.
Commemorated – Tyne Cot Memorial, Belgium; Mossley WM; St George's Church, Mossley, RoH; Mossley Town Hall WM; R Vaughan, page 93, and the **Drill Hall WM panel 3, column 1.**

CHAMBERS Charles Edward – 240111 Sergeant.
Born in Kirkburton to Henry and Emma, resided at Honley and enlisted at Kirkburton. Embarked for France in April, 1915.
1/5th Battalion DWR; killed in action 07 8 1917, aged 25, Nieuport.
Buried – Ramscapelle Road Military Cemetery, 2, A, 4.
Commemorated - All Hallows Parish Church, Kirkburton, WM (G Company); M Stansfield, page 87, and the **Drill Hall WM panel 3, column 1.**
Mentioned in the Huddersfield Examiner (announcement of death) on 16 and 23 8 1917; (killed in action, official casualty list) on 14 9 1917; the Unit War Diary (attached to the Portuguese Expeditionary Force 22 to 25 5 1917) on 31 5 1917.
TREASURED MEMORIES OF ONE DEARLY LOVED.

CHAPMAN William Henry – 5858 Private.
Born in Bradford to William Henry and Mary. Resided and enlisted at Bradford.
1/5th Battalion DWR; killed in action 04 7 1916, aged 23, Battle of the Somme.
Buried – Connaught Cemetery, 1, E, 1.
Commemorated - the **Drill Hall WM panel 3, column 1.**
FOREVER WITH THE LORD.

CHAPPELL Stanley – 3392 Private.
Born Huddersfield 14 5 1892 to Eleanor of Birkby. Resided in Birkby and enlisted at Huddersfield 04 11 1914.
1/5th Battalion DWR; killed in action 14 8 1915, Ypres.
Buried – Talana Farm Cemetery, 4, A, 9.
Commemorated – Fartown and Birkby WM; Great Northern Street Congregational Church WM; M Stanfield, page 89, and the **Drill Hall WM panel 3, column 1.**
Mentioned in the Huddersfield Examiner (death by gunshot wound) on 17 8 1915.

CHARLESWORTH George Vernon – 2nd Lieutenant.
Born 03 3 1892 in Huddersfield to John William and Elizabeth Ann, of Lockwood, Huddersfield. Resided Huddersfield and enlisted into the 1/5th DWR as a Private soldier on 12 10 1914. Embarked for France in April, 1915.
6th Battalion DWR; killed in action 28 9 1918, aged 26, Advance to Victory.
Buried – Grand Ravine British Cemetery, A, 3.
Commemorated – St Stephen's Church, Rashcliffe RoH; M Stansfield, page 90, and the **Drill Hall WM panel 3, column 1.**
Mentioned in the Unit War Diary (killed in action, Marcoing) on 30 9 1918; the Huddersfield Examiner (wounded) on 13 7 1916, (killed in action) on 08 10 1918. The Examiner published memorial notices on the anniversary of his death for at least three years.
VICTORIOUS SHALL RISE THEY WHO HAVE DRUNK CHRIST'S CUP OF SACRIFICE.

CHARLTON William Henry – 35157 Private.
Born in Beverley to Thomas and Sarah. Enlisted at Hull.
5th Battalion DWR; died of wounds 16 11 1918, aged 18, Advance to Victory.
Buried – St Sever Cemetery Extension, S, 3, R, 17.
Commemorated - the **Drill Hall WM panel 3, column 1.**
Originally 2/5th Battalion.

LOVED AND REMEMBERED.

CHASE Charlie – 242599 Private.
Born in Stalybridge, Cheshire, and enlisted into F Company 1/7th DWR at Micklehurst, Mossley.
1/5th Battalion DWR; killed in action 20 7 1918.
Buried – Marfaux British Cemetery, 7, A, 9.
Commemorated – R Vaughan, page 25, and the **Drill Hall WM panel 3, column 1.**

CHEETHAM Arthur – 5410 (later 241940) Private.
Born in Mirfield to Ben and Nancy. Resided in Mirfield. Enlisted at Huddersfield.
2/5th Battalion DWR; killed in action 03 5 1917, aged 27, Battle of Bullecourt.
Commemorated – Arras Memorial, France; Mirfield WM and the **Drill Hall WM panel 3, column 1.**
Mentioned in Goodall collection.

CHERRY Tom – 26518 Private.
Born and resided in Wombwell. Enlisted at Silkstone.
1/5th Battalion DWR; killed in action 20 11 1917, Battle of Passchendaele.
Buried - Perth (China Wall) Cemetery, 5, J, 5.
Commemorated - the **Drill Hall WM panel 3, column 1.**

CHERRY William – 33629 Private.
Resided at Wellingborough (Northants) and enlisted at London.
5th Battalion DWR; killed in action 27 3 1918, German Spring Offensive.
Buried – no trace in CWGC records.
Commemorated - the **Drill Hall WM panel 3, column 1.**
Originally 1/5th DWR.

CHIPPINDALE Norman – 4396 Private.
Born Longwood, Huddersfield, to Walter and Emily. Husband of Agnes. Resided Linthwaite.
Enlisted at Huddersfield. Embarked for France in May, 1916.
1/5th Battalion DWR; killed in action 25 10 1916, aged 23, Battle of the Somme.
Buried – Foncquevillers Military Cemetery, 1, K, 23.
Commemorated – St Mark's Parish Church, Longwood; Salendine Nook Chapel Yard, 443E; Huddersfield Mission, Milnsbridge; Crow Lane Board School, Milnsbridge; Fisher History, page 114; M Stansfield, page 92, and the **Drill Hall WM panel 3, column 1.**
CAUSEWAY SIDE LINTHWAITE HUDDERSFIELD.

CHRISTON John William – 23729 Private.
Born and enlisted in Hartlepool.
2/4th Battalion DWR; killed in action 25 8 1918, aged 28, Advance to Victory.
Buried – Gommecourt South Cemetery, 1, E, 9.
Commemorated – the **Drill Hall WM panel 3, column 1.**
HIS DUTY NOBLY DONE, DEEPLY REGRETTED BY HIS WIFE AND SON.

CLAPHAM Edgar – Lieutenant.
Born in Keighley to John and Mabel. Joined the 2/6th DWR, transferred to 1/5th DWR.
5th Battalion DWR; died of wounds 5 11 1918, aged 23, Advance to Victory.
Buried – Awoingt British Cemetery, 3, A, 3.
Commemorated - the **Drill Hall WM panel 3, column 1.**
Mentioned in 2/6th DWR War Diary (joined Bn) on 22 3 1917; 1/5th DWR War Diary (joined Bn) on 27 10 1917, (to hospital) on 05 12 1917, (to UK 22 12 1917) on 30 12 1917; 5th DWR War Diary (joined Bn 19 9 1918) on 30 9 1918, (wounded in action and died of wounds) on 30 11 1918.
HE LAID ALL ON THE ALTAR OF DUTY, HIS LIFE.

CLARIDGE Harry – 34397 Private.
Born in Huntingdon to William and Clara. Enlisted at Huntingdon.
5th Battalion DWR; killed in action 26 8 1918, aged 19, Advance to Victory.
Buried – Queens Cemetery, Bucquoy, 2, B, 1.
Commemorated - the **Drill Hall WM panel 3, column 1.**
Formerly 35110 Yorkshire Regiment.
AT REST.

CLARK (CLARKE?) Alfred – 21029 Private.
Born in Barrow on Soar, Leics. Enlisted in Loughborough.
1/5th Battalion DWR; killed in action 12 8 1917, aged 26.
Buried – Coxyde Military Cemetery, 2, G, 10.
Commemorated – the **Drill Hall WM panel 3, column 1.**
Formerly 24949 Leicestershire Regiment.
CWGC shows spelling as CLARKE.

CLARK Alfred – 240116 Sergeant.
Born in Islington, resided at Highgate Hill and enlisted in Kirkburton.
1/5th Battalion DWR; died of wounds 20 3 1917.
Commemorated – Loos Memorial, France; Kirkburton WM and the **Drill Hall WM panel 3, column 1.**

CLARK Archibald Grasson – 204566 Private.
Born in Falkirk on 06 2 1885, to John. Married and resided at Lockwood. Enlisted at Huddersfield, July 1915.
2/5th Battalion DWR; reported missing 27 11 1917, Battle of Cambrai (Bourlon Wood).
Commemorated – Cambrai Memorial (Louverval), France; St Stephen's Church, Rashcliffe, RoH; Stansfield, page 93, and the **Drill Hall WM panel 3, column 1.**
SDGW shows his place of birth as Huddersfield.

CLAY Louis – 4905 Private.
Born in Golcar, husband of Sarah and resided at Linthwaite. Enlisted at Huddersfield on 04 3 1916. Embarked for France January, 1917.
2/5th Battalion DWR; died of wounds, shrapnel, 4 Casualty Clearing Station, Lozinghem, 23 2 1917.
Buried – Varennes Military Cemetery, 1, I, 7.
Commemorated – Linthwaite WM, St John's Church, Golcar; Golcar Baptist Church; Colne Valley Almanac; M Stansfield, page 94, and the **Drill Hall WM panel 3, column 1.**
Mentioned in the Huddersfield Examiner (announcement of death) 02 3 1917, (official casualty list) on 22 3 1917.
AT REST.

CLAYTON Norman – 36 Lance Corporal.
Born in Huddersfield to William and Kate. Enlisted at Huddersfield in August, 1914. Embarked for France April, 1915.
1/5th Battalion DWR; killed in action 05 7 1916, Battle of the Somme.
Commemorated – Thiepval Memorial, France; Huddersfield Parish Church RoH; J J Fisher, page 110; M Stansfield, page 95, and **the Drill Hall WM panel 3, column 1.**
Mentioned in the Huddersfield Examiner, (killed in action shellfire) on 01 8 1916, (mia official casualty list) on 07 8 1916. The Examiner published memorial notices on the anniversary of his death for at least three years.

CLEGG Frank – 5561 Private

Born in Milnsbridge to Edwin and Grace. Resided in Milnsbridge and enlisted at Huddersfield on 30 3 1916. Embarked for France in August, 1916.
1/5th Battalion DWR; reported missing 03 9 1916, aged 19, Battle of the Somme (Thiepval).
Commemorated – Thiepval Memorial, France; J J Fisher, page 114; M Stansfield, page 96, and the **Drill Hall WM panel 3, column 1.**
The Huddersfield Examiner (previously reported missing now reported killed in action, official casualty list) on 05 3 1917.

CLEMENT Arthur John – 6051 Private.
Born in Keighley, to Ann and the late John. Resided and enlisted at Keighley.
1/5th Battalion DWR; killed in action 17 9 1916, aged 20, Battle of the Somme.
Commemorated – Thiepval Memorial, France, and the **Drill Hall WM panel 3, column 1.**
Attached to 10th Battalion King's Own Yorkshire Light Infantry.

CLEMENT (CLEMMET) Henry (Harry) James – 6052 Private.
Born in Northallerton to John and Sarah Clemmet. Resided in Sedbergh. Enlisted at Keighley.
1/5th Battalion DWR; killed in action 22 9 1916, aged 22, Battle of the Somme.
Commemorated – Thiepval Memorial, France, and the **Drill Hall WM panel 3, column 1.**
Attached 10th Battalion King's Own Yorkshire Light Infantry.
SDGW shows Henry James **CLEMENT**. CWGC shows Harry James **CLEMMET**.

CLIFF G E
No trace.
Probably 3330 Private CLIFFE George Edward.
Born in Huddersfield to Whitehead and Bessie. Resided and enlisted at Huddersfield on 10 11 1914. Embarked for France in April 1915.
1/5th Battalion DWR; killed in action 11 11 1915, aged 18, Ypres.
Buried – Talana Farm Cemetery, 4, D, 1.
Commemorated - M Stansfield, page 96, and the **Drill Hall WM panel 3, column 1.**
Mentioned in the Huddersfield Examiner (killed by a trench mortar bomb) on 17 11 1915.
LOVING MEMORIES.

CLOUGH Ernest – 4902 (later 241509) Private.
Born in Brighouse on 21 4 1885 to William of Lindley. Resided in Forres, Elgin, with his wife, Rachel. Enlisted Huddersfield on 02 3 1917.
2/5th Battalion DWR; wounded in action 01 12 1917, and died of wounds, 49 Casualty Clearing Station, Achiet le Grand, aged 32, 02 12 1917.
Buried – Achiet le Grand Communal Cemetery Extension, 1, Q, 31.
Commemorated – St James Presbyterian Church RoH, Lindley Zion Methodist Church; St Stephen's Church, Lindley; M Stansfield, page 97, and the **Drill Hall WM panel 3, column 1.**
Mentioned in the Goodall collection.

COATES Oscar Marshall – 35096 Private.
Born in Gateshead to Henry and Olive. Enlisted at Newcastle upon Tyne.
5th Battalion DWR; died of wounds 08 10 1918, aged 18, Advance to Victory.
Buried – Terlincthun British Cemetery, 4, F, 35.
Commemorated – the **Drill Hall WM panel 3, column 2.**
Formerly 12914 East Yorkshire Regiment.
ONLY A BOY BUT FAITHFUL UNTO DEATH.

COCKER Leonard – 19151 Lance Corporal.
Born and enlisted in Bradford.
2/5th Battalion DWR; killed in action 20 11 1917, Battle of Cambrai.

Commemorated – Hermies Hill British Cemetery, Special Memorial B1, and the **Drill Hall WM panel 3, column 2.**
THEIR GLORY SHALL NOT BE BLOTTED OUT.

COCKS Robert – 24299 Private.
Born and enlisted in Beverley.
2/5th Battalion DWR; killed in action 29 3 1918, German Spring Offensive.
Commemorated – Arras Memorial, France, and the **Drill Hall WM panel 3, column 2.**
Formerly 38207 the York and Lancaster Regiment.

COCKSHOTT Wright – 7063 Private.
Born and resided in Steeton and enlisted at Bradford.
1/6th Battalion DWR; reported missing, killed in action, 03 9 1916, Battle of the Somme (Thiepval).
Commemorated – Thiepval Memorial, France; Craven's Part in the Great War, page 168, & the cpgw.org.uk website, and the **Drill Hall WM panel 3, column 2.**
Mentioned in S Barber (reported missing on 03 9 1916, with photograph) page 85.

COE George B – 34393 Private.
Born in Backworth, Northumberland, to Richard and Margaret. Resided in Pelton, Co Durham, husband of Ester. Enlisted at Chester le Street.
5th Battalion DWR; killed in action 12 9 1918, aged 25, Advance to Victory.
Commemorated – Vis en Artois Memorial, France, and the **Drill Hall WM panel 3, column 2.**
Formerly 46548 Yorkshire Regiment. Originally 2/5th Battalion.

COLDWELL Hubert – 203618 Corporal.
Born in Holmfirth. Mobilised with the Holmfirth Territorials, 04 8 1914. Embarked for France on 14 4 1915. Discharged as time expired, 1916. Re-enlisted 03 5 1917.
5th Battalion DWR; reported missing 21 3 1918, informed family that he was captured 28 3 1918. Died of wounds as a POW 07 10 1918, Advance to Victory.
Buried – Mons Communal Cemetery, 8, B, 3.
Commemorated - Holmfirth Hospital WM; parents' headstone in St George's Churchyard, Brockholes; M Stansfield, page 100, and the **Drill Hall WM panel 3, column 2.**
Mentioned in the Huddersfield Examiner: (official casualty roll) on 12 12 1917 and (report of death as a POW) on 02 7 1919.
Originally 1/5th DWR, rejoined 2/5th DWR.

COLDWELL Seth – 241435 Private.
Born in Holmfirth, resided Thongsbridge and enlisted at Huddersfield on 16 2 1916.
1/5th Battalion DWR; reported missing 03 9 1916, Battle of the Somme (Thiepval).
Buried – Mill Road Cemetery, 1, H, 8.
Commemorated – Wooldale WM; M Stansfield, page 100, and the **Drill Hall WM panel 3, column 2.**
Mentioned in the Huddersfield Examiner (request for information from family) on 17 10 1916; (reported missing now presumed killed in action) on 30 8 1916.

COLE Harry - 241340 Private.
Resided at Kirkheaton. Enlisted at Lower Hopton.
1/5th Battalion DWR; killed in action 03 9 1916, Battle of the Somme (Thiepval).
Buried – Mill Road Cemetery, 1, D, 18.
Commemorated – Mirfield WM; Upper Hopton WM; R Leedham, pages 157-158; M Stansfield, page 100, and the **Drill Hall WM panel 3, column 2.**

COLEMAN Frederick Henry – 16110 (later 242798) Private.
Born, resided and enlisted in Hull.

2/5th Battalion DWR, D Company; killed in action 03 5 1917, Battle of Bullecourt.
Commemorated – Arras Memorial, France, and the **Drill Hall WM panel 3, column 2.**
Formerly 33185 East Yorkshire Regiment.
Mentioned in the Goodall collection.

COLLINGWOOD John Thomas – 16086 (later 242775) Private.
Born in Hull to Elijah and Harriet. Resided and enlisted at Hull.
2/5th Battalion DWR, D Company; died of wounds 17 5 1917, aged 32, Battle of Bullecourt.
Buried – Boulogne Eastern Cemetery, 4, B, 25.
Commemorated - the **Drill Hall WM panel 3, column 2.**
Mentioned in the Goodall collection.
A LIGHT FROM MY HOME TO A MANSION ABOVE – FROM DEAR MOTHER.

COMPTON John Leslie – 34395 Private.
Born in Balscote, Oxon, and enlisted in Banbury.
5th Battalion DWR; died of wounds, home, 10 10 1918.
Buried – Balscote (St Mary's) Churchyard Cemetery.
Commemorated - the **Drill Hall WM panel 3, column 2.**
Originally 2/5th DWR.

CONNELL Herbert – 34737 Private.
Born Bramley, Leeds, and enlisted at Chesterfield.
5th Battalion DWR; killed in action 12 9 1918, Advance to Victory.
Buried – Ruyalcourt Military Cemetery, J, 21.
Commemorated – the **Drill Hall WM panel 3, column 2.**
Formerly 31695 Notts and Derby Regiment.

CONNOLLY Anthony – 35161 Private.
Born in Hebburn, Tyne and Wear, to Mary. Resided and enlisted at West Hartlepool.
5th Battalion DWR; killed in action 12 9 1918, aged 18, Advance to Victory.
Buried – Ruyalcourt Military Cemetery, L, 10.
Commemorated – the **Drill Hall WM panel 3, column 2.**
Originally 2/5th DWR.

CONWAY Wilfred Bernard – 25070 Private.
Born in Tatchbrook, Warks, on 11 2 1898. Enlisted at Rugby.
5th Battalion DWR; killed in action, shellfire, 20 10 1918, Advance to Victory.
Buried – Quivey Communal Cemetery Extension, C, 54.
Commemorated – Wolston, Warks, WM; St Margaret's Church, Wolston, RoH; ww1wargraves.co.uk, and the **Drill Hall WM panel 3, column 2.**
Originally 2/5th DWR.
Letter from Platoon Commander held in DWR Archive.

COOPER Henry – 34523 Private.
Born Calverton, Notts, to Sarah (later Binch). Enlisted Hucknall, Notts.
5th Battalion DWR; killed in action 25 8 1918, aged 19, Advance to Victory.
Buried – Gommecourt South Cemetery, 1, C, 5.
Commemorated - the **Drill Hall WM panel 3, column 2.**
Formerly 75635 Durham Light Infantry. Originally 2/5th DWR.
FAITHFUL UNTO DEATH.

COUPLAND R.
No trace. Possible duplication of Coupland R R.

COUPLAND R B.
No trace. Possibly duplication of Coupland R R.

COUPLAND Robert Robinson – 5066 (later 241649) Private.
Born in Dumfries, to James and Mary. Resided and enlisted, February, 1916, at Huddersfield.
2/5th Battalion, C Company, DWR; reported missing, killed in action, 03 5 1917, aged 22, Battle of Bullecourt.
Commemorated - Arras Memorial, France; M Stansfield, page 105, and the **Drill Hall WM panel 3, column 2.**
Mentioned in the Goodall collection (Battalion Routine Order shows award of Commanding Officer's Commendation, for actions between 20 and 28 February, 1917) dated 06 3 1917.
Initials shown as R and R B on Memorial Boards; shown as R in SDGW. Shown as R R in CWGC.

COWARD Herbert – 5806 Private.
Born and enlisted Sheffield.
1/5th Battalion DWR; died of wounds 23 9 1916, (Battle of the Somme).
Buried – Etaples Military Cemetery, 16, C, 8.
Commemorated – the **Drill Hall WM panel 3, column 2.**

COWGILL Allen – 4723 Private.
Born in Honley, Huddersfield. Resided in Honley. Enlisted February 1916.
1/5th Battalion DWR; wounded in action 07 9 1916, died as Prisoner of War, aged 23, on 24 9 1916.
Buried – Niederzwehren Cemetery, 4, H, 2.
Commemorated - Honley WM; C Ford, page 23; M Stansfield, page 105, and the **Drill Hall WM panel 3, column 2.**
Mentioned in the Huddersfield Examiner (wia, reported missing and POW, Germany) on 05 10 1916, (died as POW) on 19 10 1916.
BELOVED SON OF FRED AND ELIZABETH COWGILL – DEARLY LOVED.

COWGILL Ernest – 240781 Private.
Born in Huddersfield. Enlisted at Huddersfield.
1/5th Battalion DWR; killed in action 03 9 1916, Battle of the Somme (Thiepval).
Commemorated - Thiepval Memorial, France, M Stansfield, page 105, and the **Drill Hall WM panel 3, column 2.**

COWGILL Herbert – 205207 Private.
Born in Huddersfield, Resided with his wife, Isabel, in Marsden. Enlisted at Halifax on 11 4 1917. Embarked for France July, 1917.
1/5th Battalion DWR; wounded in action 11 10 1917, died on the same day at 44 Casualty Clearing Station, Nine Elms, aged 28.
Buried – Nine Elms British Cemetery, 4, D, 12.
Commemorated – Marsden WM; M Stansfield, page 105, and the **Drill Hall WM panel 3, column 2.**
GREATER LOVE HATH NO MAN THAN THIS, THAT HE LAY DOWN HIS LIFE FOR HIS FRIENDS.

COWLING Fred – 242056 Private.
Born Lees, Oldham, to John and Annie. Resided Lees. Enlisted at Springhead.
1/5th Battalion DWR; killed in action 07 8 1917, aged 24, 3rd Battle of Ypres (Passchendaele).
Buried - Ramscappelle Road Military Cemetery, 2, A, 8.
Commemorated – J J Fisher, page 115, and the **Drill Hall WM panel 3, column 2.**
HIS COUNTRY CALLED – HE ANSWERED.

COX Charles – 2678 Company Sergeant Major. Military Medal.

Born in Harston, Cambs. Resided in Slaithwaite. Enlisted Huddersfield, August 1914. Embarked for France in April, 1915.
1/5th Battalion DWR; killed in action 05 8 1916, Battle of the Somme.
Buried – Connaught Cemetery, 3, M, 6.
Commemorated – the **Drill Hall WM panel 3, column 2**.
Mentioned in the Huddersfield Examiner: (award of MM) on 07 8 1916, (killed in action, shellfire) on 18 8 1916, (death) 30 8 1916 and 15 9 1916).
Formerly East Yorks Regiment, awarded Boer War Queen's South Africa Medal with Clasps Johannesburg, Cape Colony and Orange Free State, and the King's South Africa Medal, with clasps South Africa 1901 and South Africa 1902. Awarded the Military Medal, London Gazette 01 9 1916, page 8654.

COX G
No trace in DWR.
Possibly 71490 Private GERALD COX.
Born 23 12 1888 in Lindley, Huddersfield, to Mary. Resided and enlisted at Huddersfield on 15 11 1916.
17th Nottinghamshire & Derbyshire Regt, formerly 32250 North Staffordshire Regt, killed in action 31 7 1917.
Commemorated – Menin Gate (Ypres) WM; St Stephen's Church, Lindley; Marsh RoH; M Stansfield, page 106, and the **Drill Hall WM panel 3, column 2.**

CRABTREE Angus – 263031 Private.
Born at Low Moor, Bradford, to Harry and Annie. Husband of Lena. Enlisted at Halifax.
2/5th Battalion DWR; killed in action 03 5 1917, Battle of Bullecourt.
Commemorated - Arras Memorial, France, and the **Drill Hall WM panel 3, column 3.**

CRABTREE Ernest – 6707 Private.
Born Bradford to Willie and Annie Elizabeth. Resided and enlisted at Bradford.
1/5th Battalion DWR; killed in action 13 10 1916, aged 20, Battle of the Somme.
Buried – Foncquevillers Military Cemetery, 1, J, 12.
Commemorated – the Drill **Hall WM panel 3, column 3**.
THY WILL BE DONE.

CRABTREE Frank – 5619 Private.
Born Marsden to William. Enlisted at Marsden in March, 1916. Embarked for France 30 6 1916.
1/5th Battalion DWR; killed in action 25 9 1916, aged 19, Battle of the Somme.
Commemorated – Thiepval Memorial, France; Marsden WM; M Stansfield, page 106, and the **Drill Hall WM panel 3, column 3.**

CRABTREE Fred – 241553 Private.
Born at Slaithwaite to Edwin. Resided in Slaithwaite. Enlisted at Huddersfield, March 1916. Embarked for France and Flanders in January, 1917.
2/5th Battalion DWR; reported missing (killed in action) 03 5 1917, aged 21, Battle of Bullecourt.
Commemorated – Arras Memorial, France; Slaithwaite WM; St James Church, Slaithwaite; M Stansfield, page 106, and the **Drill Hall WM panel 3, column 3.**
Mentioned in the Huddersfield Examiner (official casualty list) on 27 6 1917.

CRABTREE Joseph – 14156 Private.
Born in Keighley to Benjamin and Sarah. Enlisted Keighley.
2/5th Battalion DWR; killed in action 20 11 1917, aged 31, Battle of Cambrai.
Buried – Metz en Couture British Cemetery, 2, D, 18.
Commemorated - the **Drill Hall WM panel 3, column 3.**

CRAGG Arthur Harry – 2794 Private.
Born 28 6 1894 in Newton Moor, Cheshire, to Arthur and Annie. Resided and enlisted at Huddersfield. Embarked for France in April, 1915.
1/5th Battalion DWR; killed in action 15 5 1915, aged 20, Fleurbaix Sector.
Buried - Rue David Military Cemetery, 1, B, 19.
Commemorated – Holy Trinity Church, Huddersfield; Almondbury Grammar School; Huddersfield Corporation Roll; M Stansfield, page 107, and the **Drill Hall WM panel 3, column 3.**
Mentioned in the Huddersfield Examiner, (killed in action) on 19 5 1915.
IN THE LIGHT WE SHALL REMEMBER – IN THE DARKNESS WE SHALL NOT FORGET.

CRAIG Fred – 241493 Private.
Born, resided and enlisted, Bradford.
1/5th Battalion DWR; killed in action 02 12 1917.
Buried – Lijssenthoek Military Cemetery, 26, B, 10A.
Commemorated – the **Drill Hall WM panel 3, column 3**.

CRANE Harry – 5860 Private.
Born Bacup, Lancs. Enlisted at Barnoldswick.
1/5th Battalion DWR; killed in action 25 9 1916, Battle of the Somme.
Commemorated – Thiepval Memorial, France; Barnoldswick WM; Craven's Part in the Great War, page 140; P Thompson, page 76 & 80, incl photograph, and the **Drill Hall WM panel 3, column 3.**

CREATON Harry Edward – 1570 (poss 5007) (later 241598) Lance Corporal.
Born 18 7 1894 in Huddersfield, to Edward and Minnie. Resided and Enlisted at Huddersfield on 11 3 1916.
2/5th Battalion DWR; killed in action 03 5 1917, aged 22, Battle of Bullecourt.
Commemorated – Arras Memorial, France; Primitive Methodist Church RoH; M Stansfield, page 108, and the **Drill Hall WM panel 3, column 3.**
Mentioned in the Goodall collection and the Huddersfield Examiner, (official casualty roll) on 27 6 1917, (Memoriam notice) on 03 5 1920.

CRITCHLEY Peter – 4124 Private.
Born in Huddersfield to Mrs Henry. Resided and enlisted at Huddersfield, May, 1915. Embarked for France in May, 1916.
1/5th Battalion DWR; killed in action 03 7 1916, Battle of the Somme.
Commemorated – Thiepval Memorial, France; J J Fisher, page 110; M Stansfield, page 108, and the **Drill Hall WM panel 3, column 3**.
Mentioned in the Huddersfield Examiner (missing in action) on 07 8 1916; (reported missing since 03 7 1916, now reported killed in action) on 20 10 1916.
CWGC has surname spelt Critchle.

CROSBY George – 16572 Private.
Born in Malton to William and Mary. Resided in Malton with his wife, Florence. Enlisted at Malton.
2/5th Battalion DWR; killed in action 27 3 1918, aged 28, German Spring Offensive.
Commemorated – Arras Memorial, France, and the **Drill Hall WM panel 3, column 3**.

CROSLAND Gilbert – 4757 Private.
Born Oakes, Huddersfield, to Jane. Resided in Oakes. Enlisted Huddersfield.
1/5th Battalion DWR; killed in action 20 11 1916, Battle of the Somme.
Buried – Foncquevillers Military Cemetery, 1, J, 33.
Commemorated – J Fisher, page 114; M Stansfield, page 109, and the **Drill Hall WM panel 3, column 3.**

Mentioned in the Huddersfield Examiner (official notification of death) on 08 12 1916.

CROSS W – Private
No Trace.
Commemorated - the Drill Hall WM panel 3, column 3.

CROSSLAND Tom – 2018 (later) 240118 Corporal.
Born Holmfirth, to John Crosland. Joined the Territorials pre war. Enlisted at Holmfirth.
1/5th Battalion DWR, originally F Coy; killed in action, shrapnel, 04 8 1917. Nieuport.
Commemorated – Nieuport Memorial, Belgium; Holme Valley Memorial Hospital WM (plaque 2, Underbank and Cartworth); Holy Trinity Churchyard, Holmfirth; M Stansfield, page 110, and the **Drill Hall WM panel 3, column 2.**
Mentioned in the Huddersfield Examiner (killed in action) on 22 8 1917.
Some sources show Crosland.

CROSSLEY J – Private.
Unable to positively identify.
Commemorated – the **Drill Hall WM panel 3, column 3.**

CROSSLEY J – Private.
Unable to positively identify.
Commemorated – the **Drill Hall WM panel 3, column 3.**
Both names appear on the RoH Board.

CROWE Fred Thewlis – 268353 Private.
Born 03 5 1882 in Taylor Hill, to Anthony and Susannah. Resided in Huddersfield with his wife, Lucy. Enlisted in Honley on 18 10 1916.
5th Battalion DWR; killed in action 29 8 1918, aged 36, Advance to Victory.
Buried – Vaulx Hill Cemetery, 1, H, 9.
Commemorated – Armitage Bridge WM; M Stansfield, page 112, and the **Drill Hall WM panel 3, column 3.**
Mentioned in the Huddersfield Examiner (killed in action) on 19 9 1918.
THY WILL BE DONE.

CROWTHER Ebison (Ellison?) – 2337 Private.
Born Sowerby Bridge to Albert and Betty. Resided Battyeford and enlisted at Mirfield.
1/5th Battalion DWR; killed in action 15 5 1915, aged 21, Fleurbaix Sector.
Buried – Rue David Military Cemetery, 1, B, 21.
Commemorated – Battyeford WM; Brighouse WM; Mirfield WM; J Fisher, page 106, and the **Drill Hall WM panel 3, column 2.**
HE GAVE HIS LIFE THAT OTHERS MIGHT LIVE.

CROWTHER Hubert – 5241 (later 241797) Corporal.
Born in Lindley 30 11 1891 to Joe William and Florence. Resided in Lindley. Enlisted at Huddersfield on 20 3 1916.
2/5th Battalion DWR; wounded in action and died of wounds 03 5 1917, Battle of Bullecourt.
Commemorated – Arras Memorial, France; St Stephens Church, Lindley, St Philips Church, Birchencliffe; M Stansfield, page 113, and the **Drill Hall WM panel 3, column 3.**
Mentioned in the Goodall collection; the Huddersfield Examiner (reported as POW) on 20 7 1917.

CROWTHER Leslie Taylor – 2nd Lieutenant
Born in Edgerton, Huddersfield, to Norman and Gertrude. Resided at Edgerton and joined the Territorials in 1911. Promoted Sergeant by the outbreak of war and was commissioned on 21 10 1914. Embarked for France in April, 1915.

1/5th Battalion DWR, D Company; killed in action 16 6 1915, aged 23, Ypres.
Buried – Rue David Military Cemetery, 1, B, 11.
Commemorated – Holy Trinity Church, Huddersfield; St Stephen's Church, Lindley; Huddersfield College School; J Fisher, pages 107-108 & 128; B Heywood, page 48; M Stansfield, page 113, and the **Drill Hall WM panel 3, column 2.**
Mentioned in the Huddersfield Examiner (details of death) on 18 6 1915.

CRYER Charlie – 267241 Private.
Born in Farnley, Otley, to Fred and Mary. Enlisted at Otley.
5th Battalion DWR; died of wounds 13 9 1918, aged 24, as Prisoner of War.
Buried – Berlin South Western Cemetery, 11, C, 5.
Commemorated - the **Drill Hall WM panel 3, column 3.**
DEARER TO US THAN WORDS CAN TELL, AND LIVES IN MEMORY DEAR.

CRYER Joseph Harker – 242319 Private.
Enlisted at Birtley, Durham.
1/5th Battalion DWR; killed in action 08 10 1917, 3rd Battle of Ypres (Passchendaele).
Commemorated – Tyne Cot Memorial, Belgium, and the **Drill Hall WM panel 3, column 3.**
Formerly 3342 Durham Light Infantry.

CULPAN Arthur Raymond – 202153 Private.
Born Halifax to Milford, of Stainland. Resided in Stainland, enlisted at Halifax.
2/5th Battalion DWR; died of wounds 04 12 1917, aged 25, Battle of Cambrai.
Buried – Etaples Military Cemetery, 31, A, 16.
Commemorated - the **Drill Hall WM panel 3, column 3.**

CUNNINGHAM Clifford Thomas Sidney – 2488 (later 240267) Private.
Born in Hoyland Common to William and Elizabeth of Denby Dale. Enlisted at Holmfirth. Embarked for France in April, 1915.
1/5th Battalion DWR, originally F Company; killed in action 03 9 1916, aged 20, Battle of the Somme (Thiepval).
Commemorated – Thiepval Memorial, France; Denby Dale and Cumberworth WM; G H Norton RoH; J Fisher, page 113; M Stansfield, page 115, and the **Drill Hall WM panel 3, column 3.**
Mentioned in the Huddersfield Examiner (killed in action) on 21 9 1916.

CURTIS Percy Arthur – 25074 Private.
Resided with wife, Edith Emmeline, in Islington, London.
2/5th Battalion DWR; died of wounds, home, aged 30, 21 6 1918.
Buried – Southampton (Holybrook) Cemetery, B, 01, 3.
Commemorated - the **Drill Hall WM panel 3, column 3**.
Formerly 446 Army Service Corps.
IN MEMORY EVER PRESENT.

CURTOIS Harry – 5133 (later 241709) Private.
Born Stixwould, Lincs, to Priscilla. Enlisted at Louth on 14 3 1916.
2/5th Battalion DWR, D Company, 15 Platoon; killed in action 03 5 1917, aged 25, Battle of Bullecourt.
Commemorated – Arras Memorial, France, and the **Drill Hall WM panel 3, column 3.**
Mentioned in Goodall collection, Lewis Gun Shooting Team, 1917; awarded Commanding Officer's Commendation for actions between 13 and 17 February, 1917.

CUTTS Kelvin Ewart – 3162 Private.
Son of William Henry and Elizabeth of Crosland Moor, Huddersfield. Resided in Hemsworth. Enlisted in Huddersfield.

1/5th Battalion DWR; died of wounds, 23 General Hospital, Etaples, 04 10 1916, aged 20, Battle of the Somme.
Buried – Etaples Military Cemetery, 11, F, 15A.
Commemorated – J Fisher, page 113; M Stansfield, page 115, and the **Drill Hall WM panel 3, column 3.**
Mentioned in the Huddersfield Examiner (killed in action) on 09 10 1916.

DALE George Alfred – 204540 Private.
Born Batley, to Mary Jane and the late Alfred. Resided in Batley, enlisted at Mirfield.
2/5th Battalion DWR; died of wounds, 31 3 1918, aged 20, Advance to Victory.
Buried – St Sever Cemetery Extension, P, 9, G, 6A.
Commemorated - the **Drill Hall WM panel 3, column 4.**
THY WILL BE DONE.

DARNBOROUGH (DARNBROUGH?) Arthur – 205578 Private.
Resided in Bingley. Enlisted at Keighley
2/5th Battalion DWR; killed in action 27 3 1918, German Spring Offensive.
Commemorated – Arras Memorial, France, and the **Drill Hall WM panel 3, column 4.**
CWGC and SDGW both show DARNBROUGH.

DARNBROOK Herbert – 24607 Lance Corporal.
Born in Birstall to Charlotte and the late John. Enlisted at Birstall.
2/5th Battalion DWR; killed in action 27 11 1917, Battle of Cambrai.
Commemorated - Cambrai Memorial (Louverval), France, and the **Drill Hall WM panel 3, column 4.**

DARRAGH Matthew Sloan – 2nd Lieutenant.
1/5th Battalion DWR; killed in action 20 3 1917.
Commemorated – Loos Memorial, France, and the **Drill Hall WM panel 3, column 4.**
From 6th DWR.
Mentioned in 1/6th DWR War Diary (C Company, Martinsart Wood) on 03 9 1916. 1/5th DWR War Diary (joined Bn 22 9 1916) on 30 9 1916, (killed in patrol action, 20 3 1917) on 20 3 1917.

DAVIDSON David Robert – 3831 (later 235929) Private.
Resided Liversedge and enlisted at Mirfield on 27 1 1915.
Originally 2/5th Battalion DWR, transferred to 3/4th Battalion DWR in 1917; killed in action 24 4 1917. Had been posted to 5th Battalion Yorkshire Regiment at time of death.
Commemorated – Arras Memorial, France, St Peter's Church, Hartshead, Plaque, and the **Drill Hall WM panel 3, column 4.**
Mentioned in Goodall Collection (D Company).

DAVIES David – 25075 Private.
Born Beaumaris, Anglesey, to John. Enlisted at Menai Bridge.
2/5th Battalion DWR; killed in action 20 11 1917, aged 20, Battle of Cambrai.
Commemorated - Hermies Hill British Special Memorial A16, and the **Drill Hall WM panel 3, column 4.**
Formerly 287256 Army Service Corps.
ALWAYS REMEMBERED BY ALL AT HOME.

DAVIES William – 240661 Sergeant. Military Medal.
Born Marsden to Annie Sadler. Resided Marsden and enlisted at Huddersfield in November, 1914.
2/5th Battalion DWR; killed in action, GSW, 26 3 1918, aged 23, German Spring Offensive.
Commemorated - Arras Memorial, France; Marsden WM; M Stansfield, page 117, and the **Drill Hall WM panel 3, column 4.**

Mentioned in the London Gazette (award of MM for Cambrai, 21 11 1917) on 13 3 1918, page 3231.

DAVIES Walter Owen – 2nd Lieutenant.
Born 08 3 1895 at Moldgreen. Joined the Territorials pre war. Embarked for France in April, 1915. Commissioned from the ranks,
2/5th Battalion DWR; killed in action 27 11 1917, Battle of Cambrai (Bourlon Wood).
Commemorated – Cambrai Memorial (Louverval), France; Christ Church, Moldgreen RoH; Almondbury Grammar School RoH; B Heywood, page 49; M Stansfield, page 117, and the **Drill Hall WM panel 3, column 4.**
Mentioned in the Huddersfield Examiner (via official casualty list) on 07 8 1916; Goodall collection (B Company, 2/5th DWR) and 2/5th DWR War Diary (joined Bn) on 21 6 1917, (killed in action) on 27 11 1917.
Originally 1/5th DWR, on commissioning, June 1917.

DAWSON Charles – 6710 Private.
Born and resided in Baildon. Enlisted at Shipley.
1/5th Battalion DWR; killed in action 16 9 1916, Battle of the Somme.
Buried – Authuile Military Cemetery, H, 1.
Commemorated - the **Drill Hall WM panel 3, column 3**.

DAWSON C.
No trace - duplication of name on **column 3?**
Commemorated - the **Drill Hall WM panel 3, column 4**.

DAWSON Frank – 5292 Private.
Born Lockwood to Walter and Edith. Resided in Huddersfield. Enlisted Huddersfield on 22 10 1916.
2/5th Battalion DWR, A Company; killed in action 27 2 1917, aged 23.
Commemorated – Thiepval Memorial, France; St Stephen's Church, Rashcliffe, RoH; M Stansfield, page 118, and the **Drill Hall WM panel 3, column 4.**

DAWSON James – 203641 Sergeant.
Born 03 1 1889 in Huddersfield. Resided with his wife in Almondbury. Enlisted Huddersfield on 04 8 1914.
1/5th Battalion DWR, A Company; killed in action 27 11 1917, Battle of Passchendaele.
Commemorated – Tyne Cot Memorial, Belgium; Almondbury WM; Huddersfield Parish Church; Huddersfield Corporation RoH; M Stansfield, page 118, and the **Drill Hall WM panel 3, column 4.**

DAY Albert (Littlewood) – 235317 Company Sergeant Major.
Born in New Mill, Holmfirth, 20 11 1887 to William. Enlisted in the 2nd Volunteer Battalion in 1894. Served 1900 to 1901 with the 1st Volunteer Service Company in South Africa.
5th Battalion DWR; wounded in action, gas, 20 11 1917, Battle of Passchendaele. Evacuated to England, died, home, Ipswich Military Hospital, 19 9 1918.
Buried – Huddersfield (Edgerton) Cemetery, 36, C, 9.
Commemorated – the **Drill Hall WM panel 3, column 4.**
Mentioned in the Huddersfield Examiner (with Volunteer Service Company, South Africa) on 14 6 1917, (died of wounds, Ipswich) on 19 9 1917, 10 9 1917 and 24 9 1917.
Boer War papers show his name as Albert Littlewood Day, not mentioned in WW1 records.

DEAN Frank – 3412 Private.
Born 28 11 1892 at Newsome to William and Annie. Resided Newsome. Enlisted in Huddersfield on 13 11 1914.

1/5th Battalion DWR; died as result of accident with ammunition box, 13 11 1915, aged 22, Ypres.
Buried – Hospital Farm Cemetery, C, 14.
Commemorated – St John's Church, Newsome; M Stansfield, page 119, and the **Drill Hall WM panel 3, column 4.**
Mentioned in Huddersfield Examiner (awarded Distinguished Conduct Certificate for action on 26 9 1915) on 17 11 1915, (died of wounds, explosion of ammunition box) on 17 11 1917.
EVER REMEBERED.

DEAN Handel Oliver – 3205 Private.
Born in Lindley on 18 3 1893. Resided in Lindley. Enlisted at Huddersfield, October, 1914.
1/5th Battalion DWR; died of wounds at 10 Casualty Clearing Station, Remy Siding, 22 11 1915, aged 23, Advance to Victory.
Buried – Lijssenthoek Military Cemetery, 2, D, 2A.
Commemorated – Lindley Zion United Methodist Church; St Stephen's Church, Lindley; M Stansfield, page 119, and the **Drill Hall WM panel 3, column 4.**
Mentioned in the Huddersfield Examiner (death) on 29 11 1915.
Some sources show Handle and Handal.
EVER IN OUR THOUGHTS, MOTHER, FATHER AND FAMILY – LINDLEY, HUDDERSFIELD.

DEANS John William – 7102 (later 5218) Private.
Born in Gateshead and enlisted at Newcastle.
Originally 5th Battalion DWR; died 02 9 1916, Battle of the Somme.
Commemorated – Thiepval Memorial, France, and the **Drill Hall WM panel 3, column 4.**
Formerly 5th DWR; died serving as 5218 Private with the 1/6th Battalion Northumberland Fusiliers.
CWGC shows date of death as 03 9 1916.

DEARNLEY Ernest – 3074 Private.
Born in Almondbury on 19 1 1898 to John William. Resided in Almondbury. Enlisted at Huddersfield on 21 9 1914.
1/5th Battalion DWR; killed in action 21 12 1915, Ypres.
Commemorated – Ypres (Menin Gate) Memorial, Belgium; Almondbury WM; St Stephen's Church, Lindley; J Fisher, page 110; M Stansfield, page 120, and the **Drill Hall WM panel 3, column 4.**
Mentioned in the Huddersfield Examiner (killed in action, MG fire) on 07 1 1916.

DEARNLEY George Frederick – 2606 (later 240340) Private.
Born in Birkby on 10 4 1897 to John H of Crosland Moor. Enlisted at Huddersfield in August, 1914.
2/5th Battalion DWR; killed in action, 04 7 1917.
Buried – Queant Road Cemetery, Buissy, 2, H, 30.
Commemorated – Crosland Moor Wesleyan Church RoH; St Stephens' Church, Rashcliffe, RoH; St Barnabas Church, Crosland Moor, RoH; Almondbury Grammar School RoH; Lockwood Cemetery memorial; Colne Valley Almanac; M Stansfield page 120, and the **Drill Hall WM panel 3, column 4.**
Mentioned in the Goodall collection; the Huddersfield Examiner (Trench Mortar battery, killed in action) on 10 7 1917; (killed in action, official casualty list) on 02 8 1917; (in memoriam) on 04 7 1918.

DEIONE Alfred Stewart – 26855 Private.
Born Hackney, London, to Frederick James and Eleanor. Resided Chingford and enlisted at St Pancras.
5th Battalion DWR; died 30 10 1918, as Prisoner of War, aged 22.
Buried – Niederzwehren Cemetery, 4, F, 17.
Commemorated – the **Drill Hall WM panel 3, column 4.**

From 32182 Essex Regiment.
LOVED BY ALL.

DEMPSTER George Glen – 26436 Private.
Born in Govan, Lanarkshire, to George and Mary. Resided and enlisted at Glasgow.
5th Battalion DWR; killed in action 29 8 1918, aged 21, Advance to Victory.
Buried – Vaulx Hill Cemetery, 3, H, 10.
Commemorated – the **Drill Hall WM panel 3, column 4.**
Formerly 37943 Royal Scots Fusiliers.

DENBY Jonas – 263013 Private.
Born Oxenhope to Isaac and Sarah. Resided in Oxenhope. Enlisted at Keighley.
1/5th Battalion DWR; killed in action 05 8 1917, aged 34.
Buried – Coxyde Military Cemetery, 2, D, 28.
Commemorated – the **Drill Hall WM panel 3, column 4.**
EVER REMEBERED.

DENNISON Norman – 4528 (later 241342) Lance Corporal.
Resided Lees, enlisted at Mirfield.
1/5th Battalion DWR; killed in action 03 9 1916, Battle of the Somme (Thiepval).
Buried – Mill Road Cemetery, 1, G, 7.
Commemorated – the **Drill Hall WM panel 3, column 4.**

DENT William – 3043 Private.
Born Saddleworth to Sam and Elizabeth. Resided with his wife, Mary Alice, in Delph. Enlisted at Huddersfield.
1/5th Battalion DWR; killed in action 28 9 1915, aged 39, Ypres.
Commemorated – Ypres (Menin Gate) Memorial, France, and the **Drill Hall WM panel 3, column 4.**

DENTON Charles Singleton - 17394 Lance Corporal.
Born 19 6 1895 in Huddersfield to Mr and Mrs Alfred Denton. Enlisted at Huddersfield 1914.
5th Battalion DWR; reported missing, presumed killed in action, 29 3 1918, German Spring Offensive.
Buried – Gommecourt British Cemetery No2, 5, A, 2.
Commemorated – St Thomas's Church, Huddersfield, M Stansfield, page 121, and the **Drill Hall WM panel 3, column 4.**
Mentioned in the Huddersfield Examiner (wounded in action 14 9 1916) on 25 9 1916, (missing, news requested by relatives) on 20 7 1917, (in Memoriam) on 29 3 1920.

DENTON Fred – 4506 Private.
Son of Sam and Mary Jane, of Lepton. Resided Lepton. Enlisted at Huddersfield.
1/5th Battalion DWR; killed in action 03 9 1916, aged 19, Battle of the Somme (Thiepval).
Commemorated - Thiepval Memorial, France; Lepton Parish Church RoH; M Stansfield, page 121, and the **Drill Hall WM panel 3, column 4.**
Mentioned in the Huddersfield Examiner (wounded in action, official casualty list) on 07 8 1916, (missing, news requested by relatives) on 20 7 1917.

DEWHURST George Dyson – 3311 (later 240678) Private.
Born 25 12 1893 in Lockwood to John William and Jane. Enlisted at Huddersfield in October, 1914.
2/5th Battalion DWR; reported missing, killed in action, 03 5 1917, Battle of Bullecourt.
Commemorated – Arras Memorial, France; M Stansfield, page 122, and the **Drill Hall WM panel 3, column 4.**

Mentioned in the Goodall collection and the Huddersfield Examiner (reported missing, official casualty list) on 27 6 1917.
OH FOR THE TOUCH OF A VANISHED HAND AND THE SOUND OF A VOICE THAT IS STILL.

DINSDALE Ralph – 242147 Private.
Son of Alfred and Mary Elizabeth, of Bradford. Enlisted at Bradford.
2/5th Battalion DWR; killed in action 30 3 1918, aged 23, German Spring Offensive.
Commemorated – Arras Memorial, France, and the **Drill Hall WM panel 4, column 1.**

DITCHBURN James Benjamin – 2631 Private.
Born in Huddersfield, to James and Clara. Resided Paddock. Re-enlisted on outbreak of war, 1914
1/5th Battalion DWR, A Company; died of wounds, 23 Canadian General Hospital, Etaples, 24 7 1915, aged 22. Repatriated to England for burial.
Buried – Huddersfield (Edgerton) Cemetery, 30, C, 199.
Commemorated – All Saints Church, Paddock; Huddersfield College School; Almondbury Grammar School RoH; M Stansfield, page 123; Parish Memorial Board, Huddersfield Drill Hall, and the **Drill Hall WM panel 3, column 4.**
Mentioned in the Huddersfield Examiner (wia, shellfire) on 06 7 1915, (dow, Etaples, 24 7 1915) on 26 7 1915, (in memoriam) on 24 7 1917, 24 7 1918 and 24 7 1919.

DIXON William Robert – 241464 Private.
Born and resided in Haworth.
1/5th Battalion DWR; killed in action 03 9 1916, Battle of the Somme (Thiepval).
Buried – Mill Road Cemetery, 1, C, 15.
Commemorated – the **Drill Hall WM panel 4, column 1.**

DOBSON Horace Charles – 32908 Private.
Born in Battersea, enlisted at Bradford.
5th Battalion DWR; died, home, 15 7 1918.
Buried – Eton Wick (St John – Bucks) Cemetery, NE part.
Commemorated – the **Drill Hall WM panel 4, column 1.**

DODD David Leonard – 33438 Sergeant.
Son of James Richard and Emily. Enlisted in Leeds.
2/5th Battalion DWR; killed in action 27 3 1918, aged 35, German Spring Offensive.
Commemorated – Arras Memorial, France, and the **Drill Hall WM panel 4, column 1.**
Formerly 20255 Kings Own Yorkshire Light Infantry.

DODSON Percival - 3388 Private.
Born on 27 7 1895 at Farnley Tyas to Shaw and Clara. Enlisted at Huddersfield in 1914. Embarked for France in April, 1915.
1/5th Battalion DWR; killed in action, GSW, 18 11 1915, aged 20, Ypres.
Buried – Talana Farm Cemetery, 4, F, 13.
Commemorated – St Stephen's Church, Rashcliffe; Mount Pleasant Chapel, Lockwood; M Stansfield, page 123, and the **Drill Hall WM panel 4, column 1.**
THE SOUND OF THE LAST TRUMPET WILL GIVE HIM BACK TO ME.

DONALD Albert – 13186 Private.
Born in Oldham to Samuel and Annie. Enlisted at Skipton.
5th Battalion DWR; killed in action 26 3 1918, aged 27, German Spring Offensive.
Commemorated – Arras Memorial, France, and the **Drill Hall WM panel 4, column 1.**
Originally 2/5th Battalion.

DONKERSLEY William – 240003 Private.
Born in Lockwood to Frank and Mary. Enlisted at Huddersfield on 04 8 1914.
1/5th Battalion DWR; wounded in action 26 12 1917, died of wounds at 10 Casualty Clearing Station, Remy Siding, 27 12 1917, aged 29.
Buried - Lijssenthoek Military Cemetery, 22, CC, 1A.
Commemorated – Rehoboth Baptist Chapel; St Barnabas Church, Crosland Moor; M Stansfield, page 124, the Rising Sun Public House, Crosland Hill, and the **Drill Hall WM panel 4, column 1.**
SDGW shows name as Don Kersley, William.
Mentioned in the Huddersfield Examiner (wia) on 20 10 1916.
HE WHO HATH DIED IN BATTLE, GRANT HIM THY PEACE O LORD.

DONNELLAN William – 240649 Private.
Born on 19 10 1898 in Huddersfield. Resided with his wife, Moldgreen. Enlisted Huddersfield in October, 1914.
2/5th Battalion DWR; killed in action 03 5 1917, Battle of Bullecourt.
Commemorated – Arras Memorial, France; Moldgreen RoH; M Stansfield, page 124, and the **Drill Hall WM panel 4, column 1.**
Mentioned in the Huddersfield Examiner (killed in action) on 08 6 1917.

DOOK Charles Sanderson – 15178 Private.
Born in Doncaster to Alberta. Enlisted at Huddersfield.
5th Battalion DWR; killed in action 23 5 1918, aged 22.
Buried – Bienvillers Military Cemetery, 20, B, 9.
Commemorated - the **Drill Hall WM panel 4, column 1.**
HE DIED FOR ALL – R.I.P.

DOOLAN E
No trace, possibly:
DOOLAN Patrick – 223808 Private.
Born in Willington Quay, enlisted at North Shields.
2nd Battalion DWR; killed in action 10 10 1917.
Commemorated - Tyne Cot Memorial, Belgium; Bruce History, page 222, and the **Drill Hall WM panel 4, column 1.**

DOOLEN Edward – 22474 Private.
Born in Sunderland, resided Darnell, Sheffield, and enlisted at Sheffield.
5th Battalion DWR; killed in action 28 9 1918, Advance to Victory.
Buried – Grand Ravine British Cemetery, A, 10.
Commemorated - the **Drill Hall WM panel 4, column 1.**
Originally 2/5th DWR.

DORLING Bert – 235616 Private.
Son of John (stepmother Ruth), of Ely, Cambs. Enlisted in Cambridge.
5th Battalion DWR; killed in action 25 8 1918, aged 21, Advance to Victory.
Commemorated – Vis en Artois Memorial, France; Ely Cathedral WM, and the **Drill Hall WM panel 4, column 1.**
Originally 2/5th DWR.

DOUGHTY Lawrence – 203406 Private.
Born on 29 10 1894 in Huddersfield. Enlisted at Huddersfield on 04 8 1914.
2/4th Battalion DWR; killed in action 25 11 1917, Cambrai.
Commemorated – Cambrai Memorial (Louverval), France; M Stansfield, page 125, and the **Drill Hall WM panel 12, column 4.**

DOVE J – Private.
No trace, possibly:
DOVE H – 2381 Private.
1/6th Battalion DWR; died of wounds, shellfire, British Red Cross Hospital, 03 8 1915, aged 29.
Buried - Le Touquet-Paris Plage Communal Cemetery, 2, A, 1.
Commemorated - the **Drill Hall WM panel 4, column 1.**
Mentioned in 1/6th DWR War Diary (D Company, wia shellfire) on 30 7 1915; S Barber (wounded in action, shrapnel, on 31 7 1915, died of wounds 31 7 1915) page 31.

DOVER Lawrence Watmough – 22516 Private.
Born in Bradford to George and Susannah, of Allerton. Enlisted at Bradford.
5th Battalion DWR; killed in action 23 7 1918, aged 19, Battle of Tardenois.
Buried – Marfaux British Cemetery, 5, K, 2.
Commemorated - the **Drill Hall WM panel 4, column 1.**

DRANSFIELD Ernest – 241302 Private.
Born 11 10 1885 at Crosland Hill to Tom. Enlisted at Huddersfield on 01 8 1915.
1/5th Battalion DWR; died of wounds at 10 Casualty Clearing Station, Remy Sidings, 18 11 1917, aged 32, Battle of Passchendaele.
Buried – Lijssenthoek Military Cemetery, 27, AA, 6A.
Commemorated – The Rising Sun Public House; M Stansfield, page 125, and the **Drill Hall WM panel 4, column 1.**
Mentioned in the Huddersfield Examiner (wia, September, 1917) on 19 9 1917.
His brother, 10682 Private Norman Dransfield, served with 2nd DWR; killed in action, Hill 60, on 18 4 1915.
THERE IS A LINK DEATH CANNOT SEVER, LOVE AND REMEMBRANCE LAST FOREVER.

DRAPER Archibald John – 49703 Private.
Born and enlisted Northampton.
5th Battalion DWR; killed in action 29 8 1918, Advance to Victory.
Buried – Vaulx Hill Cemetery, 3, J, 8.
Commemorated - the **Drill Hall WM panel 4, column 1.**
Formerly 5468 Yorkshire Regiment.

DREW George (W H) – 6795 Private.
Born in King's Lynn. Enlisted at Dereham, Norfolk.
1/5th Battalion DWR; killed in action 14 1 1917 aged 20.
Buried – Berlies au Bois Churchyard Cemetery Extension, N, 2.
Commemorated - the **Drill Hall WM panel 4, column 1.**
CWGC shows initials as G W H.
NOT FORGOTTEN.

DRINKWATER Isaac Watts (Walter?) – 6711 Private.
Born in Milnsbridge to Harry and Florence. Resided in Milnsbridge. Enlisted Huddersfield on 27 1 1916. Embarked for France 23 8 1916.
1/5th Battalion DWR; died of wounds, GSW, at 2 Stationary Hospital, 24 9 1916, aged 19, Battle of the Somme.
Buried – Abbeville Communal Cemetery Extension,1, C ,9.
Commemorated – J Fisher, page 114; M Stansfield, page 126, and the **Drill Hall WM panel 4, column 1.**
Mentioned in the Huddersfield Examiner (kia, head wound) 29 9 1916, (dow official casualty list) 25 10 1916.
SDGW shows middle name as Walter.
AT REST.

DRUMMOND Tom Milner – 13019 Lance Corporal.
Born in Skipton to Mr and Mrs George Drummond. Enlisted at Skipton on 05 9 1914.
2/5th Battalion DWR, D Company; killed in action 19 5 1918, aged 25.
Buried – Bagneux British Cemetery, 2, B, 29.
Commemorated – Craven's Part in the Great War, page 351, and the **Drill Hall WM panel 4, column 1.**
Mentioned in the Goodall Collection.
NOT GONE FROM MEMORY OR FROM LOVE, BUT TO OUR FATHER'S HOME ABOVE.

DUNSHEE Ernest Rowland – 2nd Lieutenant.
Husband of Mrs E R Dunshee of Smethwick, Staffs.
5th Battalion DWR, C Company; killed in action, air raid, 11 8 1918, aged 26.
Buried – Etaples Military Cemetery, 28, O, 2.
Commemorated – Bruce History, page 213, and the **Drill Hall WM panel 4, column 1.**
From 1st DWR, and 2nd DWR, and 2/5th DWR.
Mentioned in the Goodall collection and 5th DWR War Diary (to hospital sick) on 30 6 1918, (rejoined Bn) 31 7 1918, (dow) 30 8 1918.

DURKIN John – 240216 Corporal.
Born Huddersfield. Enlisted in local Territorials on 13 6 1912.
2/5th Battalion DWR; reported missing, killed in action, 03 5 1917, Battle of Bullecourt.
Commemorated – Arras Memorial, France, parent's headstone, Edgerton Cemetery; M Stansfield, page 127, and the **Drill Hall WM panel 4, column 1.**
Mentioned in the Goodall collection; the Huddersfield Examiner (reported missing) on 04 6 1917.

DURRANS Fred – 2845 Lance Sergeant.
Born 29 11 1883 to Arthur and Elizabeth, of Oakes. Married. Enlisted at Huddersfield on 04 1914.
1/5th Battalion DWR; wounded in action 03 9 1916, died of wounds, 14 General Hospital, Wimereux, 14 9 1916, aged 33, Battle of the Somme (Thiepval).
Buried – Wimereux Communal Cemetery, 1, Q, 9A.
Commemorated – Lindley Church Yard Memorial; St Stephen's Church, Lindley, RoH; M Stansfield, page 128, and the **Drill Hall WM panel 4, column 1.**
SWEET TO REMEMBER ONE WHO ONCE WAS HERE AND WHO THOUGH ABSENT IS STILL JUST AS DEAR.

DUXBURY (DUCKSBURY?) Charles – 34736 Private.
Born in Kendal, Westmoreland. Resided, with his wife, Kendal and enlisted at Kendal.
5th Battalion DWR; killed in action 28 9 1918, Advance to Victory.
Buried - Grand Ravine British Cemetery, A, 14.
Commemorated - the **Drill Hall WM panel 4, column 1.**
Some sources show Ducksbury.

DYCHE Wilfred (Harold?) – 4031 (later 241119) Private.
Born in Netherton. Resided Netherton and enlisted at Huddersfield in April, 1915.
2/5th Battalion DWR; killed in action 20 11 1917, Battle of Cambrai.
Commemorated – Cambrai Memorial (Louverval), France, South Crosland and Netherton RoH; M Stansfield, page 128, and the **Drill Hall WM panel 4, column 2.**
Mentioned in the Goodall collection; the Huddersfield Examiner (in memoriam) on 20 11 1918.

DYER Frank Morgan – 2602 Corporal.
Born Abergavenny, Mon. Resided Huddersfield, and enlisted at Huddersfield.
1/5th Battalion DWR; killed in action 23 8 1915, Ypres.
Buried – Artillery Wood Cemetery, 2, A, 14.

Commemorated – London and North Western Railway Company RoH; M Stansfield, page 128, and the **Drill Hall WM panel 4, column 1.**

DYSON Arnold Garside – 2844 Private.
Born 05 3 1895 in Lindley, to Mr and Mrs Joe Dyson. Enlisted at Huddersfield on 03 9 1914.
1/5th Battalion DWR; wounded in action 08 11 1915, died of wounds at 17 Casualty Clearing Station, Remy Siding, 10 11 1915, aged 20, Ypres.
Buried – Lijssenthoek Military Cemetery, 4, B, 7A.
Commemorated – St Stephen's Church, Lindley; Lindley Zion Methodist Chapel; M Stansfield, page 128, and the **Drill Hall WM panel 4, column 1.**
Mentioned in the Huddersfield Examiner (died of wounds) on 17 11 1915.
EVER IN OUR THOUGHTS, FATHER, MOTHER AND FAMILY – LINDLEY, HUDDERSFIELD.

DYSON Frank Crossley – 3765 (later 240948) Sergeant.
Born 27 2 1896, in Dalton Green, to Tom Edward and Martha. Enlisted at Huddersfield.
5th Battalion DWR; killed in action 12 9 1918, aged 22, Advance to Victory.
Commemorated – Vis en Artois Memorial, France; St John's Church, Kirkheaton, RoH; Family headstone, Kirkheaton Cemetery, M Stansfield, page 130, and the **Drill Hall WM panel 4, column 2.**
Mentioned on the Goodall collection; the Huddersfield Examiner (wia, official casualty list, 05 6 1916).
Originally 2/5th DWR.
Brother of John Rowland Dyson, see below.

DYSON Harold Freeman – 240039 Company Sergeant Major.
Born 10 6 1892 in Dalton, Huddersfield, to John and Emily. Enlisted in the local Territorials on 14 6 1909.
1/5th Battalion DWR; killed in action 03 9 1916, aged 24, Battle of the Somme (Thiepval).
Buried – Mill Road Cemetery, 1, B, 19.
Commemorated – Almondbury WM; Huddersfield Parish Church RoH; J Fisher, page 113, M Stansfield, page 131, and the **Drill Hall WM panel 4, column 2.**

DYSON Herbert – 241800 Private.
Born in Marsden to John and Martha Ann. Resided in Huddersfield. Enlisted at Huddersfield.
2/5th Battalion DWR; taken prisoner 03 5 1917 at Bullecourt. Died, pneumonia, 17 6 1917, as Prisoner of War, aged 23.
Buried – Cologne Southern Cemetery, 18, A, 19.
Commemorated – Marsden WM; Colne Valley Almanac; M Stansfield, page 131, and the **Drill Hall WM panel 4, column 2.**

DYSON John Rowland – 6626 (later 267722) Private.
Born 20 1 1893 in Dalton Green, to Tom and Sarah. Resided at Kirkheaton. Enlisted in Halifax in August, 1916.
1/5th Battalion DWR; died of wounds 09 8 1917 (but see below).
Buried – New Irish Farm Cemetery, 13, F, 7.
Commemorated – St John's Church, Kirkheaton; family headstone in Kirkheaton cemetery; M Stanfield, page 132, and the **Drill Hall WM panel 4, column 2.**
M Stansfield shows he was wounded on 09 8 1917 and died of his wounds at the Field Ambulance Advanced Dressing Station on 11 8 1917.
Mentioned in the Goodall collection; the Huddersfield Examiner (wounded in action 09 8 1917, official casualty list) on 14 9 1917, (reported missing, official casualty list) on 18 10 1917.
Brother of Frank Crossley Dyson, see above.

DYSON Ralph – 240380 Sergeant.

Born Mirfield. Resided in Lower Hopton and enlisted at Huddersfield.
1/5th Battalion DWR; killed in action 03 9 1916, Battle of the Somme (Thiepval).
Commemorated - Thiepval Memorial, France; Mirfield WM and the **Drill Hall WM panel 4, column 2.**

DYSON Tom – 5361 (later 241896) Private.
Born Milnsbridge to Fred and Clara. Resided in Milnsbridge. Enlisted at Huddersfield. Embarked for France in January, 1917.
2/5th Battalion DWR; reported missing, killed in action, 03 5 1917, aged 23, Battle of Bullecourt.
Commemorated – Arras Memorial, France; Huddersfield Mission, Milnsbridge, RoH; St John's Church, Golcar, RoH; Crow Lane Board School, Milnsbridge; M Stansfield, page 133, and the **Drill Hall WM panel 4, column 2.**

EARNSHAW Albert – 240462 Private.
Born in Kirkheaton to Mr and Mrs E Earnshaw, of Shawcross. Resided Kirkheaton, enlisted at Huddersfield.
1/5th Battalion DWR; killed in action 03 9 1916, Battle of the Somme (Thiepval).
Buried - Mill Road Cemetery, 1, F, 11.
Commemorated – St John's Church, Kirkheaton; M Stansfield, page 134, and the **Drill Hall WM panel 4, column 2.**

EARNSHAW Harold – 4943 (later 241542) Private.
Born in Huddersfield, resided at Paddock and enlisted at Huddersfield.
2/5th Battalion DWR; reported missing, killed in action 03 5 1917, Battle of Bullecourt.
Commemorated – Arras Memorial, France; All Saints Parish Church RoH, Paddock; M Stansfield, page 134; Paddock Parish RoH (now in Huddersfield Drill Hall) and the **Drill Hall WM panel 4, column 2.**
Mentioned in the Goodall collection

EARNSHAW Willie – 3678 (later 240891) Private.
Born to Mr and Mrs John Willie Earnshaw, of Holmfirth. Resided in Holmfirth and enlisted in January, 1915, at Huddersfield. Embarked for France in January, 1916.
2/5th Battalion DWR; killed in action 27 3 1918, German Spring Offensive.
Commemorated – Arras Memorial, France; Underbank WM; M Stansfield, page 136, and the **Drill Hall WM panel 4, column 2.**
Mentioned in the Goodall collection.

EASTWOOD Benjamin – 5881 Private.
Born in Calverley Bridge, Leeds. Enlisted at Yeadon.
1/5th Battalion DWR; killed in action 03 7 1916, aged 21, Battle of the Somme.
Buried – Bouzincourt Communal Cemetery Extension, 2, D, 19.
Commemorated - the **Drill Hall WM panel 4, column 2.**
PEACE PERFECT PEACE.

EASTWOOD Frederick Eddison – 3380 (later 240715) Private.
Born in Ossett and enlisted at Mirfield.
2/5th Battalion DWR; killed in action 03 5 1917, aged 20, Battle of Bullecourt.
Commemorated – Arras Memorial, France, and the **Drill Hall WM panel 4, column 2.**
Mentioned in the Goodall collection.

EASTWOOD George Henry – 2852 Corporal.
Born in Huddersfield on 5 July, 1890. Resided in Newsome and enlisted at Huddersfield in September, 1914.
1/5th Battalion DWR; died of wounds, shellfire, 17 9 1916, aged 26, Battle of the Somme.

Commemorated – Thiepval Memorial, France; Almondbury WM; Almondbury Cemetery WM; March WM; J J Fisher, page 113; M Stansfield, page 137, and the **Drill Hall WM panel 4, column 2.**
Mentioned in the Huddersfield Examiner, 09 10 1916.

EASTWOOD Harry Ross – 3385 (later 240719) Sergeant. Military Medal
Resided Ravensthorpe. Enlisted at Mirfield on 10 11 1914.
5th Battalion DWR, D Company; killed in action 25 8 1918, aged 24, Advance to Victory.
Buried – Douchy les Ayette Cemetery, 4, A, 8
Commemorated – D Tattersfield, pp 381 & 382, and the **Drill Hall WM panel 4, column 2.**
Originally 2/5th Battalion,
Mentioned in Goodall collection; L Magnus (medal award) page 293; London Gazette (award of MM for operations at the Battle of Cambrai, 1917) on 13 3 1918, page 3232.
UNTIL THE DAY DAWNS.

EATON Harry – 6520 Private.
Born and enlisted, Nottingham.
1/5th Battalion DWR; died of wounds 19 1 1917.
Buried – Warlincourt Halte British Cemetery, 3, J, 12.
Commemorated - the **Drill Hall WM panel 4, column 2.**

EDWARDS William Edward – 7056 Private.
Enlisted at Newcastle under Lyne, Staffs.
1/5th Battalion DWR; killed in action 16 9 1916, aged 19, Battle of the Somme.
Commemorated - Thiepval memorial, France, and the **Drill Hall WM panel 4, column 2.**

EGLINGTON (EGLINTON?) Claude – 240981 Corporal. Military Medal.
Born Newsome Cross, Huddersfield, 21 4 1897, to Alice. Enlisted 6 1 1915, at Huddersfield.
2/5th Battalion DWR; killed in action 27 11 1917, Battle of Cambrai.
Commemorated – Cambrai Memorial (Louverval), France; Newsome United Methodist Church RoH; St John's Church, Newsome, RoH; M Stansfield, page 139, and the **Drill Hall WM panel 4, column 2.**
Mentioned in Goodall collection and the Magnus History medal roll. Awarded the Military Medal for operations at the Battle of Cambrai, 1917, London Gazette 13 3 1918, page 3232.
Name spelt Eglinton in SDGW as well as one of the Goodall entries.

ELLIOTT (Elliot?) Joseph George – 4166 (later 241185) Private.
Resided in Mirfield and enlisted at Huddersfield.
2/5th Battalion DWR, D Company; killed in action 03 5 1917, aged 26, Battle of Bullecourt.
Commemorated – Arras Memorial, France; Battyeford WM; Mirfield WM and the **Drill Hall WM panel 4, column 2.**
Mentioned in the Goodall collection.
CWGC shows name as Elliot.

ELLIS George – 240569 Private.
Born in East Thorpe, Yorks. Resided New Worley, Leeds, and enlisted at Huddersfield.
1/5th Battalion DWR; killed in action 03 9 1916, Battle of the Somme (Thiepval).
Commemorated - Thiepval Memorial, France, and the **Drill Hall WM panel 4, column 2.**

ELLIS Harry – 4949 (later 241547) Private.
Born Primrose Hill to Mr and Mrs W Ellis of Milnsbridge. Resided at Milnsbridge and enlisted at Huddersfield.
2/5th Battalion DWR; reported missing, killed in action 03 5 1917, Battle of Bullecourt.

Commemorated - Arras Memorial, France; M Stansfield, page 140, and the **Drill Hall WM panel 4, column 2.**

ELLIS Herbert – 5662 (later 242072) Private.
Born Longroyd Bridge on 21 8 1894, to Walter and Mary of Crosland Moor. Resided Paddock and enlisted at Huddersfield on 07 4 1916.
1/5th Battalion DWR; reported missing, killed in action 03 9 1916, aged 22, Battle of the Somme (Thiepval).
Commemorated – Thiepval Memorial, France; Shared Church RoH, Paddock; M Stansfield, page 140, and the **Drill Hall WM panel 4, column 2.**
SDGW shows he enlisted at Halifax.

ELLIS William – 25078 Private. Military Medal.
Born Norfolk. Enlisted at Huddersfield.
2/5th Battalion DWR; killed in action 27 11 1917, Battle of Cambrai.
Commemorated – Cambrai Memorial, France, and the **Drill Hall WM panel 4, column 2.**
Mentioned in Goodall collection; L Magnus History (medal roll), page 295; Mentioned in the London Gazette (award of MM for operations at the Battle of Cambrai, 1917) on 13 3 1918, page 3232.

ELSTON W – Private.
No trace. Possibly Northumberland Fusiliers.
Commemorated - the **Drill Hall WM panel 4, column 2.**

ELY George William – 5879 Private.
Born Spilsby, Lincs. Resided in Keighley and enlisted at Bradford.
1/5th Battalion DWR; killed in action 03 9 1916, Battle of the Somme (Thiepval).
Commemorated - Thiepval Memorial, France, and the **Drill Hall WM panel 4, column 2.**

EMMOTT Thomas Oldfield – 267659 Private.
Born in Skipton to Edward and Isabella Ann. Resided in Skipton and enlisted at Keighley.
2/5th Battalion DWR; killed in action 27 11 1917, Battle of Cambrai.
Commemorated – Cambrai Memorial, France; Cravens Part in the Great War, page 37, & the cpgw.org.uk website, and the **Drill Hall WM panel 4, column 3.**

EMSLEY John – 5883 (later 242151) Private.
Born Little Horton, Bradford, to Sam and Sarah A Emsley. Enlisted at Bradford.
1/5th Battalion DWR; killed in action 03 9 1916, aged 21, Battle of the Somme (Thiepval).
Buried – Mill Road Cemetery, 1, D, 10.
Commemorated – St Oswald's Church, Little Horton, WM; and the **Drill Hall WM panel 4, column 2.**
CWGC shows 1/4th DWR.

ENGLISH Thomas – 242320 Private.
Born Edmondsley, Durham. Resided in West Stanley and enlisted at Stanley.
1/5th Battalion DWR; killed in action 07 8 1917.
Buried – Ramscappelle Road Military Cemetery, 2, A, 29.
Commemorated – J J Fisher, page 115, and the **Drill Hall WM panel 4, column 3**

ERRINGTON William Strong - 35630 Private.
Born and enlisted Hanley, Staffs.
5th Battalion DWR; died 14 1 1919, home, aged 22.
Buried - South Moor (St George) Cemetery, North part.
Commemorated – the **Drill Hall WM panel 4, column 3.**

Originally 2/5th DWR. SDGW shows date of death as 13 1 1919.
Formerly 76152 West Yorkshire Regiment.

EVANS Ernest – 35168 Private.
Born Castleford and enlisted at Middlesbrough.
5th Battalion DWR; killed in action 14 9 1918, Advance to Victory.
Buried – Sunken Road, Boisleux, Cemetery, 2, A, 22.
Commemorated - the Drill Hall WM panel 4, column 3.
Originally 2/5th DWR.

FAHY Michael – 4114 Private.
Resided Huddersfield. Enlisted at Huddersfield in June, 1915.
1/5th Battalion DWR; reported missing, killed in action 03 9 1916, Battle of the Somme (Thiepval).
Buried – Mill Road Cemetery, 3, F, 6.
Commemorated – J J Fisher, page 113, M Stansfield, page 144, and the **Drill Hall WM panel 4, column 3.**
Mentioned in the Huddersfield Examiner (reported wounded, official casualty list) 07 8 1916; (body found), 05 10 1916.

FAIRLESS William – 16777 Private.
Born in Bentinck, Northumberland. Enlisted in Elswick, Lancs.
2/5th Battalion DWR; killed in action 28 3 1916, German Spring Offensive.
Buried – Foncquevillers Military Cemetery, 3, E, 19.
Commemorated - the Drill Hall WM panel 4, column 3.

FARRAR James Edward – 203680 Private.
Born Lockwood on 26 April, 1896, to Mr and Mrs W H Farrar. Resided Lockwood and enlisted at Huddersfield on 1 March 1916.
1/5th Battalion DWR; reported missing, killed in action 20 3 1918, Advance to Victory.
Commemorated – Loos Memorial, France; Lockwood Baptist Church RoH; Emmanuel Church RoH, Lockwood; M Stansfield, page 144, and the **Drill Hall WM panel 4, column 3.**
CWGC shows forenames as James Ernest.

FARRELL Robert P – 3894 (later 241030) Lance Corporal. Military Medal.
Resided in Heckmondwike. Enlisted at Mirfield on 19 2 1915.
5th Battalion DWR D Company (Stokes Mortar detachment); died of wounds 19 11 1918, Advance to Victory.
Buried – St Sever Cemetery Extension, S, 3, O, 16.
Commemorated - the Drill Hall WM panel 4, column 3.
Originally 2/5th DWR. Attached 168 Trench Mortar Battery.
Mentioned in the Goodall collection; London Gazette (award of MM) on 13 3 1919, page 3430.
Initials shown as R; R F or R P, depending on source.

FEATHER Ernest Arthur – 5888 Private.
Born and enlisted Keighley.
1/5th Battalion DWR; killed in action 03 9 1916, Battle of the Somme (Thiepval).
Commemorated – Thiepval Memorial, France, and the **Drill Hall WM panel 4, column 3.**

FERGUSON Alfred – 2017 (later 240150) Corporal. Military Medal.
Born Bramley, Leeds. Resided in Leeds and enlisted at Mirfield.
1/5th Battalion DWR; killed in action 03 9 1916, aged 22, Battle of the Somme (Thiepval).
Commemorated – Thiepval Memorial, France, and the **Drill Hall WM panel 4, column 3.**
Originally 2/5th DWR, H, then D, Company. Volunteered for foreign service and posted to 1/5th DWR.

Mentioned in the Goodall collection. The Unit War Diary (announced award of Gallantry Card, and Military Medal) on 31 7 1916; (Military Medal award) on 30 9 1916.
Military Medal award announced in the London Gazette on 01 9 1916, page 8655.

FIDLER Clifford – 2266 Private.
Born Leeds 14 4 1897, to Fred and Lily, of Huddersfield. Resided at Turnbridge. Enlisted in the Territorials in April, 1913.
1/5th Battalion DWR, A Company; killed in action 18 9 1915, aged 18, Ypres.
Buried – New Irish Farm Cemetery, 17, E, 3.
Commemorated – Fartown and Birkby WM; Milton Independent Church RoH; St Andrew's Church, Leeds Road, RoH (thought to have been destroyed), Parents' headstone, Edgerton Cemetery; M Stansfield, page 146, and the **Drill Hall WM panel 4, column 3.**
DEEP IN OUR HEARTS THE MEMORY OF OUR DEAR ONE WE CHERISH.

FIRN Arthur – 202800 Lance Corporal.
Born in Gomersall to James William and Mary Jane. Resided Gomersall. Enlisted at Birstall.
2/5th Battalion DWR; killed in action 28 11 1917, aged 27, aged 27, Battle of Cambrai.
Buried - Rocquigny-Equancourt Road Cemetery, 3, D, 16.
Commemorated – Cleckheaton WM; Spenborough WM; C Turpin, page 8, and the **Drill Hall WM panel 4, column 3.**

FIRTH Leonard – 5549 Private.
Born Nettleton, Kirkheaton, on 27 9 1880 to Tom and Catherine. Resided Kirkheaton and enlisted at Huddersfield on 04 4 1916.
1/5th Battalion DWR; wounded in action 03 9 1916 and died of wounds 13 9 1916, aged 21, Battle of the Somme.
Buried – Warloy Baillon Communal Cemetery Extension, 2, H, 3.
Commemorated – St John's Church, Kirkheaton, RoH; Headstone in Kirkheaton Cemetery; M Stansfield, page 149, and the **Drill Hall WM panel 4, column 3.**
Mentioned in the Huddersfield Examiner (died of wounds, hospital, France) on 29 9 1916.
HE BRAVELY ANSWERED DUTY'S CALL, HE GAVE HIS LIFE, HIS LOVE, HIS ALL.

FIRTH Richard – 3985 (later 241087) Private.
Resided Liversedge and enlisted at Huddersfield.
5th Battalion DWR; died of wounds 28 7 1918, Advance to Victory.
Buried – St Sever Cemetery Extension, Q, 3, O, 15.
Commemorated – Spenborough (Cleckheaton) WM; Turpin, page 8, and the **Drill Hall WM panel 4, column 3.**
Mentioned in the Goodall collection.
Originally 2/5th DWR.

FISHER Allott – 20534 Private.
Born Heckmondwike. Resided in Liversedge. Enlisted at Heckmondwike.
2/5th Battalion DWR; killed in action 03 5 1917, Battle of Bullecourt.
Commemorated – Arras Memorial, France, and the **Drill Hall WM panel 4, column 3.**

FISHER Dyson Armsworth – 1813 Private.
Born Luddenden, Halifax, to Mr and Mrs Harry Fisher of Longroyd Bridge. Resided Birkby and enlisted at Huddersfield, 1914. Embarked for France in April, 1915.
1/5th Battalion DWR; killed in action 24 6 1915, aged 21, Ypres.
Buried – Rue David Military Cemetery, 1, B, 10.
Commemorated – M Stansfield, page 150, and the **Drill Hall WM panel 4, column 3.**
Mentioned in the Huddersfield Examiner (death announced) on 28 6 1915.
PEACE PERFECT PEACE.

FISHER Hobson – 3908 (later 241040) Private.
Resided Liversedge, enlisted at Mirfield on 27 2 1915.
2/5th Battalion DWR, D Company; reported missing, killed in action 03 5 1917, aged 23, Battle of Bullecourt.
Commemorated – Arras Memorial, France; Spenborough (Cleckheaton) WM; Turpin, page 9, and the **Drill Hall WM panel 4, column 3.**
Mentioned in the Goodall collection.

FISHER John Hailton (Haylton?) – 2nd Lieutenant.
Son of John William and Mary Ann, of Gateshead. Resided London.
1/5th Battalion DWR; killed in action, sniper, 29 11 1916, aged 20, Battle of the Somme.
Buried – Foncquevillers Military Cemetery, 1, J, 35.
Commemorated - the **Drill Hall WM panel 4, column 3.**
Mentioned in unit War Diary on numerous occasions: (joined Bn) 07 8 1916; (appointed Transport Officer) 30 9 1916; (awarded Gallantry Card) 30 11 1916; (author of Raid Report) 20 11 1916.
THY WILL BE DONE.

FISHER William – 33633 Private.
Born in Ealing, London, to William and Fanny. Enlisted at Ealing.
5th Battalion DWR; died of wounds 01 4 1918, aged 19, German Spring Offensive.
Buried – St Sever Cemetery Extension, P, 9, K, 7A.
Commemorated - the **Drill Hall WM panel 4, column 3.**
From 60985 Royal West Surrey Regiment.
DEARLY LOVED AND DEEPLY MOURNED.

FITZJOHN Arthur Thomas – 16113 (later 242801) Lance Corporal.
Born, resided and enlisted at Hull.
2/5th Battalion DWR; killed in action 03 5 1917, Battle of Bullecourt.
Commemorated – Arras Memorial, France, and the **Drill Hall WM panel 4, column 3.**
Mentioned in the Goodall collection.

FLETCHER David – 8652 Private.
Born in Halifax. Resided in Halifax with his wife, Alice. Enlisted at Halifax.
1/5th Battalion DWR; killed in action 20 1 1917, aged 35.
Buried – Humbercamps Communal Cemetery Extension, 1, B, 14.
Commemorated – Halifax RoH; Calderdale War Dead, page 120, and the **Drill Hall WM panel 4, column 3.**
MIZPAH.

FLETT Thomas William – 35632 Private.
Born Monk Wearmouth, Durham to John of Fulwell, Sunderland. Enlisted at Newcastle upon Tyne.
5th Battalion DWR; killed in action 12 9 1918, aged 19, Advance to Victory.
Buried - Sunken Road, Boisaux, Cemetery, 2, A, 9.
Commemorated - the **Drill Hall WM panel 4, column 3.**
From 76144 West Yorkshire Regiment.
AT REST.

FLINTON Thomas – 2185 (later 240174) Private.
Born Almondbury on 19 9 1892 to Thomas and Rachel. Enlisted at Huddersfield on 04 8 1914.
2/5th Battalion DWR, C Company; killed in action 27 11 1917, Battle of Cambrai.
Commemorated – Cambrai Memorial (Louverval), France; Almondbury WM; M Stansfield, page 152, and the **Drill Hall WM panel 4, column 3.**

FOGG Walter – 269103 Private.
Born and enlisted at Sheffield.
1/5th Battalion DWR; killed in action 09 10 1917.
Commemorated – Tyne Cot Memorial, Belgium, and the **Drill Hall WM panel 4, column 4.**

FOREST (FORREST?) Henry Dacre – 2nd Lieutenant.
Son of MR T W A Forrest, of Loxholme, Darwen, Lancs.
5th Battalion DWR; killed in action 07 4 1918, German Spring Offensive.
Buried – Bienvillers Military Cemetery, 9, B, 14.
Commemorated – the **Drill Hall WM panel 4, column 4.**
From West Yorkshire Regiment.
Mentioned in 62nd Divisional History (killed in action); mentioned in 2/5th DWR Unit War Diary, (in action) 16 1 1917; and 5th DWR War Diary (killed in action) 30 4 1918.
CWGC shows spelling as FORREST.

FORESHAW Albert Edward – 25081 Private.
Born and enlisted in Upholland, Lincs.
2/5th Battalion DWR; killed in action 08 8 1917.
Buried – Queant Road Cemetery, 3, H, 12.
Commemorated - the **Drill Hall WM panel 4, column 4.**
From 284939 Army Service Corps.
CWGC shows spelling as FORSHAW.

FORSTER James Thomas - 26214 Private.
Born Benshaw, Durham. Enlisted in Gateshead.
5th Battalion DWR; killed in action 11 4 1918, aged 27, German Spring Offensive.
Buried – Bienvillers Military Cemetery, 9, C, 8.
Commemorated - the **Drill Hall WM panel 4, column 4.**
Originally 2/5th DWR. From 39365 Durham Light Infantry.
BLESSED ARE THE PURE IN HEART, FOR THEY SHALL SEE GOD.

FOX John – 241331 Private.
Resided Lockwood with his wife, Nellie. Enlisted at Huddersfield.
1/5th Battalion DWR; killed in action 03 9 1916, Battle of the Somme (Thiepval).
Commemorated – Thiepval Memorial, France; Emmanuel Church, Lockwood, RoH; M Stansfield, page 154, , and the **Drill Hall WM panel 4, column 3.**

FRAINE (FRAIN) John – 4976 (later 241573) Private.
Born and resided Birstall. Enlisted at Halifax.
5th Battalion DWR; died 31 10 1918, as Prisoner of War, aged 30.
Buried – Berlin South Western Cemetery, 9, A, 5.
Commemorated - the **Drill Hall WM panel 4, column 4.**
Originally 2/5th DWR
All other sources, apart from the WM Board, show Frain.

FRANCIS (FRANCES) Harry – 4780 Private.
Born Saddleworth to Charles and Emma Jane. Resided in Delph with his wife, Alice Jane, of Diggle. Enlisted at Uppermill.
1/5th Battalion DWR; killed in action 05 7 1916, aged 25, Battle of the Somme.
Commemorated - Thiepval Memorial, France; Fisher, page 110, and the **Drill Hall WM panel 4, column 4.**
All other sources, apart from the 5 DWR WM Board, show Frances.
4780 Private **J** Frances is also commemorated on the 7th Battalion Roll of Honour Board.

FRANKLIN Ernest – 25969 Private.
Born Gloucester and enlisted at Woolwich.
5th Battalion DWR; killed in action 20 10 1918.
Buried – Quivey Communal Cemetery Extension, C, 65.
Commemorated - the **Drill Hall WM panel 4, column 4.**
Originally 2/5th DWR.

FRANKLIN Harry – 33632 Private.
Born in Toddington, Beds, to William and Elizabeth. Enlisted at Luton.
5th Battalion DWR; killed in action 20 7 1918, aged 20.
Buried – Courmas British Cemetery, 2, C, 2.
Commemorated – the **Drill Hall WM panel 4, column 4.**
Originally 2/5th DWR. Formerly 60986 Royal West Surrey Regiment.
HIS DUTY WELL DONE, HIS CROWN NOBLY WON.

FRASER William David – 2667 Sergeant. MID, Military Medal.
Born Talybont, Brecon, Wales. Resided Chapel Hill, Huddersfield. Served in the Boer War and was re-enlisted 08 8 1914. Embarked for France on 15 4 1915.
1/5th Battalion DWR; died of wounds as Prisoner of War 08 9 1916.
Buried – Morchies Communal Cemetery, 2.
Commemorated – Fisher, page 79, M Stansfield, page 156, and the **Drill Hall WM panel 4, column 4.**
Mentioned in the Goodall collection (medals awards roll for MID and MM); the Huddersfield Examiner (award of MID) 20 9 1916, (announcement of death) 15 2 1917; Unit War Diary (announcement of MID award) 30 6 1917; (MM award) 31 3 1917.

FREEMAN William Leonard – 25082 Private.
Born Bermondsey and enlisted at Lambeth.
2/5th Battalion DWR; killed in action 27 3 1918, German Spring Offensive.
Commemorated - Arras Memorial, France, and the **Drill Hall WM panel 4, column 4.**

FROGGATT George – 5309 (later 241855) Private.
Born Wakefield, of Mr and Mrs Matthew Froggatt, of Lepton. Resided Lepton and enlisted at Huddersfield in March, 1916.
2/5th Battalion DWR; killed in action 26 11 1917, Battle of Cambrai.
Commemorated - Cambrai Memorial (Louverval), France; Lepton Parish Church RoH; Emley Churchyard memorial; M Stansfield, page 157, and the **Drill Hall WM panel 4, column 4.**
Mentioned in the Goodall collection.

GALLAGHER James William – 240815 Private.
Born in Huddersfield. Served in the Boer War and re-enlisted in January, 1915.
5th Battalion DWR; killed in action 28 9 1918, Advance to Victory.
Buried – Grand Ravine British Cemetery, A, 5.
Commemorated – M Stansfield, page 159, and the **Drill Hall WM panel 4, column 4.**
The Huddersfield Examiner (announcement of death) 18 10 1918; (memoriam notice) 30 9 1919.
Originally 2/5th DWR.

GALLAGHER William George – 242158 Private.
Born in Hebburn upon Tyne to Robert, of Bradford. Enlisted at Bradford.
1/5th Battalion DWR; killed in action 03 9 1916, aged 23, Battle of the Somme (Thiepval).
Buried - Mill Road Cemetery, 9, A, 4.
Commemorated - the **Drill Hall WM panel 4, column 4.**

GANNON John – 202638 Private.

Born and enlisted at Newcastle under Lyne.
2/5th Battalion DWR; killed in action 29 3 1918, aged 21, German Spring Offensive.
Commemorated – Arras Memorial, France, and the **Drill Hall WM panel 4, column 4.**
Attached 168 Trench Mortar Battery.

GARFITT Walter – 3625 Private.
Resided in Ravensthorpe. Enlisted at Mirfield.
1/5th Battalion DWR; died of wounds 05 9 1916, aged 20, Battle of the Somme.
Buried – Forceville Communal Cemetery, 3, C, 2.
Commemorated – D Tattersfield, page 136 & 383, and the **Drill Hall WM panel 4, column 4.**

GARFORTH Frank – 205655 Private.
Born in Shipley to Thomas and Anna. Resided in Shipley and enlisted at Bradford.
2/5th Battalion DWR; killed in action 28 3 1918, aged 30, German Spring Offensive.
Commemorated – Arras Memorial, France, and the **Drill Hall WM panel 4, column 4.**

GARROD Frederick – 25703 Private.
Born Bermondsey, London. Enlisted Rotherhithe.
2/5th Battalion DWR; killed in action 22 7 1918, Battle of Tardenois.
Commemorated – Soissons Memorial, France, and the **Drill Hall WM panel 4, column 4.**

GARSIDE Joseph – 16434 Private.
Born in New Mill, Holmfirth. Resided in Huddersfield. Enlisted at Earsdon, Northumberland.
5th Battalion DWR, D Company, 13 Platoon; reported missing, killed in action 26 3 1918, German Spring Offensive.
Commemorated – Arras Memorial, France; Fulstone WM; Mirfield WM; New Mill Working Men's Club RoH; M Stansfield, page 161, and the **Drill Hall WM panel 4, column 4.**
Originally 2/5th DWR.
Mentioned in the Goodall collection and the Huddersfield Examiner (wounded, official casualty roll) 06 11 1916.

GARSIDE Thomas Henry – 5259 (later 241814) Private.
Born in Longwood, Huddersfield, to Richard and Elizabeth. Resided in Lindley. Enlisted at Huddersfield.
2/5th Battalion DWR; reported missing, killed in action 03 5 1917, aged 25, Battle of Bullecourt.
Commemorated – Arras Memorial, France; M Stansfield, page 161, and the **Drill Hall WM panel 4, column 4.**
Mentioned in the Goodall collection; the Huddersfield Examiner, official casualty list, reported missing, on 27 6 1917.

GARWOOD James Watson – 2456 (later 265566) Private.
Born Skipton to John and Margaret. Resided and enlisted at Skipton. Embarked for France 14 4 1915.
1/5th Battalion DWR; killed in action 12 4 1917, aged 22.
Buried – Le Touret Military Cemetery, 4, C, 19.
Commemorated – Skipton WM; Craven's Part in the Great War, page 237, and the **Drill Hall WM panel 4, column 4.**
Originally 1/6th DWR. CWGC is the only source showing 5 DWR.
THY WILL BE DONE.

GAWTHORPE Stanley – 3635 (later 240867) Corporal.
Born in Shipley. Resided in Ravensthorpe and enlisted at Mirfield.
1/5th Battalion DWR; killed in action 03 9 1916, aged 19, Battle of the Somme (Thiepval).

Commemorated – Thiepval Memorial, France; D Tattersfield, pages 135 & 383, and the **Drill Hall WM panel 4, column 4.**

GEE Benjamin – 4395 Private.
Resided in Stainland and enlisted at Huddersfield.
1/5th Battalion DWR; killed in action 03 9 1916, Battle of the Somme (Thiepval).
Commemorated – Thiepval Memorial, France, and the **Drill Hall WM panel 4, column 4.**

GIBBS William – 202639 Private. Military Medal.
Born North Carolina, USA. Resided in Stoke and enlisted at Tunstall, Staffs, 15 11 1915.
2/5th Battalion DWR, D Company, 14 Platoon; killed in action 27 11 1917, Battle of Cambrai.
Commemorated - Cambrai Memorial (Louverval), France, and the **Drill Hall WM panel 5, column 1**.
Mentioned in the Goodall collection (Medal Award and Nominal Rolls); L Magnus (Medal Award Roll) page 295; the London Gazette (award of MM) on 13 3 1918, page 3233.

GIBSON Gladstone – 2865 Lance Corporal.
Born High Hoyland to Alma and Elizabeth. Resided at Clayton West and enlisted at Huddersfield.
1/5th Battalion DWR; killed in action, shellfire, 03 7 1916, aged 26, Battle of the Somme.
Buried – Connaught Cemetery, 12, J, 4.
Commemorated – Clayton West and High Hoyland WM; M Stansfield, page 163, and the **Drill Hall WM panel 4, column 4.**
Mentioned in the Huddersfield Examiner (details of death) 17 7 1916.
SAVIOUR IN THY GRACIOUS KEEPING, LEAVE WE NOW OUR BROTHER SLEEPING.

GIBSON William Henry – 200927 Private.
Resided in Sowerby Bridge and enlisted at Halifax.
2/5th Battalion DWR; killed in action 20 11 1917, aged 24, Battle of Cambrai.
Commemorated – Cambrai Memorial (Louverval), France, and the **Drill Hall WM panel 4, column 4.**

GIFFORD Walter – 23893 Corporal.
Born Huddersfield on 24 11 1893 to Mrs A Gifford. Enlisted at Huddersfield in January, 1915.
2/5th Battalion DWR; reported missing, killed in action 21 11 1917, Battle of Cambrai.
Commemorated – Cambrai Memorial (Louverval), France; Huddersfield Parish Church RoH; M Stansfield, page 164, and the **Drill Hall WM panel 5, column 1.**
Mentioned in the Huddersfield Examiner (official date of death) 23 8 1918; (in memoriam notice) 22 11 1920.

GILL Wilfred – 241057 Private.
Born in Batley to Fred and Mary Ann. Resided in Batley. Enlisted at Mirfield.
1/5th Battalion DWR, B Company; killed in action 19 9 1916, aged 20, Battle of the Somme.
Commemorated - Thiepval Memorial, France, and the **Drill Hall WM panel 4, column 4.**

49th Division undergoing Trench instruction, Fleurbaix, 1915.

49th Division in action, Battle of the Somme, September, 1916.

GILL. W. A. PTE.	GRIMES. G. PTE.	HANSON. A. PTE.	HALEY. J. PTE.
GILMOUR. J. R. "	GRAHAM. W. H. SGT.	HURT. E. "	HAINSWORTH. H. L/CPL.
GIFFORD. W. CPL.	GRAHAM. HARRY. PTE.	HARRISON. J. W. "	HALL. J. A. PTE.
GIBBS. W. PTE.	GRAHAM. HIRST. M.M. "	HARRISON. S. "	HALL. FRANK. "
GLEDHILL. N. "	GRAHAM. F. T. "	HARRISON. M. "	HALL. F. "
GLEDHILL. G. R. 2/LT.	GREENHOUGH. M. "	HARRISON. W. "	HALL. E. "
GLEDHILL. R. R. L/CPL.	GREENFIELD. S. "	HARRISON. F. H. "	HARPIN. H. R. "
GLASS. W. M.M. PTE.	GREAVES. J. "	HARDY. W. F. L/CPL.	HARGREAVES. S. "
GOLLAND. F. "	GREEN. A. "	HARDY. F. "	HARGREAVES. H. "
GOODRICK. H. "	GREEN. F. "	HARDY. HERBERT. CPL.	HAMPSHIRE. L. "
GOODALL. E. "	GRANT. F. "	HARDY. HAROLD. PTE.	HALE. H. F. "
GOODER. W. H. CPL.	GRAY. W. B. "	HARDY. E. CPL.	HAWKSLY. J. R. "
GOLDSELLER. L. D. LT.	GREAVES. V. 2/LT.	HARDAKER. F. PTE.	HAWKSWORTH. H. CPL.
GOLDSBROUGH. H. PTE.	GREAVES. W. CPL.	HARTLEY. G. "	HARWOOD. H. PTE.
GODDARD. B. "	GRIFFITHS. P. PTE.	HARTLEY. F. "	HATTON. A. "
GOREHAM. E. J. A/CPL.	GRUNDY. A. J. "	HARTLEY. W. "	HAILWOOD. T. "
GOUGH. J. W. C. PTE.	GUNN. H. "	HASSALL. W. J. "	HALLAS. J. "
GODFREY. G. "	JACKSON. D. R. F. LT.	HAIGH. G. "	HEAPS. A. "
GOMERSALL. W. E. "	HARRIS. S. L/CPL.	HAIGH. J. "	HERBERT. R. "
GODFREY. E. A. A. "	HAMMOND. G. A. PTE.	HAIGH. J. "	HERBERT. F. "
GRACE. E. E. "	HAMER. C. "	HAIGUE. W. "	HELLAWELL. W. "
GRAYSON. J. R. L/SGT.	HAMER. TOM. "	HAIGH. W. "	HELLAWELL. E. "
GREENWOOD. H. L/CPL.	HAMER. THOMAS. "	HAIGH. J. A. LT.	HELLAWELL. L. "
GREENWOOD. G. A. PTE.	HANSON. B. L/CPL.	HAIGH. N. SGT.	HELLIWELL. F. "
GREENWOOD. F. W. "	HANSON. E. PTE.	HAGUE. C. H. PTE.	HELLEWELL. W. "
GREENWOOD. S. "	HANSON. C. "	HANSON. H. CPT.	HEADEY. P. L/CPL.

HEY. F. PTE.	HIRD. S. PTE.	HORNE. J. W. PTE.	JARDINE. A. M. PTE.
HEATON. W. 2/LIEUT.	HOBSON. G. "	HOSKIN. T. SGT.	JEFFERSON. D. P. "
HEMINGWAY. H. PTE.	HOBSON. D. W. CPL.	HOFFMAN. E. PTE.	JEWSBURY. A. "
HEATH. H. "	HOLT. W. PTE.	HUNT. G. L. "	JENNINGS. A. G. "
HENTHORNE. S. SGT.	HOLT. T. "	HUNT. A. "	JENNINGS. J. "
HEYWOOD. J. W. PTE.	HOPKINSON. J. E. "	HUTCHINSON. H. "	JESSOP. A. W. "
HEESOM. G. "	HOPKINSON. J. "	HUTCHINSON. J. "	JESSOP. L. H. "
HOLLINGWORTH. J. H. "	HORNSBY. G. H. "	HUXLEY. T. "	JESSOP. E. "
HIRST. A. B. "	HOOD. C. "	HUGHES. J. "	JEPSON. A. W. "
HIRST. F. "	HOLROYD. H. "	HUGHES. A. "	JEPSON. P. "
HIRST. S. "	HOLMES. C. H. SGT.	HUDSON. J. W. "	JOHNSON. J. G. "
HIRST. H. E. "	HOLMES. F. PTE.	HUDSON. A. A. CPL.	JOHNSON. P. "
HIRST. H. I. "	HOLMES. H. DMR.	HYDE. T. PTE.	JOHNSON. T. C. "
HIRST. HAROLD "	HOLMES. G. F. PTE.	IBBOTSON. J. "	JOHNSON. F. M.M. "
HIRST. J. E. "	HOLMES. C. E. SGT.	IDDON. G. "	JOHNSON. A. E. "
HIRST. H. M.M. SGT.	HOYLE. T. SGT.	INGHAM. H. "	JOHNSTONE. A. "
HINCHLIFFE. E. "	HOYLE. H. S. PTE.	ISSATT. J. "	JONES. J. "
HINCHCLIFFE. F. PTE.	HOYLE. H. "	IZZARD. H. "	JONES. A. B. "
HINCHCLIFFE. A. "	HOBLEY. J. "	JACKSON. H. SGT.	JONES. J. D. "
HINCHCLIFFE. H. "	HORSFALL. E. "	JACKSON. W. PTE.	JONES. J. V. D.C.M. C.S.M.
HINCHCLIFFE. H. CPL.	HORSFALL. F. "	JACKSON. H. N. "	JONES. J. W. PTE.
HILL. C. T. PTE.	HOWARTH. W. "	JACKSON. A. "	JONES. C. "
HILL. E. "	HOWARTH. M. L/CPL.	JACKSON. G. "	JOHNSEY. H. "
HIBBIRD. G. "	HOUGHLAND. T. CPL.	JACKSON. J. B. SGT.	JURY. R. 2/LIEUT.
HIBBARD. G. R. "	HORSFIELD. S. "	JACKSON. J. PTE.	KAYE. C. W. D. LIEUT.
HIGHAM. F. L/CPL.	HOCKLEY. J. PTE.	JAGGAR. W. "	KAYE. O. PTE.

GILL William Akeroyd – 3917 (later 241046) Private.
Resided Birstall and enlisted at Mirfield on 24 2 1915.
5th Battalion DWR, D Company; died of wounds 12 4 1918, German Spring Offensive.
Buried – Doullens Communal Cemetery Extension, 6, B, 16.
Commemorated – the **Drill Hall WM panel 5, column 1.**
Mentioned in the Goodall collection.
Originally 2/5th DWR.

GILLING George Frederick – 3396 Private.
Born Huddersfield, 08 12 1894 to George and Mary Ellen. Joined the local Territorials prior to the war and re-enlisted at Huddersfield in October, 1914.
1/5th Battalion DWR; killed in action, shrapnel, 04 8 1916, Battle of the Somme.
Buried - Connaught Cemetery, 3, M, 1.
Commemorated – Huddersfield Parish Church RoH; M Stansfield, page 164, and the **Drill Hall WM panel 4, column 4.**
Mentioned in the Huddersfield Examiner (killed in action, official casualty list,) on 09 6 1916; (killed in action by shellfire) on 09 8 1916.

GILMOUR James Ross – 242850 Private.
Born in Kiveton Park, Yorks. Resided in Holywell Green. Enlisted at Elland.
1/5th Battalion DWR; killed in action 17 7 1917 aged 19.
Buried – Noix les Mines Communal Cemetery, 2, E, 35.
Commemorated – the **Drill Hall WM panel 5, column 1.**

GLASS William – 26337 Private. Military Medal.
Born and enlisted at Hamilton.
5th Battalion DWR; killed in action 05 11 1918, Advance to Victory.
Commemorated – Vis en Artois Memorial, France; Magnus, page 295, and the **Drill Hall WM panel 5, column 1.**
Originally 2/5th Battalion. Formerly 086502 Army Service Corps.
Mentioned in the Goodall collection (Gallantry Awards Nominal Roll); the London Gazette, (award of MM) on 11 12 1918, page 14659.

GLEDHILL George Richard – 2nd Lieutenant
Born Huddersfield 24 11 1896 to Walter and Hannah of Thongsbridge. Resided Huddersfield and enlisted at Huddersfield on 03 9 1914.
1/5th Battalion DWR; killed in action 03 9 1916, Battle of the Somme.
Commemorated – Thiepval Memorial, France; Holme Valley Memorial Hospital WM (plaque 5 Netherthong & Thongsbridge); Huddersfield College School RoH; Fisher, page 129; M Stansfield, page 167, and the **Drill Hall WM panel 5, column 1.**
Mentioned in the Huddersfield Examiner (reported missing) on 13 9 1916. Mentioned in the Unit War Diary (joined the Battalion) on 07 10 1915; (in action with B Company) on 03 9 1916; (listed as missing) on 30 9 1916.

GLEDHILL Norman – 3176 Private.
Born Lindley. Resided Elland and enlisted at Huddersfield.
1/5th Battalion DWR; died of wounds 23 8 1915, aged 16, Ypres.
Buried - Etaples Military Cemetery, 4, D, 9A.
Commemorated – Fisher, page 106, and the **Drill Hall WM panel 5, column 1.**
SDGW shows date of death as 24 8 1915.
Mentioned in the Huddersfield Examiner (died of wounds) on 31 8 1915.

GLEDHILL Robert Randolph – 5357 (later 241894) Lance Corporal.

Born Golcar to James and Sarah. Resided in Golcar. Enlisted at Milnsbridge in March, 1916. Embarked for France on 10 1 1917.
2/5th Battalion DWR; killed in action 03 5 1917, aged 29, Battle of Bullecourt.
Commemorated - Arras Memorial, France; St John's Church, Golcar, RoH; M Stansfield, page 168, and the **Drill Hall WM panel 5, column 1.**
Mentioned on the Goodall collection; the Huddersfield Examiner (family request for further details) 12 6 1917; (reported missing, official casualty list) 27 6 1917.

GODDARD Brandon – 5404 (later 241934) Lance Corporal.
Born in Saddleworth to Thomas and Mary, of Delph. Resided and enlisted at Oldham.
2/5th Battalion DWR, C Company; reported missing, killed in action 03 5 1917, aged 22, Battle of Bullecourt.
Commemorated – Arras Memorial, France, and the **Drill Hall WM panel 5, column 1.**
Mentioned in Goodall collection (awarded Commanding Officer's Commendation for actions between 20-28 2 1917); the Huddersfield Examiner (reported missing) on 07 6 1917.

GODFREY Edwin Arthur Alfred – 34047 Private.
Son of Lena, of Peckham, London. Enlisted at Camberwell, London.
5th Battalion DWR; killed in action 05 11 1918, aged 26, Advance to Victory.
Buried – Ruesnes Communal Cemetery, 1, B, 4.
Commemorated - the **Drill Hall WM panel 5, column 1.**
Originally 2/5th DWR.
AT REST.

GODFREY George – 26438 Private.
Born Highgate, Middlesex to F and Alice, of Whitchurch, Oxon. Enlisted at Woolwich.
5th Battalion DWR; killed in action 27 8 1918, aged 30, Advance to Victory.
Buried – Mont Huon Military Cemetery, 7, C, 4A.
Commemorated - the **Drill Hall WM panel 5, column 1.**
Originally 2/5th DWR. Formerly 840 Army Service Corps.
LIFE'S WORK DONE, A CROWN WELL WON, NOW PERFECT PEACE.

GOLDSBOROUGH Horace – 5372 (later 241905) Private.
Born in Mirfield on 23 8 1895 to Walter and Ellen, of Blackpool. Resided in Huddersfield. Enlisted at Halifax, 16 3 1916.
2/5th Battalion DWR; reported missing, killed in action 03 5 1917, aged 21, Battle of Bullecourt.
Commemorated - Arras Memorial, France; St Mark's Parish Church, Longwood, RoH; M Stansfield, page 169, and the **Drill Hall WM panel 5, column 1.**
Mentioned in the Huddersfield Examiner (official casualty list, reported missing) 27 6 1917.
CWGC shows name as GOLDSBROUGH.

GOLDSELLER Leon David – Lieutenant.
The son of Ben and Bertha of Manchester.
2/5th Battalion DWR, Signals Officer; wounded in action on patrol and died of wounds 14 4 1917, aged 21.
Buried - Mory Abbey Military Cemetery, 1, C, 1.
Commemorated - the **Drill Hall WM panel 5, column 1.**
Mentioned in the Goodall collection; the Unit War Diary (Signals Officer) on 31 1 1917; (on recce patrol, dow) on 15 4 1917; (buried at Mory Abbey) on 15 4 1917; (brought in by Stretcher Bearers from B Company, 2/7th Battalion) on 30 4 1917.
INTO THY HANDS O LORD.

GOLLAND Frank – 5893 Private.
Born in Collingham. Resided in North Collingham. Enlisted in Bradford.

1/5th Battalion DWR; died of wounds 28 7 1916, aged 20, Battle of the Somme.
Buried – Puchevillers British Cemetery, 2, B, 31.
Commemorated - the **Drill Hall WM panel 5, column 1.**
IN LOVING MEMORY OF OUR DEAR BOY FRANK.

GOMERSALL Ernest Wilfred – 34277 Private.
Born in September, 1899, in Hull, to William and Mary Ann, of Hessle Road, Hull. Enlisted at Hull on 25 5 1917.
5th Battalion DWR; killed in action 28 9 1918, Advance to Victory.
Buried – Grand Ravine British Cemetery, A, 12.
Commemorated - the **Drill Hall WM panel 5, column 1.**
Originally 2/5th DWR.

GOODALL Edward – 5892 (later 242156) Private.
Born in Baildon to William and Sarah. Resided in Baildon. Enlisted at Shipley.
1/5th Battalion DWR; killed in action 03 9 1916, aged 22, Battle of the Somme (Thiepval).
Commemorated – Thiepval Memorial, France, and the **Drill Hall WM panel 5, column 1.**

GOODER William Hall – 242559 Corporal.
Born in Rastrick to Thomas Edwin and Jane, of Soyland, Ripponden. Resided in Ripponden. Enlisted at Halifax.
1/5th Battalion DWR; killed in action 07 10 1917, aged 27.
Commemorated - Tyne Cot Memorial, France, and the **Drill Hall WM panel 5, column 1.**

GOODRICK Herbert – 2872 Private.
Born Hill House, Huddersfield, on 22 7 1889, to Ashley and Annie. Resided in Aspley with his wife, Frances Mary. Enlisted at Huddersfield on 03 9 1914.
1/5th Battalion DWR; reported missing, killed in action 17 9 1916, aged 27, Battle of the Somme.
Commemorated – Thiepval Memorial, France; St Paul's Church, Southgate, Huddersfield, RoH; Christ Church, Moldgreen, RoH; J J Fisher, page 113; M Stansfield, page 169, and the **Drill Hall WM panel 5, column 1.**
Mentioned in the Huddersfield Examiner (killed in action) on 04 10 1916; (killed in action, official casualty list) on 13 10 1916.

GOREHAM Edward James – 242502 Corporal.
Enlisted in Fakenham, Norfolk.
5th Battalion DWR; killed in action 10 4 1918, German Spring Offensive.
Commemorated – Pozieres Memorial, France, and the **Drill Hall WM panel 5, column 1.**
Originally 2/5th DWR.

GOUGH John William Charles – 26236 Private.
Enlisted at Newbury.
5th Battalion DWR; killed in action 20 7 1918, Advance to Victory.
Commemorated - Soissons Memorial, France, and the **Drill Hall WM panel 5, column 1.**
Originally 2/5th DWR.

GRACE Ernest Edwin – 2650 Private.
Born Crewe, Cheshire, to Frederick and Louise. Husband of May, of Fartown. Enlisted at Huddersfield.
1/5th Battalion DWR; killed in action 10 7 1915, aged 29, Ypres.
Buried - Bard Cottage Cemetery, 1, A, 41.
Commemorated – St Andrew's Church, Leeds Road, RoH (thought to have been destroyed); Salvation Army Citadel RoH; M Stansfield, page 171, and the **Drill Hall WM panel 5, column 1.**
Mentioned in the Huddersfield Examiner (announcement of death) 21 7 1915.

GRAHAM F T – Private
No trace.
Commemorated – the **Drill Hall WM panel 5, column 2.**

GRAHAM Harry – 242699 Private.
Born in Cornholme, Todmorden to Arthur and Ann. Resided in Cornholme. Enlisted at Todmorden.
1/5th Battalion DWR; died of wounds 26 12 1917, aged 26.
Buried – Lijssenthoek Military Cemetery, 27, CC, 2A
Commemorated - the **Drill Hall WM panel 5, column 2.**
NOBLY HE DID HIS DUTY BRAVELY, HE FOUGHT AND FELL.

GRAHAM Hirst – 240310 Private. Military Medal.
Born in Huddersfield on 16 9 1893 to Kossuth and Lavini, of Lockwood. Enlisted into the local Territorials in June, 1914.
5th Battalion DWR; died of wounds 16 3 1918, aged 24, German Spring Offensive.
Buried – Marouille British Cemetery, 4, H, 10.
Commemorated – Lockwood Cemetery memorial; St Stephen's Church, Rashcliffe, RoH; M Stansfield, page 172, and the **Drill Hall WM panel 5, column 2.**
Originally 2/5th DWR.
Mentioned in L Magnus (medal roll), page 251; the London Gazette, (award of MM) on 28 1 1918, page 1386.
EVER REMEMBERED.

GRAHAM Walter Huddlestone – 240113 Sergeant.
Born and resided in Lockwood. Enlisted in Huddersfield.
1/5th Battalion DWR; killed in action 03 9 1916, Battle of the Somme (Thiepval).
Commemorated – Thiepval Memorial, France; St Stephen's Church, Rashcliffe, RoH; M Stansfield, page 172, and the **Drill Hall WM panel 5, column 2.**
Mentioned in the Huddersfield Examiner (wounded in action, official casualty list) on 07 8 1916

GRANT Fred – 5430 (later 241955) Private.
Born in Chapeltown, Sheffield. Resided and enlisted at Sheffield.
2/5th Battalion DWR; killed in action 03 5 1917, Battle of Bullecourt.
Commemorated - Arras Memorial, France, and the **Drill Hall WM panel 5, column 2.**
Mentioned in the Goodall collection.

GRAY William Best – 15346 Private.
Born in Hetton le Hole, Northumberland. Enlisted at Houghton le Spring, Northumberland.
2/5th Battalion DWR; killed in action 03 5 1917, Battle of Bullecourt
Commemorated – Arras Memorial, France, and the **Drill Hall WM panel 5, column 2.**

GRAYSON Joseph Rupert – 2567 Lance Sergeant.
Born in Huddersfield to John and Ellen. Resided in Stalybridge, Cheshire, with his wife, Martha. Enlisted at Huddersfield.
1/5th Battalion DWR; killed in action 23 8 1915, aged 32, Ypres.
Commemorated - Ypres (Menin Gate) Memorial, Belgium, and the **Drill Hall WM panel 5, column 1.**

GREAVES John – 241577 Private.
Born Honley to Mr and Mrs Friend Greaves. Enlisted at Huddersfield in March, 1916.
2/5th Battalion DWR; reported missing, killed in action 03 5 1917, Battle of Bullecourt.
Commemorated - Arras Memorial, France, Honley WM; C Ford, page 23; M Stansfield, page 173, and the **Drill Hall WM panel 5, column 2.**

Mentioned in the Huddersfield Examiner (official casualty roll) 12 6 1917; (request by relatives for more information) 27 6 1917; (presumed killed at Bullecourt with memoriam notice) 03 5 1920.

GREAVES Victor – 2nd Lieutenant.
Son of Thomas and Ellen of Clay Cross, Derbyshire.
2/5th Battalion DWR; killed in action 28 11 1917, aged 28, Battle of Cambrai (Bourlon Wood).
Buried – Rocquigny-Equancourt Road Cemetery, 3, E, 9.
Commemorated – 62 Div History, page 192, and the **Drill Hall WM panel 5, column 2.**
Mentioned in Goodall Diary, page 29, and Unit War Diary (in action Havringcourt) 20 11 1917; (died of wounds, at Bourlon Wood) 27 11 197.

GREAVES William – 11449 Corporal.
Born in Ipswich, the son of Mrs Adelaid Sheard, of Huddersfield.
2/5th Battalion DWR; reported missing, killed in action 27 11 1917, aged 24, Battle of Cambrai.
Commemorated – Cambrai Memorial (Louverval), France; St Andrew's Church, Leeds Road, RoH (thought to have been destroyed), M Stansfield, page 173, and the **Drill Hall WM panel 5, column 2.**

GREEN Arthur – 241782 Private.
Born Dewsbury Moor. Resided and enlisted at Mirfield.
2/5th Battalion DWR; reported missing, killed in action 03 5 1917, Battle of Bullecourt.
Commemorated - Arras Memorial, France; Mirfield WM and the **Drill Hall WM panel 5, column 2.**
Mentioned in the Huddersfield Examiner (reported missing, official casualty list) 27 6 1917.

GREEN Fred – 242029 Private.
Born in Holmbridge to Mr and Mrs F W Green. Resided and enlisted at Holmfirth.
2/5th Battalion DWR; wounded in action 23 7 1918 and died of wounds at 12 General Hospital on 25 7 1918.
Buried – St Sever Cemetery Extension, Q, 3, J, 7.
Commemorated – Holme and Holmbridge RoH; M Stansfield, page 173, and the **Drill Hall WM panel 5, column 2.**

GREENFIELD Samuel – 241972 Private.
Born in Attercliffe to Walter and Frances. Resided and enlisted at Sheffield.
2/5th Battalion DWR; died of wounds 18 3 1917, aged 29.
Buried – Varrennes Military Cemetery, 1, J, 43.
Commemorated - the **Drill Hall WM panel 5, column 2.**
SAFE HOME.

GREENHOUGH Mark – 5894 (later 242157) Private.
Born and enlisted at Bradford.
1/5th Battalion DWR; killed in action 03 9 1916, Battle of the Somme (Thiepval).
Buried – Mill Road Cemetery, 9, B, 9.
Commemorated - the **Drill Hall WM panel 5, column 2.**

GREENWOOD George Alfred – 2163 Private.
Born Lindley on 26 3 1894 to Emma, of Longroyd Bridge. Served with local Territorial pre war and re-enlisted 04 8 1914. Embarked for France in April, 1915.
1/5th Battalion DWR; killed in action, shellfire, 02 7 1916, Battle of the Somme.
Commemorated – Thiepval Memorial, France; St Thomas's Church, Longroyd Bridge, RoH; M Stansfield, page 175, and the **Drill Hall WM panel 5, column 1.**
Mentioned in the Huddersfield Examiner (killed in action, shellfire) on 24 7 1916; (wounded in action) 25 7 1916.

GREENWOOD Herbert Richardson – 3365 Lance Corporal
Born in Ravensthorpe to William Albert and Elizabeth Hannah. Resided in Ravensthorpe and enlisted at Mirfield.
1/5th Battalion DWR; killed in action 22 12 1915, aged 19, Ypres.
Buried -Talana Farm Cemetery, 4, I, 23.
Commemorated - the **Drill Hall WM panel 5, column 1.**
REST IN PEACE.

GREENWOOD S – Private .
Unable to positively identify.
Possibly 7075 Private **GREENWOOD Smith**, 1/6th DWR, killed in action 03 9 1916.
Commemorated – Thiepval Memorial, France, and the **Drill Hall WM panel 5, column 1.**

GRIFFITHS Philip (Henry) – 238052 Private.
Born in Caergwrle, Flintshire, to Philip Henry and Rosa Hannah. Resided in Gwversyllt, Denbighshire and enlisted at Brymbo, Denbighshire.
5th Battalion DWR; killed in action 25 8 1918, aged 22, Advance to Victory.
Buried – Gommecourt South Cemetery, 1, C, 7.
Commemorated – the **Drill Hall WM panel 5, column 2.**
CWGC shows names as Philip Henry; SDGW shows Phillips.
HE NOBLY DID HIS DUTY.

GRIMES George – 6844 Private. Territorial Force War Medal.
Born King's Lynn, Norfolk, to James and Sophia. Resided with his wife, Liza Elizabeth, in West Rudham, King's Lynn. Enlisted at East Dereham, Norfolk.
1/5th Battalion DWR; killed in action 19 9 1916, aged 33, Battle of the Somme.
Commemorated – Thiepval Memorial, France, and the **Drill Hall WM panel 5, column 2.**
Formerly 2220 Norfolk Regiment, possibly 5/5777 5th Northumberland Fusiliers.
Awarded the Territorial Force War Medal, posthumously, on 20 4 1922.

GRUNDY Arthur James – 34282 Private.
Born Swanland, East Riding, to Harry and Fanny of Anlaby, Hull. Resided and enlisted at Hull.
5th Battalion DWR; killed in action 28 9 1918, aged 18, Advance to Victory.
Buried – Grand Ravine British Cemetery, A, 4.
Commemorated - the **Drill Hall WM panel 5, column 2.**
Originally 2/5th DWR.
REST IN THE LORD.

GUNN Harold – 5010 (later 241601) Private.
Born Chesterton, Staffs, on 14 11 1885 to Josiah James and Elizabeth, of Lockwood. Resided in Lockwood and enlisted at Huddersfield on 10 3 1916.
2/5th Battalion DWR; killed in action 03 5 1917, Battle of Bullecourt.
Commemorated – Arras Memorial, France; M Stansfield, page 176, and **the Drill Hall WM panel 5, column 2.**
Mentioned in the Goodall collection and the Huddersfield Examiner (reported missing) 08 6 1917; (official casualty list) 27 6 1917; (reported missing now presumed dead) 08 7 1918.

HAGUE Charles Harold – 34533 Private.
Born and enlisted at Nottingham.
5th Battalion DWR; died of wounds 25 8 1918, aged 29, Advance to Victory.
Buried – Douchy les Ayette Cemetery, 4, A, 10.
Commemorated - the **Drill Hall WM panel 5, column 3.**
Formerly 176505 Royal Engineers.
Mentioned in the Huddersfield Examiner (buried with cross) 08 5 1919.

HAGUE Willie – 3858 (later 241005) Private.
Born Shelley. Enlisted at Huddersfield.
2/5th Battalion DWR; reported missing 03 5 1917, Battle of Bullecourt.
Commemorated – Arras Memorial, France; Emmanuel Church (Shelley), M Stansfield, page 177, and the **Drill Hall WM panel 5, column 3.**
Mentioned in Goodall collection.
5 DWR RoH Board shows HAIGUE W.

HAIGH George – 203744 Private.
Born Golcar to Mr and Mrs George Haigh. Resided in Golcar and enlisted at Huddersfield.
1/5th Battalion DWR; killed in action 07 8 1917.
Buried – Ramscappelle Road Cemetery, 2, A, 30.
Commemorated – St John's Church, Golcar, RoH; Colne Valley Almanac; M Stansfield, page 180, and the **Drill Hall WM panel 5, column 3.**
Mentioned in the Huddersfield Examiner (official casualty list) 14 9 1917.

HAIGH James Aspinall – Lieutenant
Born in Huddersfield, on 09 9 1894, to Alan. Resided with mother in Birkby. Joined the local Territorials in Spring, 1911. Commissioned 21 2 1915 into DWR.
2/5th Battalion DWR, B Company; died of wounds 21 CCS, at Ytres, 22 11 1917, aged 23, Battle of Cambrai.
Buried – Rocquigny-Equancourt Road Cemetery, 3, B, 10.
Commemorated – Fartown and Birkby WM; Fisher, page 129; M Stansfield, page 182, and the **Drill Hall WM panel 5, column 2.**
Mentioned in Goodall collection; 62nd Div History, page 191, and the Unit War Diary (appointed Sniper Officer) on 10 1 1917; (collecting wounded at Bullecourt) on 03 5 1917; (died of wounds at Havringcourt) on 20 11 1917.
IN MANY A HEART HIS GRAVE IS GREEN.

HAIGH Joe – 240133 Private. Territorial Force War Medal.
Born in Crosland Moor on 12 1 1893 to James William and Emma. Enlisted at Huddersfield on 04 8 1914.
2/5th Battalion DWR; reported missing, killed in action 03 5 1917, Battle of Bullecourt.
Commemorated – Arras Memorial, France; Huddersfield Parish Church ROH, M Stansfield, page 182, and the **Drill Hall WM panel 5, column 3.**
Awarded the Territorial Force War Medal, posthumously, 20 4 1922.

HAIGH Joel – 3995 Private.
Born in Huddersfield to Joseph and Sarah. Resided and enlisted at Huddersfield.
2/5th Battalion DWR; killed in action 14 2 1917, aged 33.
Buried – Auchonvillers Military Cemetery, 2, K, 11.
Commemorated – Huddersfield Corporation RoH; M Stansfield, page 183, and the **Drill Hall WM panel 5, column 3.**
SDGW shows date of death as 15 2 1917.
Mentioned in the Huddersfield Examiner (official casualty list) 16 3 1917.
THOUGH DEATH DIVIDES STILL MEMORY CLINGS.

HAIGH Norman – 2604 (later 240338) Sergeant. Mentioned In Despatches.
Born Huddersfield on 27 3 1897 to Walter and Sarah Jane, of Birkby. Resided in Birkby and enlisted at Huddersfield.
2/5th Battalion DWR; wounded in action 20 11 1917, died of wounds 21 11 1917, aged 20, Battle of Cambrai.
Buried – Hermies Hill British Cemetery, 3, E, 28.

Commemorated – Fartown and Birkby WM; St Andrew's Church, Leeds Road RoH; M Stansfield, page 183, and the **Drill Hall WM panel 5, column 3.**
Awarded a Mention in Despatches by Sir Douglas Haig on 07 11 1917.
Mentioned in Goodall collection (Gallantry Award Roll). London Gazette (announcement of award of MID) on 18 12 1917, page 13287.

HAIGH Willie – 241833 Private.
Born Kirkburton to Mary of High Burton. Resided in High Burton and enlisted at Huddersfield in March 1916.
2/5th Battalion DWR; reported missing, killed in action 03 5 1917, Battle of Bullecourt.
Commemorated – Arras Memorial, France; All Hallows parish Church, Kirkburton, RoH; M Stansfield, page 185, and the **Drill Hall WM panel 5, column 3.**

HAIGUE W.
No trace of Haigue, probably 241005 Private Hague W.
Commemorated – the **Drill Hall WM panel 5, column 4.**

HAILWOOD Thomas – 35108 Private.
Born in Bolton to William Thomas. Enlisted at Bolton.
5th Battalion DWR; killed in action 28 9 1918, aged 18, Advance to Victory.
Buried - Grand Ravine British Cemetery, A, 5.
Commemorated - the **Drill Hall WM panel 5, column 4.**
Formerly 98958 Durham Light Infantry.
GREATER LOVE HATH NO MAN THAN THIS, THAT HE LAY DOWN HIS LIFE FOR HIS FRIEND.

HAINSWORTH Hubert – 242426 Lance Corporal.
Born Bradford. Resided in Great Horton and enlisted at Bradford.
1/5th Battalion DWR; killed in action 09 10 1917, aged 24, 3rd Battle of Ypres (Passchendaele).
Commemorated – Tyne Cot Memorial, Belgium, and the **Drill Hall WM panel 5, column 4.**

HALE Horace Frederick – 5415 (later 241943) Private.
Born in Walsall to Frederick William and Florence Resided with his wife, Edith May in Walsall. Enlisted at Sheffield.
2/5th Battalion DWR; killed in action 03 5 1917, aged 27, Battle of Bullecourt.
Commemorated – Arras Memorial, France, and the **Drill Hall WM panel 5, column 4.**
Mentioned in Goodall collection.

HALEY John – 306479 Private.
Born in Cleckheaton to Albert William. Enlisted at Cleckheaton.
7th Battalion DWR; killed in action 21 11 1917.
Commemorated – Tyne Cot Memorial, Belgium, and the **Drill Hall WM panel 5, column 4.**
SDGW states 1/5th DWR, all other sources show 7 DWR.

HALL Edward – 34434 Private.
Born in Liverpool to Peter and Margaret Ann. Enlisted at Liverpool.
5th Battalion DWR, C Company; killed in action 30 9 1918, aged 19, Advance to Victory.
Buried - Grand Ravine British Cemetery, C, 10.
Commemorated – the **Drill Hall WM panel 5, column 4.**
GREATER LOVE HATH NO MAN.

HALL Frank – 16902 (later 242781) Private.
Born in Bishop Burton, East Riding to Charles, of Beverley. Enlisted at Beverley.
2/5th Battalion DWR; killed in action 03 5 1917, aged 19, Battle of Bullecourt.

Commemorated – Arras Memorial, France, and the **Drill Hall WM panel 5, column 4.**
Mentioned in Goodall collection.

HALL Joseph Armitage – 242058 Private.
Born Stalybridge. Resided in Greenfield and enlisted at Uppermill.
1/5th Battalion DWR; killed in action 14 10 1917, aged 20.
Buried - Nine Elms British Cemetery, 5, B, 3.
Commemorated - the **Drill Hall WM panel 5, column 4.**
Mentioned in the Huddersfield Examiner (notification of death) 20 10 1917.

HALLAS Joe – 241993 Private.
Born and resided Lepton. Enlisted at Huddersfield.
5th Battalion DWR; died of wounds 56 CCS, Grevillers, 05 10 1918, Advance to Victory.
Buried - Grevillers Cemetery, 15, D, 7.
Commemorated – Lepton Parish Church RoH, M Stansfield, page 187, and the **Drill Hall WM panel 5, column 4.**
Originally 2/5th DWR.

HAMER Charles – 3310 (later 242058?) Private.
Born Dalton on 20 10 1895, to Jacob. Resided in Berry Brow and enlisted into the Huddersfield Territorials on 07 1 1914. Embarked for France in April, 1915.
1/5th Battalion DWR; killed in action, sniper, 09 11 1915, Ypres.
Buried – Talana Farm Cemetery, 4, F, 7.
Commemorated – Armitage Bridge WM; M Stansfield, page 188, and the **Drill Hall WM panel 5, column 2.**
Mentioned in the Huddersfield Examiner (announcement of death by sniper) 17 11 1915.
SDGW shows number as 242058.

HAMER Thomas – 3302 (later 240673) Private.
Born Lockwood on 10 5 1893. Resided Huddersfield with aunt and uncle. Enlisted at Huddersfield in November, 1914.
2/5th Battalion DWR; reported missing, killed in action 03 5 1917, Battle of Bullecourt.
Commemorated – Arras Memorial, France; M Stansfield, page 189, and the **Drill Hall WM panel 5, column 2.**
Mentioned in the Huddersfield Examiner (reported missing) 04 6 1917.

HAMER Tom – 3374 Private.
Enlisted at Mirfield on 09 11 1914.
2/5th Battalion DWR, D Company (bomber); killed in action, shellfire, 09 2 1917, aged 28.
Buried – Auchonvillers Military Cemetery, 2, K, 17.
Commemorated – Mirfield WM and the **Drill Hall WM panel 5, column 2.**
Mentioned in Goodall collection.
IN LOVING REMEMBRANCE FROM WIFE AND CHILDREN.

HAMMOND George Arthur – 3761 Private.
Born in Ravensthorpe, Dewsbury, to Francis. Resided in Ravensthorpe. Enlisted at Mirfield.
1/5th Battalion DWR; killed in action 26 10 1915, aged 20, Ypres.
Buried – Talana Farm Cemetery, 3, D, 8.
Commemorated – D Tattersfield, pages 77 & 384, and the **Drill Hall WM panel 5, column 2.**

HAMPSHIRE Lewis – 5356 (later 241893) Private.
Born, resided and enlisted at Huddersfield.
2/5th Battalion DWR; killed in action 03 5 1917, Battle of Bullecourt.

Commemorated – Arras Memorial, France; M Stansfield, page 189, and the **Drill Hall WM panel 5, column 4.**
Mentioned in the Goodall collection; the Huddersfield Examiner (reported missing, official casualty list) 05 6 1917; (request for further information from relatives) 27 6 1917; (reported missing, now presumed to have died) 12 12 1917.

HANSON Alfred – 202923 Private.
Born in Halifax, to John and Elizabeth Ann (later of Edenbridge, Kent). Resided in Mixenden. Enlisted at Halifax.
2/5th Battalion DWR; killed in action 22 7 1918, aged 20, Battle of Tardenois
Commemorated – Soissons Memorial, France, and the **Drill Hall WM panel 5, column 3.**

HANSON Ben – 2042 Lance Corporal.
Born Barnsley to George Henry and Lucy. Resided in Honley and enlisted in Huddersfield in 1914. Embarked for France in April, 1915.
1/5th Battalion DWR; killed in action, shell on dugout, aged 20, 07 3 1916.
Commemorated – Thiepval Memorial, France; Honley WM; C Ford, page 23; Heywood, page 127; M Stansfield, page 190, and the **Drill Hall WM panel 5, column 2.**
Brother of Colin, qv.

HANSON Colin – 241556 Private.
Born Monk Bretton to George and Lucy. Resided in Honley and enlisted in Huddersfield.
2/5th Battalion DWR; reported missing, killed in action 03 5 1917, aged 20, Battle of Bullecourt.
Commemorated – Arras Memorial, France; Honley WM; C Ford, page 23; M Stansfield, page 91, and the **Drill Hall WM panel 5, column 2.**
Mentioned in the Huddersfield Examiner (official casualty list) 27 6 1917.
Brother of Ben, qv.

HANSON Ernest – 3088 (later 240565) Private.
Born Primrose Hill, Huddersfield, on 28 4 1895 to Fred and Mary. Resided Primrose Hill and enlisted at Huddersfield on 30 10 1914.
2/5th Battalion DWR, D Company; reported missing, killed in action 03 5 1917, Battle of Bullecourt.
Commemorated – Arras Memorial, France; Memorial in Almondbury cemetery; M Stanfield, page 191, and the **Drill Hall WM panel 5, column 2.**
Mentioned in Goodall collection (Commanding Officer's Commendation for operations from 20-28 2 1917, awarded 06 3 1917).

HARDAKER Frank – 242170 Private.
Born in Lister Hills, Bradford, to John William. Enlisted at Bradford.
1/5th Battalion DWR; killed in action 03 9 1916, aged 22, Battle of the Somme (Thiepval).
Commemorated – Thiepval Memorial, France, and the **Drill Hall WM panel 5, column 2.**

HARDY Eric – 34418 Corporal.
Born and enlisted in Nottingham.
5th Battalion DWR; killed in action 15 9 1918, aged 19, Advance to Victory.
Buried - Hermies Hill British Cemetery, 2, A, 16.
Commemorated – the **Drill Hall WM panel 5, column 3.**
REST IN PEACE.

HARDY Fred – 240386 Lance Corporal.
Born in Meltham to James. Husband of Mary and resided Huddersfield. Enlisted at Huddersfield on 08 8 1914.
1/5th Battalion DWR; killed in action 07 8 1917, Nieuport.

Buried - Ramscappelle Road Military Cemetery, 2, A, 6.
Commemorated – St Mark's Parish Church, Longwood, RoH; M Stansfield, page 193, and the **Drill Hall WM panel 5, column 3.**
Mentioned in the Huddersfield Examiner (memoriam notice) 07 8 1918.

HARDY Harold – 242026 Private.
Born Paddock on 19 3 1897 to Mr and Mrs Charles Edward. Resided in Paddock and enlisted at Huddersfield on 29 3 1915.
2/5th Battalion DWR; killed in action 04 2 1918, aged 20.
Buried – Roclincourt Military Cemetery, 4, A, 4.
Commemorated – All Saints Church, Paddock, RoH; M Stansfield, page 194, and the **Drill Hall WM panel 5, column 3.**
FAITHFUL UNTO DEATH.

HARDY Herbert – 2488 (later 240288) Corporal. Territorial Force War Medal.
Born Huddersfield on 23 4 1896. Resided Thornton Lodge, Huddersfield, and enlisted into the local Territorials in May, 1914.
2/5th Battalion DWR; reported missing, killed in action 03 5 1917, Battle of Bullecourt.
Commemorated – Arras Memorial, France; St Barnabas Church, Crosland Moor; M Stansfield, page 194, and the **Drill Hall WM panel 5, column 3.**
Awarded the Territorial Force War Medal, posthumously, on 20 4 1922

HARDY Wilfred Fairburn – 240195 Lance Corporal.
Born Almondbury on 20 11 1893 to Arthur and Annie E. Resided in Moldgreen and enlisted into the local Territorials on 16 5 1913.
1/5th Battalion DWR; reported missing, killed in action 03 9 1916, aged 22, Battle of the Somme (Thiepval).
Commemorated – Thiepval Memorial, France; Almondbury WM; Christ Church, Moldgreen, RoH; M Stansfield, page 194, and the **Drill Hall WM panel 5, column 3.**

HARGREAVES Herbert – 3558 (later 240834) Private.
Born and enlisted at Huddersfield.
2/5th Battalion DWR; killed in action 27 11 1917, Battle of Cambrai.
Commemorated – Cambrai Memorial (Louverval), France; M Stansfield, page 194, and the **Drill Hall WM panel 5, column 4.**
Mentioned in the Goodall collection.

HARGREAVES Sylvester – 3875 (later 241017) Private.
Resided in Liversedge and enlisted at Mirfield, 15 2 1915.
2/5th Battalion DWR; killed in action 03 5 1917, Battle of Bullecourt.
Commemorated – Arras Memorial, France; Spenborough (Cleckheaton) WM; Turpin, page 11, and the **Drill Hall WM panel 5, column 4.**
Mentioned in the Goodall collection.

HARPIN Henri Rodgers – 2548 (later 240317) Private.
Born at Cowcliffe to Thomas Kilner. Resided in Leicester. Re-enlisted at Huddersfield on 04 8 1914.
2/5th Battalion DWR, Signals Section; killed in action 03 5 1917, Battle of Bullecourt.
Commemorated – Arras Memorial, France; St Andrew's Church, Leeds Road, RoH (thought to have been destroyed); M Stansfield, page 195, and the **Drill Hall WM panel 5, column 4.**
Mentioned in the Goodall collection. Mentioned in the Huddersfield Examiner (in memoriam) on 03 5 1920 and 03 5 1921.
Medal Display Case held in the Officer's Mess, Huddersfield Drill Hall, and other personal artefacts held in Bankfield Museum, Halifax.

He appears on the photograph of 2/5th DWR Signals Section in the gallery pages, standing, 6th from the left.

HARRIS Stanley – 1746 Lance Corporal.
Born Rashcliffe Hill, Huddersfield, on 16 12 1894 to Alfred and Caroline. Resided and enlisted at Huddersfield on 04 8 1914. Embarked for France in April, 1915
1/5th Battalion DWR, B Company; killed in action 14 6 1915, aged 21, Ypres.
Buried – Rue David Military Cemetery, 1, B, 14.
Commemorated – M Stansfield, page 196, and the **Drill Hall WM panel 5, column 2**.
Mentioned in Unit War Diary (killed in action) 14 6 1915. Mentioned in Huddersfield Examiner on (killed in action) 10 7 1915; (in memoriam) 14 6 1917.
GREATER LOVE HATH NO MAN.

HARRISON Frank Holland – 3950 (later 241068) Private.
Born Wakefield on 10 1 1897 to Henry Bailey and Mary Eleanor. Resided in Huddersfield and enlisted at Huddersfield on 02 3 1915.
2/5th Battalion DWR, C Company; reported missing, killed in action 03 5 1917, aged 20, Battle of Bullecourt.
Commemorated – Arras Memorial, France; New North Road Baptist Church RoH; M Stansfield, page 196, and the **Drill Hall WM panel 5, column 3**.

HARRISON John William – 5903 Private.
Born in Yeadon, Leeds, to Holdsworth. Enlisted at Yeadon.
1/5th Battalion DWR; killed in action 17 9 1916, aged 23, Battle of the Somme.
Commemorated – Thiepval Memorial, France and the **Drill Hall WM panel 5, column 3**.

HARRISON Munroe – 7078 Private.
Born in Earby, to John William. Resided in Keighley. Enlisted at Skipton.
1/5th Battalion DWR; killed in action 20 1 1917, aged 22.
Buried - Humbercamps Communal Cemetery Extension, 1, B, 13.
Commemorated - the **Drill Hall WM panel 5, column 3**.

HARRISON Sam 4261 Private.
Born Huddersfield, resided in Linthwaite and enlisted at Huddersfield. Embarked for France and Flanders in April, 1915.
1/5th Battalion DWR; reported missing, killed in action 03 9 1916, Battle of the Somme (Thiepval).
Commemorated – Thiepval Memorial, France; Linthwaite WM; M Stansfield, page 196, and the **Drill Hall WM panel 5, column 3**.

HARRISON Wilfred – 8626 Private.
Born in Cullingworth. Resided in Keighley with his wife, Ada. Enlisted at Keighley.
1/5th Battalion DWR; killed in action 20 1 1917, aged 26.
Buried – Humbercamps Communal Cemetery Extension, 1, A, 5.
Commemorated – the **Drill Hall WM panel 5, column 3**.
HE HAD A KINDLY WORD FOR EACH AND DIED BELOVED BY ALL.

HARTLEY Frank – 242855 Private.
Born in Bradford to Samuel and Annie. Enlisted at Bradford.
1/5th Battalion DWR; killed in action 09 10 1917, aged 20, 3rd Battle of Ypres (Passchendaele).
Commemorated – Tyne Cot Memorial, Belgium, the **Drill Hall WM panel 5, column 3**.

HARTLEY George – 6065 Private.
Born Keadby, Yorks, resided in Spofforth, enlisted at Keighley.
1/5th Battalion DWR; killed in action 25 9 1916, Battle of the Somme.

Commemorated – Thiepval Memorial, France, and the **Drill Hall WM panel 5, column 3.**

HARTLEY W – Private
Unable to identify – possibly:
265645 Private W Hartley, 2nd Battalion DWR – killed in action 02 10 1917.
268239 Private W Hartley, 1/6th Battalion DWR – killed in action 18 4 1918.
Commemorated – the **Drill Hall WM panel 5, column 3.**

HARWOOD Harry – 20408 Private.
Born in Wadsworth, Hebden Bridge, to Smith. Resided in Pecket Well, Hebden Bridge. Enlisted at Halifax.
5th Battalion DWR; killed in action 10 4 1918, aged 21, German Spring Offensive.
Buried - Douchy les Ayette Cemetery, 4, G, 9.
Commemorated – Wadsworth WM and the **Drill Hall WM panel 5, column 4.**
SDGW shows his date of death as 09 4 1918.
AT REST.

HASSALL William Jones – 242748 Private.
Born in Christchurch, Staffs, and enlisted at Stafford.
1/5th Battalion DWR; killed in action 07 8 1917.
Buried - Ramscappelle Road Military Cemetery, 2, A, 9.
Commemorated - the **Drill Hall WM panel 5, column 3.**
Formerly 3861 Northumberland Fusiliers.

HATTON Albert – 34425 Private.
Born in Tamworth, Staffs, to John and Mary. Enlisted at Athestone, Warks.
5th Battalion DWR; killed in action 27 8 1918, aged 36, Advance to Victory.
Buried – Mory Abbey Military Cemetery, 5, A, 8.
Commemorated - the **Drill Hall WM panel 5, column 4.**
Originally 2/5th DWR.
THE LORD'S WILL BE DONE.

HAWKSLY (HAWKSLEY?) John Reginald – 5422 (later 241949) Private.
Born, resided and enlisted in Sheffield.
2/5th Battalion DWR; killed in action 20 11 1917, Battle of Cambrai.
Commemorated – Cambrai Memorial (Louverval), France, and the **Drill Hall WM panel 5, column 4.**
Mentioned in Goodall collection.
CWGC shows spelling as Hawksley.

HAWKSWORTH Harry – 240599 Corporal.
Born in Lockwood, 06 12 1886. Resided with his wife, Agnes, in Paddock. Enlisted at Huddersfield on 08 8 1917.
2/5th Battalion DWR; killed in action 26 3 1918, aged 31, German Spring Offensive.
Commemorated – Arras Memorial, France; St Stephen's Church, Rashcliffe, RoH; All Saint's Church, Paddock, RoH; M Stansfield, page 198, and the **Drill Hall WM panel 5, column 4.**
Mentioned in the Huddersfield Examiner (in memoriam) 26 3 1919.

HEADEY Percy – 240512 Lance Corporal.
Born in Huddersfield on 06 10 1882, to William Henry and Elizabeth. Resided with his wife, Annie, in Huddersfield. Enlisted at Huddersfield on 05 9 1914.
1/5th Battalion DWR; killed in action 07 8 1917, aged 34, Nieuport.
Buried – Ramscappelle Road Military Cemetery, 2, A, 27.

Commemorated – St James' Presbyterian Church, Huddersfield, RoH, M Stansfield, page 200, and the **Drill Hall WM panel 5, column 4.**
Mentioned in the Huddersfield Examiner (notification of death) on 16 8 1917; (memoriam notices) on 07 8 1918 and 07 8 1919.

HEAPS Arthur – 2338 Private.
Born in Huddersfield, to Dyson and Hannah, of Battyeford. Enlisted at Mirfield.
1/5th Battalion DWR, D Company; killed in action 17 10 1915, aged 20, Ypres.
Buried – Lijssenthoek Military Cemetery, 1, B, 18.
Commemorated – Battyeford WM; Mirfield WM and the **Drill Hall WM panel 5, column 4.**
Mentioned in Goodall Collection (volunteered for foreign service, 1914).
IN LOVING MEMORY OF A DEAR SON, GOD'S WILL BE DONE.

HEATH Harry – 25090 Private.
Born Marylebone. Resided with his wife, Edith Mary, in Ilford. Enlisted on 11 12 1916 at Park Royal, London.
2/5th Battalion DWR, D Company; killed in action 17 7 1917, aged 39.
Buried – Favreuil British Cemetery, 1, B, 15.
Commemorated – the **Drill Hall WM panel 6, column 1.**
Mentioned in Goodall Collection (pre war occupation – decorator).

HEATON William – 2nd Lieutenant.
Son of Eva and the late Fred, of Keighley.
2/5th Battalion DWR; reported missing, killed in action 03 5 1917, Battle of Bullecourt.
Commemorated – Arras Memorial, France; Morley WM, and the **Drill Hall WM panel 6, column 1.**
Mentioned in 62nd Division History (missing in action) page 185; mentioned in Unit War Diary (missing in action) on 03 5 1917. Also Divisional Cyclist Company.

HEESOM George – 34455 (34435?) Private.
Born and enlisted at Liverpool.
5th Battalion DWR; killed in action 13 9 1918, Advance to Victory.
Commemorated – Vis en Artois Memorial, France, and the **Drill Hall WM panel 6, column 1.**
Originally 2/5th DWR.
SDGW shows his number as 34435.

HELLAWELL Ernest – 5399 (later 241930) Private.
Born in Kirkheaton, Resided in Huddersfield. Enlisted at Holmfirth on 27 3 1916.
2/5th Battalion DWR, D Company; reported missing, killed in action 03 5 1917, Battle of Bullecourt.
Commemorated – Arras Memorial, France; Holme Valley Memorial Hospital WM (plaques 5 & 6, Fulstone); Newmill Working Men's Club RoH; M Stansfield, page 204, and the **Drill Hall WM panel 5, column 4.**
Mentioned in Goodall collection (pre war employment Spinner. Company Lewis gunner, 14 Platoon; the Huddersfield Examiner (request for further information by relatives) on 13 6 1917.

HELLAWELL Luther – 14981 Private.
Born in Holmfirth to Mr & Mrs Charles Hellawell. Resided Thongsbridge. Enlisted in December, 1914 and embarked for France and Flanders in July, 1915.
2/5th Battalion DWR; died of wounds at 21 Casualty Clearing Station, Ytres, on 21 11 1917, Battle of Cambrai.
Buried – Rocquigny-Equancourt Road Cemetery, 2, D, 25.

Commemorated – Holme Valley Memorial Hospital WM (plaque 5, Netherthong and Thongsbridge); St Andrew's Church, Netherthong, RoH; St Bartholemew's Church, Meltham, RoH; M Stansfield, page 204, and the **Drill Hall WM panel 5, column 4.**

HELLAWELL Wilfred – 241428 Private.
Born in Golcar. Enlisted at Huddersfield.
1/5th Battalion DWR; reported missing, killed in action 03 9 1916, Battle of the Somme (Thiepval).
Commemorated – Thiepval Memorial, France; St John's Church, Golcar, RoH; Pole Moor Baptist Church, RoH; M Stansfield, page 205, and the **Drill Hall WM panel 5, column 4.**

HELLEWELL (HELLIWELL?) Willie – 203740 Private.
Enlisted at Halifax.
2/5th Battalion DWR; killed in action 23 7 1918, Battle of Tardenois.
Buried – Bouilly Cross Roads Military Cemetery, 1, C, 16.
Commemorated - Calderdale War Dead, page 153, and the **Drill Hall WM panel 5, column 4.**
CWGC and SDGW show spelling as HELLIWELL.

HELLIWELL Fred – 204260 Private.
Resided Wheatley, Halifax. Enlisted at Halifax.
5th Battalion DWR; killed in action 20 7 1918, Battle of Tardenois.
Buried – Courmas British Cemetery, 2, C, 6.
Commemorated – Calderdale War Dead, page 152, and the **Drill Hall WM panel 5, column 4.**

HEMINGWAY Harry – 241931 Private.
Born in Mirfield to Alfred. Resided in Mirfield. Enlisted at Halifax.
2/5th Battalion DWR; killed in action 03 5 1917, aged 26, Battle of Bullecourt.
Buried – Tilloy British Cemetery, 12, B, 8.
Commemorated – Mirfield WM and the **Drill Hall WM panel 6, column 1.**
FOR KING AND COUNTRY – EVER REMEBERED.

HENTHORNE Samuel – 241667 Lance Sergeant.
Born in Oldham, to Charles and Martha Ellen, of Audenshaw, Manchester. Enlisted at Manchester.
2/5th Battalion DWR; killed in action 20 1 1917, aged 25, Battle of Cambrai.
Commemorated – Cambrai Memorial (Louverval), France, Colne Valley Almanac, 1917, and the **Drill Hall WM panel 6, column 1.**
CWGC shows spelling as HENTHORN.

HERBERT Fred A – 4032 (later 241120) Private.
Born in Marsden, 25 12 1897, to Robert and Elizabeth. Resided Marsden. Enlisted at Huddersfield in May 1915. Embarked for France and Flanders in January, 1917.
2/5th Battalion DWR; reported missing, killed in action 03 5 1917, Battle of Bullecourt.
Commemorated – Arras Memorial, France; Marsden WM; M Stansfield, page 207, and the **Drill Hall WM panel 5, column 4.**
Mentioned in the Goodall collection; the Huddersfield Examiner (reported missing 03 5 1917) on 27 6 1916.
Brother of Robert, qv.

HERBERT Robert – 5618 Private.
Born in Grimsby. Resided Marsden. Enlisted at Huddersfield on 04 4 1916.
1/5th Battalion DWR; died of wounds, 9th General Hospital, Rouen, on 15 9 1916, Battle of the Somme.
Buried - St Sever Cemetery, B, 21, 46.
Commemorated - Marsden WM; Fisher, page, 113; M Stansfield, page 207, and the **Drill Hall WM panel 5, column 4.**

Mentioned in the Huddersfield Examiner (died of wounds in hospital) on 21 9 1916.
Brother of Fred qv.

HEY Fred – 241239 Private.
Born in Ravensthorpe, to Job and Susan. Resided in Dewsbury. Enlisted at Huddersfield.
1/5th Battalion DWR; killed in action 14 10 1917, aged 29.
Buried – Wimereux Communal Cemetery, 6, D, 4A.
Commemorated – B Heywood, page 207; D Tattersfield, pp 238 & 384, and the **Drill Hall WM panel 6, column 1.**

HEYWOOD Joseph – 241513 Private.
Born in Thurstonland on 23 4 1885, the son of Eliza, of Crosland Moor. Resided in Crosland Moor. Enlisted at Huddersfield in December, 1915. Embarked for France and Flanders in January, 1917.
2/5th Battalion DWR; killed in action 27 3 1918, aged 33, German Spring Offensive.
Commemorated – Arras Memorial, France; The Rising Sun Public house, Crosland Hill, RoH; St Barnabus Church, Crosland Moor, RoH; M Stansfield, page 207, and the **Drill Hall WM panel 6, column 1.**

HIBBARD G R
No trace, probably:
HIBBERD George Robert – 235432 Private.
Born in Newmarket. Resided Burnwell, Cambs. Enlisted at Maidstone, Kent.
2/5th Battalion DWR; killed in action 26 11 1917, Battle of Cambrai.
Commemorated – Cambrai Memorial (Louverval), France, and the **Drill Hall WM panel 6, column 1.**

HIBBIRD George – 3389 Private.
Born in Colne Bridge, Kirkheaton, on 04 2 1891, to Mrs Lumb of Dalton. Enlisted at Huddersfield on 09 11 1914. Embarked for France and Flanders in April, 1915.
1/5th Battalion DWR; died, cerebral meningitis, at No 12 Stationary Hospital on 25 12 1916, aged 25.
Buried – St Pol Communal Cemetery Extension, C, 12.
Commemorated – Christ Church, Moldgreen, RoH, M Stansfield, page 208, and the **Drill Hall WM panel 6, column 1.**

HIGHAM Frank – 242388 Lance Corporal.
Born in Wetherby to John and Annie. Resided Rylston. Enlisted at Skipton.
1/5th Battalion DWR; wounded in action and died of wounds at the Field Ambulance Dressing Station on 24 4 1917.
Buried – Vieille Chapelle New Military Cemetery, 1, D, 6.
Commemorated - the **Drill Hall WM panel 6, column 1.**

HILL Charles Thomas – 5913 Private.
Born in Yeadon to James and Mary. Resided in Yeadon. Enlisted at Guiseley.
1/5th Battalion DWR; died of wounds 19 9 1916, aged 22, Battle of the Somme.
Buried - Etaples Military Cemetery, 15,C, 3.
Commemorated - the **Drill Hall WM panel 6 column 1.**
SADLY MISSED.

HILL Ernest – 241593 Private.
Born in Bradford to Eliza. Resided in Bradford. Enlisted at Bradford.
2/5th Battalion DWR; killed in action 03 5 1917, Battle of Bullecourt.
Commemorated – Arras Memorial, France, and the **Drill Hall WM panel 6, column 1.**

HINCHCLIFFE Alan – 2213 (later 235069) Private.
Born in Holmfirth on 12 12 1893. Resided at Hinchcliffe Mill. Enlisted at Holmfirth. Embarked for France and Flanders in April, 1915. Was in action with another unit and wounded in September, 1916, on the Somme. Evacuated to UK and returned to France in 1917, joined 2/4th Battalion.
2/4th Battalion DWR; reported missing, killed in action 03 5 1917, Battle of Bullecourt.
Commemorated – Arras Memorial, France; Home and Holmbridge WM; M Stansfield, page 210, and the **Drill Hall WM panel 6, column 1.**

HINCHCLIFFE (HINCHLIFFE?) Frank – 5403 Private.
Born in Holmbridge on 22 8 1891 to Ben and Mary, of Fartown. Resided in Huddersfield. Enlisted at Huddersfield in January, 1916.
2/5th Battalion DWR; killed in action 14 2 1917.
Buried - Auchonvillers Military Cemetery, 2, K, 8.
Commemorated – Fartown and Birkby WM; Christ Church, Woodhouse Hill, RoH; M Stansfield, page 211, and the **Drill Hall WM panel 6, column 1.**
SDGW shows spelling as HINCHCLIFFE.

HINCHCLIFFE (HINCHLIFFE?) Harold – 5378 (later 241910) Private.
Born in Honley to Alfred and Annie. Resided Honley. Enlisted at Huddersfield.
2/5th Battalion DWR; died of wounds 04 5 1917, Battle of Bullecourt.
Buried – Achiet le Grand Communal Cemetery Extension, 1, E, 24.
Commemorated – Honley WM; C Ford, page 23, M Stansfield, page 211, and the **Drill Hall WM panel 6, column 1.**
M Stansfield shows Hinchliffe.

HINCHCLIFFE Herbert – 241570 Private.
Born Huddersfield, 02 1 1897, resided at Marsh and enlisted Huddersfield on 08 3 1916. Embarked for France January, 1917.
2/5th Battalion DWR; killed in action 20 11 1917, aged 20, Battle of Cambrai
Commemorated – Cambrai Memorial (Louverval), France; Huddersfield Parish Church; Huddersfield GPO Memorial; M Stansfield, page 211, and the **Drill Hall WM panel 6, column 1.**

HINCHLIFFE Ernest – 240141 Sergeant.
Born in Paddock. Resided in Ravensthorpe and enlisted at Mirfield.
1/5th Battalion DWR; killed in action 03 9 1916, Battle of the Somme (Thiepval).
Commemorated – Thiepval Memorial, France; D Tattersfield, pp 136 & 384, and the **Drill Hall WM panel 6, column 1.**
Mentioned in the Huddersfield Examiner (information requested by family) on 12 10 1916; (officially reported killed, as at June 1917) on 29 6 1917.
CWGC shows spelling as HINCHCLIFFE.

HIRD Samuel – 266948 Private. Military Medal.
Born and resided in Bingley. Enlisted at Skipton.
2/6th Battalion DWR; killed in action 29 3 1918, German Spring Offensive.
Commemorated – Arras Memorial, France, J J Fisher, page 87, and the **Drill Hall WM panel 6, column 2.**
Mentioned in the 2/6th DWR War Diary (award of MM) on 30 9 1917 (shows Regtl number as 266968); the London Gazette (award of MM) on 19 11 1917, page 11967.
The citation reads, *"For conspicuous gallantry and devotion to duty while in the trenches."* (Fisher page 87).
SDGW shows unit as 2/5th DWR.

HIRST Arthur Boothroyd – 4255 Private.

Born in Deighton, Huddersfield, in 1883, to Harry Boothroyd. Resided Huddersfield. Enlisted at Huddersfield in 1915.
1/5th Battalion DWR; killed in action 12 7 1916, Battle of the Somme.
Commemorated – Thiepval Memorial, France; M Stansfield, page 214, and the **Drill Hall WM panel 6, column 1.**
Mentioned in the Huddersfield Examiner (announcement of death) on 07 8 1916.
M Stansfield does not show Drill Hall commemoration.
CWGC shows spelling as HURST.

HIRST Fred 241361 Private.
Born in Brockholes to Sarah Ann. Resided in Brockholes. Enlisted at Huddersfield in 1916.
1/5th Battalion DWR; reported missing, killed in action 03 9 1916, aged 19, Battle of the Somme (Thiepval).
Buried – Connaught Cemetery, 1, C, 26.
Commemorated – Honley WM; Holme Valley Memorial Hospital WM (plaques 5 & 6, Fulstone); C Ford, pp 9, 11 & 24, M Stansfield, page 215, and the **Drill Hall WM panel 6, column 1.**
Mentioned in the Huddersfield Examiner (as wounded on the official casualty list) on 14 8 1916; (reported missing as at 03 9 1916) on 06 10 1916.

HIRST Harold – 5225 (later 241784) Private.
Born in South Crosland, Huddersfield, to Edward and Hannah. Resided in Ravensthorpe and enlisted at Marsden on 20 3 1916. Embarked for France and Flanders in January, 1917.
2/5th Battalion DWR, D Company; killed in action 03 5 1917, Battle of Bullecourt.
Commemorated – Arras Memorial, France; Marsden WM; Marsden Churchyard Memorial; M Stansfield, page 216, and the **Drill Hall WM panel 6, column 1.**
Mentioned in the Huddersfield Examiner (reported missing, official casualty list) on 27 6 1917.
Mentioned in the Goodall collection: (pre war employment, Mill hand. 13 Platoon and D Company Signaller).

HIRST H E – Private
No trace of H E Hirst.
Probably 4495 Private Henry (Harry) HIRST.
Born Marsden, resided and enlisted at Huddersfield.
3/5th Battalion DWR; died (pneumonia) Clipstone Camp, 03 1 1916.
Buried – Marsden (St Bartholomews) Parish Churchyard, South, 29, 5.
Commemorated – Marsden WM; M Stansfield, page 217, and the **Drill Hall WM panel 6, column 1.**

HIRST Hubert Irvin – 5360 Private.
Born in Golcar to Mitchell. Resided in Golcar. Enlisted at Huddersfield on 27 3 1916.
2/5th Battalion DWR; killed in action 14 2 1917.
Buried – Auchonvillers Military Cemetery, 2, K, 7.
Commemorated – St John's Church, Golcar, RoH; M Stansfield, page 218, and the **Drill Hall WM panel 6, column 1.**
Mentioned in the Huddersfield Examiner (announcement of death) on 02 3 1917; (official casualty list) on 16 3 1917. Mentioned in the Colne Valley Almanac (official casualty list).

HIRST John Eli – 22843 Private.
Born in Greetland, Halifax, to Mary Jane and the late James. Enlisted at Halifax.
5th Battalion DWR; killed in action 28 3 1918, aged 25, German Spring Offensive.
Buried – Gezaincourt Communal, 1, H, 7.
Commemorated – the **Drill Hall WM panel 6, column 1.**
DEAR SON OF JAMES A AND MARY J HIRST, GREETLAND, HALIFAX.

HIRST Sam (Samuel?) – 2748 Private.
Born in Greenfield, to Joseph and Ann Maria. Resided in Greenfield. Enlisted at Huddersfield.
1/5th Battalion DWR; died of wounds 20 9 1916, aged 40, Battle of the Somme.
Buried – Bolougne Eastern, 8, C, 149.
Commemorated – J Fisher, page 114, and the **Drill Hall WM panel 6, column 1.**
Mentioned in the Huddersfield Examiner (died of wounds) on 28 9 1918.
WORTHY OF EVERLASTING REMEMBRANCE, THORN BANK, GREENFIELD.

HOBLEY James – 308104 Private.
Born in Oakham, Dudley, Staffs, to James and Isabella. Resided with his wife, Elizabeth, in Dudley (widow later moved to Handsworth). Enlisted at Old Hill, Staffs.
8th Battalion DWR; died of wounds 10 8 1917, aged 26.
Buried – Dozinghem Military Cemetery, 3, D, 14.
Commemorated – the **Drill Hall WM panel 6, column 2.**
THY WILL BE DONE.

HOBSON David William – 2226 (later 240189) Corporal.
Born Hill House, Huddersfield, 02 3 1895, to Charles Edward and Emily. Resided in Fartown. Enlisted into the Territorial Force in 1913 at Huddersfield. Embarked for France and Flanders in April, 1915.
1/5th Battalion DWR; killed in action 03 9 1916, aged 19, Battle of the Somme (Thiepval).
Commemorated – Thiepval Memorial, France; Fartown and Birkby WM, M Stansfield, page 220, and the **Drill Hall WM panel 6, column 2.**
Mentioned in the Huddersfield Examiner (previously reported missing now presumed dead) on 27 6 1917.

HOBSON George – 2901 Private.
Born in Upperthong to Joseph E. Resided in Doncaster. Enlisted at Huddersfield in September, 1914. Embarked for France in April, 1915.
1/5th Battalion DWR; killed in action, shellfire, 01 10 1915, Ypres.
Commemorated – Ypres (Menin Gate) Memorial, France; Fartown and Birkby WM; M Stansfield, page 220. and the **Drill Hall WM panel 6, column 2.**

HOCKLEY Jesse – 25093 Private.
Born in South Norwood, London. Enlisted at Croydon.
2/5th Battalion DWR; killed in action 26 11 1917, aged 32, Battle of Cambrai.
Commemorated – Cambrai Memorial (Louverval), France, and the **Drill Hall WM panel 6, column 2.**

HOFFMAN Ernest – 16104 (later 242789) Private.
Born and enlisted in Hull on 10 10 1916.
2/5th Battalion DWR, D Company; killed in action 20 7 1918, Battle of Tardenois.
Commemorated – Soissons Memorial, France, and the **Drill Hall WM panel 6, column 3.**
Mentioned in the Goodall collection: (pre war employment as glazier. Was in 15 and 16 Platoons of D Company).

HOLLINGWORTH John Henry – 3563 (later 240837) Private.
Born in Holmfirth. Resided Burn Lea, Holmfirth. Enlisted at Huddersfield in October, 1914.
2/5th Battalion DWR; killed in action 03 5 1917, Battle of Bullecourt.
Commemorated – Arras Memorial, France, and the **Drill Hall WM panel 6, column 1.**
Mentioned in the Goodall collection.

HOLMES Charles Edward – 204495 Sergeant.
Born Huddersfield, Enlisted at Huddersfield in September, 1914.

2/5th Battalion DWR; died of wounds 20 7 1918, Battle of Tardenois.
Buried – Marfaux British Cemetery, 3, BB, 3.
Commemorated – Christchurch (Woodhouse Hill) Huddersfield, M Stansfield, page 225, and the **Drill Hall WM panel 6, column 2.**
CWGC shows initials as G E.

HOLMES Charles Herbert – 247 (later 240017) Sergeant.
Born in Huddersfield. Resided in Darlington. Enlisted at Mirfield.
1/5th Battalion DWR; killed in action 07 8 1917.
Buried – Ramscappelle Road Military Cemetery, 3, A, 3.
Commemorated – J Fisher, page 115, and the **Drill Hall WM panel 6, column 2.**
Mentioned in the Huddersfield Examiner (official casualty list) on 14 9 1917.
Mentioned in Goodall collection: (D Company, 2/5th DWR; volunteered for foreign service and transferred to 1/5th DWR).

HOLMES Fred – 242399 Private.
Born in Halifax. Enlisted at Bradford.
1/5th Battalion DWR; killed in action 07 8 1917.
Buried – Ramscappelle Road Military Cemetery, 2, A, 10.
Commemorated – J Fisher, page 115, and the **Drill Hall WM panel 6, column 2.**

HOLMES George Frederick – 5456 (later 241976) Private.
Born in Huddersfield on 14 7 1881, to Frederick of Marsh. Resided in Marsh. Enlisted at Huddersfield on 28 3 1916.
2/5th Battalion DWR; reported missing, killed in action 03 5 1917, Battle of Bullecourt.
Commemorated – Arras Memorial, France: Holy Trinity Church, Huddersfield, RoH; M Stansfield, page 225, and the **Drill Hall WM panel 6, column 2.**
Mentioned in the Goodall collection.

HOLMES Harry – 4939 (later 241538) Drummer.
Born in Holmfirth in 1886. Resided in Holmfirth. Enlisted at Holmfirth in March, 1916.
2/5th Battalion DWR; killed in action 03 5 1917, Battle of Bullecourt.
Commemorated – Arras Memorial, France; Underbank WM; M Stansfield, page 225, and the **Drill Hall WM panel 6, column 2.**
Mentioned in the Goodall collection (Casualty Return dated 22 8 1917); the Huddersfield Examiner (reported missing) on 18 6 1917.

HOLROYD Harry – 5072 (later 241655) Private.
Born and resided in Linthwaite. Enlisted at Halifax.
2/5th Battalion DWR; killed in action 03 5 1917, Battle of Bullecourt.
Commemorated – Arras Memorial, France; Linthwaite WM; M Stansfield, page 227, and the **Drill Hall WM panel 6, column 2.**
Mentioned in the Goodall collection.

HOLT Thomas – 203148 Private.
Born in Heptonstall. Resided in Hebden Bridge. Enlisted at Halifax.
5th Battalion DWR; killed in action 30 8 1918, Advance to Victory.
Buried – Vaulx Hill Cemetery, 1, F, 6.
Commemorated – the **Drill Hall WM panel 6, column 2.**

HOLT Walter - 2754 Private.
Born in Halifax. Resided in Primrose Hill. Previously a Volunteer and enlisted at the outbreak of war.
1/5th Battalion DWR; died of wounds 07 7 1916, Battle of the Somme.

Buried - Puchevillers British Cemetery, 1, C 43.
Commemorated – Arras Memorial, France; St Matthew's Church, Primrose Hill, RoH; London & NW Railway Company Nominal Roll; J Fisher, page 110; M Stansfield, page 229, and the **Drill Hall WM panel 6, column 2.**
Mentioned in the Huddersfield Examiner (died of wounds) on 02 11 1916; (the official casualty list) on 13 12 1916.

HOOD Charles – 4886 (later 241503) Private.
Born in Addingham to Isaac and Susanna. Resided in Ilkley. Enlisted at Rotherham.
1/5th Battalion DWR; killed in action 03 9 1916, Battle of the Somme (Thiepval)
Commemorated – Thiepval Memorial, France; Addingham WM; Addingham Bowling Club WM; St Peter's Church, Addingham, RcH; Cravens Part in the Great War (book, page 280, & the cpgw.org.uk website) and the **Drill Hall WM panel 6, column 2.**

HOPKINSON John – 240595 Private.
Resided Lees, Lancs. Enlisted at Huddersfield.
1/5th Battalion DWR; killed in action 08 10 1917.
Commemorated – Tyne Cot Memorial, Belgium, and the **Drill Hall WM panel 6, column 2.**

HOPKINSON John Edward – 241170 Private.
Resided Liverpool, Lancs. Enlisted at Huddersfield.
1/5th Battalion DWR; killed in action 03 9 1916, Battle of the Somme (Thiepval).
Commemorated – Thiepval Memorial, France, and the **Drill Hall WM panel 6, column 2.**

HORNE John William – 22523 Private.
Born and enlisted at Lincon.
5th Battalion DWR; killed in action 27 3 1918, German Spring Offensive.
Buried – Doulens Communal Cemetery Extension, 5, E, 13.
Commemorated – the **Drill Hall WM panel 6, column 3.**

HORNSBY George Herbert – 240886 Private.
Born in Dewsbury. Resided with his wife, Mary Ann, in Dewsbury. Enlisted at Mirfield.
1/5th Battalion DWR; killed in action 03 9 1916, aged 35, Battle of the Somme (Thiepval).
Buried - Mill Road Cemetery, 1, D, 7.
Commemorated – the **Drill Hall WM panel 6, column 2.**
THY WILL BE DONE.

HORSFALL Ernest Arthur – 3707 Private.
Born in Huddersfield to Arthur and Lilly of Birkby. Enlisted at Huddersfield 27 12 1914.
1/5th Battalion DWR; wounded in action 03 9 1916 and died of wounds, King George's Hospital, London, on 27 9 1916, aged 21, Battle of the Somme (Thiepval).
Buried – Huddersfield (Edgerton) Cemetery, 10, B, 174.
Commemorated – Fartown and Birkby WM; J Fisher, page 114; M Stansfield, page 230, and the **Drill Hall WM panel 6, column 2.**
Mentioned in the Huddersfield Examiner (wounded in action) on 11 9 1916; (official casualty list) on 20 10 1916; (died of wounds, official casualty list) on 20 10 1916.
> *"11 9 1916 - Information was received on Saturday by Mr and Mrs Horsfall, 190 Halifax Old Road, Birkby, that their eldest son, Private Ernest Horsfall, of the West Riding Regiment, is lying in the Stationary Hospital, France, suffering from a severe wound in the groin. Private Horsfall has been in France for 15 months and has twice been wounded previously."*

TO LIVE IN THE HEARTS OF THOSE WE LOVE IS NOT TO DIE.

HORSFALL Frank – 5068 (later 241651) Private.

Born in Marsden to Edwin and Rebecca. Resided in Marsden. Enlisted at Huddersfield in March, 1916. Embarked for France and Flanders in January, 1917.
2/5th Battalion DWR; reported missing, killed in action 03 5 1917, Battle of Bullecourt.
Commemorated – Arras Memorial, France; Marsden WM; M Stansfield, page 230, and the **Drill Hall WM panel 6, column 2.**
Mentioned in the Huddersfield Examiner (reported missing) on 07 6 1917. Mentioned in the Goodall collection.

HORSFIELD Stanley – 4937 (later 241536) Corporal.
Born in Paddock on 19 5 1884. Resided in Paddock. Enlisted at Huddersfield.
2/5th Battalion DWR; reported missing killed in action 03 5 1917, Battle of Bullecourt.
Commemorated – Arras Memorial, France; New North Road Baptist Church RoH; All Saints Church, Paddock, RoH; M Stansfield, page 231, and the **Drill Hall WM panel 6, column 2.**
Mentioned in the Huddersfield Examiner (reported missing) on 04 6 1917; (previously reported missing now reported killed in action) on 06 7 1917 and 17 7 1917. Mentioned in the Goodall collection: (casualty return, dated 22 8 1917).

HOSKIN Tom – 240419 Sergeant.
Born in Rashcliffe, Huddersfield, to Hannah. Resided with his wife, Mary Alice, in Mexborough. Pre war Volunteer and Territorial soldier, 14 years. Enlisted at Huddersfield.
2/5th Battalion DWR, D Company; killed in action 14 4 1918, aged 35, German Spring Offensive.
Buried – Bienvillers Military Cemetery, 9, C, 18.
Commemorated – M Stansfield, page 231, and the **Drill Hall WM panel 6, column 3.**
AT REST.

HOUGHLAND Thomas – 4186 (later 241201) Corporal.
Born in Kirkheaton. Resided at Thornton le Fylde. Enlisted at Huddersfield.
2/5th Battalion DWR; reported missing, killed in action 03 5 1917, Battle of Bullecourt.
Commemorated – Arras Memorial, France; St John's Church, Kirkheaton, RoH; Lepton Parish Church RoH; M Stansfield, page 231, and the **Drill Hall WM panel 6, column 2.**
Mentioned in the Goodall collection.

HOWARTH Maurice – 241507 Lance Corporal.
Born in Hoyland, to Binns and Mary Elizabeth, of Ripponden. Resided in Ripponden. Enlisted at Halifax.
5th Battalion DWR; killed in action 28 3 1918, aged 24, German Spring Offensive.
Commemorated – Arras Memorial, France; Ripponden WM and the **Drill Hall WM panel 6, column 2.**
Originally 2/5th DWR.

HOWARTH Walter – 5311 Private.
Born in Marsh on 13 7 1896. Resided Marsh. Enlisted at Huddersfield on 15 3 1916. Embarked for France in January, 1917.
2/5th Battalion DWR; killed in action 28 2 1917, aged 20.
Commemorated – Thiepval Memorial, France; Marsh WM; Holy Trinity Church, Huddersfield, RoH; M Stansfield, page 232, and the **Drill Hall WM panel 6, column 2.**

HOYLE Harold – 22863 Private.
Born in Britannia, Lancs, to Albert Johnson and Pauline Mary. Resided in Earby. Enlisted at Keighley.
2/5th Battalion DWR; killed in action 25 8 1918, aged 25, Advance to Victory.
Commemorated – Vis en Artois Memorial, France; Earby WM; Cravens Part in the Great War (book, page 359, & the cpgw.org.uk website) and the **Drill Hall WM panel 6, column 2.**

HOYLE Herbert Stanley – 4940 (later 241539) Private.
Born in Huddersfield to John and Emily of Primrose Hill. Resided in Huddersfield. Enlisted at Huddersfield in 1916.
2/5th Battalion DWR; died of wounds at 48 Casualty Clearing Station, Ytres, on 27 11 1917, aged 30, Battle of Cambrai.
Buried – Rocquigny-Equancourt Road Cemetery, 3, D, 18.
Commemorated – M Stansfield, page 234, and the **Drill Hall WM panel 6, column 2**.
Mentioned in the Goodall collection.

HOYLE Thomas (Henry) – 240578 Sergeant.
Born May 1892, in Outcoat Bank, Huddersfield, to Joseph and Mary Hannah. Resided in Huddersfield. Enlisted at Huddersfield in December, 1914.
1/5th Battalion DWR; died of wounds in Number 3 General Hospital at Le Treport on 27 10 1917, aged 24.
Buried – Mont Huon Military Cemetery, 6, A, 12A.
Commemorated – M Stansfield, page 235, and the **Drill Hall WM panel 6, column 2**.
Mentioned in the Huddersfield Examiner (in memoriam) on 27 10 1918.
A LOVING SON, A BROTHER, KIND A BEAUTIFUL MEMORY LEFT BEHIND.

HUDSON Albert Alfred – 306035 Corporal.
Resided Milnsbridge. Enlisted at Doncaster.
5th Battalion DWR; killed in action 15 9 1918, Advance to Victory.
Buried - Hermies Hill British Cemetery, 2, E, 24.
Commemorated – Longwood WM; M Stansfield, page 236, and the **Drill Hall WM panel 6, column 3**.

HUDSON John William – 16080 (later 242769) Private.
Resided and enlisted at Hull
2/5th Battalion DWR; killed in action 21 11 1917, Battle of Cambrai.
Commemorated – Cambrai Memorial (Louverval), France, and the **Drill Hall WM panel 6, column 3**.
Mentioned in the Goodall collection.

HUGHES Abraham – 26199 Private.
Born in Cwmyglo, Carnaervon. Enlisted at Llanberis.
5th Battalion DWR; killed in action 04 11 1918, aged 34, Advance to Victory.
Buried - Ruesnes Communal Cemetery, 1, C, 8.
Commemorated – Arras Memorial, France, and the **Drill Hall WM panel 6, column 2**.
SDGW shows date of death as 05 11 1918.
Originally 2/5th DWR.

HUGHES James – 5368 (later 241902) Private.
Resided in Moldgreen. Enlisted at Halifax on 25 3 1916.
2/5th Battalion DWR, D Company; died of wounds on the same day, 20 11 1917, Battle of Cambrai (Graincourt).
Commemorated – Hermies Hill British Special Memorial, A 15, France; Christ Church, Moldgreen, RoH; M Stansfield, page 236, and the **Drill Hall WM panel 6, column 3**.
Mentioned in the Goodall collection and Goodall Collection (pre war employment warehouseman. 13 Platoon, D Company at time of death).
THEIR GLORY SHALL NOT BE BLOTTED OUT.

HUNT George Lewis – 6781 Private.
Born in Shotesham, Norfolk. Resided in Wroxham. Enlisted in East Dereham.
1/5th Battalion DWR; killed in action 17 9 1916, aged 18, Battle of the Somme.

Commemorated – Thiepval Memorial, France, and the **Drill Hall WM panel 6, column 3.**

HURT Ernest - 4139 Private.
Resided in Sheffield. Enlisted at Huddersfield.
1/5th Battalion DWR; killed in action 04 7 1916, Battle of the Somme.
Buried – Connaught Cemetery, 6, A, 1.
Commemorated – the **Drill Hall WM panel 5, column 3.**

HUTCHINSON Herman – 240131 Private.
Born in Liversedge. Enlisted at Mirfield.
1/5th Battalion DWR; killed in action 15 10 1917, Ypres.
Buried – Nine Elms British Cemetery, 4, D, A.
Commemorated – Mirfield WM and the **Drill Hall WM panel 6, column 3.**
SDGW shows date of death as 11 10 1917.

HUTCHINSON John – 5108 (later 241786) Private.
Born in Sutton on Trent, Notts. Resided in Marton. Enlisted at Gainsborough.
5th Battalion DWR, D Company; reported missing, Prisoner of War, died of wounds in German hands on 30 5 1917, aged 34.
Buried – Tournai Communal Cemetery Extension, 5, H, 13.
Commemorated – J Fisher, page 143, and the **Drill Hall WM panel 6, column 3.**
Mentioned in Goodall collection and Goodall Collection (13 Platoon, D Company).
CWGC shows number as 241687.

HUXLEY Thomas – 29433 Private.
Born in Whixhall, Shrops. Resided in Shropshire. Enlisted at Ilkley.
2/5th Battalion DWR; killed in action 30 6 1917, aged 29.
Buried – Queant Road Cemetery, 3, A, 9.
Commemorated – Newtown WM, Salop; Whixhall Wesleyan Chapel WM, Salop, and the **Drill Hall WM panel 6, column 3.**
ALWAYS THOUGHTFUL TRUE AND KIND A BEAUTIFUL MEMORY LEFT BEHIND.

HYDE Thomas – 2408 Private.
Born in Moldgreen, of Frank and Lena, of Newsome. Resided Newsome. Enlisted at Huddersfield in August, 1914. Embarked for France and Flanders in April, 1915.
1/5th Battalion DWR; killed in action 11 7 1915, AGED 19, Ypres.
Buried – Bard Cottage Cemetery, 1, A, 40.
Commemorated – Almondbury WM; M Stansfield, page 237, and the **Drill Hall WM panel 6, column 3.**
SWEET REST AT LAST.

IBBOTSON Joseph – 5445 (later 241966) Private.
Born in Sheffield, to Frederick and Laura. Resided in Sheffield. Enlisted at Sheffield.
2/5th Battalion DWR; killed in action 03 5 1917, aged 20, Battle of Bullecourt.
Commemorated – Arras Memorial, France, and the **Drill Hall WM panel 6, column 3.**
Mentioned in the Goodall collection.

IDDON George – 2783 Private.
Born in Rochdale in 21 1 1897 to Joseph and Anne, of Huddersfield. Enlisted at Huddersfield 02 9 1914.
1/5th Battalion DWR; wounded in action 03 9 1916, died of wounds at No 6 General Hospital, Rouen, on 11 9 1916, aged 19, Battle of the Somme (Thiepval).
Buried – St Sever Cemetery, B, 25, 20.

Commemorated – Fartown and Birkby WM; St Andrew's Church, Leeds Road, RoH (thought to have been destroyed); Salvation Army RoH; J Fisher, page 113; M Stansfield, page 238, and the **Drill Hall WM panel 6, column 3.**
Mentioned in the Huddersfield Examiner (wounded in action) on 11 9 1916; (official; casualty list) on 13 9 1916; (died of wounds) on 02 10 1916.
WE KNOW HE DIED FOR THE LOVE OF US AND HE COULD NOT DO MORE.

INGHAM Harry – 242177 Private.
Born in Allerton, Bradford, to Calvin and Sarah. Resided in Allerton. Enlisted at Bradford.
1/5th Battalion DWR; killed in action 15 8 1917, aged 23.
Buried – Coxyde Military Cemetery, 2, H. 30.
Commemorated – the **Drill Hall WM panel 6, column 3.**
FAR AWAY BUT TO MEMORY DEAR.

ISSATT John – 33106 Private.
Born and enlisted in Leeds.
5th Battalion DWR; died of wounds 24 7 1918.
Buried – Terlincthun British Cemetery, 17, D, 7.
Commemorated – the **Drill Hall WM panel 6, column 3.**

IZZARD Horace – 203350 Private.
Resided in Wheathampstead, Herts. Enlisted in Hertfordshire.
5th Battalion DWR; killed in action 06 9 1918, Advance to Victory.
Buried - St Sever Cemetery Extension, Q, 4, G, 17.
Commemorated – the **Drill Hall WM panel 6, column 3.**
Formerly 4249 Hertfordshire Regiment.

JACKSON Allan – 21595 Private.
Born in Govan, to William and Kate, of Partick. Resided in Glasgow. Enlisted at Partick.
5th Battalion DWR; killed in action 20 7 1918, aged 20.
Buried - Courmas British Cemetery, 2, C, 3.
Commemorated – the **Drill Hall WM panel 6, column 3.**
Originally 2/5th DWR.
CWGC shows initials as A D.
GOODNIGHT BRAVE HEART, GOODNIGHT, GOODNIGHT.

JACKSON Donald Richard Field – Lieutenant.
Born Scissett, Huddersfield, to Sir Percy and Lady Jackson, of Woodlands, Scissett.
Enlisted as a Private soldier into DWR on 04 9 1914 and was commissioned in March 1915.
Embarked for France and Flanders in September, 1915.
5th Battalion DWR; killed in action 27 8 1917, aged 24, Ypres.
Commemorated – Tyne Cot Memorial, Belgium: Scissett WM; St Aidan's Church, Skelmanthorpe, RoH; J Fisher, pp 116 & 129; M Stansfield, page 242, and the **Drill Hall WM panel 5, column 2.**
Mentioned in the 1/5th DWR War Diary, joined the Battalion on 21 8 1916. Mentioned in the 8th DWR War Diary, killed in action, on 28 8 1917.
Mentioned in the Huddersfield Examiner (enlisted 04 9 1914; commissioned March, 1915, and killed in action September, 1917) on 06 9 1917.

JACKSON George – 26298 Private.
Born in Pontefract, to James and Lois, of Tanshelf. Enlisted at Pontefract.
2/5th Battalion DWR; killed in action 22 7 1918, aged 20, Battle of Tardenois.
Commemorated – Soissons Memorial, France, and the **Drill Hall WM panel 6, column 3.**
Formerly 37244 Army Service Corps.

JACKSON Harry – 240010 Sergeant.
Born in Primrose Hill on 21 9 1886 (son of ex Colour Sergeant Jackson of the Duke of Wellington's Regiment, retired after 30 years service). Resided Primrose Hill, married with one child. Mobilised 03 8 1914.
1/5th Battalion DWR; killed in action 03 9 1916, Battle of the Somme (Thiepval).
Commemorated – Thiepval Memorial, France; St Matthew's Church, Primrose Hill, RoH; M Stansfield, page 242, and the **Drill Hall WM panel 6, column 3.**
Mentioned in the Huddersfield Examiner (previously reported missing, now reported killed in action) on 27 6 1916; (reported missing, 03 9 1916) on 29 9 1918.

JACKSON Herbert Norton – 5003 (later 241594) Private.
Born in Denby to Allen and Martha Ann, of Denby. Resided in Upper Denby. Enlisted in Huddersfield.
2/5th Battalion DWR, B Company; killed in action 03 5 1917, aged 24, Battle of Bullecourt.
Commemorated – Arras Memorial, France; Denby Dale and Cumberworth WM; M Stansfield, page 242, and the **Drill Hall WM panel 6, column 3.**
Mentioned in the Huddersfield Examiner (news requested by relatives) on 14 6 1917; (reported missing on the official casualty list) on 27 6 1917. Mentioned in the Goodall collection.

JACKSON James – 33116 Private.
Born in York, to Richard and Margaret. Resided in Crosby Garrett, Cumberland. Enlisted at Leeds.
5th Battalion DWR; killed in action 12 9 1918, aged 34, Advance to Victory.
Commemorated – Vis en Artois Memorial, France; J Fisher, page 115, and the **Drill Hall WM panel 6, column 3.**
Originally 2/5th DWR.

JACKSON John Bulmer – 265607 Sergeant. Territorial Force War Medal.
Enlisted at Guiseley.
2/5th Battalion DWR; died of wounds 24 7 1918, Battle of Tardenois.
Buried - Marfaux British Cemetery, 5, I, 2.
Commemorated – the **Drill Hall WM panel 6, column 3.**
Awarded the Territorial Force War Medal, 20 4 1922, posthumously.

JACKSON William T – 241595 Private.
Born in Luddenden Foot. Resided in Linthwaite. Enlisted at Huddersfield in March, 1916.
2/5th Battalion DWR; killed in action 16 3 1917.
Buried – Queens Cemetery, 3, E, 9.
Commemorated – Linthwaite WM; M Stansfield, page 243, and the **Drill Hall WM panel 6, column 3.**

JAGGAR W – Private
No trace.
Possibly 204043 Private JAGGER W 2nd DWR.
2nd Battalion DWR; killed in action 10 10 1917.
Buried – Cement House Cemetery, 14, B, 24.
Commemorated – Bruce History, page 226, and the **Drill Hall WM panel 6, column 3.**

JARDINE Alexander Matthew – 25097 Private.
Born and enlisted at Keighley.
5th Battalion DWR; killed in action 21 7 1918, Battle of Tardenois.
Buried – Jonchery sur Vesle British Cemetery, 1, E, 26.
Commemorated – the **Drill Hall WM panel 6, column 4.**

JEFFERSON Donald Percy – 2908 Private.
Born in Birkby on 28 9 1891 to Frederick Henry and Mary Jane. Resided Birkby. Enlisted at Huddersfield on 02 9 1914. Embarked for France and Flanders in April, 1915.
1/5th Battalion DWR; killed in action 15 5 1915, aged 23, Fleurbaix Sector.
Buried – Rue David Military Cemetery, 1, B, 17.
Commemorated – Fartown and Birkby WM; M Stansfield, page 244, and the **Drill Hall WM panel 6, column 4.**
Mentioned in the Huddersfield Examiner (announcement of death) on 19 5 1915.
HE GAVE HIMSELF FOR US.

JENNINGS Andrew Gorman – 5071 Private.
Born and enlisted in Bradford.
1/5th Battalion DWR; killed in action 25 9 1916, aged 22, Battle of the Somme.
Commemorated – Thiepval Memorial, France, and the **Drill Hall WM panel 6, column 4.**

JENNINGS John – 240877 Private.
Born in Dewsbury, to Walter and Hannah. Resided in Dewsbury. Enlisted at Mirfield on 30 12 1914.
2/5th Battalion DWR; died of wounds 21 11 1917, aged 20, Battle of Cambrai.
Buried – Rocquigny-Equancourt Road Cemetery, 2, F, 2.
Commemorated – the **Drill Hall WM panel 6, column 4.**
Mentioned in the Goodall collection: (pre war employment miner; 15 Platoon, D Company, on joining. Posted to Transport Section as a cook in 1917. Returned to D Coy as Lewis gunner. Wounded in action, casualty return dated 24 8 1917. Wounded on 20 11 1917, died of wounds the day afterwards).

JEPSON A W – Private.
No trace.
Possibly duplicate of JESSOP A W, below.
Commemorated – the **Drill Hall WM panel 6, column 4.**

JEPSON Percy – 5429 (later 241954) Private.
Born in Woodhouse. Resided in Shrewsbury. Enlisted at Sheffield.
2/5th Battalion DWR; killed in action 03 5 1917, Battle of Bullecourt.
Commemorated – Arras Memorial, France, and the **Drill Hall WM panel 6, column 4.**
Mentioned in the Goodall collection.

JESSOP Arthur William – 5062 Private.
Born and resided in Fenay Bridge. Enlisted in Huddersfield in March, 1916.
2/5th Battalion DWR; died of acute bronchitis and pneumonia at 4 Casualty Clearing Station, in Lozinghem, on 06 3 1917.
Buried – Varennes Military Cemetery, 1, I, 78.
Commemorated – Lepton Parish Church RoH; M Stansfield, page 246, and the **Drill Hall WM panel 6, column 4.**

JESSOP Ernest – 240797 Private.
Born in Slaithwaite on 30 1 1897 to Richard and Emma. Resided in Dewsbury. Enlisted at Mirfield in November, 1914.
2/5th Battalion DWR; killed in action 20 11 1917, aged 20, Battle of Cambrai.
Commemorated – Cambrai Memorial (Louverval), France; Mount Pleasant Chapel, Lockwood, RoH; M Stansfield, page 246, and the **Drill Hall WM panel 6, column 4.**
Mentioned in the Huddersfield Examiner (in memoriam) 20 11 1918.

JESSOP Lewis Hallas – 4262 Private.

Born in Lascelles Hall, Lepton, in 1892. Resided in Lockwood. Enlisted at Huddersfield in October, 1915.
1/5th Battalion DWR; died of wounds on board HMHS Asturias on 08 7 1916, Battle of the Somme.
Buried – Netley Military Cemetery, CE, 1802.
Commemorated – St Stephen's Church, Rashcliffe, RoH; St Paul's Church, Southgate; J Fisher, page 110; M Stansfield, page 246, and the **Drill Hall WM panel 6, column 4.**

JEWSBURY Albert – 3387 Private.
Born in Swinton, Yorks, to Edith (later Holloman), of Ravensthorpe. Resided at Ravensthorpe. Enlisted at Mirfield.
1/5th Battalion DWR; killed in action 23 10 1915, aged 19, Ypres.
Buried - Talana Farm Cemetery, 4, C, 1.
Commemorated – D Tattersfield, pp 77 & 385, and the **Drill Hall WM panel 6, column 4.**
I OFTEN THINK OF THE DAYS GONE BY WHEN WE WERE ALL TOGETHER.

JOHNSEY Herbert – 5474 (later 241991) Private.
Born in Dogley, Kirkheaton. Resided in Kirkheaton. Enlisted at Huddersfield.
5th Battalion DWR; killed in action 22 7 1918, Battle of Tardenois.
Commemorated – Soissons Memorial, France; St John's Church, Kirkheaton, RoH; M Stansfield, page 246, and the **Drill Hall WM panel 6, column 4.**
Mentioned in the Huddersfield Examiner (announcement of death) 22 8 1918. Mentioned in the Goodall collection.
Originally 2/5th DWR.

JOHNSON Arthur Ernest – 34361 Private.
Born in Far Cotton, Northants, to William and Ada. Resided Northamptonshire, Enlisted in Northampton.
2/4th Battalion DWR; died of wounds 05 9 1918, aged 17, Advance to Victory.
Buried - St Sever Cemetery Extension , Q 5, F, 6.
Commemorated – the **Drill Hall WM panel 6, column 4.**
GONE BUT NOT FORGOTTEN, FROM HIS SORROWING MOTHER AND ALL AT HOME.

JOHNSON Fred – 13201 Private. Military Medal.
Born in Bramley, Leeds, to Sarah, of Yeadon. Resided in Yeadon. Enlisted at Guiseley.
2/5th Battalion DWR; killed in action 17 9 1917.
Buried – Favreuil British Cemetery, 1, F, 8.
Commemorated – J Fisher, page 87, and the **Drill Hall WM panel 6, column 4.**
Formerly 9th DWR.
Mentioned in the London Gazette (award of MM) on 03 6 1916, page 5592.

JOHNSON Thomas Curtis – 5177 (later 241745) Private.
Born and resided in Grantby, Lincs. Enlisted at Scunthorpe on 13 3 1916.
2/5th Battalion DWR; killed in action 03 5 1917, Battle of Cambrai.
Commemorated – Arras Memorial, France, and the **Drill Hall WM panel 6, column 4.**
Mentioned in the Goodall collection and Goodall Collection (pre war employment groom; 15 Platoon, D Company).

JOHNSTONE Alexander – 26290 Private.
Born in Stonekirk, Wigtonshire, to Robert and Annie, of Port William. Enlisted at Stranraer.
2/5th Battalion DWR; killed in action 27 3 1918, aged 21, German Spring Offensive.
Commemorated – Arras Memorial, France, and the **Drill Hall WM panel 6, column 4.**

JONES Arthur Barron – 240574 Private.

Born in Moldgreen on 03 1 1889. Resided with his wife, Alice, of Shore Head, in Huddersfield. Enlisted Huddersfield on 07 10 1914.
2/5th Battalion DWR, C Company; killed in action 09 4 1918, aged 29, German Spring Offensive.
Buried – Bienvillers Military Cemetery, 9, B, 9.
Commemorated – St Paul's Church, Southgate, RoH; M Stansfield, page 247, and the **Drill Hall WM panel 6, column 4.**
IN MY HEART AND MIND HE WILL EVER BE MY DEAREST, SWEETEST MEMORY.

JONES Charles – 40516 Private.
Born in Tinsley. Enlisted at Barnsley.
5th Battalion DWR; killed in action 05 11 1918, Advance to Victory.
Commemorated – Vis en Artois Memorial, France, and the **Drill Hall WM panel 6, column 4.**
Originally 2/5th DWR.

JONES George Victor (J V) – 240222 Company Sergeant Major, Distinguished Conduct Medal.
Born in the Tower, Middlesex. Resided in Aspley. Enlisted at Huddersfield. Joined Huddersfield Territorials pre war, from the Gordon Highlanders. Mobilised on 04 8 1914. Embarked for France and Flanders in April, 1915.
5th Battalion DWR; killed in action 23 7 1918, Battle of Tardenois.
Commemorated – Arras Memorial, France; Magnus History, page 293; M Stansfield, page 248, and the **Drill Hall WM panel 6, column 4.**
Originally 2/5th DWR.
Awarded the DCM, London Gazette dated 03 9 1918, page 10312. Unit War Diary shows DCM was awarded for operations from 25 3 1918, dated 31 5 1918.
Mentioned in Huddersfield Examiner (notification of death) on 12 8 1918; (award of DCM) on 12 9 1918; (in memoriam) on 22 7 1919.
Mentioned in the Goodall collection (Medal Award Roll).
Board shows initials at J V, incorrectly.

JONES Joseph – 241393 Private.
Born in Huddersfield. Resided in Moldgreen. Enlisted at Huddersfield.
1/5th Battalion DWR; killed in action 07 8 1917.
Buried – Ramscappelle Road Military Cemetery, 2, A, 11.
Commemorated – Moldgreen WM; J Fisher, page 115; M Stansfield, page 248, and the **Drill Hall WM panel 6, column 4.**
Mentioned in the Huddersfield Examiner (announcement of death) on 06 9 1917; (official casualty list) on 14 9 1917.

JONES John Daniel – 25095 Private.
Born in Aberystwith, to Daniel and Catherine. Enlisted at Llandimiolen, Carmarthenshire.
5th Battalion DWR; killed in action 20 7 1918, aged 24.
Buried – Courmas British Cemetery, 2, C, 7.
Commemorated – the **Drill Hall WM panel 6, column 4.**
CARIAD MWY NA HWN NID OES GAB NEB SEF, BOD I UN ROI EI DROS EI GYFEILLION.

JONES J V – see George Victor.

JONES John William – 49674 Private.
Born in Hadley, Shropshire. Resided in Blackpool. Enlisted at Salford.
5th Battalion DWR; killed in action 12 9 1918, Advance to Victory.
Buried - Ruyalcourt Military Cemetery, L, 12.
Commemorated – Sherrifhales WM, Salop, and the **Drill Hall WM panel 6, column 4.**
Formerly 6243 Yorkshire Regiment.

JURY Reginald – 2nd Lieutenant.
Born in Marsh on 04 11 1893 to Francis and Emma, of Birkby. Resided Birkby. Joined the Territorials in 1910. Mobilised in August, 1914. Embarked for France and Flanders, as a Private soldier, in April, 1915. Commissioned from the rank of Sergeant on 28 3 1917. Rejoined the Battalion on 19 5 1917.
1/4th Battalion DWR; wounded in air raid while attending a course in Dunkirk, 29 9 1917. Died of wounds at Queen Alexandra's Hospital at Malo les Bains on 06 10 1917, aged 23.
Buried – Malo les Bains Communal Cemetery, A, 16.
Commemorated – Fartown and Birkby WM; Christ Church, Woodhouse Hill, RoH; Bales History, page 299; J Fisher, page 116; M Stansfield, page 257, and the **Drill Hall WM panel 6, column 4.**
Mentioned in the Huddersfield Examiner (commissioned 1916 and died of wounds following an air raid) on 08 10 1917.
DIED OF WOUNDS, PEACE PERFECT PEACE, WITH LOVED ONES FAR AWAY.

KAY James Edward – 241351 Private.
Resided in Dewsbury. Enlisted at Mirfield.
1/5th Battalion DWR; killed in action 03 9 1916, Battle of the Somme (Thiepval).
Commemorated – Thiepval Memorial, France, and the **Drill Hall WM panel 7, column 1.**

KAYE Charles William Donaldson – Lieutenant.
Born Bradford, 15 7 1888, to Jane Ann, of Deganwy, Carnavonshire. Commissioned into 2/5th Battalion DWR. Retired due to ill health.
Joined Royal Navy, October, 1915, as an Engine Room Artificer, 3rd Class. Died of pneumonia on board HMS Juno on 10 2 1917.
Buried – Muscat New Naval Cemetery, Oman, 3, 4, aged 28.
Commemorated – St John's Church, Kirkheaton; M Stansfield, page 258, and the **Drill Hall WM panel 6, column 4.**
REST IN PEACE.

KAYE Fred – 240247 Private.
Born in Huddersfield to Mary Ellen, on 10 5 1896. Resided in Fartown. Enlisted at Huddersfield and mobilised on 04 8 1914 as a Territorial.
5th Battalion DWR; died, meningitis, at Welsh Metropolitan War Hospital, Cardiff, on 23 4 1917.
Buried – Huddersfield (Edgerton) Cemetery, 10B, 41.
Commemorated – Fartown and Birkby WM; High Street United Methodist Church RoH, Christ Church Woodhouse Hill RoH; M Stansfield, page 259, and the **Drill Hall WM panel 7, column 1.**
Mentioned in the Huddersfield Examiner (died 23 4 1917, of meningitis, in Cardiff) on 26 4 1917; (official casualty list) on 04 6 1917; (memoriam notice) on 23 4 1919.
Son of 3712 (240912) Private Oliver Kaye, qv.

KAYE Fred – 242869 Private.
Born Lockwood. Enlisted at Huddersfield.
1/5th Battalion DWR; killed in action 12 4 1917.
Buried – Le Touret Military Cemetery, 4, C 18.
Commemorated – M Stansfield, page 260, and the **Drill Hall WM panel 7, column 1.**

KAYE Harry – 2437 (later 240266) Corporal. Territorial Force War Medal.
Resided in Huddersfield. Enlisted into F Company at Holmfirth, pre war.
2/5th Battalion DWR, D Company; killed in action 03 5 1917, Battle of Bullecourt.
Commemorated – Arras Memorial, France; M Stansfield, page 260, and the **Drill Hall WM panel 7, column 1.**
Mentioned in the Goodall collection; the Huddersfield Examiner (reported missing in the official casualty list) on 27 6 1917.
TFWM awarded posthumously on 20 4 1922.

KAYE Harold Sykes – 3951 (later 241069) Private.
Born in Huddersfield. Resided with his wife, Sarah, in Moldgreen. Enlisted at Huddersfield in December, 1914.
2/5th Battalion DWR, D Company; wounded in action and taken prisoner on 03 5 1917, Battle of Bullecourt; died of wounds and pneumonia, as POW, at Soltau 15 10 1918, aged 25.
Buried – Hamburg Cemetery, 2, G, 2.
Commemorated – St Andrew's Church RoH, Christ Church, Moldgreen, RoH; Huddersfield Parish Church RoH; J Fisher, page 144; M Stansfield, page 260, and the **Drill Hall WM panel 7, column 1.**
Mentioned in the Goodall collection; the Huddersfield Examiner (news requested by relatives) on 14 6 1917; (notified as wounded and POW) on 19 6 1917; (reported missing, official casualty list) on 27 6 1917; (wounded and POW, official casualty list) on 20 7 1917.
OF HUDDERSFIELD, YORKSHIRE, IN LOVING MEMORY, AT REST.

KAYE Oliver – 3712 (later 240912) Private.
Born in Huddersfield on 15 9 1875, husband of Mary Ellen and resided in Huddersfield. Enlisted at Huddersfield on 31 12 1914.
1/5th Battalion DWR; reported missing, killed in action, 03 9 1916, Battle of the Somme (Thiepval).
Commemorated – Thiepval Memorial, France; Fartown and Birkby WM; Christ Church, Woodhouse Hill, RoH; M Stansfield, page 262, and the **Drill Hall WM panel 6, column 4.**
Mentioned in the Huddersfield Examiner (reported missing, not heard of since) on 26 4 1916; (reported missing from 03 9 1916) on 04 10 1916; (previously reported missing now reported killed in action) on 28 6 1917.
Father of 240247 Private Fred Kaye, qv.

B Company, 2/5th Battalion DWR at Henham Park, July, 1916.

D Company, 2/5th Battalion DWR at Henham Park, July, 1916.

KAYE. F.	PTE.	LITTLEWOOD. A.	PTE.	LITTLEWOOD. F.	PTE	MAY. E.	PTE.
KAYE. FRED.	"	LABOURN. F.	"	LITTLEWOOD. W.	"	MALONE. P.	CPL.
KAYE. H.	CPL.	LAWTON. C.	"	LIDDLE. T.	"	MATTHEWS. A.	PTE.
KAYE. H.S.	PTE.	LAWTON. W.	"	LITTLE. A.	"	MATTHEWS. A.W.	"
KAYE. P.	"	LAWRENCE. M.	"	LINGARD. W.	"	MATTHEWS. J.	"
KAY. J.E.	"	LANGRICK. C.L.	"	LINCOLN. A.A.	"	MARTIN. T.	"
KENYON. H.	"	LACEY. A.H.	"	LLEWELLYN. W.	"	MANUEL. J.	"
KERFOOT. J.E.	"	LANCASTER. J.A.	"	LONG. E.	"	MADDEYS. H.	"
KELSALL. E.	"	LAMB. A.A.	"	LONG. J.	"	MARSHALL. J.	L/CPL.
KELLY. J.	"	LAMB. C.A.	"	LONGLEY. E.M.	"	MARSHALL. E.	PTE.
KELLET. C.	"	LAWSON. G.	"	LOCKWOOD. T.	"	MACKMAN. A.	"
KERWIN. J. M.M.	SGT.	LEGGETT. A.	"	LOCKWOOD. J.E.	L/CPL.	MARRIOTT. J.G.	"
KENNY. J.	PTE.	LEE. G.	"	LOVELL. T.	PTE.	MARRIOTT. J.L.	"
KENNY. A.	"	LEE. L.	CPL.	LODGE. W.	"	MARSH. J.W.	L/CPL.
KERSHAW. A.	"	LEE. S.M. D.C.M.	SGT.	LODGE. H.	L/CPL.	MATHERS. S.	PTE.
KEIGHLEY. H.	"	LEWIS. A.F.	CPL.	LOADER. G.	PTE.	MANN. J.N.	"
KENWORTHY. J.	"	LEWIS. F.	PTE.	LOWDEN. T.	"	MACKWELL. C.	"
KEENAN. J.	"	LEWIS. W.	"	LOWERY. T.	"	MANCHESTER. L.	"
KILLARNEY J.	"	LEESON. H.	"	LOBLEY. W.J.	CPL.	MANNING. F.T.	"
KILBURN. W.	"	LEADBEATER. L.C.	"	LUCAS. J.	L SGT.	MALLINSON. P.	"
KIMMINGS. S.	"	LEMON. H.	"	LUCAS. R.V.	PTE.	MALTBY. H.	"
KNAPTON. E.R.	"	LEDGER. C.	"	LUCY. J.	"	MARWOOD. G.H.	"
KNIFE F.	"	LEEMING. J.T.	"	LUKER. P.A.	"	MACDONALD. J.	"
KNAPTON. A.	"	LISTER. F.J.	"	LUGSDEN. A.	"	McBRIDE.	"
KRAMER. A.	"	LISTER. J.	"	LUMSDALE. J. M.M.	"	McDERMOTT.	"
KEHOE. M.	"	LISTER. N.	"	LYONS. E.	"	McAVOY.	CPL.

McDONALD. T.	CPL.	MITCHELL. E.	PTE.	MURPHY. T.	PTE.	OLDROYD. H.	PTE.
McEWAN. J.	PTE.	MITCHELL. G.H. M.M	CPL.	MURRELL. A.	"	OLDFIELD. J.	"
McGRATH. M.	"	MITCHELL. J.	PTE.	MURRAY. J.	"	ONION. W.	"
McGUIRE. J.	"	MITCHELL. H.N.	"	MUDD. G.	SGT.	O'NIELL. W.	"
McGREGOR. J.	"	MITCHELL. F.	"	MULHEARN. A.	PTE.	O'MELIA. F.	"
MACKENZIE. J.	"	MILNER. J.	"	NAYLOR. H.	"	O'MELIA. H.	"
MACKENZIE. E.G.	2/LT.	MILES. E.T.	"	NAYLOR. R.	"	ORMEROD. F.	"
McLINTOCK. A.	LT.	MIDDLEBROOK. A.W.	L/CPL.	NASH. F.	"	OUGHTON. J.H.	"
McLAUGHLIN. A.	PTE.	MIDGLEY. H.	PTE.	NEWSOME. W.	L/CPL.	OVERSBY. J.E.	"
McMANUS. R.	"	MILSON. H.	"	NEILD. J.E.	PTE.	OVERTON. A.	"
MELLOR. L.	"	MOSS. R.S.	"	NESS. D.	"	OWEN. R.S.	"
MELLOR. M.	"	MORRISON. H.	"	NEWTON. J.	"	OXLEY. J.J.	"
MELLOR. J.E.	"	MOFFITT. C.	"	NEWTON. C.	"	OXLEY. H.	L/CPL.
MELLOR. C.	"	MORRIS. F.	"	NEDDERMAN. R.M.	"	OXLEY. W.	PTE.
MELLOR. R.	"	MOORE. G.	"	NICKERSON. A.	L/CPL.	PAXMAN. B.	CPL.
MELLOR. S.	"	MOORE. J.C.D.	2/LT.	NICKOLSON. J.K.	PTE.	PARKER. F.	PTE.
MELLOR. ALFRED	"	MORRELL. G.	PTE.	NICHOLSON. H.	L/CPL.	PARKER. R.	"
MELLOR. ARTHUR	"	MORGAN. J.L.	L/CPL.	NORTON. A.	PTE.	PARKER. R.	"
MORRIS. F.	"	MORGAN. W.H.	"	NOBLE. H.	"	PARKER. A.	L/CPL.
MELVILLE. J.	2/LT.	MOXON. D.	PTE.	NORRIS. H.	"	PATTERSON. G.	PTE.
MEWETT. W.	PTE.	MOSLEY. A.	L/CPL.	NUNN. H.	"	PARR. J.W.	"
MICKLETHWAITE. A.	"	MOSLEY. P.	2/LT.	NUTTALL. J.	"	PAGE. F.	"
MILLER. S.C.	"	MOUNCEY. J.T.	PTE.	OATES. C.R.	CPL.	PARKIN. W.	"
MILNES. S.	L/CPL.	MONELLY. T.	"	OATES. F.	PTE.	PARKIN. R.	"
MILNES. H.	PTE.	MORTON. E.	"	O'BRIEN. J.P.	SGT.	PALETHORPE. J.	"
MILNES. J.H.	"	MURPHY. E.	"	O'HANLON. E.	L/CPL.	PAYNE. C.F.	"

KAYE Percy – 241326 Private.
Resided and enlisted at Huddersfield.
1/4th Battalion DWR; killed in action 25 2 1918, Advance to Victory.
Buried – Aeroplane Cemetery, 7, C, 3.
Commemorated – the **Drill Hall WM panel 7, column 1.**
Mentioned in the 4th DWR Casualty Record, AB 136, (originally buried at grid J.10.b.10.65, Map sheet 28) page 35.

KEENAN John – 35604 Private.
Born in Wallsend, Northumberland, to William and Hannah. Enlisted at Newcastle upon Tyne.
5th Battalion DWR; killed in action 05 11 1918, aged 19, Advance to Victory.
Buried – Frasnoy Communal Cemetery, A, 4.
Commemorated – the **Drill Hall WM panel 7, column 1.**

KEHOE Michael – 26470 Private.
Born in Liverpool. Enlisted at Liverpool on 01 11 1916.
2/5th Battalion, DWR, D Company; reported missing, killed in action, on 27 11 1917, Ypres.
Buried – Anneux British Cemetery, 2, F, 26.
Commemorated – the **Drill Hall WM panel 7, column 1.**
Mentioned in the Goodall collection.
Formerly 38339 South Wales Borderers.
CWGC shows his date of death as 17 11 1917.

KEIGHLEY Harold – 3588 (later 240845) Private.
Born in Manchester on 29 9 1895, to Sam and Louisa. Resided in Huddersfield. Enlisted at Huddersfield on 11 12 1914.
2/5th Battalion DWR, D Company; killed in action 03 5 1917, aged 21, Battle of Bullecourt.
Buried – Bailleul Road East Cemetery, 2, B, 29.
Commemorated – Almondbury WM; St Paul's Church, Southgate, RoH; M Stansfield, page 263, and the **Drill Hall WM panel 7, column 1.**
Mentioned in the Goodall collection; the Huddersfield Examiner (killed in action) on 27 5 1917; (reported missing, official casualty list) on 27 6 1917.
HIS NAME LIVETH FOREVER.

KELLETT Charles – 5927 Private.
Resided in Preston. Enlisted at Barnoldswick.
1/5th Battalion DWR; killed in action 03 9 1916, Battle of the Somme (Thiepval).
Commemorated – Thiepval Memorial, France, and the **Drill Hall WM panel 7, column 1.**

KELLY J – not trace, probably:
KELLY James (Edward) – 31745 Private.
Born Huddersfield, 12 9 1889. Married and resided in Huddersfield. Enlisted at Huddersfield, 28 5 1917. Embarked for France 03 10 1917.
2/4th Battalion DWR; killed in action 21 11 1917, Battle of Cambrai.
Commemorated – Cambrai Memorial (Louverval), France; Huddersfield Corporation Roll of Honour, M Stansfield, page 264, and the **Drill Hall WM panel 7, column 1.**

KELSALL Eric – 4468 Private.
Born in Nelson, Lancs, on 18 4 1899 to Thomas and Grace, of Oakes, Huddersfield. Enlisted at Huddersfield on 13 8 1915. Embarked for France in April 1916.
1/5th Battalion DWR; killed in action 28 7 1916, aged 17, Battle of the Somme.
Buried – Connaught Cemetery, 3, M, 8.
Commemorated – St Stephen's Church, Lindley, RoH; M Stansfield, page 264, and the **Drill Hall WM panel 7, column 1.**

ALWAYS REMEMBERED BY ALL AT HOME.

KENNY Albert – 34299 Private.
Born and enlisted at Leeds.
5th Battalion DWR; killed in action 30 8 1918, Advance to Victory.
Buried – Shrine Cemetery, 2, C, 9.
Commemorated – the **Drill Hall WM panel 7, column 1.**

KENNY John – 10956 Private.
Born and enlisted at Leeds.
1/5th Battalion DWR; killed in action 09 10 1917, Ypres.
Commemorated – Tyne Cot Memorial, France, and the **Drill Hall WM panel 7, column 1.**
SDGW shows number as 10958.

KENWORTHY John – 5220 (later 241779) Private.
Born Waterhead, Lancs. Resided in Oldham. Enlisted at Springhead
2/5th Battalion DWR, D Company; killed in action 03 5 1917, Battle of Bullecourt.
Commemorated – Arras Memorial, France, and the **Drill Hall WM panel 7, column 1.**
Mentioned in the Goodall collection; the Huddersfield Examiner (reported missing) on 27 6 1917.

KENYON Henry – 2915 Private.
Born In Lees, Oldham. Resided with his wife, Sarah, in Lees. Enlisted at Huddersfield.
1/5th Battalion DWR; killed in action 13 7 1915, aged 32, Ypres.
Commemorated – Ypres (Menin Gate) Memorial, Belgium, and the **Drill Hall WM panel 7, column 1.**

KERFOOT John Edward – 2918 Private.
Born in Holywell, Flintshire, North Wales, to John Edward. Resided with his wife, Emily, of Newsome, in Berry Brow. Enlisted at Huddersfield on 04 9 1914.
1/5th Battalion DWR; wounded in action on 13 11 1915 and died of wounds, St John Ambulance Brigade Hospital, Etaples, on 18 11 1915, aged 28, Ypres.
Buried – Etaples Military Cemetery, 3, G, 1.
Commemorated – Armitage Bridge WM; St John's Church, Newsome; M Stansfield, page 266, and the **Drill Hall WM panel 7, column 1.**
Mentioned in the Huddersfield Examiner (killed in action, shot in head by sniper) on 23 11 1915.
LOVED.

KERSHAW Arthur – 3386 (later 240720) Private.
Resided in Dewsbury. Enlisted at Mirfield.
2/5th Battalion DWR, D Company; killed in action 03 5 1917, Battle of Bullecourt.
Commemorated – Arras Memorial, France; D Tattersfield, pages 283 & 385 with photograph, and the **Drill Hall WM panel 7, column 1.**
Mentioned in the Goodall collection.

KERWIN (KERWYN?) John – 6579 (later 242336) Sergeant. Military Medal.
Enlisted at Durham.
5th Battalion DWR; killed in action 10 10 1917.
Buried – Tyne Cot Cemetery, 24, D, 4.
Commemorated – Magnus RoH, page 251, and the **Drill Hall WM panel 7, column 1.**
Formerly 3884 Durham Light Infantry.
Mentioned in the Goodall collection; the Unit War Diary (awarded a Gallantry Card for trench raid) on 30 11 1916; the Huddersfield Examiner (award of MM for raid carried out on 27 11 1916) on 11 1 1917.
Military Medal award announced in London Gazette dated 22 1 1917, page 832.

Goodall and War Diary show spelling as Kerwyn.

KILBURN Wilfred – 4934 (later 241586) Private.
Born in Aspley, Huddersfield, on 18 4 1885, to Councillor Henry and Margaret. Resided in Huddersfield. Enlisted at Huddersfield.
2/5th Battalion DWR, D Company; reported missing, killed in action, 03 5 1917, aged 32, Battle of Bullecourt.
Commemorated – Arras Memorial, France; M Stansfield, page 267, and the **Drill Hall WM panel 7, column 1.**
Mentioned in the Goodall collection; the Huddersfield Examiner (reported missing, possibly POW) on 04 6 1917;(reported missing, official casualty list) on 27 6 1917.

KILLARNEY – John – 2913 Private.
Born in Huddersfield on 28 8 1892 to John Henry and Annie. Previous service in the local Territorials, and re-enlisted in September, 1914. Embarked for France in April, 1915.
1/5th Battalion DWR, D Company; wounded in action and died of wounds on 23 8 1915, aged 22, Ypres.
Commemorated – Ypres (Menin Gate) Memorial, Belgium; Huddersfield Parish Church RoH; M Stansfield, page 267, and the **Drill Hall WM panel 7, column 1.**
Mentioned in the Huddersfield Examiner (killed in action) on 31 8 1915.

KIMMINGS Smith – 23907 Private.
Resided in Dewsbury. Enlisted at Mirfield.
5th Battalion DWR; killed in action 20 7 1918.
Buried – Courmas British Cemetery, 2, D, 9.
Commemorated – the **Drill Hall WM panel 7, column 1.**

KNAPTON Albert – 5171 (later 241739) Private.
Born in North Cockington, Lincs. Resided North Thoresby. Enlisted at Louth on 13 3 1916.
2/5th Battalion DWR, D Company stretcher bearer; killed in action 03 5 1917, aged 21, Battle of Bullecourt.
Commemorated – Arras Memorial, France, and the **Drill Hall WM panel 7, column 1.**
Mentioned in the Goodall collection.

KNAPTON Ernest Robert – 2916 Private.
Born in Huddersfield to Albert and Agnes of Armitage Bridge. Enlisted at Huddersfield in 1914. Embarked for France and Flanders in April, 1915.
1/5th Battalion DWR; killed in action 15 5 1915, aged 36, Fleurbaix Sector.
Buried – Rue David Military Cemetery, Fleurbaix, 1, B, 23.
Commemorated – Armitage Bridge WM; C Ford, page 27; M Stansfield, page 270 and the **Drill Hall WM panel 7, column 1.**
C Ford shows name as Ernest Raymond KNAPTON; CWGC and M Stansfield show his name as Ernest Robert KNAPRIVATEN.
Mentioned in the Huddersfield Examiner (death announced) on 19 5 1915.
IN THE MIDST OF LIFE WE ARE IN DEATH.

KRAMER Arthur – 4987 (later 241582) Private.
Born in Bradford on 15 3 1896 to John and Annie, of Moldgreen. Resided Moldgreen. Enlisted at Halifax in March, 1916.
2/5th Battalion DWR; reported missing, presumed killed, 03 5 1917, Battle of Bullecourt.
Commemorated – Arras Memorial, France; St Paul's Methodist Church, Dalton; Christ Church, Moldgreen; M Stansfield, page 270, and the **Drill Hall WM panel 7, column 1.**
Mentioned in the Goodall collection; the Huddersfield Examiner (reported missing, information requested by the family) on 05 6 1917; (reported missing, official casualty list) on 27 6 1917.

LABOURN Fred – 3790 Private.
Born in Childswell, Yorks. Resided in Batley. Enlisted at Mirfield.
1/5th Battalion DWR, A Company; died of wounds 17 6 1915, Ypres.
Buried – Merville Communal Cemetery, 2, K, 7.
Commemorated – Thiepval Memorial, France, and the **Drill Hall WM panel 7, column 2.**

LACY Arthur Harry – 2046 Private.
Born in Kingston on Thames. Resided in Scissett. Enlisted at Kirkburton.
1/5th Battalion DWR; killed in action 09 11 1915, Ypres.
Commemorated – Ypres (Menin Gate) Memorial, Belgium; Scisset WM; All Hallows Parish Church, Kirkburton, RoH; Emmanuel Church, Shelley, RoH; M Stansfield, page 271, and the **Drill Hall WM panel 7, column 2.**

LAMB Alexander Andrew – 16102 (later 242790) Private.
Born in Edinburgh. Resided and enlisted at Hull.
2/5th Battalion DWR, D Company; killed in action 03 5 1917, Battle of Bullecourt.
Commemorated – Arras Memorial, France, and the **Drill Hall WM panel 7, column 2.**
Mentioned in the Goodall collection.

LAMB Charles Archibald – 34445 Private.
Born in Sheffield. Enlisted at Sheffield.
5th Battalion DWR; killed in action 26 8 1918, Advance to Victory.
Buried – Gommecourt South Cemetery, 1, D, 1.
Commemorated – Thiepval Memorial, France, and the **Drill Hall WM panel 7, column 2.**

LANCASTER John Albert – 16783 Private.
Born in Newcastle upon Tyne, to William and Mary Ann. Resided in Newcastle. Enlisted at Elswick upon Tyne.
1/5th Battalion DWR; killed in action 06 10 1917, aged 20.
Commemorated – Tyne Cot Memorial, Belgium, and the **Drill Hall WM panel 7, column 2.**

LANGRICK Charles Lindley – 1939 Private.
Born in Barrow in Furness to Benjamin and Marion Thirza, of Berry Brow. Resided in Berry Brow. Enlisted at Huddersfield. Pre war Territorial and mobilised 04 8 1914. Embarked for France in April, 1915.
1/5th Battalion DWR; wounded in action by a sniper on 22 8 1915. Died of wounds at 17 Casualty Clearing Station, Remy Sidings, on 23 8 1915, aged 20, Ypres.
Buried – Lijssenthoek Military Cemetery, 3, C, 25.
Commemorated – Armitage Bridge WM; M Stansfield, pages xv-xvi & 271, and the **Drill Hall WM panel 7, column 2.**
Mentioned in the Huddersfield Examiner (shot in neck) on 26 8 1915; (published last letter home) on 01 9 1915.
HIS MEMORY IS EVER BLESSED.

LAWRENCE Matthew – 2399 Private.
Born in Tadcaster on 15 2 1892. Resided Huddersfield. Enlisted at Huddersfield. Pre war Territorial and mobilised in August, 1914. Embarked for France and Flanders in April, 1915
1/5th Battalion DWR; killed in action, sniper, at La Bassee, on 23 8 1915, Ypres.
Commemorated – Ypres (Menin Gate) Memorial, Belgium: St Thomas' Church, Longroyd Bridge RoH; M Stansfield, page 272, and the **Drill Hall WM panel 7, column 2.**

LAWSON George – 19651 Private.
Born in Skipton to William and Jane. Resided in Skipton. Enlisted at Barnoldswick.
2/5th Battalion DWR; died of wounds 04 6 1917, aged 22.

Buried – Etaples Military, 25, G, 14.
Commemorated – Barnoldswick WM (name added 2013); and the **Drill Hall WM panel 7, column 2.**
Mentioned in P Thompson, pages 125 & 131.
EVER REMEMBERED.

LAWTON Cyril – 3305 Private.
Born in Huddersfield to Thomas Henry and Mary Anne, of Gledholt. Resided in Huddersfield. Enlisted at Huddersfield October, 1914.
1/5th Battalion DWR; wounded in action (shot in head by sniper) and died of wounds the same day in the Brigade Field Ambulance Dressing Station on 7 8 1915, aged 20, Ypres.
Buried – Ferme Olivier Cemetery, 1, H, 2.
Commemorated – All Saints Church, Paddock, RoH (now located in Huddersfield Drill Hall); on parents' headstone, Edgerton Cemetery; M Stansfield, page 272, and the **Drill Hall WM panel 7, column 2.**

LAWTON William – 241369 Private.
Born in Huddersfield to Sam, of Brockholes. Resided in Brockholes. Enlisted at Huddersfield October, 1915. Embarked for France and Flanders in early 1916.
1/5th Battalion DWR; reported missing (presumed killed) on 03 9 1916, aged 20, Battle of the Somme (Thiepval).
Commemorated – Thiepval Memorial, France, Brockholes WM; Honley WM; C Ford, pages 9, 11 & 24; M Stansfield, page 273, and the **Drill Hall WM panel 7, column 2.**
Mentioned in the Huddersfield Examiner (missing in action) on 15 9 1916; (reported missing, now reported killed in action 03 9 1916, by shellfire) on 26 1 1917.

LEADBEATER Luke Clegg – 26576 Private.
Born in Newcastle upon Tyne, to Luke and Sarah Elizabeth. Resided in Dewsbury Enlisted at Dewsbury.
1/5th Battalion DWR; killed in action, by shellfire, on 22 11 1917, aged 19.
Buried – Aeroplane Cemetery, 2, A, 23.
Commemorated – the **Drill Hall WM panel 7, column 2.**
Mentioned in D Tattersfield, pages 247 & 385, with photo.
UNTIL THE DAY BREAKS.

LEDGER Cyril – 3904 (later 241038) Corporal.
Born and Enlisted at Doncaster.
2/5th Battalion DWR; died of wounds at home 01 7 1918, aged 21.
Buried – Doncaster Old Cemetery, C, 383.
Commemorated – the **Drill Hall WM panel 7, column 2.**
Mentioned in the Goodall collection.
SDGW shows number as 241033.

LEE George – 1985 Private.
Born in Batley. Married to Agnes and resided in Holywell Green. Enlisted at Huddersfield.
1/5th Battalion DWR; killed in action 04 11 1915, aged 22, Ypres.
Buried – Bard Cottage Cemetery, 1, D, 24.
Commemorated – St Bartholomew's Church, Meltham, RoH; St Andrew's Church, Stainland RoH; M Stansfield, page 274, and the **Drill Hall WM panel 7, column 2.**
HE SLEEPS WITH THE GLORIOUS DEAD WHO DIED THAT WE MIGHT LIVE.

LEE Leonard – 240220 Corporal.

Born in Huddersfield on 21 9 1895 to John William and Emma, of Huddersfield. Resided in Huddersfield. Pre war territorial, enlisted in 1913. Mobilised in August, 1914, and embarked for France and Flanders in April, 1915.
1/5th Battalion DWR, A Company, reported missing, presumed killed, 03 9 1916, aged 21, Battle of the Somme (Thiepval).
Commemorated – Thiepval Memorial, France; M Stansfield, page 275, and the **Drill Hall WM panel 7, column 2.**

LEE Stephen Margill (probably Hargill) – 240076 Sergeant. Distinguished Conduct Medal and Bar.
Born on 25 5 1894 in Marsh, Huddersfield, to Henry and Ada. Resided Marsh. Enlisted 04 8 1914.
1/5th Battalion DWR; killed in action 07 11 1918, aged 24, Advance to Victory – at Mecquignies, near Maubeuge.
Buried – Maubeuge Centre Cemetery, B, 17.
Commemorated – Holy Trinity Church, Huddersfield, RoH; M Stansfield, page 275, and the **Drill Hall WM panel 7, column 2.**
Mentioned in Magnus, the medal roll pages 250 & 293; the Unit War Diary, on 30 1 1918 and 31 1 1919; the Huddersfield Examiner (died of wounds) on 21 11 1918; (DCM awards) on 05 2 1919 & 13 3 1919; the London Gazette (award of DCM) on 17 4 1918, page 4673; (Bar to DCM), on 02 12 1919, page 41814 (posthumously).
SDGW shows date of death as 05 11 1918. CWGC shows Stephen Hargill.
GOD REMEMBERS WHEN THE WORLD FORGETS.

LEEMING John Thomas – 18904 Private.
Born in West Bradford, Lancs, to David and Ruth. Enlisted at Clitheroe.
5th Battalion DWR; killed in action 22 7 1916, aged 22, Battle of Tardenois.
Buried – Marfaux British Cemetery, 10, G, 5.
Commemorated –the **Drill Hall WM panel 7, column 2.**
LEAD THOU ME ON.

LEESON Herbert – 24331 Private.
Born in Bridlington, to George and Emma, of Buckton. Resided in Bempton. Enlisted at Bridlington.
1/5th Battalion DWR; killed in action 08 10 1917, aged 23, 3rd Battle of Ypres (Passchendael).
Buried – Tyne Cot Cemetery, 35, G, 7.
Commemorated – the **Drill Hall WM panel 7, column 2.**
Formerly 24633 York and Lancaster Regiment.

LEGGETT Arthur – 5936 Private.
Born in Bradford, to Jesse and Mary. Enlisted at Bradford.
1/5th Battalion DWR; killed in action 09 8 1916, aged 22, Battle of the Somme.
Commemorated – Thiepval Memorial, France, and the **Drill Hall WM panel 7, column 2.**

LEMON Hubert – 3355 (later 240699) Private.
Born in Huddersfield on 16 11 1898 to Peter and Mary. Enlisted at Huddersfield in November, 1914.
2/5th Battalion DWR; died of wounds 05 5 1917, Battle of Bullecourt.
Buried – Sauchy Lestree Communal Cemetery, 1, A.
Commemorated – M Stansfield, page 276, and the **Drill Hall WM panel 7, column 2.**
Mentioned in the Goodall collection; the Huddersfield Examiner (reported missing) on 04 6 1917; (reported missing, official casualty list) on 27 6 1917; (reported as having died as a Prisoner of War, in Germany) in 1917 [*buried in an area of France held by the Germans in 1917*].

LEWIS Arthur Frederick – 1592 (1952?) Corporal.

Born Halifax. Resided in Kirkburton, the husband of Harriet. Enlisted at Kirkburton. Embarked for France and Flanders in August, 1915.
1/5th Battalion DWR; wounded on 17 9 1916, and died of wounds at Etaples Base Hospital on 24 9 1916, aged 31, Battle of the Somme.
Buried – Etaples Military Cemetery, 11, A, 12A.
Commemorated – Kirkburton WM (G Company); All Hallows Parish Church, Kirkburton, RoH; M Stansfield, page 277, and the **Drill Hall WM panel 7, column 2.**
CWGC shows number as 1952.
LOVED HONOURED AND MOURNED.

LEWIS Fred – 17082 Private.
Born in Northampton, to William. Resided with his wife, Kate Howse Lewis, in Northampton. Enlisted at Northampton.
1/5th Battalion DWR; killed in action 08 10 1917, aged 26, Ypres.
Commemorated – Tyne Cot Memorial, Belgium, and the **Drill Hall WM panel 7, column 2.**
Formerly 2836 Army Service Corps.

LEWIS Willie – 4915 (later 241519) Private.
Born in Huddersfield on 07 8 1885 to George. Resided in Huddersfield, the husband of Edith. Enlisted in Huddersfield in February, 1916.
2/5th Battalion DWR; reported missing, presumed killed, on 03 5 1917, Battle of Bullecourt.
Commemorated – Arras Memorial, France; Deighton United Methodist Chapel RoH; Huddersfield Corporation RoH, M Stansfield, page 277, and the **Drill Hall WM panel 7, column 2.**
Mentioned in the Goodall collection; the Huddersfield Examiner (officially reported missing, killed by a sniper) on 12 6 1917; (reported missing, official casualty list) on 27 6 1917.

LIDDLE T – Private.
No trace.
Commemorated – the **Drill Hall WM panel 7, column 3.**

LINCOLN Albert Arthur – 34444 Private.
Born in Grangetown, Middlesbrough. Resided in Warrenby. Enlisted at Middlesbrough.
5th Battalion DWR; killed in action 15 9 1918, aged 24, Advance to Victory.
Buried – Hermies Hill British Cemetery, 2, A, 18.
Commemorated – the **Drill Hall WM panel 7, column 3.**

LINGARD Walter – 31552 Private.
Born in Boothtown, Halifax. Enlisted at Bradford.
5th Battalion DWR; killed in action 22 7 1918, Battle of Tardenois.
Buried – Marfaux British Cemetery, 8, E, 9.
Commemorated – the **Drill Hall WM panel 7, column 2.**

LISTER Frank Jessop – 2761 Private.
Born in Huddersfield on 13 4 1894 to Captain Albert Edward (also 5 DWR) and Elizabeth Jane, of Huddersfield. Resided at Moldgreen. Enlisted in Huddersfield in August, 1914. Embarked for France and Flanders in April, 1915.
1/5th Battalion DWR; wounded in action, GSW to both thighs on 02 7 1916 and died of wounds at No 2 Stationary Hospital, Abbeville, on 06 7 1916, aged 22, Battle of the Somme.
Buried – Abbeville Communal Cemetery, 4, F, 16.
Commemorated – Almondbury WM; M Stansfield, page 279, and the **Drill Hall WM panel 7, column 2.**
Mentioned in the Huddersfield Examiner (died of wounds) on 10 7 1916.

LISTER Joseph – 205365 Private.

Born Bradford. Resided in Bradford. Enlisted at Bradford on 15 6 1917.
2/5th Battalion DWR, D Company; wounded in action 20 11 1917 and died of wounds on 22 11 1917, Battle of Cambrai.
Buried – Rocquigny-Equancourt Road Cemetery, 2, D, 14.
Commemorated – Mirfield WM and the **Drill Hall WM panel 7, column 2.**
Mentioned in the Goodall collection.

LISTER Norman – 202882 Private.
Born in Wyke, Bradford, to John and Hannah. Enlisted at Wyke.
2/5th Battalion DWR; killed in action 28 11 1917, aged 21, Battle of Cambrai.
Buried – Abbeville Communal Cemetery Extension, 3, E, 18.
Commemorated – the **Drill Hall WM panel 7, column 2.**

LITTLE A - Private.
No trace.
Commemorated – the **Drill Hall WM panel 7, column 3.**

LITTLEWOOD Allan – 240737 Private.
Born in Brighouse. Enlisted at Mirfield.
1/5th Battalion DWR; killed in action 03 9 1916, Battle of the Somme (Thiepval).
Commemorated – Mirfield WM; Thiepval Memorial, France, and the **Drill Hall WM panel 7, column 2.**

LITTLEWOOD Frank – 5406 (241936) Private.
Born in Huddersfield, son of Mrs Green, of Paddock. Resided in Halifax. Enlisted at Huddersfield.
2/5th Battalion DWR; killed in action 03 5 1917, Battle of Bullecourt.
Commemorated – Arras Memorial, France; M Stansfield, page 280, and the **Drill Hall WM panel 7, column 3.**
Mentioned in the Huddersfield Examiner (reported missing, information requested by family) on 12 6 1917; (reported missing, official casualty list) on 27 6 1917; (previously reported missing, now reported killed in action) on 04 10 1917; (memoriam notice) on 03 5 1921.
Stepbrother of 24122 Norman Green, 8 DWR, also killed in action, at Langemark, on 11 8 1917.

LITTLEWOOD W – Private.
No trace in DWR.
Possibly Private 19220 Private William Littlewood, 10th Battalion York and Lancaster Regiment, formerly 16687 Private King's Own Yorkshire Light Infantry.
Born Emley, enlisted at Barnsley.
10 York and Lancaster Regiment; killed in action 09 2 1916, aged 26, Ypres.
Buried – Rue David Military Cemetery, 1, H, 32.
Commemorated – Emley WM, M Stansfield, page 280, and the **Drill Hall WM panel 7, column 3.**

LLEWELLYN William – 204642 Private.
Born in London. Resided in Bradford. Enlisted at Bradford.
10th Battalion DWR; died of wounds 21 9 1917, Ypres.
Buried – Lijssenthoek Military Cemetery, 23, D, 8A.
Commemorated – the **Drill Hall WM panel 7, column 3.**
Mentioned in the Tunstill's Men Blog – tunstillsmen.blogspot.com.

LOADER George – 2356 (later 240235) Private.
Born in Mirfield. Enlisted at Mirfield, pre war territorial, H Company, and volunteered for foreign service.
2/5th Battalion DWR, D Company; killed in action 03 5 1917, Battle of Bullecourt.

Commemorated – Arras Memorial, France; R Leedham, page 115, and the **Drill Hall WM panel 7, column 3.**
Mentioned in the Goodall collection; the Dewsbury Reporter (reported missing on the same day as his cousin Arthur Loader, serving with 2 DWR) on 30 6 1917 & 16 3 1918 & 23 3 1918.

LOBLEY William Jennings – 306595 Corporal.
Resided in Bradford. Enlisted at Halifax.
5th Battalion DWR; killed in action 23 7 1918, aged 22, Battle of Tardenois.
Buried – Sezanne Communal Cemetery, B, 3.
Commemorated – Arras Memorial, France, and the **Drill Hall WM panel 7, column 3.**
TILL WE MEET AGAIN.

LOCKWOOD John Edward – 4601 (later 241381) Lance Corporal.
Resided in Huddersfield. Enlisted at Huddersfield in November, 1915.
2/5th Battalion DWR; reported missing, presumed killed, 03 5 1917, Battle of Bullecourt.
Commemorated – Arras Memorial, France; M Stansfield, page 282, and the **Drill Hall WM panel 7, column 3.**
Mentioned in the Huddersfield Examiner (official casualty list) on 27 6 1917.
Electronic image of 'Death Penny' held in DWR Archives.

LOCKWOOD Thomas – 240734 Private.
Born in Brockholes. Resided in Huddersfield. Enlisted at Holmfirth in November, 1914.
Embarked for France and Flanders in April, 1915.
1/5th Battalion DWR; killed in action 03 9 1916, Battle of the Somme.
Buried – Mill Road Cemetery, 9, C, 7.
Commemorated – Brockholes WM; Thurstonland WM; J Fisher, page 110; M Stansfield, page 283, and the **Drill Hall WM panel 7, column 3.**
Mentioned in the Huddersfield Examiner (reported missing) on 05 10 1916; (previously reported missing, now reported killed in action, shellfire) on 26 1 1917.

LODGE Harold – 241083 Lance Corporal.
Born in Holmfirth to John. Resided in Holmfirth. Enlisted at Huddersfield in March, 1915.
Embarked for France and Flanders in June, 1916.
2/5th Battalion DWR; reported missing, presumed killed, 03 5 1917, Battle of Bullecourt.
Commemorated – Arras Memorial, France; Holme Valley Memorial Hospital WM (plaque 2, Underbank & Cartworth); M Stansfield, page 284, and the **Drill Hall WM panel 7, column 3.**
Mentioned in the Huddersfield Examiner (previously reported missing, now reported killed in action, official casualty list) on 30 10 1917.

LODGE William – 2351 (later 240233) Private.
Born in Farnley Tyas to Fred of Almondbury.
2/5th Battalion DWR; killed in action 03 5 1917, aged 20, Battle of Bullecourt.
Commemorated – Arras Memorial, France; Almondbury WM; Farnley Tyas WM (erected in 2014); M Stansfield, page 285, and the **Drill Hall WM panel 7, column 3.**

LONG Ernest – 5935 Private.
Born in Yeadon to Caleb and Mary Alice, of Yeadon. Enlisted at Yeadon.
1/5th Battalion DWR; killed in action 05 7 1916, aged 20, Battle of the Somme.
Buried – Puchevillers Cemetery, 1, C, 35.
Commemorated – the **Drill Hall WM panel 7, column 3.**
GOD'S WILL BE DONE.

LONGLEY E M – Private.
No trace, possibly Private Longley E H, 1/4th Battalion DWR.

Commemorated – the **Drill Hall WM panel 7, column 3.**

LOVELL T – Private.
No trace.
Commemorated – the **Drill Hall WM panel 7, column 3.**

LOWDEN Thomas – 35641 Private.
Born in Benwell, Northumberland, to James and Rose Hannah, of Wallsend. Enlisted at Stanley.
5th Battalion DWR; killed in action 13 9 1918, aged 20, Advance to Victory.
Buried – Hermies Hill British Cemetery, 2, E, 23.
Commemorated – the **Drill Hall WM panel 7, column 3.**
Formerly 76128 West Yorkshire Regiment.
CWGC shows spelling as LOWDON.
DEATH DIVIDES, MEMORY CLINGS.

LOWERY Thomas – 16079 (later 242768) Private.
Born in Leeds, to Ellen, of New Wortley. Resided in Hull. Enlisted at Hull.
2/5th Battalion DWR, D Company, killed in action 03 5 1917, aged 34, Battle of Bullecourt.
Commemorated – Arras Memorial, France, and the **Drill Hall WM panel 7, column 3.**
Mentioned in the Goodall collection.

LUCAS Joseph – 2555 Lance Sergeant.
Born in Dalton on 27 6 1892 to Frederick Arthur and Clara. Resided in Dalton. Pre war Territorial in Huddersfield. Mobilised on 04 8 1914.
1/5th Battalion DWR; killed in action, rifle bullet, 01 8 1915, aged 23, Ypres.
Buried – Bard Cottage Cemetery, 1, B, 22.
Commemorated – Christ Church, Moldgreen, RoH,; St Andrew's Church, Moldgreen, RoH; M Stansfield, page 287, and the **Drill Hall WM panel 7, column 3.**
Mentioned in the Huddersfield Examiner (shot in head) on 04 8 1915.

LUCAS Reginald Victor – 26465 Private.
Born in Highcliffe, Hants. Resided with his wife, Jessie Lillian, in Winchester. Enlisted at Winchester.
2/5th Battalion DWR; killed in action 21 11 1917, aged 28, Battle of Cambrai.
Commemorated – Cambrai Memorial (Louverval), France, and the **Drill Hall WM panel 7, column 3.**

LUCY James – 2424 Private.
Born in Paddington. Resided at Lowtown, Kirkburton. Enlisted at Kirkburton.
1/5th Battalion DWR; killed in action, sniper, 09 11 1915, Ypres.
Commemorated – Ypres (Menin Gate) Memorial, Belgium; Kirkburton WM (G Company); All Hallows Parish Church, Kirkburton, RoH; M Stansfield, page 287, and the **Drill Hall WM panel 7, column 3.**

LUGSDEN Amos – 17408 Private.
Enlisted at Luton.
5th Battalion DWR; killed in action 20 7 1918, Battle of Tardenois.
Buried – Marfaux British Cemetery, 7, A, 7.
Commemorated – the **Drill Hall WM panel 7, column 3.**
Originally 2/5th DWR.

LUKER Percy Alfred – 6849 Private.
Born in Marylebone. Resided with his wife, Tilly, in Paddington. Enlisted at Hampstead.
1/5th Battalion DWR; killed in action 14 11 1916, aged 26, Battle of the Somme.

Buried – Foncquevillers Military Cemetery, 1, J, 29.
Commemorated – the **Drill Hall WM panel 7, column 3.**
IN EVER LOVING MEMORY OF MY DARLING HUSBAND – TILLY.

LUMSDALE John – 34447 Private. Military Medal.
Born in Bishop Auckland. Resided in South Shields with his wife, Alice. Enlisted at South Shields.
5th Battalion DWR; killed in action 27 8 1917, aged 35.
Buried – Mory Abbey Military Cemetery, 5, A, 7.
Commemorated – the **Drill Hall WM panel 7, column 3.**
Military Medal award announced in the London Gazette dated 13 9 1918, page 10768.

LYONS Edward – 16857 Private.
Born in Newcastle upon Tyne, to William and Aliza, of Benwell, Newcastle. Resided in Newcastle upon Tyne. Enlisted at Elswick.
1/5th Battalion DWR; killed in action 09 10 1917, aged 24, Ypres.
Commemorated – Tyne Cot Memorial, Belgium, and the **Drill Hall WM panel 7, column 3.**

MACDONALD Josiah – 4212 Private.
Resided in Liversedge with his wife, Frances Elizabeth, of Hartshead. Resided in Liversedge. Enlisted at Huddersfield.
1/5th Battalion DWR; killed in action 03 9 1916, aged 25, Battle of the Somme (Thiepval).
Commemorated – Thiepval Memorial, France, and the **Drill Hall WM panel 7, column 4.**

MACKENZIE Erik George – 2nd Lieutenant.
Born in Chatham in 1884. Resided in London with his wife, Marion, married in 1909. Embarked for France and Flanders on 21 9 1914 as a Private soldier in the Army Service Corps. Commissioned into the West Yorkshire Regiment on 30 10 1917 and was attached to the 5th Battalion on 13 1 1918.
5th Battalion DWR; reported missing in action on 20 1 1918. Later reported as wounded in action and taken prisoner of war. Reported Prisoner of War by Cox and Co, Bankers, and repatriated 17 12 1918.
Commemorated – the **Drill Hall WM panel 8, column 1.**
Mentioned in the Goodall collection; the 62nd Division History (missing in action) page 194; Unit War Diary (shot) on 20 1 1918.
From MS/3650 Army Service Corps, then West Yorkshire Regiment.

MACKENZIE James – 4458 Private.
Born to Daniel and Frances. Resided in Liverpool. Enlisted at Huddersfield.
1/5th Battalion DWR; died of wounds 05 9 1916, aged 38, Battle of the Somme.
Buried – Puchevillers British Cemetery, 4, A, 32.
Commemorated – the **Drill Hall WM panel 8, column 1.**

MACKMAN Arthur – 3738 (later 240929) Private.
Born in Pinchbeck, Lincs, on 19 1 1896 to Samuel and Betsy, of Birkby. Resided in Huddersfield. Enlisted at Huddersfield in January, 1915.
2/5th Battalion DWR; killed in action 03 5 1917, aged 21, Battle of Bullecourt.
Commemorated – Arras Memorial, France: Fartown and Birkby WM; M Stansfield, page 290, and the **Drill Hall WM panel 7, column 4.**
Mentioned in the Goodall collection; the Huddersfield Examiner (reported missing, official casualty list) on 27 6 1917.

MACKWELL Charles – 29462 Private.
Son of Joseph and Emma. Husband of Mary Ellen, of Denholme. Enlisted at Keighley.

5th Battalion DWR; killed in action 21 7 1918, aged 35, Battle of Tardenois.
Commemorated – Soissons Memorial, France, and the **Drill Hall WM panel 7, column 4.**
Originally 2/5th DWR.

MADDEYS Henry – 242520 Private.
Born, resided and enlisted at Great Yarmouth.
1/6th Battalion DWR; killed in action 13 4 1918, aged 22, German Spring Offensive.
Commemorated – Tyne Cot Memorial, Belgium, and the **Drill Hall WM panel 7, column 4.**
Mentioned in S Barber (reported missing, presumed killed, 13 4 1918) page 177.
CWGC shows second forename as Arthur.

MALLINSON Percy – 205417 Private.
Born, resided and enlisted at Bradford.
5th Battalion DWR; killed in action 10 4 1918, German Spring Offensive.
Buried – Douchy les Ayette Cemetery, 2, E, 20.
Commemorated – the **Drill Hall WM panel 7, column 4.**

MALONE Patrick – 3031 Corporal.
Born in Turnbridge, Huddersfield, on 19 5 1891. Resided in Huddersfield with his wife, Mary. Enlisted at Huddersfield in August. 1914.
1/5th Battalion DWR; wounded in action, gunshot to wrist and thigh, on 21 3 1916. Died of wounds at 29 Casualty Clearing Station, Gezaincourt, on 26 3 1916.
Buried – Gezaincourt Communal Cemetery, 1, A, 9.
Commemorated – M Stansfield, page 291, and the **Drill Hall WM panel 7, column 4.**

MALTBY Hubert – 308155 Private.
Resided and enlisted at Long Eaton, Derbyshire.
5th Battalion DWR; killed in action 29 7 1918, Battle of Tardenois.
Commemorated – Soissons Memorial, France, and the **Drill Hall WM panel 7, column 4.**
Originally 2/5th DWR.

MANCHESTER Leonard – 32158 Private.
Born in Meltham to James and Hannah. Resided in Meltham with his wife, Hilda. Enlisted at Huddersfield on 06 8 1917. Embarked for France and Flanders in early 1918.
5th Battalion DWR, D Company; killed in action 27 3 1918, aged 28, German Spring Offensive.
Commemorated – Arras Memorial, France; St Mary's Church, Wilshaw, stone memorial; St Bartholomew's Church, Meltham, RoH; M Stansfield, page 291, and the **Drill Hall WM panel 7, column 4.**
Mentioned in the Goodall collection;
Originally 2/5th DWR.

MANN John Nelson – 4974 (later 241751) Private.
Born in Farsley. Resided in Calverley. Enlisted at Bradford.
2/5th Battalion DWR; killed in action 20 11 1917, Battle of Cambrai.
Commemorated – Cambrai Memorial (Louverval), France, and the **Drill Hall WM panel 7, column 4.**
Mentioned in the Goodall collection.

MANNING Frederick Thomas – 26292 Private.
Born in Helmingham, Suffolk, to Thomas and Emily of Stowmarket, Suffolk. Enlisted in Ipswich.
5th Battalion DWR; died of wounds 28 3 1918, aged 21, German Spring Offensive.
Buried – Doullens Communal Cemetery Extension, 5, D, 4.
Commemorated – the **Drill Hall WM panel 7, column 4.**
Formerly 13923 Army Service Corps.

DEEPLY MOURNED, SADLY MISSED, FROM MOTHER, FATHER, SISTERS AND BROTHERS.

MANUEL James – 307780 Private.
Born in Beeston, Leeds. Resided in Leeds. Enlisted at Mirfield.
1/5th Battalion DWR; killed in action 09 10 1917, Ypres.
Commemorated – Tyne Cot Memorial, Belgium, and the **Drill Hall WM panel 7, column 4.**

MARRIOTT Joseph George – 4944 (later 241543) Private.
Born in Mirfield, to Maud. Resided and enlisted at Mirfield.
2/5th Battalion DWR; killed in action 03 5 1917, aged 21, Battle of Bullecourt.
Commemorated – Arras Memorial, France; Mirfield WM and the **Drill Hall WM panel 7, column 4.**
Mentioned in the Goodall collection; the Huddersfield Examiner (reported missing, official casualty list) on 27 6 1917.

MARRIOTT James Leo – 40492 Private.
Born in Nottingham. Enlisted at Melby, Yorks.
5th Battalion DWR; killed in action 21 10 1918, Advance to Victory.
Buried – Delsaux Farm Cemetery, 2, D, 9.
Commemorated – the **Drill Hall WM panel 7, column 4.**

MARSH John William – 5433 (later 241957) Lance Corporal.
Born in Heeley. Resided in Sheffield. Enlisted at Sheffield.
2/5th Battalion DWR; killed in action 03 5 1917, Battle of Bullecourt.
Commemorated – Arras Memorial, France, and the **Drill Hall WM panel 7, column 4.**
Mentioned in the Goodall collection.

MARSHALL Ernest – 241626 Private.
Born in Gosburton, Lincs. Resided and enlisted at Spalding, Lincs.
2/5th Battalion DWR; killed in action 08 8 1917.
Buried – Grevillers British Cemetery, 6, C, 17.
Commemorated – the **Drill Hall WM panel 7, column 4.**

MARSHALL Joseph – 240785 Lance Corporal.
Born in Birkby on 17 7 1897 to John and Clara of Grimescar. Enlisted at Huddersfield in November, 1914.
2/5th Battalion DWR, C Company; reported missing, presumed killed, 03 5 1917, aged 20, Battle of Bullecourt.
Commemorated – Arras Memorial, France; Fartown and Birkby WM; St John's Church, Birkby, RoH; Huddersfield Parish Church RoH; Cowcliffe Wesleyan Church, RoH; M Stansfield, page 293, and the **Drill Hall WM panel 7, column 4.**
Mentioned in the Huddersfield Examiner (information requested by the family) on 14 6 1917; (reported missing, official casualty list) on 27 6 1917.

MARTIN Thomas – 24336 Private.
Born in Londesborough, to George and Selina. Resided in Londesborough. Enlisted at Beverley.
1/5th Battalion DWR; killed in action 27 8 1917, aged 21, Nieuport Sector.
Buried – Coxyde Military Cemetery, 3, C, 18.
Commemorated – the **Drill Hall WM panel 7, column 4.**
Formerly 38246 York and Lancaster Regiment.
HE NOBLY ANSWERED DUTY'S CALL, HIS LIFE HE GAVE FOR ONE AND ALL.

MARWOOD George Henry – 34491 Private.
Born in Norton, to William and Annie, of Middelsbrough. Enlisted at Middlesbrough.

5th Battalion DWR; killed in action 20 10 1918, aged 27, Advance to Victory.
Buried – Quivey Communal Cemetery Extension, C, 35.
Commemorated – the **Drill Hall WM panel 7, column 4.**
Originally 2/5th DWR.
HE SLEEPS WITH ENGLAND'S HEROES IN THE WATCHFUL CARE OF GOD.

MATHERS Sydney – 28793 (later 263025) Private.
Born in Skelmanthorpe to David and Alice. Resided in Skelmanthorpe. Enlisted at Huddersfield.
2/5th Battalion DWR; killed in action 03 5 1917, aged 21, Battle of Bullecourt.
Commemorated – Arras Memorial, France; St Aidan's Church, Skelmanthorpe, RoH; M Stansfield, page 294, and the **Drill Hall WM panel 7, column 4.**
Mentioned in the Goodall collection; the Huddersfield Examiner (previously reported missing, now reported killed in action) on 04 10 1917.

MATTHEWS Aquilla – 4517 Private.
Resided in Kirkburton. Enlisted in Huddersfield.
1/5th Battalion DWR; reported missing, presumed killed, 03 9 1916, Battle of the Somme (Thiepval).
Commemorated – Thiepval Memorial, France; All Hallows Parish Church, Kirkburton; M Stansfield, page 294, and the **Drill Hall WM panel 7, column 4.**

MATTHEWS Arthur William – 34458 Private.
Born in Fareham, Hants, to Arthur and Alice Mary, of Upper Chilcomb. Enlisted at Winchester.
5th Battalion DWR; killed in action 28 8 1918, aged 26, Advance to Victory.
Buried – Mory Abbey Military Cemetery, 5, A, 10.
Commemorated – the **Drill Hall WM panel 7, column 4.**
Formerly 42403 Yorkshire Regiment. Originally 2/5th DWR.
A PLACE IS VACANT IN OUR HOME WHICH NEVER CAN BE FILLED.

MATTHEWS John – 4073 Private.
Enlisted at Huddersfield.
1/5th Battalion DWR; died of wounds, at home, on 07 8 1916, Battle of the Somme.
Buried – Huddersfield (Lockwood) Cemetery, C, C, 654.
Commemorated – M Stansfield, page 295, and the **Drill Hall WM panel 7, column 4.**
Mentioned in the Huddersfield Examiner (died of wounds) on 11 9 1916.

MAY Ephraim – 3040 Private.
Born in Linthwaite. Resided in Dobcross with his wife, Eva. Enlisted at Huddersfield in 1914.
Embarked for France and Flanders in April, 1915.
1/5th Battalion DWR; killed in action, shellfire, 23 8 1915, aged 43, Ypres.
Commemorated – Ypres (Menin Gate) Memorial France; Linthwaite WM; M Stansfield, page 295, and the **Drill Hall WM panel 7, column 4.**

McAVOY John – 242330 Corporal.
Born in Birtley, Co Durham. Resided with his wife, Mary, in Birtley. Enlisted at Chester le Street.
1/5th Battalion DWR; reported missing 29 4 1918, aged 36, German Spring Offensive.
Commemorated – Tyne Cot Memorial, Belgium, and the **Drill Hall WM panel 7, column 4.**
Attached 1/4th Bn DWR.
Mentioned in the 4th DWR Casualty Record, AB 136, (originally buried at grid N.8.a.3.3, Map sheet 28) page 39, and also listed on unit documents as having been killed at grid reference Sheet 28, N.8.a.3.5, Erquinghem Lys, dated 03 5 1918.

McBRIDE William – 26240 Private.
Born Ayr. Enlisted at Ayr, Scotland, on 01 6 1916.

2/5th Battalion DWR, D Company; killed in action 28 9 1918, aged 33, Advance to Victory.
Buried – Grand Ravine British Cemetery, A, 11.
Commemorated – the **Drill Hall WM panel 7, column 4.**
Formerly 24211 Cameron Highlanders.
Mentioned in the Goodall collection.
THY PURPOSE LORD WE CANNOT SEE, BUT ALL IS WELL THAT IS DONE BY THEE.

McDERMOTT John James – 2658 Private.
Born in Sunderland, to James and Alice. Resided in Sunderland. Enlisted at Sunderland.
1/5th Battalion DWR; killed in action 03 1 1918, aged 19, Ypres.
Commemorated – Tyne Cot Memorial, Belgium, and the **Drill Hall WM panel 7, column 4.**

McDONALD Tom – 12667 Corporal.
Born in Heckmondwike, on 14 11 1894, to John and Clara. Enlisted at Huddersfield in September, 1914.
2/5th Battalion DWR; killed in action 27 11 1917, aged 23, Battle of Cambrai.
Commemorated – Cambrai Memorial (Louverval), France, M Stansfield, page 295, and the **Drill Hall WM panel 8, column 1.**

McEWAN J
No trace, possibly McEWAN C, below:
McEWAN Crawford – 4840 Private.
Born in West Bowling, Bradford, to William and Mary. Enlisted at Bradford.
1/5th Battalion DWR; killed in action 12 7 1916, aged 24, Battle of the Somme.
Buried – Aveluy Wood Cemetery, 1, D, 2.
Commemorated – Arras Memorial, France, and the **Drill Hall WM panel 8, column 1.**
ETERNAL REST GIVE UNTO HIM O LORD.

McGRATH Michael – 4533 Private.
Born in Huddersfield. Resided in Huddersfield. Enlisted at Huddersfield in September, 1915. Embarked for France and Flanders in May, 1916.
1/5th Battalion DWR; reported missing, presumed killed 03 9 1916, aged 35, Battle of the Somme (Thiepval).
Commemorated – Thiepval Memorial, France; Huddersfield Corporation RoH; M Stansfield, page 296, and the **Drill Hall WM panel 8, column 1.**
Mentioned in the Huddersfield Examiner (reported missing) on 05 10 1916.
M Stansfield shows his number as 45333.

McGREGOR James – 35115 Private.
Born in Southwick, Durham. Enlisted at Sunderland.
5th Battalion DWR; killed in action 29 9 1918, Advance to Victory.
Buried – Terlincthun British Cemetery, 4, D, 6.
Commemorated – the **Drill Hall WM panel 8, column 1.**
Formerly 12997 East Yorkshire Regiment.
FROM MEMORY'S PAGE I'LL NEVER BLOT TRUE LITTLE WORDS – FORGET ME NOT.

McGUIRE James – 238212 Private.
Resided in Wilton Park, Durham. Enlisted at Bishop Auckland.
5th Battalion DWR; killed in action 15 9 1918, Advance to Victory.
Buried – Hermies Hill British Cemetery, 2, A, 3.
Commemorated – Arras Memorial, France, and the **Drill Hall WM panel 8, column 1.**

McLAUGHLIN Alfred – 205640 Private.

Born in Cleator Moor, Cumberland, to Henry and Isabella. Resided in Ingleton. Enlisted at Keighley.
5th Battalion DWR; killed in action 25 8 1918, aged 22, Advance to Victory.
Buried – Gommecourt South Cemetery, 1, D, 4.
Commemorated – Ingleton WM; A Brooks; Craven's Part in the Great War, page 322, & the cpgw.org.uk website, with photo, and the **Drill Hall WM panel 8, column 1.**
MISSED MOST BY THOSE WHO LOVED HIM BEST.

McLINTOCH Arnold – Captain. Mention in Despatches.
Born in Marsden on 23 4 1885 to Doctor and Mrs M E McLintoch. Resided in Huddersfield.
Enlisted at the outbreak of war and was commissioned in October, 1914. Embarked for France and Flanders in April, 1915.
1/5th Battalion DWR, OC A Company; reported missing 03 9 1916, aged 31, Battle of the Somme.
Buried – Mill Road Cemetery, 13, C, 2.
Commemorated –Holy Trinity Church, Huddersfield, RoH, M Stansfield, page 296, and the **Drill Hall WM panel 7, column 4.**
Mentioned in Sir John French's Despatch of 15 10 1915, London Gazette dated 01 1 1916, and Sir Douglas Haig's Despatch of 30 4 1916, London Gazette dated 15 6 1916.
Mentioned in the Colne Valley Almanac; the Huddersfield Examiner, MID awarded, on 03 1 1916; reported missing, on 13 9 1916; previously reported missing now known as killed in action, on 31 1 1917; Will administered, £5,500.00 left to his mother, on 09 2 1917.
Mentions in the unit war diary for 31 12 1915; 30 1 1916; 30 6 1916; 03 9 1916; 30 9 1916;

McMANUS Robert (F?) – 26234 (26294?) Private.
Born in Dundee. Enlisted at Perth.
5th Battalion DWR; killed in action 25 3 1918, aged 32, German Spring Offensive.
Commemorated – Arras Memorial, France, and the **Drill Hall WM panel 8, column 1.**
SDGW has the number 26294. Formerly 086485 Army Service Corps. Originally 2/5th DWR.
CWGC shows Robert Fairweather.

MELLOR Alfred – 242926 Private.
Born in South Crosland. Resided in Netherton. Enlisted at Huddersfield.
5th Battalion DWR; killed in action 22 7 1918, Battle of Tardenois.
Commemorated – Soissons Memorial, France; South Crosland and Netherton RoH; M Stansfield, page 298, and the **Drill Hall WM panel 8, column 1.**
Originally 2/5th DWR.

MELLOR Arthur – 5020 (later 241610) Private.
Born in Hepworth to Joshua and Alice, of Hepworth. Resided in Holmfirth. Enlisted at Homlfirth on 13 3 1916.
2/5th Battalion DWR, D Company; reported missing, presumed killed, 03 5 1917, aged 23, Battle of Bullecourt.
Commemorated – Arras Memorial, France, The Holme Valley Memorial Hospital WM (plaque 6, Hepworth & Scholes); Hepworth Parish Church RoH; M Stansfield, page 298, and the **Drill Hall WM panel 8, column1.**
Mentioned in the Goodall collection.

MELLOR Clement – 5772 (later 242101) Private.
Born Honley, mother came from Netherton. Resided in Huddersfield. Enlisted at Huddersfield, Easter 1916.
1/5th Battalion DWR; reported missing, presumed killed, 03 9 1916, Battle of the Somme (Thiepval).
Commemorated – Thiepval Memorial, France; South Crosland and Netherton WM; M Stansfield, page 298, and the **Drill Hall WM panel 8, column 1.**

Mentioned in the Huddersfield Examiner (reported missing) on 04 10 1916.
Not on Honley WM.

MELLOR James Edward – 242024 Private.
Born in Holmfirth, to James. Resided in Holmbridge. Enlisted at Holmfirth.
1/5th Battalion DWR; killed in action 03 9 1916, aged 20, Battle of the Somme (Thiepval).
Commemorated – Thiepval Memorial, France; The Holme Valley Memorial Hospital WM, (plaques 1 & 2, Holme and Holmbridge), and the **Drill Hall WM panel 8, column 1.**
Mentioned in T Ashworth (killed on first day in trenches) page 87.

MELLOR Leonard – 6719 Private.
Born in Elland to Amelia. Enlisted at Elland.
1/5th Battalion DWR; died 30 10 1916, aged 20, Battle of the Somme.
Buried – Couin British Cemetery, 4, C, 19.
Commemorated – the **Drill Hall WM panel 8, column 1.**
Mentioned in the Huddersfield Examiner (November 1916 official casualty list) on 04 12 1916.
GONE BUT NOT FORGOTTEN.

MELLOR Milton – 2932 Private.
Born and resided in Greenfield. Enlisted at Huddersfield.
1/5th Battalion DWR; killed in action 07 11 1915, Ypres.
Commemorated – Ypres (Menin Gate) Memorial, Belgium, and the **Drill Hall WM panel 8, column 1.**
Mentioned in the Huddersfield Examiner (killed by sniper) on 16 11 1915.

MELLOR Ralph – 305821 Private.
Resided in Oldham. Enlisted at Milnsbridge.
5th Battalion DWR; killed in action 23 7 1918, Battle of Tardenois.
Buried – St Sever Cemetery Extension, Q, 3, J, 24.
Commemorated – the **Drill Hall WM panel 8, column 1.**
Mentioned in the Huddersfield Examiner (official casualty list) on 07 8 1916.
Originally 2/5th DWR.

MELLOR Squire – 306333 Private.
Resided in Oldham. Enlisted at Milnsbridge.
5th Battalion DWR; killed in action 20 7 1918.
Buried – Marfaux British Cemetery, 2, A, 4.
Commemorated – the **Drill Hall WM panel 8, column 1.**
Mentioned in the Huddersfield Examiner (official casualty list) on 11 8 1918.
Originally 2/5th. Possibility of also being Originally 2/7th DWR.

MELVILLE John – 2nd Lieutenant.
Son of William and Elizabeth, of Newlands, Glasgow.
2/5th Battalion DWR; killed in action 27 11 1917, aged 24, Battle of Cambrai.
Commemorated – Cambrai Memorial (Louverval), France, and the **Drill Hall WM panel 8, column 1.**
Mentioned in 62nd Division History (missing in action Cambrai) page 192; Unit War Diary (reported missing at Bourlon Wood) on 27 11 1917.

MEWETT William – 241180 Private.
Resided in Twickenham. Enlisted at Huddersfield.
5th Battalion DWR; killed in action 20 7 1918.
Buried – Courmas British Cemetery, 2, D, 4.
Commemorated – the **Drill Hall WM panel 8, column 1.**

Originally 2/5th DWR.

MICKLETHWAITE Arthur – 2083 Private.
Born in Kirkheaton. Enlisted at Mirfield in D Company, 2/5th DWR, but volunteered for foreign service and embarked for France and Flanders in April, 1915, with 1/5th DWR.
1/5th Battalion DWR; killed in action 09 5 1915, Fleurbaix Sector.
Buried – Rue David Military Cemetery, 1, H, 30.
Commemorated – Mirfield WM; M Stansfield, page 3001, and the **Drill Hall WM panel 8, column 1.**

MIDDLEBROOK Arthur William – 241675 Lance Corporal.
Born and resided in Swineshead, Lincs. Enlisted at Lincoln.
2/5th Battalion DWR; killed in action 16 3 1917.
Buried – Queens Cemetery, 3, E, 5.
Commemorated – the **Drill Hall WM panel 8, column 2.**

MIDGLEY Herbert – 241604 Private.
Born in Baildon, to Mary Ann. Resided in Baildon. Enlisted at Shipley.
2/5th Battalion DWR; killed in action 03 5 1917, aged 25, Battle of Bullecourt.
Commemorated – Arras Memorial, France, and the **Drill Hall WM panel 8, column 2.**

MILES Edward Thompson – 26584 Private.
Born in Ashington to Edward and Mary. Resided in Ashington. Enlisted at Morpeth.
1/5th Battalion DWR; killed in action 14 12 1917, aged 19, Ypres.
Buried – Nine Elms British Cemetery, 9, D, 15..
Commemorated – Ashington WM; the **Drill Hall WM panel 8, column 2.**
SAFE IN THE CARE OF THE LORD.

MILLER Samuel (C?) – 242703 Private.
Born in Chester. Resided and enlisted at Halifax.
1/4th Battalion DWR; killed in action 03 9 1916, Battle of the Somme (Thiepval).
Commemorated – Thiepval Memorial, France, and the **Drill Hall WM panel 8, column 1.**

MILNER John – 6536 Private.
Born in Southburn. Resided with his wife, Edith, in Driffield. Enlisted at Driffield.
1/5th Battalion DWR; killed in action 20 1 1917, aged 25.
Buried – Humbercamps Communal Cemetery Extension, 1, A, 14.
Commemorated – the **Drill Hall WM panel 8, column 2.**
THY WILL BE DONE.

MILNES Herbert – 241825 Private.
Born in Almondbury to J and Edith. Resided in Almondbury. Enlisted at Huddersfield on 24 3 1916.
2/5th Battalion DWR; reported missing, presumed killed 03 5 1917, Battle of Bullecourt.
Commemorated – Arras Memorial, France; Almondbury WM; M Stansfield, page 304, and the **Drill Hall WM panel 8, column 1.**

MILNES John Henry - 241407 Private.
Born in Huddersfield to James Henry and Annie. Enlisted at Huddersfield on 12 12 1915.
5th Battalion DWR, B Company; killed in action 05 11 1918, aged 23, Advance to Victory.
Buried – Frasnoy Communal Cemetery, A, 7.
Commemorated – St Mark's Parish Church, Longwood,; M Stansfield, page 304, and the **Drill Hall WM panel 8, column 1.**
M Stansfield shows initials as J R.

REST IN PEACE.

MILNES Stanley – 3407 Lance Corporal.
Born in Almondbury on 17 8 1896 to Mary Ormerod, of Huddersfield. Resided in Dalton. Enlisted at Huddersfield in December, 1914. Embarked for France and Flanders in April, 1915.
1/5th Battalion DWR; killed in action 04 7 1916, aged 19, Battle of the Somme.
Buried – Connaught Cemetery, 4, M, 7.
Commemorated – Almondbury WM; Headstone in Kirkheaton Cemetery; J Fisher, page 110; M Stansfield, page 304, the **Drill Hall WM panel 8, column 1.**
Mentioned in the Huddersfield Examiner, in memoriam, 03 7 1918 and 04 7 1919.
HE DIED FOR FREEDOM AND HONOUR.

MILSON Harold – 241639 Private.
Born, resided and enlisted at Barton on Humber. Stepson of John Gosling of Barton.
5th Battalion DWR, D Company; killed in action 06 11 1918, aged 23, Advance to Victory.
Buried – Fontaine au Bois Communal Cemetery, E, 8.
Commemorated – the **Drill Hall WM panel 8, column 2.**
Mentioned in the Goodall collection (left behind at Depot - undated).
Originally 2/5th Bn.

MITCHELL Ernest – 4513 Private.
Born in Holmfirth to George William and Emily, of Lockwood. Resided in Lockwood. Enlisted at Huddersfield in August, 1915. Embarked for France in May, 1916.
1/5th Battalion DWR; killed in action, shrapnel 31 7 1916, aged 20, Battle of the Somme.
Buried – Connaught Cemetery, 3, M, 10.
Commemorated – South Crosland and Netherton WM; Emmanuel Church, Lockwood, RoH; J Fisher, page 113; M Stansfield, page 305, and the **Drill Hall WM panel 8, column 2.**
Mentioned in the Huddersfield Examiner (official casualty list) on 06 9 1916; (killed in action, shrapnel) on 11 8 1916.

MITCHELL Fred – 31487 Private.
Born at Morton, Keighley. Resided with his wife, Georgina, in Morton. Enlisted at Keighley
5th Battalion DWR; killed in action 23 7 1918, aged 31, Advance to Victory.
Buried – Marfaux British Cemetery, 6, I, 7.
Commemorated – the **Drill Hall WM panel 8, column 2.**
Originally 1/5th Bn.
EVER REMEMBERED.

MITCHELL George Herbert – 3136 (later 240588) Corporal. Military Medal.
Born in Almondbury to George and Ruth. Resided in Almondbury. Enlisted at Huddersfield.
Embarked for France and Flanders in April, 1915.
1/5th Battalion DWR; killed in action 06 10 1917, aged 23, Ypres (Passchendaele).
Commemorated – Tyne Cot Memorial, Belgium; Almondbury WM; J Fisher, page 86; M Stansfield, page 305, and the **Drill Hall WM panel 8, column 2.**
Mentioned in the Goodall collection; the Huddersfield Examiner, award of Military Medal, on 04 10 1916; awarded MM, on 09 10 1916; memoriam notice, on 06 10 1920.
Award of Military Medal in London Gazette, dated 16 11 1916, page 11141.
Honoured by Brighouse Town Council.

MITCHELL Hubert Norman – 205602 Private.
Born and enlisted at Halifax.
5th Battalion DWR; killed in action 10 4 1918, Advance to Victory.
Buried – Douchy les Ayette Cemetery, 2, G, 17.
Commemorated – Calderdale War Dead, page 200, and the **Drill Hall WM panel 8, column 2.**

Originally 2/5th DWR.

MITCHELL James – 5750 Private.
Born in Clayton, to Harry and Ann. Enlisted at Halifax.
1/5th Battalion DWR; died of wounds 16 9 1916, aged 37, Battle of the Somme.
Buried – Clayton Chapelyard Cemetery, E, B, 3.
Commemorated – the **Drill Hall WM panel 8, column 2.**
WITH CHRIST WHICH IS FAR BETTER.

MOFFITT C – Private
No trace DWR.
Possibly 9th Battalion Kings Own Yorkshire Light Infantry?
Commemorated – the **Drill Hall WM panel 8, column 2.**

MONELLY Thomas - 300161 Private.
Born in Swinford, County Mayo, to James and Alice of Bradford. Resided and enlisted at Bradford.
5th Battalion DWR; killed in action 26 5 1918, aged 31, German Spring Offensive.
Buried – Beinvillers Military Cemetery, 20, C, 9.
Commemorated – the **Drill Hall WM panel 8, column 2.**
TO MEMORY EVER DEAR.

MOORE George – 242917 Private.
Enlisted at Hinckley, Leics.
1/5th Battalion DWR; killed in action 05 6 1917.
Buried – Rue Petillon Cemetery, 1, N, 46.
Commemorated – the **Drill Hall WM panel 8, column 2.**

MOORE John Clifford Dawson – 2nd Lieutenant.
Born in Keighley on 08 5 1896 to Emmanuel and Emma Elizabeth, of Keighley. Resided in Oakworth, Keighley. Embarked for France and Flanders as a Private soldier on 14 4 1915 and was promoted Lance Corporal. Commissioned into DWR.
5th Battalion DWR; died of wounds 20 7 1918, aged 22.
Buried – St Imoges Churchyard Cemetery, C, 10.
Commemorated – the **Drill Hall WM panel 8, column 2.**
Mentioned in the 5th DWR Unit War Diary, (died of wounds) on 31 7 1918; the 62nd Division History (died of wounds) page 201.
Originally 2579 (later 265628) 6th and 7th DWR.
BECAUSE I LIVE YE SHALL LIVE ALSO

MORGAN James Cornelius – 3098 (later 240572) Lance Corporal.
Born in Burton on Trent, Staffs, on 11 1 1893 to John and Bridget, of Huddersfield. Resided and enlisted at Huddersfield on 04 9 1914.
2/5th Battalion DWR C Company; reported missing, presumed killed, 03 5 1917, aged 24, Battle of Bullecourt.
Commemorated – Arras Memorial, France; M Stansfield, page 310, and the **Drill Hall WM panel 8, column 2.**
Mentioned in the Goodall collection; the Huddersfield Examiner, information requested by the family, on 05 6 1917; official casualty list, on 27 6 1917.

MORGAN William Henry – 238187 Corporal.
Enlisted at Middlesbrough.
5th Battalion DWR; killed in action 27 8 1918, Advanced to Victory.
Buried – Mory Abbey Military Cemetery, 5, A, 5.

Commemorated – the **Drill Hall WM panel 8, column 2.**
Originally 2/5th DWR.

MORRELL Gill – 267210 Private.
Born in Keighley.
1/5th Battalion DWR; killed in action 16 8 1917, Ypres.
Buried – Coyde Military Cemetery, 2, J, 6.
Commemorated – the **Drill Hall WM panel 8, column 2.**
Mentioned in Swaledale and Wharfedale Remembered, page 209.

MORRIS Fred – 7035 Private.
Born in Kirby Hill, Yorks. Resided at Langthorpe, Yorks. Enlisted at Kirby Hill.
1/5th Battalion DWR; killed in action 13 10 1916, Battle of the Somme.
Buried – Humbercamps Communal Cemetery Extension 1, C, 3.
Commemorated – the **Drill Hall WM panel 8, column 1.**
Formerly 24526 Yorkshire Regiment.

MORRIS F – Private.
No trace, probably a duplicate of 7035 Private F Morris on the previous column.
Commemorated – the **Drill Hall WM panel 8, column 2.**

MORRISON Harry – 3116 Private
Born in Huddersfield in October, 1895 to Ernest and Mary of Fartown. Resided at Fartown.
Enlisted at Huddersfield on his 19th birthday, in October 1914. Embarked for France and Flanders in April, 1915.
1/5th Battalion DWR, A Company; killed in action 03 7 1916, aged 20, Battle of the Somme.
Buried – Connaught Cemetery, 13, B, 3
Commemorated – Fartown and Birkby WM; Christ Church, Woodhouse Hill, RoH; J Fisher, page 110; M Stansfield, page 311, and the **Drill Hall WM panel 8, column 2.**
Mentioned in the Huddersfield Examiner, killed in action, on 24 7 1916; in memoriam, on 03 7 1916 and 03 7 1919.
SDGW shows his number as 3119.

MORTON Ernest – 40207 Private.
Born in Mirfield, to Fred and Mary Ellen. Enlisted at Halifax.
2/5th Battalion DWR; killed in action 28 9 1918, aged 21, Advance to Victory.
Buried – Ruyalcourt Military Cemetery, N, 22.
Commemorated – Mirfield WM and the **Drill Hall WM panel 8, column 2.**
REST IN PEACE.

MOSLEY Arnold – 5353 (later 241890) Lance Corporal.
Born in Shepley to Fred. Resided Shepley. Enlisted at Huddersfield on 03 10 1914.
2/5th Battalion DWR, D Company; reported missing, presumed killed in action, 03 5 1917, Battle of Bullecourt.
Commemorated – Arras Memorial, France; Shepley WM; M Stansfield, page 312, and the **Drill Hall WM panel 8, column 2.**
Mentioned in the Goodall collection; the Huddersfield Examiner, reported missing, on 07 6 1917.

MOSLEY Percy – 2nd Lieutenant.
Born in Shepley to John, of Shepley. Joined the Battalion on 13 1 1918.
5th Battalion DWR; killed in action 28 3 1918, aged 24, German Spring Offensive.
Commemorated – Arras Memorial, France; Shepley WM; M Stansfield, page 312, and the **Drill Hall WM panel 8, column 2.**

Mentioned in the Goodall collection; the 62nd Divisional History, page 196; the Unit war Diary, killed in action, on 31 3 1918.

MOSS Ralph Sunderland – 1917 Private.
Born in Hebden Bridge on 07 10 1893 to Charles Walter and Elizabeth of Moldgreen. Pre war Territorial and mobilised on the outbreak of war. Embarked for France and Flanders in April, 1915.
1/5th Battalion DWR; killed in action 16 8 1915, aged 21, Ypres.
Commemorated – Ypres (Menin Gate) Memorial, Belgium; Christ Church, Moldgreen, RoH; J Fisher, page 106; M Stansfield, page 312, and the **Drill Hall WM panel 8, column 2.**

MOUNCEY John Thomas – 5172 (later 241740) Private.
Born in Grimsby, to John and Rebecca Jane. Resided in Grimsby. Enlisted at Grimsby on 13 3 1916.
2/5th Battalion DWR, D Company Lewis Gunner; died of wounds, shrapnel, 20 7 1917, aged 22.
Buried – Vaulx Australian Field Ambulance Cemetery, A, 22, on 21 7 1917.
Commemorated – the **Drill Hall WM panel 8, column 2.**
Mentioned in the Goodall collection.
ROCK OF AGES CLEFT FOR ME LET ME HIDE MYSELF IN THEE.

MOXON David – 5319 (later 241863) Private.
Born in Moldgreen to David, of Kirkheaton. Resided in Kirkheaton. Enlisted at Huddersfield.
2/5th Battalion DWR; reported missing, presumed killed, 03 5 1917, aged 21, Battle of Bullecourt.
Commemorated – Arras Memorial, France; St John's Church, Kirkheaton, RoH; M Stansfield, page 313, and the **Drill Hall WM panel 8, column 2.**
Mentioned in the Goodall collection; the Huddersfield Examiner (reported missing, official casualty list) on 27 6 1917.

MUDD Geoffrey – 265794 Sergeant.
Resided in Menston. Enlisted at Guiseley.
5th Battalion DWR; killed in action 29 3 1918, Germany Spring Offensive.
Buried – Gommecourt Military Cemetery No2, 5, A, 4.
Commemorated – the **Drill Hall WM panel 8, column 3.**

MULHEARN Andrew – 26935 Private.
Born in Liverpool to Martin and Bridget. Resided with his wife, Mary Ann, in Liverpool. Enlisted at Liverpool.
5th Battalion DWR; killed in action 23 7 1918, aged 33.
Buried – Cezanne Communal Cemetery, C, 14.
Commemorated – the **Drill Hall WM panel 8, column 3.**

MURPHY Ernest – 4822 Private.
Born in Moldgreen on 19 3 1890 to Dennis and Sarah Hannah, of Almondbury. Enlisted in Huddersfield in February, 1916. Embarked for France and Flanders in June, 1916.
1/5th Battalion DWR; killed in action 25 9 1916, aged 26, Battle of the Somme.
Buried – Guards (Lesbouef) Cemetery, 3, L, 7.
Commemorated – Almondbury WM; Lowerhouses WM; Almondbury Cemetery memorial; M Stansfield, page 314, and the **Drill Hall WM panel 8, column 2.**
Mentioned in the Huddersfield Examiner (official casualty list) on 13 11 1916.
THY WILL BE DONE.

MURPHY Thomas – 34457 Private.
Born in Wexford, to Martin and Johanna. Resided with his wife, Margaret, in Enniscorthy, County Wexford, Ireland. Enlisted at Enniscorthy.
5th Battalion DWR; killed in action 25 8 1918, aged 41, Advance to Victory.

Buried – Douchy les Ayette Cemetery, 4, A, 7.
Commemorated – the **Drill Hall WM panel 8, column 3.**
Mentioned in the Huddersfield Examiner (killed in action) on 08 5 1919.
Originally 2/5th DWR.
SACRED HEART OF JESUS HATH MERCY ON HIM.

MURRAY John (Luison) – 26229 Private.
Born in Plaistow, London. Enlisted at Canning Town, London.
5th Battalion DWR, D Company; died of wounds 25 4 1918, aged 29, German Spring Offensive.
Buried – East Ham (St Mary Magdelene) Cemetery.
Commemorated – the **Drill Hall WM panel 8, column 3.**

MURRELL Ambrose – 242550 Private.
Born and resided in Huddersfield. Enlisted at Huddersfield.
1/5th Battalion DWR; reported missing, presumed killed, 16 8 1917, Nieuport.
Commemorated – Nieuport Memorial, Belgium; M Stansfield, page 314, and the **Drill Hall WM panel 8, column 3.**
Mentioned in the Huddersfield Examiner (killed in action) on 11 10 1917.

NASH Frederick – 242479 Private.
Born in Fulham, to Charles and Alice. Resided in Fulham. Enlisted in West London.
1/5th Battalion DWR; killed in action 07 8 1917, aged 34.
Buried – Ramscapelle Road Military Cemetery, 2, A, 34.
Commemorated – the **Drill Hall WM panel 8, column 3.**
Formerly 20271 East Surry Regiment.
PEACE PERFECT PEACE.

NAYLOR Harold – 3547 Private.
Born in Holmbridge to Fred and Emily. Resided in Holmbridge. Enlisted at Huddersfield in 1914.
Embarked for France and Flanders in April, 1915.
1/5th Battalion DWR; wounded in the head, 23 12 1915, and died of wounds at 10 Casualty Clearing Station, Remy Sidings, on 26 12 1915, aged 22, Ypres.
Buried – Lijssenthoek Military Cemetery, 2, B, 27.
Commemorated – Holme Valley Memorial Hospital WM (plaques 1 & 2, Holme & Holmbridge); J Fisher, page 110; M Stansfield, page 315, and the **Drill Hall WM panel 8, column 3.**
Personal papers held in the DWR Archives.
WITH GOD HE CONQUERED.

NAYLOR Robert – 5782 Private.
Born in Manchester, to Alfred and Ellen, of Dobcross. Resided with his wife, Margaret, in Oldham. Enlisted at Manchester.
1/5th Battalion DWR, B Company; killed in action 03 9 1916, aged 26, Battle of the Somme (Thiepval).
Commemorated – Thiepval Memorial, France; Saddleworth WM, and the **Drill Hall WM panel 8, column 3.**

NEDDERMAN Robert Moses – 240594 Private. Military Medal.
Born in Oldham, to James William and Sarah Ellen. Resided in Lees. Enlisted at Huddersfield.
5th Battalion DWR; killed in action 20 7 1918, aged 24, Battle of Tardenois.
Buried – Marfaux British Cemetery, 7, A, 8
Commemorated – the **Drill Hall WM panel 8, column 3.**
Mentioned in the Goodall collection; Unit War Diary (award of Military Medal for operations from 25 3 1918 - shows number as 240954); the London Gazette (award of MM) on 29 8 1918, page 10130; L Magnus (medal award) page 294.

Originally 2/5th DWR.

NESS Douglas – 5204 (later 241765) Private.
Born in Sheepridge, to Edward. Enlisted at Huddersfield on 17 3 1916.
2/5th Battalion DWR, C Company; reported missing, presumed killed. 03 5 1917, aged 24, Battle of Bullecourt.
Commemorated – Arras Memorial, France; St Andrew's Church, Leeds Road, RoH (thought to have been destroyed); M Stansfield, page 316, and the **Drill Hall WM panel 8, column 3.**
Mentioned in the Goodall collection; the Huddersfield Examiner (official casualty list) on 27 6 1917.

NEWSOME Willie – 3755 Lance Corporal.
Born in Dewsbury, to John and Hannah, of Gawthorpe, Ossett. Resided in Gawthorpe. Enlisted at Mirfield.
1/5th Battalion DWR; killed in action 20 9 1916, aged 21, Battle of the Somme.
Buried – Lonsdale Cemetery, 5, P. 4.
Commemorated – the **Drill Hall WM panel 8, column 3.**
HE DIED THAT WE MIGHT LIVE.

NEWTON George – 10621 Private.
Born in Barnsley. Enlisted at Halifax.
5th Battalion DWR; killed in action 21 5 1918, German Spring Offensive.
Buried – Bienvillers Military Cemetery, 20, A, 13.
Commemorated – G Sargeant, Annex C (see below), and the **Drill Hall WM panel 8, column 3.**
Originally 2nd DWR, in action at Mons in August, 1914, reported missing twice during the retreat and rejoined both times. Evacuated and transferred.
> Extract from Sargeant G, et al, Death of the 'Dukes' (2017): *8 Platoon, B Company, (probably identical with 10502 Newton G on the BEF List). Reported as 'Missing' twice. Recovered both times. Evacuated and transferred. Died while serving with 2/5th DWR.*

NEWTON Joe – 5350 (later 241838) Private.
Born in Holmfirth to John and Mary Anne, of Meltham. Resided in Meltham. Enlisted at Huddersfield in March, 1916. Embarked for France and Flanders in January, 1917.
2/5th Battalion DWR D Company, bomber; died of wounds at 48 Casualty Clearing Station, Ytres, on 28 11 1917, aged 38.
Buried – Rocquigny-Equancourt Road Cemetery, 4, A, 16.
Commemorated – St Bartholomew's Church, Meltham, RoH; M Stansfield, page 319, the **Drill Hall WM panel 8, column 3.**
Mentioned in Goodall collection, including a letter from his sister.
AT REST.

NICHOLSON Herbert – 235084 Lance Corporal.
Born in Ingrow, to George and Alice. Resided with his wife, Lois, at Lees, Keighley. Enlisted at Haworth.
2/5th Battalion DWR; killed in action 03 5 1917, aged 31, Battle of Bullecourt.
Commemorated – Arras Memorial, France, and the **Drill Hall WM panel 8, column 3.**

NICKOLSON (NICHOLSON?) James Kilner – 242624 Private.
Born in Parton, Lancs. Resided in Ingrow. Enlisted at Keighley.
1/5th Battalion DWR; died 18 6 1917, aged 22.
Buried – Vieulle Chapelle New Military Cemetery, 1, E, 3.
Commemorated – the **Drill Hall WM panel 8, column 3.**
CWGC shows name as NICHOLSON. Probably a spelling error by the woodcarver.
REST IN PEACE.

NICKERSON Alfred (William Victor?) – 6837 Lance Corporal.
Born in Bradford, to Sarah, of Neatishead, Norwich. Resided in Irstead, Norfolk. Enlisted at East Dereham, Norfolk.
1/5th Battalion DWR; killed in action 20 9 1916, aged 19, Battle of the Somme.
Commemorated – Thiepval Memorial, France, and the **Drill Hall WM panel 8, column 3.**
Formerly 3032 Norfolk Regiment.
GWGC shows his forenames as Alfred William Victor.

NOBLE Herbert – 242692 Private.
Born in Halifax, to Hannah, of Gibbet Street. Enlisted at Halifax.
2/5th Battalion DWR; killed in action 25 11 1917, aged 20, Battle of Cambrai.
Commemorated – Cambrai Memorial (Louverval), France, and the **Drill Hall WM panel 8, column 3.**

NORRIS Harry – 204735 Private.
Born in Dalton on 26 6 1889. Resided with his sister at Almondbury Bank. Enlisted at Huddersfield on 16 2 1916.
2/5th Battalion DWR; killed in action 27 11 1917, Battle of Cambrai.
Commemorated – Cambrai Memorial (Louverval), France; M Stansfield, page 320, and the **Drill Hall WM panel 8, column 3.**

NORTON Arthur Edwin – 2219 Private.
Born in Westminster, London, to Arthur Edwin and Alice, of Lambeth. Resided Flockton Moor. Enlisted at Kirkburton.
1/5th Battalion DWR; killed in action, shellfire, 03 7 1916, aged 21, Battle of the Somme.
Buried – Connaught Cemetery, 1, E, 2.
Commemorated – All Hallows Church, Kirkburton, RoH; M Stansfield, page 322, and the **Drill Hall WM panel 8, column 3.**

NUNN Halstead – 3072 Private.
Born in Lightcliffe, Halifax, to William and Sarah Ann, of Akroydon, Halifax. Resided in Boothtown, Halifax. Enlisted at Huddersfield.
1/5th Battalion DWR; killed in action 13 7 1915, aged 19, Ypres.
Buried – Bard Cottage Cemetery, 1, C, 13.
Commemorated – Calderdale war Dead, page 212; J Fisher, page 106, and the **Drill Hall WM panel 8, column 3.**

NUTTALL Joseph – 4961 (later 241559) Private.
Born in Meltham, to George Thomas and Martha Hannah, of Golcar. Resided in Golcar. Enlisted at Huddersfield.
5th Battalion DWR; killed in action 20 7 1918, aged 21, Tardenios.
Buried – Courmas British Cemetery, 2, D, 8.
Commemorated – St John's Church, Golcar, RoH; Crow Lane Board School, Milnsbridge, RoH; M Stansfield, page 323, and the **Drill Hall WM panel 8, column 3.**
Mentioned in the Goodall collection.
LEST WE FORGET.

OATES Charles Richard – 3832 (later 240987) Corporal.
Resided in Mirfield. Enlisted at Mirfield on 31 1 1915. Embarked for France and Flanders in January 1917.
2/5th Battalion DWR, D Company, later Battalion Bombing Section; reported missing 03 5 1917, Battle of Bullecourt.
Commemorated – Arras Memorial, France; Battyeford WM; Mirfield WM and the **Drill Hall WM panel 8, column 3.**

Mentioned in the Goodall collection and the Huddersfield Examiner (reported missing, official casualty list) on 27 6 1917.
Mentioned in Battalion Routine Orders (Awarded a Commanding Officer's Commendation Certificate for gallantry between 13-17 2 1917 and 20-28 2 1917) on 06 3 1917..

OATES Frederick – 241822 Private.
Born in Huddersfield on 28 5 1888 to Julietta. Resided in Hillhouses. Enlisted 21 3 1916 at Huddersfield.
2/5th Battalion DWR; reported missing, presumed killed on 03 5 1917, Battle of Bullecourt.
Commemorated – Arras Memorial, France; Fartown and Birkby WM; St John's Church, Birkby, RoH; M Stansfield, page 324, and the **Drill Hall WM panel 8, column 3.**

O'BRIEN Joseph Patrick – 240944 Sergeant.
Born in Huddersfield, Resided with his wife and two children at Moldgreen. Enlisted at Huddersfield.
2/5th Battalion DWR; reported missing, presumed killed on 03 5 1917, Battle of Bullecourt.
Commemorated – Arras Memorial, France; Christ Church, Moldgreen, RoH; Huddersfield Corporation RoH; M Stansfield, page 323, and the **Drill Hall WM panel 8, column 3.**
Mentioned in the Huddersfield Examiner (reported missing, official casualty list) on 27 6 1917.

O'HANLON Edward – 241747 Lance Corporal.
Born in Sunderland. Resided in Bedford. Enlisted at Huddersfield.
2/5th Battalion DWR; reported missing, presumed killed on 03 5 1917, Battle of Bullecourt.
Commemorated – Arras Memorial, France, and the **Drill Hall WM panel 8, column 3.**
Mentioned in the Huddersfield Examiner (reported missing, official casualty list) on 27 6 1917.

OLDFIELD John – 3899 (later 241034) Private.
Resided in Liversedge and enlisted at Mirfield on 11 1 1915.
2/5th Battalion DWR, D Company; killed in action 27 3 1918, German Spring Offensive.
Commemorated – Arras Memorial, France, and the **Drill Hall WM panel 8, column 4.**
Mentioned in the Goodall collection.

OLDROYD Horace – 235086 Private.
Born in Bradley Mills, Huddersfield, to Charlie and Sarah. Resided and enlisted at Huddersfield on 25 10 1915.
2/5th Battalion DWR; reported missing, presumed killed on 03 5 1917, aged 20, Battle of Bullecourt.
Commemorated – Arras Memorial, France; Fartown and Birkby WM; St Andrew's Church, Leeds Road, RoH (thought to have been destroyed); M Stansfield, page 326, and the **Drill Hall WM panel 8, column 4.**
Mentioned in the Huddersfield Examiner (reported missing, believed killed) on 15 6 1917; (reported missing, official casualty list) on 27 6 1917.

O'MELIA Fred – 2939 Lance Corporal.
Born in Upperthong. Resided at Holmfirth with his wife. Enlisted at Huddersfield in 1914.
1/5th Battalion DWR; wounded in action on 03 9 1916, died of wounds at 23 General Hospital, Etaples (later 7th Canadian Hospital) on 09 9 1916, Battle of the Somme.
Buried – Etaples Military Cemetery, 10, C, 13.
Commemorated – Holme Valley Memorial Hospital WM (plaque 3, Holmfirth); J J Fisher, page 113; M Stansfield, page 324, and the **Drill Hall WM panel 8, column 4.**

O'NEIL(O'NEILL?) William – 242626 Private.
Born in Skipton, to John and Hannah. Enlisted at Skipton.
1/5th Battalion DWR; killed in action 08 2 1918, aged 20.

Buried – Boisguillame Communal Cemetery Extension, D, 25, A.
Commemorated – the **Drill Hall WM panel 8, column 4.**
CWGC shows spelling as O'NEILL.
THY WILL BE DONE, R.I.P.

ONION Willie – 268562 Private.
Born in Bradford, to Joe and Amy, of Laisterdyke. Enlisted at Bradford.
1/5th Battalion DWR; killed in action 05 8 1917, aged 21, Ypres.
Buried – Coxyde Military Cemetery, 2, D, 29.
Commemorated – the **Drill Hall WM panel 8, column 4.**
PEACE PERFECT PEACE.

ORMEROD Fred – 26469 Private.
Born and enlisted at Haslingden, Lancs.
2/5th Battalion DWR; killed in action 04 2 1918.
Buried – Roclincourt Military Cemetery, 4, A, 3.
Commemorated – the **Drill Hall WM panel 8, column 4.**
Formerly 26230 Private East Lancashire Regiment.

OUGHTON James Harrison – 242331 Private.
Born in Witton Gilbert, Co Durham, to James Wharrie and Jane. Resided in Sacriston, Durham. Enlisted at Durham.
1/5th Battalion DWR, D Company; killed in action 14 4 1918, aged 23, Advance to Victory.
Buried – Beinvillers Military Cemetery, 9, C, 17.
Commemorated – the **Drill Hall WM panel 8, column 4.**
ETERNAL REST GIVE UNTO HIM O LORD AND LET PERPETUAL LIGHT SHINE UPON HIM.

OVERSBY John Edward – 205635 Private.
Born in Dent to Edward and Elizabeth. Resided in North Sedbergh. Enlisted at Barnard Castle.
5th Battalion DWR; killed in action 22 7 1918, aged 26, Battle of Tardenois.
Commemorated – Soissons Memorial, France; Cowgill WM; and the **Drill Hall WM panel 8, column 4.**
Originally 2/5th DWR.

OVERTON Arthur – 35082 Private.
Born in Skegness. Enlisted at Scunthorpe.
5th Battalion DWR; killed in action 13 9 1918, Advance to Victory.
Buried – Hermies Hill British Cemetery, 2, A, 20.
Commemorated – the **Drill Hall WM panel 8, column 4.**

OWEN Robert Stanley – 3303 Private.
Born and enlisted at Sheffield.
5th Battalion DWR; killed in action 27 8 1918, Advance to Victory.
Buried – Douchy les Ayette Cemetery, 4, J, 13.
Commemorated – the **Drill Hall WM panel 8, column 4.**
SDGW shows number as 33030.

OXLEY Hubert – 3799 Lance Corporal.
Born in Ravensthorpe on 01 4 1893 to John Henry. Resided in Ravensthorpe. Enlisted at Mirfield in 1915.
5th Battalion DWR; died of disease at home (ptomaine (food) poisoning) at Sheffield Northern General Hospital on 12 9 1915, aged 22.
Buried – Huddersfield (Edgerton) Cemetery, 6B, 50.

Commemorated – St Thomas's Church, Longroyd Bridge, RoH; M Stansfield, page 327, and the **Drill Hall WM panel 8, column 4.**
Mentioned in D Tattersall, pp 58 & 386; the Huddersfield Examiner (funeral notice) on 15 9 1915; (memoriam notice) on 12 12 1917.

OXLEY John Joseph – 6540 Private.
Resided with his wife, Margaret Ann, of Newbiggin by the Sea. Enlisted in Ashington, Northumberland.
1/5th Battalion DWR; killed in action 21 9 1916, Battle of the Somme.
Commemorated – Thiepval Memorial, France, and the **Drill Hall WM panel 8, column 4.**
Formerly 3404 Private Northumberland Fusiliers.

OXLEY William – 238216 Private.
Enlisted at Gateshead, Northumberland.
5th Battalion DWR; killed in action 15 9 1918, Advance to Victory.
Buried - Sunken Road, Boisleux, Cemetery, 1, F, 6.
Commemorated – the **Drill Hall WM panel 8, column 4.**

PAGE Fred – 5124 (later 241701) Private.
Born in Kelsey, Lincs. Resided in Lincoln. Enlisted at Brigg on 13 3 1916.
2/5th Battalion DWR, D Company; wounded in action on 02 12 1917 and died of wounds 03 12 1917.
Buried – Grevillers British Cemetery, 9, A, 7.
Commemorated – the **Drill Hall WM panel 8, column 4.**
Mentioned in the Goodall collection.

PALETHORPE Jim – 26477 Lance Corporal.
Born in Redford, Sussex, to Daniel and Mary Ann, of Attercliffe, Sheffield. Resided in Attercliffe. Enlisted at Sheffield on 13 8 1915.
2/5th Battalion DWR, D Company; reported missing 27 11 1917, aged 21, Battle of Cambrai.
Commemorated – Cambrai Memorial (Louverval), France, and the **Drill Hall WM panel 8, column 4.**

PARKER Albert – 5049 (later 241635) Lance Corporal.
Born Ulceby, Lincs. Resided and enlisted at Barton on Humber.
2/5th Battalion DWR, D Company, sniper; reported as POW by Goodall from 26 3 1918, died as POW on 21 7 1918, aged 25, German Spring Offensive.
Buried – Valenciennes Communal Cemetery, 5, D, 6.
Commemorated – the **Drill Hall WM panel 8, column 4.**
GONE BUT NOT FORGOTTEN.

PARKER Frank – 4005 Private.
Born in Lockwood, Huddersfield, to Henry and Elizabeth. Resided in Stainland with wife Ellen Agnes (married June , 1916). Enlisted at Huddersfield in March, 1915.
1/5th Battalion DWR; reported missing, presumed killed on 03 9 1916, aged 28, Battle of the Somme (Thiepval).
Buried – Mill Road Cemetery, 4, C, 1
Commemorated – St Stephen's Church, Lindley, RoH; M Stansfield, page 327, and the **Drill Hall WM panel 8, column 4.**
Mentioned in the Huddersfield Examiner (reported missing, presumed dead) on 02 7 1917; (reported missing) on 19 9 1918.
REQUIESCANT IN PACE.

PARKER Richard – 241946 Private.

Born at Haddenham, Cambs, to Richard and Hannah, of Attercliffe, Sheffield. Resided with his wife, Alattea Mary, of Balbrorough, Chesterfield, in Attercliffe, Sheffield. Enlisted at Sheffield. 2/5th Battalion DWR; killed in action 03 5 1917, aged 25, Battle of Bullecourt.
Commemorated – Arras Memorial, France, and the **Drill Hall WM panel 8, column 4.**

PARKIN Richard – 4946 (later 241545) Private.
Born Sutton, Yorks, to Rose Ami, of Haley Hill, Halifax. Enlisted at Huddersfield.
2/5th Battalion DWR, A Company; killed in action 03 5 1917, aged 32, Battle of Bullecourt.
Commemorated – Arras Memorial, France, and the **Drill Hall WM panel 8, column 4.**
Mentioned in the Goodall collection; the Huddersfield Examiner (reported missing, official casualty list) on 27 6 1917.

PARKIN William – 235087 Private.
Born in Saddleworth. Enlisted a Mossley.
2/5th Battalion DWR; killed in action 27 11 1917, Battle of Cambrai.
Commemorated – Cambrai Memorial (Louverval), France; Saddleworth WM and the **Drill Hall WM panel 8, column 4.**
Mentioned in R Vaughan, page 104.

PARR John William – 3967 (later 241074) Private.
Born in Almondbury in 1877. Resided in Marsden with his wife, Rosina, and four children. Enlisted at Huddersfield on 15 3 1915.
2/5th Battalion DWR; reported missing 03 5 1917, aged 39, Battle of Bullecourt.
Commemorated – Arras Memorial, France; Marsden WM; M Stansfield, page 329, and the **Drill Hall WM panel 8, column 4.**
Mentioned in the Goodall collection; the Colne Valley Almanac (killed in action); the Huddersfield Examiner (information requested by family) on 06 6 1917; (previously reported missing, now reported killed in action) on 04 10 1917

PATTERSON George – 6894 Corporal
Born in Huddersfield on 17 8 1892 to George and Emily Ann, of Paddock. Resided in Paddock. Enlisted at Huddersfield in 1914.
1/5th Battalion DWR; died (gangrene) at No 3 General Hospital, Le Treport, on 12 3 1917, aged 24.
Buried – Mont Huon Military Cemetery, 3, C, 9.
Commemorated – All Saints Church, Paddock, RoH (now housed in Huddersfield Drill Hall); M Stanfield, page 329, and the **Drill Hall WM panel 8, column 4.**
Mentioned in the Huddersfield Examiner (died of gangrene) on 21 3 1917.
EVER REMEMBERED AT HOME.

PAXMAN Boynton – 96 Corporal.
Born in Huddersfield. Resided in Paddock (married in April, 1915, to Edith). Pre war Territorial, embodied in 1914.
1/5th Battalion DWR; killed in action 18 8 1915, aged 23, Ypres.
Buried – White House Cemetery, 3, O, 18.
Commemorated – Gospel Mission, Huddersfield; M Stansfield, page 330, and the **Drill Hall WM panel 8, column 4.**
Mentioned in the Huddersfield Examiner (killed in action) on 25 8 1915; (killed in action, Ypres) on 15 8 1919.
EVER REMEMBERED.

5 DWR Band, 1918.

5 DWR Band, 1919

PEARSON. D. L/CPL.	POGSON. T. A. CPL.	REED. J. R. PTE.	ROBINSON. J. A. PTE.
PEARSON. G. PTE.	POTTER. A. L/CPL.	REID. G. C. C.Q.M.S.	ROBINSON. S. B. SGT.
PEATE. C. "	POWELL. R. PTE.	REAY. E. PTE.	ROBERTS. W. PTE.
PECKETT. C. "	POTTS. H. "	RENDALL. F. H. S. D.S.O. CPT.	ROBERTS. A. "
PECK. H. "	PRIESTNALL. R. L/CPL.	REES. J. W. L/CPL.	ROBERTS. P. "
PERRY. H. C. "	PRIESTLEY. F. PTE.	RHODES. T. G. SGT.	ROBERTSON. JAMES. "
PEMBERTON. P. M.M. SGT.	PRIESTLEY. L. "	RHODES. ALBERT. PTE.	ROBERTSON. JOHN. "
PEDLEY. J. C.Q.M.S.	PRIESTLEY. E. M.M. SGT.	RHODES. ARTHUR. "	ROYLE. C. CPL.
PHIPPARD. F. G. C.S.M.	PRIOR. H. PTE	RILEY. A. "	ROUTLEDGE. J. E. PTE.
PHILLIPS. A. E. PTE.	PRIOR. W. "	RILEY. J. R. N. 2/LT.	ROWE. W. "
PINDER. H. J. "	PRITCHETT. J. S. "	RIDGWAY. J. E. "	ROWE. H. "
PINDER. R. M. CPT.	PROCTOR. J. J. "	RIDLEY. P. R. M.C. LT.	ROEBUCK. L. "
PIERCE. W. L/CPL.	QUARMBY. A. "	RIDLEY. H. PTE.	ROEBUCK. F. "
PIERCY. G. R. PTE.	RASTALL. A. W. "	RIPPON. N. 2/LT.	ROTHWELL. J. T. "
PINKNEY. T. SGT.	RAMM. F. L/CPL.	RICE. A. PTE.	ROBBINS. E. "
PINKNEY. W. R. PTE.	RAISTRICK. W. PTE.	RICHARDSON. D. "	ROUSE. M. "
PINKNEY. I. SGT.	RAISTRICK. T. "	RICHARDSON. A. "	ROSSINGTON. A. 2/LT.
PIGGOTT. H. PTE.	RAINBIRD. N. A/CPL.	RICHARDSON. M. "	RUSHFIRTH. F. PTE.
PILSWORTH. W. "	RAYNER. W. PTE.	RISPIN. P. "	RUSHWORTH. F. "
PICK. F. G. "	RAYNOR. A. E. SGT.	RODDIS. C. "	RUSH. C. W. 2/LT.
PLANT. G. H. "	RAYNER. G. PTE.	ROSE. W. "	RUSSELL. R. J. PTE.
PLATT. W. "	RALPH. A. "	ROBSON. W. A. "	RYLANCE. E. "
POPPLEWELL. W. E. "	RAMSDEN. A. "	ROBINSON. F. "	SANDERSON. J. "
POLLARD. H. "	RAMSDEN. B. "	ROBINSON. SAM. "	SANDIFORTH. A. "
POUNDER. B. W. LT.	RAMSDEN. C. R. L/CPL.	ROBINSON. H. "	SANDFORD. L. "
POULSON. E. PTE.	READ. J. D. PTE.	ROBINSON. SIDNEY. "	SANDFORD. F. "

SAYLES. F. PTE.	SHAW. ERNEST. PTE.	SIMPSON. J. H. PTE.	SMITH. E. W. PTE.
SALWAY. E. G. L/CPL.	SHAW. T. H. L/CPL.	SIMPSON. H. "	SMITH. G. H. "
SAUL. H. PTE.	SHAW. F. PTE.	SIMPSON. J. M.M. "	SMITH. R. L/CPL.
SCHOFIELD. F. M. "	SHAW. W. "	SIMPSON. W. "	SMITH. ERNEST. PTE.
SCHOFIELD. J. O. CPL.	SHARPE. A. N. LT.	SINGLETON. J. H. "	SMALES. A. "
SCHOFIELD. N. PTE.	SHARPE. S. CPL.	SILVESTER. W. H. "	SNOWDON. J. W. "
SCHOFIELD. F. CPL.	SHEPPARD. W. PTE.	SIDDALL. R. N. "	SOUTHALL. W. "
SCHOFIELD. A. PTE.	SHEPHERD. WALTER. "	SISSONS. F. H. "	SPENCE. N. "
SCHOFIELD. J. E. "	SHEPHERD. E. "	SLACK. T. "	SPENCE. F. "
SCHOFIELD. H. "	SHEPHERDSON. W. CPL.	SLATER. H. M.M. L/CPL.	SPEIGHT. G. L. "
SCHOFIELD. M. "	SHACKLETON. A. PTE.	SMITH. G. N. PTE.	SPEIGHT. T. G. L. "
SCRIMSHAW. G. W. "	SHACKLETON. J. R. "	SMITH. F. A. "	SPEIGHT. J. W. "
SCOTNEY. W. "	SHACKLETON. T. W. "	SMITH. D. "	SPIVEY. F. M.M. SGT.
SENIOR. T. "	SHERBON. C. "	SMITH. ARTHUR. "	STOKES. J. H. PTE.
SENIOR. F. "	SHORE. L. SGT.	SMITH. A. B. "	STOKES. W. "
SENIOR. G. "	SHORE. A. PTE.	SMITH. J. "	STEVENSON. A. "
SECKER. N. "	SHINDLER. C. "	SMITH. G. W. "	STEVENS. H. C. "
SEWELL. T. "	SHIRES. H. "	SMITH. J. B. "	STEVENS. E. C. "
SEAMAN. W. S. "	SHUTTLEWORTH. H. "	SMITH. T. "	STOCKDALE. J. "
SEVILLE. W. H. "	SHINGLES. D. A. "	SMITH. M. "	STAMFORD. F. L/CPL.
SEDDON. C. "	SHEARD. T. H. "	SMITH. EDWIN. "	STEAD. A. PTE.
SHAW. J. L. R. "	SHEARD. S. "	SMITH. J. "	STANDISH. A. M.M. L/CPL.
SHAW. D. CPL.	SHEARSMITH. S. "	SMITH. G. "	STEEL. A. PTE.
SHAW. A. PTE.	SHEARSMITH. W. M.M. A/CPL.	SMITH. EDGAR. "	STAVELEY. F. "
SHAW. ERNEST. "	SIMPSON. F. PTE.	SMITH. F. S. "	STIRK. H. "
SHAW. EDWIN. "	SIMPSON. J. "	SMITH. A. B. "	STANTON. L. "

PAYNE Charles Frederick – 235435 Lance Corporal.
Born in London to Henry and Emily. Resided London with his wife Ida Muriel.
5th Battalion DWR; died 11 2 1919, aged 35.
Buried – Terlincthun British Cemetery, 13, C, 37.
Commemorated – the **Drill Hall WM panel 8, column 4.**
Originally 2/5th DWR.
EVER IN OUR THOUGHTS.

PEARSON Dan – 2946 Lance Corporal.
Born in Golcar, Huddersfield to Fred and Louisa, of Blackpool. Resided in Golcar. Pre war Territorial, embodied in August, 1914. Embarked for France and Flanders in April, 1915.
1/5th Battalion DWR, B Company; killed in action (shot by sniper) on 15 8 1915, aged 22, Ypres.
Commemorated – Ypres (Menin Gate) Memorial, France; St John's Church, Golcar, RoH; Golcar Baptist Church RoH; M Stansfield, page 332, and the **Drill Hall WM panel 9, column 1.**
Mentioned in the Huddersfield Examiner (shot in head) on 19 8 1915.

PEARSON George – 4293 Private.
Born in Huddersfield to David. Resided in Lascelles Hall, Huddersfield, with his wife, Elizabeth Ann. Enlisted in Huddersfield.
1/5th Battalion DWR; killed in action 03 9 1916, aged 24, Battle of the Some (Thiepval).
Commemorated – Thiepval Memorial, France; St John's Church, Kirkheaton, RoH; Lepton Parish Church RoH, M Stansfield, page 332, and the **Drill Hall WM panel 9, column 1.**
Attached to 147 Trench Mortar Battery.
Mentioned in the Huddersfield Examiner (killed in action, official casualty list) on 16 10 1916.

PEATE (E B?) Cecil – 4810 Private.
Born and enlisted at Guiseley.
1/5th Battalion DWR; killed in action 17 9 1916, aged 26, Battle of the Somme.
Buried – Varennes Military Cemetery, 1, B, 2.
Commemorated – the **Drill Hall WM panel 9, column 1.**
CWGC shows initials as E B C.

PECK Horace – 51875 Private.
Born in Sheffield to Jane.
9th Battalion DWR; killed in action 04 11 1918, aged 24, Advance to Victory.
Buried - Poix du Nord Communal Cemetery Extension, 1, B, 2.
Commemorated – the **Drill Hall WM panel 9, column 1.**
Not mentioned in SDGW.
GOD BE WITH US TILL WE MEET AGAIN.

PECKETT Charles – 242901 Private.
Resided in Salterhebble, Halifax. Enlisted at Halifax.
1/5th Battalion DWR; killed in action 04 4 1917.
Buried – Le Tourette Military Cemetery, 4, C, 16.
Commemorated – the **Drill Hall WM panel 9, column 1.**

PEDLEY Joseph – 240431 Company Quartermaster Sergeant. Meritorious Service Medal.
Born in Leek, Staffs, on 10 9 1889, to Amelia. Resided in Huddersfield with his wife. Enlisted at Huddersfield in September, 1914.
5th Battalion DWR; killed in action 17 10 1918, Advance to Victory.
Buried – Quivey Communal Cemetery Extension, D, 29.
Commemorated – Arras Memorial, France; Huddersfield Parish Church RoH; L Magnus RoH, page 293; M Stansfield, page 334, and the **Drill Hall WM panel 9, column 1.**

Mentioned in the Goodall collection (gallantry awards); the Huddersfield Examiner (killed in action, shellfire, and letter from CO to family) on 30 10 1918; (award of Meritorious Service Medal) on 22 1 1919; the London Gazette (award of MSM) on 18 1 1919, page 991; 1/5th DWR War Diary (concert party artiste, 20 4 1917) on 30 4 1917; 5th DWR War Diary (award of MSM) on 22 1 1919.

PEMBERTON Percy – 6599 (later 267955) Sergeant. Military Medal.
Born in Baildon, to Samuel and Mary Jane. Resided in Baildon. Enlisted at Shipley.
5th Battalion DWR; killed in action 25 8 1918, aged 26, Advance to Victory.
Buried – Gommecourt South Cemetery, 1, C, 3.
Commemorated – the **Drill Hall WM panel 9, column 1.**
Originally 1/6th DWR
SDGW shows date of death as 26 8 1918.
Mentioned in the 1/6th DWR Part 2 Order (change of number) on 20 4 1917; the 1/6th DWR War Diary (C Company, wounded in hand by Trench Mortar) on 12 3 1917; the London Gazette (award of MM) on 11 12 1918, page 14658; the Goodall collection (gallantry awards); L Magnus (gallantry awards), page 294; the Huddersfield Examiner (award of MM for 2nd Battle of the Marne, 1918) on 09 9 1918.
CWGC shows forename as Percival.
HE HAS FOUGHT THE FIGHT AND FINISHED HIS COURSE.

PERRY Henry Charles – 26189 Private.
Born in Stoke St Gregory, Somerset, to Mary Ann. Enlisted at Taunton.
5th Battalion DWR; killed in action 20 7 1918, aged 33, Battle of Tardenois.
Buried – Marfaux Cemetery, 2, BB, 7.
Commemorated – the **Drill Hall WM panel 9, column 1.**
Originally 2/5th DWR.

PHILLIPS Arthur Edgar – 242406 Private.
Born in Leeds to George Sunderland and Agnes Alice, of Barkerend, Bradford. Enlisted at Bradford.
2/5th Battalion DWR; killed in action 28 3 1916, aged 19.
Commemorated – Arras Memorial, France, and the **Drill Hall WM panel 9, column 1.**

PHIPPARD Frederick George – 240025 Company Sergeant Major. Mention in Despatches.
Born in Brixton. Resided in Kirkburton with his wife, Winifred. Pre war Territorial, embodied (or re-enlisted) in August, 1914. Embarked for France and Flanders in April, 1915.
1/5th Battalion DWR; died of wounds at 44 Casualty Clearing Station, Remy Siding, 08 10 1917, aged 27.
Buried – Nine Elms British Cemetery, 4, B, 5.
Commemorated – All Hallows Parish Church, Kirkburton, RoH; M Stansfield, page 336, and the **Drill Hall WM panel 9, column 1.**
Mentioned in the Goodall collection (gallantry awards); the Huddersfield Examiner (died of wounds) on 31 10 1917; 1/5th DWR War Diary (award of MID) on 31 12 1917; (MID award in despatch of 07 11 1917) on 30 1 1918; London Gazette (award of MID) on 18 12 1917, page 13287.
REST IN PEACE.

PICK Frederick George – 242343 Private.
Resided and enlisted at Hull on 08 3 1916.
2/5th Battalion DWR, D Company; wounded in action, reported missing, on 27 11 1917, Cambrai.
Commemorated – Cambrai Memorial (Louverval), France, and the **Drill Hall WM panel 9, column 1.**
Mentioned in the Goodall collection (also 1/5th DWR, reported missing).

PIERCE William – 6935 Lance Corporal.
Born in Stockport. Resided in Mossley. Enlisted at Micklehurst, Lancs.
1/5th Battalion DWR, F Company; died, 20 or 43 Casualty Clearing Station, on 23 2 1917.
Buried – Warlincourt Halte British Cemetery, 5, B, 12.
Commemorated – the **Drill Hall WM panel 9, column 1.**
Mentioned in R Vaughan, pp 25 & 67.
SDGW shows his date of death as 24 2 1917.

PIERCY George Richard – 2443 (later 240270). Territorial Force War Medal (posthumous).
Born in Ardsley, Barnsley, 0n 26 7 1897 to Richard and Martha Ann. Resided at 5, St Paul's Street, Huddersfield. Pre War Territorial, embodied in August, 1914.
5th Battalion DWR, C Company; killed in action 21 7 1918, aged 20, Battle of Tardenois.
Buried – Marfaux British, 5, F, 8.
Commemorated – St Paul's Church Southgate, Huddersfield, RoH; M Stansfield, page 337, and the **Drill Hall WM panel 9, column 1.**
Mentioned in the Huddersfield Examiner (reported missing, 21 7 1918, and officially reported killed in action on that date) on 27 8 1919.
Posthumous award of the Territorial Force War Medal on 20 4 1922.
Originally B Company 2/5th DWR.
HE DIED TO SAVE US ALL, IN THE MIDST OF LIFE WE ARE IN DEATH.

PIGGOTT Herbert – 5145 (later 24720) Private.
Born in Holbeach, Lincs, to William and Hannah. Resided in Leeds. Enlisted in Lincoln on 14 3 1916.
2/5th Battalion DWR, D Company, bomber; reported missing (killed in action) 03 5 1917, aged 24, Battle of Bullecourt.
Commemorated – Arras Memorial, France, and the **Drill Hall WM panel 9, column 1.**
Originally 2/5th DWR.

PILSWORTH William – 5147 (later 241721) Private.
Born in Epworth. Resided in Doncaster. Enlisted at Epworth.
2/5th Battalion DWR; killed in action 03 5 1917, Battle of Bullecourt.
Commemorated – Arras Memorial, France, and the **Drill Hall WM panel 9, column 1**.
Mentioned in the Goodall collection.

PINDER Horace Jenkinson – 4743 Private.
Born in Nettleton, Dalton, on 17 10 1892 to Arthur and Mary, of Birkby. Resided in Birkby. Enlisted at Huddersfield on 09 2 1916. Embarked for France and Flanders on 14 5 1916.
1/5th Battalion DWR; reported missing 03 9 1916, Battle of the Somme (Thiepval).
Commemorated – Thiepval Memorial, France; Fartown and Birkby WM; M Stansfield, page 338, and the **Drill Hall WM panel 9, column 1.**
Mentioned in the Huddersfield Examiner (presumed dead) 06 7 1916; (reported missing on 03 9 1916) on 28 9 1918.

PINDER Reginald Maw – Captain.
Born in Horsforth, Leeds, to John William and Eliza, on 30 12 1895. Member of Leeds University Officers' Training Corps at outbreak of war and commissioned into DWR. Embarked for France and Flanders on 01 12 1915.
1/5th Battalion DWR, OC C Company; killed in action 07 10 1917, aged 21.
Commemorated – Tyne Cot Memorial, Belgium; J J Fisher, page 128, and the **Drill Hall WM panel 9, column 1.**
Mentioned in J J Fisher, page 116; 1/5th DWR War Diary (numerous entries between 30 1 1916 and 31 10 1917).
Also in 2/5th DWR in 1916 (Army List).

PINKNEY I.
Possible duplication of Pinkney T, below, otherwise no trace.
Commemorated – the **Drill Hall WM panel 9, column 1.**

PINKNEY Thomas – 240818 Sergeant.
Resided in Wakefield. Enlisted at Huddersfield.
2/5th Battalion DWR; killed in action 03 5 1917, Battle of Bullecourt.
Commemorated – Arras Memorial, France, and the **Drill Hall WM panel 9, column 1.**

PINKNEY Walter Robson – 242792 Private.
Born in Sutton, Hull. Resided with his wife, Louisa, in Sutton. Enlisted at Beverley.
2/5th Battalion DWR; killed in action 03 5 1917, aged 36, Battle of Bullecourt.
Commemorated – Arras Memorial, France, and the **Drill Hall WM panel 9, column 1.**

PLANT George Henry – 241026 Private.
Resided with his wife, Mabel. Enlisted at Doncaster.
1/5th Battalion DWR; died of wounds 04 11 1917, aged 28.
Buried – Adwick le Street (St Lawrence) Cemetery, B, 136.
Commemorated – the **Drill Hall WM panel 9, column 1.**
SDGW shows number as 241036.
Mentioned in the 1/5th DWR War Diary (commended for raid on 20 11 1916 and awarded a gallantry card) on 30 11 1916.
SDGW shows his number as 241036.
PEACE PERFECT PEACE.

PLATT Walter – 4827 Private.
Born and resided in Dobcross. Enlisted at Huddersfield.
1/5th Battalion DWR; killed in action 25 9 1916, Battle of the Somme.
Commemorated – Thiepval Memorial, France; Saddleworth WM and the **Drill Hall WM panel 9, column 1.**
Mentioned in the Huddersfield Examiner (also Kings Own Yorkshire Light Infantry, killed in action) on 24 11 1916.

POGSON Thomas Alan – 5274 (later 241827) Private.
Born and resided in Slaithwaite. Enlisted at Halifax in March, 1916.
2/5th Battalion DWR; wounded in action on 29 10 1916 and died of wounds at 21 Casualty Clearing Station, Corbie, on 29 11 1917.
Buried – Rocquigney-Equancourt Road Cemetery, 4, A, 20.
Commemorated – Slaithwaite WM; St James' Church, Slaithwaite, RoH; M Stansfield, page 340, and the **Drill Hall WM panel 9, column 2.**
Mentioned in the Goodall collection.

POLLARD Harry – 4225 (later 241217) Private.
Born in Berry Brow, Huddersfield. Resided in Huddersfield with his wife, Edith Ida. Enlisted at Huddersfield.
1/5th Battalion DWR; killed in action 03 9 1916, aged 19, Battle of the Somme (Thiepval).
Commemorated – Divion Wood No2, Memorial No 1, France; Armitage Bridge WM; Mirfield WM; St Andrews Church, Leeds Road Huddersfield, RoH (now missing); M Stansfield, page 341, and the **Drill Hall WM panel 9, column 1.**

POPPLEWELL William Ewart – 3436 Private.
Born in Mirfield to Edwin and Louisa. Resided in Ravensthorpe. Enlisted at Mirfield.
1/5th Battalion DWR; killed in action 07 11 1915, aged 19, Ypres.
Buried – Talana Farm Cemetery, 4, F, 9.

Commemorated – Mirfield WM and the **Drill Hall WM panel 9, column 1.**
UNTIL DAY BREAKS AND THE SHADOWS PASS AWAY.

POTTER Arthur Samuel – 202886 Lance Corporal. Military Medal.
Born and enlisted at Middlesbrough.
10th Battalion DWR, C Company; died of wounds 17 10 1917, aged 24.
Buried – Lijssennthoek Military Cemetery, 21, B, 8A.
Commemorated – the **Drill Hall WM panel 9, column 2.**
Military Medal award announced in the London Gazette 17 12 1917, page 13194, for an action on 20 9 1917.
Originally 1/4th DWR, then 2/5th DWR.
Commemorated on Tunstill's Men Blog – tunstillsmen.blogspot.com.
ALSO IN LOVING MEMORY OF PRIVATE. F. A. POTTER BORDER REGIMENT KILLED IN ACTION DECEMBER, 1914.

POTTS Harry –269311 Private.
Born and resided in Drighlington. Enlisted at Gildersome.
2/5th Battalion DWR; killed in action 28 3 1918, German Spring Offensive.
Buried - Gommecourt British Cemetery No2, 5,D, 2.
Commemorated – the **Drill Hall WM panel 9, column 2.**

POULSON Edward – 5218 (later 241777) Private.
Born and resided in Mexborough. Enlisted at Huddersfield.
2/5th Battalion DWR; killed in action 03 5 1917, aged 37, Battle of Bullecourt.
Commemorated – Arras Memorial, France, and the **Drill Hall WM panel 9, column 1.**
Mentioned in the Goodall collection.

POUNDER Benjamin William – Lieutenant.
Born in Harrogate, on 04 7 1892, to William and Sarah, of Killinghall. Resided in Moortown, Leeds. Commissioned into the Regiment from Leeds University Officers' Training Corps in 1914. Embarked for France and Flanders on 03 11 1915.
1/5th Battalion DWR; killed in action 09 10 1917, aged 25.
Buried – White House Cemetery, 3, P, 23.
Commemorated – University of Leeds OTC RoH, pp 61-62; and the **Drill Hall WM, panel 9, column 1.**
Mentioned in J J Fisher, pp 119 & 129; the 1/5th DWR War Diary (numerous entries between 29 12 1916 to 31 10 1917); the Huddersfield Examiner (killed in action) on 25 10 1917.
IN LOVING MEMORY OF A DEAR SON AND BROTHER, KILLED IN ACTION.

POWELL Roger – 205357 Private.
Born in Harrogate, to Charles and Hannah, of Ripon. Resided with his wife, Sarah Ann, of Millwood, in Todmorden. Enlisted at Halifax.
5th Battalion DWR; killed in action 29 3 1918, aged 28, German Spring Offensive.
Buried – Doullens Communal Cemetery Extension, 5, C, 46.
Commemorated – Arras Memorial, France; Todmorden WM and the **Drill Hall WM panel 9, column 2.**

PRIESTLEY Edgar – 241414 Sergeant. Military Medal.
Born in Quarmby, Huddersfield, on 15 4 1891 to Mary. Resided Stroud, Glos. Enlisted at Huddersfield on 22 11 1915. Embarked for France and Flanders on 11 1 1917.
2/5th Battalion DWR, D Company Lewis gunner; died of pneumonia, 14 4 1919, home.
Buried – Salendine Nook Baptist Churchyard, 114, E, Huddersfield, not a CWGC grave.
Commemorated – Fartown and Birkby WM; Oakes Baptist Church RoH; L Magnus, page 293; M Stansfield, page 342, and the **Drill Hall WM panel 9, column 2.**

No trace of him in either CWGC or SDGW.
Submitted a report in support of Capt Goodall's gallantry award, 20 11 1918.
Military Medal award announced in the London Gazette 13 3 1918, page 3242, for Bravery in the Field at the Battle of Cambrai, 22 11 1917.
Mentioned in the Goodall collection; the Huddersfield Examiner (died of pneumonia after demobilisation, 14 4 1919) on 15 4 1919; (arrived home 17 4 1919, caught chill on way home, died) on 16 4 1919.

PRIESTLEY Farrar – 4594 Private.
Resided in Halifax. Enlisted at Huddersfield.
1/5th Battalion DWR; killed in action 03 9 1916, Battle of the Somme, (Thiepval).
Commemorated – Thiepval Memorial, France, Greetland WM and the **Drill Hall WM panel 9, column 2.**

PRIESTLEY Lewis – 267594 Private.
Born in Deighton, Huddersfield on 15 10 1888, to George and Mary Ann. Resided in Kirkheaton. Enlisted at Huddersfield on 01 3 1916.
1/5th Battalion DWR; killed in action 07 10 1917, Ypres (Passchendaele).
Commemorated – Tyne Cot Memorial, Belgium; St John's Church, Kirkheaton, RoH; M Stansfield, page 343, and the **Drill Hall WM panel 9, column 2.**

PRIESTNALL Reginald – 4755 Lance Corporal.
Born and resided in Leicester. Enlisted at Huddersfield.
1/5th Battalion DWR; killed in action 16 9 1916, Battle of the Somme.
Commemorated – Thiepval Memorial, France, and the **Drill Hall WM panel 9, column 2.**

PRIOR Harry – 17064 Private.
Born in London. Enlisted at Leyton, Essex.
1/5th Battalion DWR; killed in action 08 10 1917.
Commemorated – Tyne Cot Memorial, Belgium, and the **Drill Hall WM panel 9, column 2.**

PRITCHETT Joseph Stanley – 22402 Private.
Born in Hull. Enlisted at Hull.
5th Battalion DWR; killed in action 21 7 1918, aged 19, Battle of Tardenois.
Buried – Cezanne Communal Cemetery, A, 3.
Commemorated – the **Drill Hall WM panel 9, column 2.**

PROCTOR John Joseph – 14897 Private.
Born in Tarporley, Cheshire, to Frederick and Selina. Enlisted at Halifax.
5th Battalion DWR; killed in action 22 7 1918, aged 24, Battle of Tardenois.
Commemorated – Soissons Memorial, France, and the **Drill Hall WM panel 9, column 2.**
Originally 2/5th DWR.

QUARMBY Arthur – 5387 (later 241918) Private.
Born and resided in Honley. Enlisted at Holmfirth on 25 3 1916. Embarked for France and Flanders in January, 1917.
2/5th Battalion DWR, D Company Lewis gun team; killed in action, shot by sniper, 20 11 1917, Battle of Cambrai.
Commemorated – Hermies Hill Special Memorial, A, 2, France; Honley WM; Holme Valley Memorial Hospital WM (plaque 5, Netherthong & Thongsbridge); St Andrew's Church, Netherthong RoH; C Ford, page 9, 10 & 26; M Stansfield, page 345, and the **Drill Hall WM panel 9, column 2.**
Mentioned in the Goodall collection.
THEIR GLORY SHALL NOT BE BLOTTED OUT.

RAINBIRD Norman – 2556 Corporal.
Born in Wetherby on 21 7 1892, to William and Mary. Resided in Moldgreen. Enlisted at Huddersfield on 05 8 1914.
1/5th Battalion DWR; killed in action 03 9 1916, aged 24, Battle of the Somme (Thiepval).
Commemorated – Thiepval Memorial, France; Almondbury WM; Christ Church, Moldgreen, RoH; J J Fisher, page 113; M Stansfield, page 347, and the **Drill Hall WM panel 9, column 2.**
Mentioned in the Huddersfield Examiner (killed in action) on 20 9 1916.

RAISTRICK Taylor – 242439 Private. Military Medal and Bar.
Born in Girlington, Bradford, to Thomas and Emily. Resided with his wife, Mary, in Bradford. Enlisted at Bradford.
5th Battalion DWR; killed in action 22 7 1918, aged 29, Battle of Tardenois.
Commemorated – Soissons Memorial, France, and the **Drill Hall WM panel 9, column 2.**
Originally 2/5th DWR.
Military Medal award announced in the London Gazette on 28 1 1918, page 1396.
Bar to Military Medal award announced in the London Gazette on 11 12 1918, page 14651.
Mentioned in the Goodall collection (awards of Military Medal and Bar); the Huddersfield Examiner (award of Bar to MM for 2nd Battle of the Marne (Tardenois)) on 09 9 1918; the 1/5th DWR War Diary (award of MM) on 30 11 1917; 5 DWR War Diary (award of Bar to MM) on 30 8 1918.

RAISTRICK (RAINSTRICK?) William – 6078 Private.
Born and enlisted at Bradford.
1/5th Battalion DWR; killed in action 30 8 1916, aged 21, Battle of the Somme.
Buried – Faubourg d'Amiens Cemetery, 1, F, 47.
Commemorated – the **Drill Hall WM panel 9, column 2.**
Attached to 10th Battalion Kings Own Yorkshire Light Infantry.
SDGW show his name as Rainstrick.
LOVED BY ALL.

RALPH Albert – 242444 Private.
Born in Horton in Ribblesdale to Alfred and Sarah Margaret Jane. Enlisted at Keighley.
1/5th Battalion DWR; died of wounds 21 11 1917, aged 23.
Buried – Mont Huon Military Cemetery, 6, C, 65.
Commemorated – Settle WM and the **Drill Hall WM panel 9, column 2.**

RAMM Frederick (W?) – 3483 Lance Corporal.
Born in Huddersfield to Frederick and Caroline, of Norwich. Enlisted in Huddersfield.
1/5th Battalion DWR; killed in action 10 7 1916, aged 34, Battle of the Somme.
Buried – Forceville Communal Cemetery, 2, C, 8.
Commemorated – M Stansfield, page 347, and the **Drill Hall WM panel 9, column 2.**
CWGC shows middle initial as W.

RAMSDEN A.
Not positively identified but could be 2497 Private Ramsden Arthur, 15 years of age in 1914, F Company, 5 DWR, mobilised with the Territorials but underage for overseas service and posted to the second line battalions, and may be:
RAMSDEN Arthur – 204881 Private. Territorial Force War Medal.
Born in Holmfirth to John Thomas and Frances, of Holmbridge. Enlisted at Holmfirth. Embarked for France and Flanders in June, 1917.
1/7th Battalion DWR; killed in action 29 7 1917.
Commemorated – Nieuport WM; 7th DWR WM, Huddersfield Drill Hall; Holme Valley Memorial Hospital WM (plaques 1&2, Holme and Holmbridge); M Stansfield, page 347, and the **Drill Hall WM panel 9, column 2.**

Mentioned in the Huddersfield Examiner (believed killed in raid on enemy trench) on 27 8 1917.
Awarded the Territorial Force War Medal (posthumously) on 20 4 1922.

RAMSDEN Ben – 5497 (later 242010) Private.
Born in Holmfirth to Hugh and Alice. Resided at Holmfirth. Enlisted at Holmfirth under the Derby Scheme in 1917.
2/5th Battalion DWR, Signals Section; reported missing 03 5 1917, aged 31, Battle of Bullecourt.
Buried – Croissilles British Cemetery, 5, G, 2.
Commemorated – Holme Valley Memorial Hospital WM (plaque 2, Underbank); M Stansfield, page 347, and the **Drill Hall WM panel 9, column 2.**
Mentioned in the Goodall collection; the Huddersfield Examiner (request for information from relatives) on 12 6 1917; (official casualty list) on 27 6 1917; (previously reported missing, now officially reported killed in action) on 05 7 1917 & 17 7 1917.
May be on the photograph of 2/5th DWR Signals Section in the gallery pages.
MAY HIS REWARD BE AS GREAT AS HIS SACRIFICE.

RAMSDEN Charles Richard – 242944 Private.
Born in Almondbury to Samuel. Resided in Almondbury. Enlisted at Huddersfield on 02 11 1914.
5th Battalion DWR; killed in action 22 7 1918, Battle of Tardenois.
Commemorated – Soissons Memorial, France; Almondbury WM; M Stansfield, page 347, and the **Drill Hall WM panel 9, column 2.**
Originally 2/5th DWR.
Mentioned in the Huddersfield Examiner (killed in action) on 28 8 1918.

RASTALL Arthur William – 3123 Private.
Born in Huddersfield. Resided in Birkby with his wife, Nelly. Enlisted in Huddersfield in October, 1914. Embarked for France and Flanders in April, 1915.
1/5th Battalion DWR, C Company; killed in action 01 10 1915, aged 27, Ypres.
Commemorated – Ypres (Menin Gate) Memorial, Belgium Fartown and Birkby WM; M Stansfield, page 349, and the **Drill Hall WM panel 9, column 2.**
Mentioned in the Huddersfield Examiner (killed in action, shellfire) on 06 10 1915; (in memoriam) 02 10 1916 & 30 9 1919.

RAYNER (RAYNOR?) Albert Edward – 2455 (later 240276) Sergeant. Territorial Force War Medal.
Born in Lockwood, Huddersfield, on 15 9 1896 to John Edward and Jane, of Thornton Lodge. Resided in Huddersfield. Pre war Territorial, embodied in August, 1914.
2/5th Battalion DWR; killed in action 20 11 1917, aged 21, Battle of Cambrai.
Commemorated – Hermies Hill British Cemetery, Special Memorial B2, France; Mount Pleasant Chapel, Lockwood, RoH; M Stansfield, page 351, and the **Drill Hall WM panel 9, column 2.**
Awarded the Territorial Force War Medal, posthumously, 20 4 1922.
Most sources show RAYNER, listed as RAYNOR on the Drill Hall WM Boards.
Further details held in the DWR Regimental Archives.

RAYNER George – 33511 Private.
Born in Harleston, Norfolk. Enlisted at Norwich.
5th Battalion DWR; killed in action 13 9 1918, Advance to Victory.
Buried – Hermies Hill British Cemetery, 2, 2, 21.
Commemorated – the **Drill Hall WM panel 9, column 2.**
Formerly 059492 Private Army Service Corps.

RAYNER Walter – 2516 Private.
Born in Huddersfield to Fred and Emily, of Paddock. Resided in Paddock. Enlisted at Huddersfield on 04 8 1914. Embarked for France and Flanders in April, 1915.

1/5th Battalion DWR; killed in action 21 9 1916, aged 20, Battle of the Somme.
Commemorated – Thiepval Memorial, France; All Saints Church, Paddock, RoH (now in Huddersfield Drill Hall); M Stansfield, page 351, and the **Drill Hall WM panel 9, column 2.**

RAYNOR A E – see RAYNER A E

READ John Dixon – 242201 Private.
Born in Crosshills, Keighley, to William and Mary. Enlisted at Crosshills.
1/5th Battalion DWR, B Company; killed in action 09 10 1917, aged 21.
Commemorated – Tyne Cot Memorial, Belgium, and the **Drill Hall WM panel 9, column 2.**

REAY Edward – 6543 Private.
Born Horton, Northumberland. Enlisted at Ashington, Northumberland.
1/5th Battalion DWR; died of wounds 10 1 1917.
Buried – Seaton (St John) Cemetery, E, 8, 14.
Commemorated – the **Drill Hall WM panel 9, column 3.**

REED George Robert – 34544 Private.
Born in Ryhope to Ralph and Clara, of Ryhope Colliery. Resided at Harden Colliery with his wife, Enid. Enlisted at Sunderland.
5th Battalion DWR; killed in action 26 8 1918, aged 27, Advance to Victory.
Buried – Bagneux British Cemetery, 4, E, 6.
Commemorated – the **Drill Hall WM panel 9, column 3.**
Formerly 15356 Private East Yorkshire regiment.
HE HATH SACRIFICED HIS LIFE ON THE ALTAR OF DUTY.

REES John William – 235090 Lance Corporal.
Born in South Bank, Yorks, of John William and Ann. Enlisted in South Bank.
2/5th Battalion DWR; killed in action 03 5 1917, aged 23, Battle of Bullecourt.
Commemorated – Arras Memorial, France, and the **Drill Hall WM panel 9, column 3**.

REID George Clement – 235105 Company Quartermaster Sergeant.
Born in Halifax. Enlisted at Bradford in 08 9 1916.
5th Battalion DWR, D Company, Lewis gun rangefinder, then CQMS; died of wounds 18 10 1918, Advance to Victory.
Buried – Delsaux Farm Cemetery, 2, B, 25.
Commemorated – the **Drill Hall WM panel 9, column 3.**
Mentioned in the Goodall collection.

RENDALL Francis Holden Shuttleworth – Captain. Distinguished Service Order. Mention in Despatches.
Born at Darley Abbey, Deryshire, on 22 11 1879, to Francis Shuttleworth and Rachel Frances of Barrington Vicarage, Cambs. Resided with his wife Muriel. Embarked for France and Flanders on 14 4 1915.
1/5th Battalion DWR; died of wounds as Prisoner of War, 09 7 1916, aged 36.
Buried – Lebucquiere Communal Cemetery extension, 2, B, 21.
Commemorated – the **Drill Hall WM panel 9, column 3.**
From Duke of Cornwall's Light Infantry, Adjt 1/5th DWR, left to command 5th Bn York and Lancaster Regiment.
Mentioned in the Huddersfield Examiner (notification as POW) on 20 7 1916; (died of wounds as POW) on 14 8 1916; (left 5 DWR to command 5th Battalion, the York and Lancaster Regiment, October, 1915) on 29 7 1919.
Mentioned in L Magnus (gallantry medal roll), page 250; J J Fisher, page 128.
London Gazette announcements of MID on 01 1 1916, page 42, and DSO on 14 1 1916, page 574.

1/5th DWR War Diary entries between 26 4 1915 to 27 11 1915.
His medals were sent to his widow it Windsworth, Looe, Cornwall.
A GALLANT SOLDIER AND A GOOD MAN.

RHODES Albert – 2429 Private.
Born in Thurstonland to Oliver and Ada. Resided in Thurstonland. Enlisted at Holmfirth in 1914, F Company.
1/5th Battalion DWR; wounded in action on 03 9 1916 and died of wounds at 3 Casualty Clearing Station, Puchevillers, on 06 9 1916, Battle of the Somme (Thiepval).
Buried – Puchevillers British, 4, A, 43.
Commemorated – Thurstonland WM; St Thomas's Churchyard, Thurstonland, Memorial; M Stansfield, page 352, and the **Drill Hall WM panel 9, column 3**.
Mentioned in the Huddersfield Examiner (died of wounds) on 13 9 1916; J J Fisher, page 113.

RHODES Arthur – 241480 Private.
Born in Oakes, Huddersfield, to William Harry and Ellen. Resided in Oakes. Enlisted at Huddersfield in 16 2 1916.
1/5th Battalion DWR; reported missing 03 9 1916, aged 27, Battle of the Somme (Thiepval).
Commemorated – Thiepval Memorial, France; Oakes Baptist Church RoH; St Stephen's Church, Lindley, RoH; M Stansfield, page 352, and the **Drill Hall WM panel 9, column 3**.
CWGC shows number as 141480. SDGW shows his place of birth as Halifax.

RHODES Thomas George – 1681 Sergeant (later 240049 Warrant Officer Class 2) (later Lieutenant, RFC & RAF).
Born in Huddersfield on 08 8 1892 to George Henry and Ellen. Resided Huddersfield. Enlisted at Huddersfield in August, 1914. Promoted to WO2 and commissioned on 25 9 1917. Attached from 3 DWR to 57 Squadron of the Royal Flying Corps (Royal Air Force after April, 1918).
1/5th Battalion DWR; killed in action, serving with the RAF, 11 6 1918, aged 25.
Buried – Huby St Leu British Cemetery, B, 4.
Commemorated – St Thomas's Church, Longroyd Bridge, RoH; M Stansfield, page 353, and the **Drill Hall WM panel 9, column 3**.
Mentioned in the Huddersfield Examiner (wounded in action, shrapnel to the knee) on 14 7 1916; (wounded in action) on 07 8 1916.
Paddock RoH shows date of death as 11 7 1918 (although indistinct).
Originally 1/5th DWR; posted to 3 DWR, commissioned 2nd Lieutenant; posted to RFC and promoted Lieutenant.

RICE A – Private.
No trace.
Commemorated – the **Drill Hall WM panel 9, column 3**.

RICHARDSON Arthur – 24683 Private.
Resided in Mirfield. Enlisted at Liversedge.
5th Battalion DWR; killed in action 23 7 1918. (27 3 1918?)
Buried – Bouilly Cross Roads Military Cemetery, 1, C, 15.
Commemorated – Mirfield WM and the **Drill Hall WM panel 9, column 3**.

RICHARDSON D – Private
No trace.
Commemorated – the **Drill Hall WM panel 9, column 3**.

RICHARDSON Mark – 242304 Private.
Born in Alnwick. Resided in Penrith. Enlisted at Alnwick.
1/5th Battalion DWR; killed in action 26 4 1917.

Buried – Les Touret Military Cemetery, 4, C, 24.
Commemorated – the **Drill Hall WM panel 9, column 3.**
Formerly 4531 Private Northumberland Fusiliers.

RIDGWAY John Edwin – Lieutenant.
Family appeared to live in Stockport.
2/5th Battalion DWR, A Company; killed in action 20 11 1917, Battle of Cambrai.
Commemorated – Cambrai Memorial (Louverval), France, and the **Drill Hall WM panel 9, column 3.**
Mentioned in the Goodall collection; Heywood, page 216.

RIDLEY Herbert Jesse – 15910 Private.
Born in Fulham. Resided in Hammersmith with his wife, Ellen Caroline. Enlisted at Hammersmith.
5th Battalion DWR; killed in action 27 3 1918, aged 26, German Spring Offensive.
Buried – Gommecourt British Cemetery No2, 5, D, 3.
Commemorated – the **Drill Hall WM panel 9, column 3.**

RIDLEY Pattison Reay – Lieutenant. Military Cross; Territorial Force War Medal.
Born in October, 1893, at Bill Quay, Heworth, Co Durham, to Pattison and Eliza Jane, of Monkseaton, Newcastle upon Tyne. Embarked for France and Flanders in January, 1917.
2/5th Battalion DWR, D Company; reported missing (killed in action) 03 5 1917, Battle of Bullecourt.
Commemorated – Arras Memorial, France; Royal Grammar School, Newcastle, T Ashworth, page 76; L Magnus, page 292, and the **Drill Hall WM panel 9, column 3.**
Commissioned from 647 Corporal, Northern Cyclists Battalion.
Mentioned in the Goodall collection (B Company, award of CO's Commendation for action at Orchard Alley, 27/28 2 1917); the 62nd Division History (wounded) page 185; L Magnus (medal award) page 119, 121; the Huddersfield Examiner (award of MC) on 24 9 1919; B Heywood (in action 24 2 1917) page 194; the Unit War Diary (Roll of Officers) on 31 1 1917; (award of MC) on 23 3 1917; the London Gazette (award of MC for gallantry on 27/28 2 1917) on 17 4 1917, page 3685.
TFWM awarded posthumously on 23 2 1923.

RILEY Arthur – 2958 Private.
Born in Outcote Bank, Huddersfield. Resided in Lockwood with his wife, Annie, and four children. Enlisted at Huddersfield on 04 9 1914. Embarked for France and Flanders in April, 1915.
1/5th Battalion DWR; killed in action, shellfire, 09 5 1915, Fleurbaix Sector.
Buried – Rue David Military Cemetery, 1, H, 29.
Commemorated – St Stephen's Church, Rashcliffe, RoH; Huddersfield Corporation RoH; M Stansfield, page 354, and the **Drill Hall WM panel 9, column 3.**
Mentioned in the Huddersfield Examiner (killed in action, 09 5 1915) on 15 5 1915 & 10 5 1920; (killed in action, shellfire) on 17 5 1915.
IT IS GOD THAT AVENGETH ME.

RILEY John Reginald Newton – 2nd Lieutenant.
Born in 1892, in Timperley, Cheshire, to Edward James and Annie Newton. Resided in Ashton on Mersey, Cheshire.
1/5th Battalion DWR; killed in action 03 9 1916, aged 24, Battle of the Somme (Thiepval).
Buried – Mill Road Cemetery, 1, J, 19.
Commemorated – the **Drill Hall WM panel 9, column 3.**
BLESSED ARE THE PURE IN HEART FOR THEY SHALL SEE GOD.

RIPPON Norris – 2nd Lieutenant.

Born in Huddersfield on 28 9 1892 to Joseph and Elizabeth. Commissioned in October, 1914. Embarked for France and Flanders in April, 1915.
1/5th Battalion DWR, D Company; killed in action 18 11 1915, aged 23, Ypres.
Buried – Bard Cottage Cemetery, 1, L, 18.
Commemorated – Fartown and Birkby WM; Waterloo Rugby Union Football Club RoH; M Stanfield, page 355, and the **Drill Hall WM panel 9, column 3.**
Mentioned in the Huddersfield Examiner (wrote to family of Private C Langrick) on 01 9 1915; (wrote to families of Private C Hamer & Private G E Cliffe) on 17 11 1915; (D Company, killed by sniper) on 22 11 1915. Mentioned in Unit War Diary (command of working party) on 16 10 1915; (killed in action by sniper) on 18 11 1915; (buried at Bard Cottage Cemetery) on 19 11 1915; Mentioned in J J Fisher (personal details), page 129.

RISPIN Percy – 22601 Private.
Born and resided in Harrogate, grandfather, G Rispin, lived at Longscales Farm, Birstwith. Enlisted at Keighley.
5th Battalion DWR; killed in action 26 5 1918, Advance to Victory.
Buried – Bienvillers Military Cemetery, 20, C, 12.
Commemorated – Arras Memorial, France, and the **Drill Hall WM panel 9, column 3.**

ROBBINS Ellis – 267427 Private.
Incorrectly spelt on RoH Board, see ROBINS, below.

ROBERTS Percy – 33489 Private.
Born and enlisted at Cardiff.
2/5th Battalion DWR; killed in action 28 3 1918, German Spring Offensive.
Commemorated – Arras Memorial, France, and the **Drill Hall WM panel 9, column 4.**
Formerly 29450 Private Army Service Corps.

ROBERTS Willie – 3230 (later 240631) Private.
Born Primrose Hill, Huddersfield, on 09 4 1894 to Joe and Clara. Resided in Primrose Hill. Enlisted at Huddersfield on 15 10 1914.
2/5th Battalion DWR, A Company; reported missing 03 5 1917, aged 23, Battle of Bullecourt.
Commemorated – Arras Memorial, France; M Stansfield, page 357, and the **Drill Hall WM panel 9, column 4.**
Mentioned in the Goodall collection (casualty return, dated 22 8 1917); the Huddersfield Examiner (reported missing, official casualty list) on 27 6 1917; (previously reported missing, now reported as killed in action) on 19 9 1917 & 04 10 1917.

ROBERTSON James – 26441 Private.
Born in Glasgow to John and Margaret Dunn. Enlisted at Glasgow.
5th Battalion DWR; killed in action 25 8 1918, aged 21, Advance to Victory.
Commemorated – Vis en Artois Memorial, France, and the **Drill Hall WM panel 9, column 4**.
Originally 2/5th DWR.

ROBERTSON John – 26458 Private.
Born in Lanark. Enlisted at Glasgow.
2/5th Battalion DWR; killed in action 25 11 1917, Battle of Cambrai.
Commemorated – Cambrai Memorial (Louverval), France, and the **Drill Hall WM panel 9, column 4.**
Formerly 30593 Private Royal Scots Fusiliers.

ROBINS (ROBBINS?) Ellis – 267427 Private.
Born in Ridgeway, Sheffield, to John and Mary. Resided in Ridgeway. Enlisted at Halifax.
5th Battalion DWR, D Company; killed in action 22 7 1918, aged 22, Battle of Tardenois.

Commemorated – Soissons Memorial, France; Barkisland WM and the **Drill Hall WM panel 9, column 4.**
Originally 2/5th DWR.
Mentioned in the Goodall collection.

ROBINSON Frank – 8625 Private.
Born in Wilsden to Edward and Emily. Resided in Wilsden. Enlisted at Bradford.
1/5th Battalion DWR; died of wounds 20 1 1917, aged 21.
Buried – Warlincourt Halte British Cemetery, 12, C, 9.
Commemorated – the **Drill Hall WM panel 9, column 3.**

ROBINSON Harry – 241241 Private.
Born in Huddersfield to Harry and Thirza. Resided in Huddersfield. Enlisted at Huddersfield.
5th Battalion DWR; died in hospital at Mons, whilst POW 06 10 1918, aged 23, Advance to Victory.
Buried – Mons Communal Cemetery, 7, B, 6.
Commemorated – St Andrews Church, Leeds Road, RoH (now missing); M Stansfield, page 358, and the **Drill Hall WM panel 9, column 3.**
LOVED, HONOURED, MOURNED.

ROBINSON John Arthur – 24070 Private.
Born and enlisted at Bradford.
5th Battalion DWR; killed in action 28 3 1918, aged 42, German Spring Offensive.
Commemorated – Arras Memorial, France, and the **Drill Hall WM panel 9, column 4.**

ROBINSON Sam – 6373 Private.
Born and enlisted at Bradford.
1/5th Battalion DWR; died of wounds 31 1 1917.
Buried – Warlincourt Halte British Cemetery, 4, G, 7.
Commemorated – the **Drill Hall WM panel 9, column 3.**

ROBINSON Sam Benson – 240240 Private.
Born in Ripon to Tom and Mary Jane, of Linthwaite. Resided in Meltham. Enlisted at Huddersfield in 1915.
2/5th Battalion DWR; killed in action 29 3 1918, aged, 24, German Spring Offensive.
Commemorated – Arras Memorial, France; Linthwaite WM; M Stansfield, page 359, and the **Drill Hall WM panel 9, column 4.**

ROBINSON Sidney – 16829 Private.
Born in Allendale, Northumberland. Enlisted at Hexham.
2/5th Battalion DWR; killed in action 10 4 1918, German Spring Offensive.
Commemorated – Pozieres Memorial, France, and the **Drill Hall WM panel 9, column 3.**

ROBSON W A – Private.
No trace.
Commemorated – the **Drill Hall WM panel 9, column 3.**

RODDIS Charles Harry – 3071 Private.
Born in Sheffield on 06 2 1897 to Charles and Ellen, of Huddersfield. Enlisted at Huddersfield in October, 1914. Embarked for France and Flanders in April, 1915.
1/5th Battalion DWR, A Company; killed in action 25 6 1915, aged 18, Ypres.
Buried – Rue David Military Cemetery, 1, B, 7.
Commemorated – Christ Church, Woodhouse Hill, RoH; M Stansfield, page 359, and the **Drill Hall WM panel 9, column 3.**
Mentioned in the Huddersfield Examiner (in memoriam) 25 6 1918.

HE DIED THAT WE MIGHT LIVE.

ROEBUCK Frank – 5061 (later 241645) Private.
Born in Marsh, Huddersfield, to Herbert, of Huddersfield. Resided in Huddersfield. Enlisted at Huddersfield on 16 3 1916.
2/5th Battalion DWR, C Company; reported missing 03 5 1917, aged 31, Battle of Bullecourt.
Commemorated – Arras Memorial, France; St Mark's Parish Church, Longwood, RoH; Shared Church, Paddock, RoH; M Stansfield, page 360, and the **Drill Hall WM panel 9, column 4.**
Mentioned in the Goodall collection; the Huddersfield Examiner (reported missing, official casuatly list) on 27 6 1917; (reported missing from 03 5 1917, now presumed killed in action on that date) on 16 10 1918.

ROEBUCK Lawrence Cyril – 3940 (later 241061) Private.
Born in New Mill, Holmfirth, to Ben. Resided New Mill. Enlisted at Huddersfield on 01 3 1915.
2/5th Battalion DWR; reported missing, afterwards accepted as killed in action, on 05 5 1917, aged 19, Battle of Bullecourt.
Buried – Sauchy Lestree Communal Cemetery, 1.
Commemorated – Fulstone WM; Holmfirth Secondary School RoH; New Mill Working Men's Club RoH; M Stansfield, page 361, and the **Drill Hall WM panel 9, column 4.**
Mentioned in the Goodall collection; T Ashcroft, page 78, the Huddersfield Examiner (reported missing) on 07 6 1917; (reported missing, official casualty list) on 27 6 1917; (died as POW, official casualty list) on 27 10 1917.

ROSE William – 2416 Private.
Born in Lightcliffe, Halifax, to Thomas and Mary Ann, of New Mill. Resided in New Mill. Enlisted at Holmfirth, F Company.
1/5th Battalion DWR; killed in action 28 9 1915, aged 19, Ypres.
Commemorated – Ypres (Menin Gate) Memorial, Belgium; Holme Valley Memorial Hospital WM (plaque 6, Hepworth & Scholes); Hepworth Parish Church RoH; M Stansfield, page 363, and the **Drill Hall WM panel 9, column 3.**
Mentioned in the Huddersfield Examiner (killed in action, shellfire) on 04 10 1915.

ROSSINGTON Arthur – 2nd Lieutenant.
Born in Bradford, to Richard and Clara. Resided in Headingley, Leeds, with his wife. Embarked for France and Flanders on 29 12 1916. Commissioned from 6 DWR to 5 DWR on 26 2 1918.
5th Battalion DWR; killed in action 13 9 1918, aged 27, Advance to Victory.
Buried – Hermies Hill British, Cemetery 2, A, 17.
Commemorated – 62nd Divisional History, page 207; and the **Drill Hall WM panel 9, column 4.**
Mentioned in the 5th DWR War Diary (joined Battalion, 03 9 1918, and killed in action, 13 9 1918) on 30 9 1918.
From 242540 Sergeant 6th DWR.
IN HONOUR HE SERVED.

ROTHWELL John Thomas – 5221 (later 241780) Private.
Born in Halifax to William Henry and Ellen. Resided in Lindley. Enlisted at Huddersfield.
2/5th Battalion DWR; reported missing 03 5 1917, aged 29, Battle of Bullecourt.
Commemorated – Arras Memorial, France; Blackley Baptist Chapel RoH; M Stansfield, page 364, and the **Drill Hall WM panel 9, column 4.**
Mentioned in the Goodall collection; the Huddersfield Examiner (reported missing, official casualty list) on 27 6 1917; (previously reported missing, now killed in action) on 04 10 1917.

ROUSE Mark – 203321 Private.
Born and enlisted at Bradford
5th Battalion DWR; killed in action 22 7 1918, Battle of Tardenois.

Commemorated – Soissons Memorial, France, and the **Drill Hall WM panel 9, column 4.**
Originally 2/5th DWR.

ROUTLEDGE Joseph Edward Christopher – 2366 Private.
Born in Bolton, Lancs on 23 2 1897. Resided at Moldgreen. Enlisted in Huddersfield in August, 1914.
1/5th Battalion DWR; wounded in action on 03 9 1916 and died of wounds in St George's Hospital, London, on 09 9 1916, aged 19, Battle of the Somme (Thiepval).
Buried – Huddersfield (Almondbury) Cemetery, 8, C, 62.
Commemorated – Almondbury WM; Christ Church, Moldgreen, RoH; M Stansfield, page 364, and the **Drill Hall WM panel 9, column 4.**
Mentioned in the Huddersfield Examiner (died of wounds) on 27 6 1916; (buried in Almondbury 13 6 1916) on 14 9 1916.

ROWE Herbert – 5079 (later 241661) Private.
Born in Thurby, Lincs, to Henry. Resided and enlisted at Bourne, Lincs.
2/5th Battalion DWR; killed in action 03 5 1917, aged 28, Battle of Bullecourt.
Commemorated – Arras Memorial, France, and the **Drill Hall WM panel 9, column 4.**
Mentioned in the Goodall collection.

ROWE Walter – 3324 (later 240684) Private.
Born in Huddersfield Workhouse on 05 10 1885. Resided in Lockwood with his wife, Polly. Enlisted at Huddersfield on 10 11 1914.
2/5th Battalion DWR; wounded and taken prisoner 03 5 1917 and died of wounds as Prisoner of War 23 6 1917, aged 33.
Buried – Tournai Communal Cemetery Extension, 1, A, 2.
Commemorated – Emmanuel Church, Lockwood, RoH; M Stansfield, page 365, and the **Drill Hall WM panel 9, column 4.**
Mentioned in the Goodall collection; the Huddersfield Examiner (reported missing, official casualty list) on 27 6 1917; (previously reported missing, now reported POW) on 09 7 1917; (reported wounded in action, POW, casualty list) on 16 8 1917.

ROYLE Charles – 2956 Corporal.
Born in Lindley. Resided in Lindley, with his wife, Ellen. Enlisted at Huddersfield on 05 9 1914.
1/5th Battalion DWR; reported missing from patrol 14 11 1916, date of death accepted as 14 11 1916, aged 33, Battle of the Somme.
Buried – Foncquevillers Military Cemetery, 1, J, 32.
Commemorated – St Stephen's Church, Lindley, RoH; M Stansfield, page 365, and the **Drill Hall WM panel 9, column 4.**
Mentioned in the Huddersfield Examiner (reported missing) on 10 11 1916; (letter received by family informing them of his death) on 29 11 1916; (previously reported missing, now killed in action) on 10 1 1917; J J Fisher, page 114.

RUSH Clement Ward – 2nd Lieutenant.
Born in 1890 at Witnesham, Suffolk, to Robert and Amy. Resided with his wife, Alice Ellen, in Broomhall, Bradfield St George, Suffolk. Commissioned into DWR 19 7 1916.
1/5th Battalion DWR; killed in action 03 9 1916, Battle of the Somme (Thiepval).
Commemorated – Thiepval Memorial, France, and the **Drill Hall WM panel 9, column 4.**
Formerly Quarter Master Sergeant in 2nd SMCC (MTC) [*unknown unit*].

RUSHFIRTH Frank – 2951 Private.
Born in Berry Brow, Huddersfield, on 03 12 1883, to Joshua and Martha. Resided in Lockwood. Enlisted at Huddersfield on 09 9 1914.

1/5th Battalion DWR, A Company stretcher bearer; killed in action, gas attack, on 19 11 1915, aged 33, Ypres.
Buried – Talana Farm Cemetery, 4, G, 5.
Commemorated – Emmanuel Church, Lockwood, RoH; M Stansfield, page 366, and the **Drill Hall WM panel 9, column 4.**
Mentioned in the Huddersfield Examiner (stretcher bearer, A Company, killed in action) on 25 11 1915.

RUSHWORTH Frank – 23513 Private.
Born in Bradford to Josiah and Mary. Resided in Bradford with his wife, Annie Stocks. Enlisted at Bradford.
5th Battalion DWR; killed in action 29 3 1918, aged 28, German Spring Offensive.
Commemorated – Arras Memorial, France, and the **Drill Hall WM panel 9, column 4.**
Originally 2/5th DWR.

RUSSELL Robert John – 33628 Private.
Born in Wood Green, London, to George and Elizabeth. Resided in Woolwich. Enlisted at Woolwich.
5th Battalion DWR; killed in action 26 3 1918, aged 19, German Spring Offensive.
Commemorated – Arras Memorial, France, and the **Drill Hall WM panel 9, column 4.**
Originally 1/5th DWR.

RYLANCE Ernest – 3411 (later 240733) Private.
Born in Huddersfield on 25 10 1897 to John William and Ann, of Huddersfield. Enlisted at Huddersfield on 10 11 1914.
2/5th Battalion DWR; reported missing 03 5 1917, aged 19, Battle of Bullecourt.
Commemorated – Arras Memorial, France; St John's Church, Newsome, RoH; M Stansfield, page 367, and the **Drill Hall WM panel 9, column 4.**
Mentioned in the Huddersfield Examiner (news requested by relatives) on 14 6 1917.

SALWAY Ernest George – 17218 Lance Corporal.
Born in Draycott, Derbyshire. Resided at Gressmore, Derbyshire. Enlisted at Chesterfield.
5th Battalion DWR; killed in action 29 3 1918, aged 38, German Spring Offensive.
Buried – Doullens Communal Cemetery Extension, 5, C, 19.
Commemorated – the **Drill Hall WM panel 10, column 1.**
Formerly 300330 Private Army Service Corps. Originally 2/5th DWR.

SANDERSON (aka WOOD) Joseph Walker – 299 Private.
Born in Holmfirth. Resided in Holmfirth with his wife, Edith WOOD (he served as Sanderson). Enlisted at Holmfirth, F Company.
1/5th Battalion DWR; died of wounds at No 13 General Hospital, Boulogne, on 19 7 1915, Ypres.
Buried – Boulogne Eastern Cemetery, 8, B, 64.
Commemorated – Holme Valley Memorial Hospital WM (plaque 3, Holmfirth); M Stansfield, page 493, and the **Drill Hall WM panel 9, column 4.**

SANDFORD Fred – 4941 (later 241540) Private.
Born Catworth, Hunts, to John and Martha Ann. Resided in Holmfirth. Enlisted in Homfirth in March, 1916.
2/5th Battalion DWR; killed in action 03 5 1917, aged 29, Battle of Bullecourt.
Commemorated – Arras Memorial, France; Wooldale WM; M Stansfield, page 368, and the **Drill Hall WM panel 9, column 4.**
Mentioned in the Goodall collection (casualty return dated 22 8 1917); the Huddersfield Examiner (reported missing) on 07 6 1917; (reported missing, official casualty list) on 27 6 1917; (previously reported missing, now killed in action) 19 9 1917 & 04 10 1917.

SANDFORD Leonard – 4741 Private.
Born in Huddersfield to Jonathan and Mary. Resided at Underbank, Holmfirth, with his wife, Mavis. Enlisted at Holmfirth in 1916.
2/5th Battalion DWR; died of wounds at No 20 General Hospital, Camiers, on 18 9 1916, aged 23, Battle of the Somme.
Buried – Etaples Military Cemetery, 15, A, 3A.
Commemorated – Arras Memorial, France; Holme Valley Memorial Hospital WM (plaque 3, Holmfirth); Holmfirth Secondary School RoH; Holmfirth Parish Churchyard Memorial; M Stansfield, page 368, and the **Drill Hall WM panel 9, column 4.**
Mentioned in the Huddersfield Examiner (died of wounds in hospital, France) on 21 9 1916; J J Fisher, page 113.
HE SLEEPS UNTIL THE RESURRECTION MORN.

SANDIFORTH Arthur – 2967 Private.
Born in Leeds to John and Mary, of Headingley. Resided in Huddersfield. Enlisted at Huddersfield in 1914.
1/5th Battalion DWR; killed in action, shellfire, 01 10 1915, aged 22, Ypres.
Buried – New Irish Farm Cemetery, 2, B, 20.
Commemorated – M Stansfield, page 368, and the **Drill Hall WM panel 9, column 4.**

SAUL Harry – 242350 Private.
Born to George and Elizabeth, of Blackburn. Husband of the late Alice M and Enlisted in Hull.
5th Battalion DWR; killed in action 05 6 1918, aged 34, Advance to Victory.
Buried – Bienvillers Military Cemetery, 21, B, 13.
Commemorated – the **Drill Hall WM panel 10, column 1.**
Originally 2/5th DWR.

SAYLES Frank – 2784 Private.
Born in Huddersfield to Reuben and Mary, of Longroyd Bridge. Enlisted at Huddersfield on 05 9 1914.
1/5th Battalion DWR, A Company; killed in action 16 11 1915, aged 20, Ypres.
Buried – Talana Farm Cemetery, 4, F, 12.
Commemorated – M Stansfield, page 369, and the **Drill Hall WM panel 10, column 1.**

SCHOFIELD Albert (E?) – 268556 Private.
Born in Lindley to John and Edith. Resided in Lindley. Enlisted in September, 1914.
5th Battalion DWR; killed in action, 22 7 1918, aged 25, Battle of Tardenois.
Buried – Marfaux British Cemetery, 6, 1, 8.
Commemorated – M Stansfield, page 370, and the **Drill Hall WM panel 10, column 1.**
Originally 2/5th DWR.
CWGC shows initial as A E.
R.I.P.

SCHOFIELD Frank Metcalfe – 2268 Private.
Born in Huddersfield on 03 10 1895, to Eleanor Rigg and the late John. Resided in Huddersfield. Enlisted into the local Territorials at Huddersfield in 1912. Embodied at the beginning of the war and embarked for France and Flanders in April, 1915.
1/5th Battalion DWR; killed in action 17 11 1915, aged 20, Ypres.
Commemorated – Ypres (Menin Gate) Memorial, France; Almondbury WM; Huddersfield Parish Church RoH; Christ Church, Moldgreen, RoH; M Stansfield, page 370, and the **Drill Hall WM panel 10, column 1.**

SCHOFIELD Franklin – 240898 Corporal.

Born in Moldgreen on 20 9 1896 to Charlotte, of Moldgreen. Resided in Oakes. Enlisted at Huddersfield on 04 1 1915.
2/5th Battalion DWR; reported missing, presumed killed in action, 27 11 1917, aged 21, Battle of Cambrai.
Commemorated – Cambrai Memorial (Louverval), France; St Stephen's Church, Lindley, RoH; M Stansfield, page 370, and the **Drill Hall WM panel 10, column 1.**

SCHOFIELD Harry – 267699 Private.
Born in Ripponden to Elizabeth and the late John Benjamin, of Soyland. Resided in Ripponden. Enlisted at Halifax.
5th Battalion DWR; died of wounds 13 9 1918, aged 23, Advance to Victory.
Buried – Grevillers British Cemetery, 13 B, 18.
Commemorated – the **Drill Hall WM panel 10, column 1.**
Originally 2/5th DWR.

SCHOFIELD John Edward – 3638 (later 240869) Private.
Born to Joseph and Priscilla, of Dewsbury. Resided in Ravensthorpe. Enlisted at Mirfield on 28 12 1914.
5th Battalion DWR, 15 Platoon, D Company; killed in action 25 8 1918, aged 24, Advance to Victory.
Buried – Gommecourt South Cemetery, 1, C, 2.
Commemorated – the **Drill Hall WM panel 10, column 1.**
Mentioned in the Goodall collection.

SCHOFIELD Joseph Oates – 3138 (later 240589) Corporal.
Born in Huddersfield to Emma and the late Daniel. Resided in Mirfield. Enlisted at Huddersfield.
1/5th Battalion DWR D Company; killed in action 03 9 1916, aged 22, Battle of the Somme (Thiepval).
Commemorated – Thiepval Memorial, France; Battyeford WM; Mirfield WM and the **Drill Hall WM panel 10, column 1.**

SCHOFIELD Malcolm – 5188 Private.
Born and enlisted at Mosley.
2/5th Battalion DWR; killed in action 14 2 1917.
Buried – Auchonvillers Military Cemetery, 2, K, 10.
Commemorated – All Saints Church, Mossley, RoH; Micklehurst Conservative Club RoH; R Vaughan, page 155, and the **Drill Hall WM panel 10, column 1.**
SDGW shows date of death as 15 2 1917.

SCHOFIELD Norman – 3520 (later 240809) Private.
Born in Honley. Resided in Honley. Enlisted at Huddersfield in November, 1914. Embarked for France and Flanders in January, 1917.
2/5th Battalion DWR; killed in action 20 11 1917, Battle of Cambrai.
Commemorated – Hermies Hill British Cemetery Special Memorial A11, France; Honley WM; C Ford, page 26; M Stansfield, page 373, and the **Drill Hall WM panel 10, column 1.**
Mentioned in the Goodall collection.
THEIR GLORY SHALL NOT BE BLOTTED OUT.

SCOTNEY William – 241637 Private.
Born in Nocton, Lincs. Resided and enlisted at Louth.
2/5th Battalion DWR; killed in action 20 11 1917, Battle of Cambrai.
Commemorated – Cambrai Memorial (Louverval), France, and the **Drill Hall WM panel 10, column 1.**

SCRIMSHAW George William – 5161 (later 241731) Private.
Born to George William and Mary Anne, of Willingham-by-Sea, Lincs. Resided and enlisted at Gainsborough.
2/5th Battalion DWR, 15 Platoon, D Company; died of wounds, shellfire, 18 4 1917, aged 33.
Buried – Mory Abbey Military Cemetery, 1, A, 9.
Commemorated – the **Drill Hall WM panel 10, column 1.**
Mentioned in the Goodall collection.

SEAMAN Walter Stanley – 25325 Private.
Born in Middlesbrough to Walter and Katherine. Resided and enlisted at Middlesbrough.
9th Battalion DWR; killed in action 29 4 1918, aged 22, German Spring Offensive.
Buried – Forceville Communal Cemetery, 4, B, 20.
Commemorated – the **Drill Hall WM panel 10, column 1.**

SECKER Nelson – 4526 Private.
Resided in Lees. Enlisted at Mirfield.
1/5th Battalion DWR; killed in action 17 9 1916, Battle of the Somme.
Buried – Serre Road Cemetery No2, 9, M, 10.
Commemorated – the **Drill Hall WM panel 10, column 1.**

SEDDON Clifford – 201698 Private.
Enlisted at Halifax.
5th Battalion DWR; killed in action 23 7 1918, Battle of Tardenois.
Commemorated – Soissons Memorial, France; Calderdale War Dead, page 242, and the **Drill Hall WM panel 10, column 1.**
Originally 2/5th DWR.

SENIOR Fred – 4895 (later 241506) Private.
Born in Netherton on 22 6 1891 to Herbert and Mary, of Crosland Moor. Resided in Huddersfield. Enlisted at Milnsbridge in February, 1916.
1/5th Battalion DWR; killed in action 03 9 1916, Battle of the Somme (Thiepval).
Buried – Connaught Cemetery, 1, E, 7.
Commemorated – St Barnabas Church, Crosland Moor, RoH; The Rising Sun Public House, Crosland Hill, RoH; M Stansfield, page 375, and the **Drill Hall WM panel 10, column 1.**
Mentioned in the Huddersfield Examiner (reported missing) on 05 10 1916; (request for information by the family) on 28 2 1917; (previously reported missing, now reported as killed in action) on 12 12 1917.

SENIOR George – 241975 Private.
Born in Lepton to Elizabeth H. Resided in Lepton. Enlisted at Huddersfield in March, 1916
2/5th Battalion DWR; killed in action 16 3 1917.
Buried – Queens Cemetery, 3, E, 8.
Commemorated – Lepton Parish Church RoH; M Stansfield, page 375, and the **Drill Hall WM panel 10, column 1.**
Brother of Thomas, qv.

SENIOR Thomas – 5513 Private.
Born in Lepton, son of Elizabeth H. Resided in Lepton, Enlisted at Huddersfield in March 1916.
1/5th Battalion DWR; died of wounds at 13 General Hospital, Boulogne, on 11 9 1916, aged 23, Battle of the Somme.
Buried – Boulogne Eastern Cemetery, 8, 3, 133.
Commemorated – Lepton Parish Church RoH; M Stansfield, page 377, and the **Drill Hall WM panel 10, column 1.**
Mentioned in the Huddersfield Examiner (died of wounds, official casualty list) on 20 10 1916.

Brother of George, qv.

SEVILLE William Henry - 26277 Private.
Resided in Broughton, Lancs. Enlisted in Salford.
5th Battalion DWR; killed in action 24 7 1918, Tardenois.
Buried – St Sever Cemetery Extension, Q, 3, J, 12.
Commemorated – the **Drill Hall WM panel 10, column 1.**

SEWELL Tom – 235093 Private.
Born in Longwood, Huddersfield. Resided in Huddersfield. Enlisted at Huddersfield.
2/5th Battalion DWR; died of wounds 18 4 1917.
Buried – Mory Abbey Military Cemetery, 1, A, 7.
Commemorated – St Stephen's Church, Rashcliffe, RoH; M Stansfield, page 378, and the **Drill Hall WM panel 10, column 1.**
Mentioned in the Huddersfield Examiner (died of wounds, official casualty list) on 03 5 1917.

SHACKLETON Albert – 5960 Private.
Born and enlisted at Bradford.
1/5th Battalion DWR; died of wounds 13 11 1916, Battle of the Somme.
Buried – Warlincourt Halte British Cemetery, 3, D, 3.
Commemorated – the **Drill Hall WM panel 10, column 2.**
SDGW shows his number as 5966.

SHACKLETON John Robert – 6979 Private.
Enlisted at Bradford.
1/5th Battalion DWR; died of wounds 20 1 1917.
Buried – Warlincourt Halte British Cemetery, 3, J, 3.
Commemorated – the **Drill Hall WM panel 10, column 2.**

SHACKLETON Thomas William – 242847 Private.
Born in Todmorden to James and Betsy. Enlisted at Todmorden.
1/5th Battalion DWR; killed in action 27 8 1917, aged 19, Nieuport Sector.
Buried – Coxyde Military Cemetery, 3, C, 19.
Commemorated – the **Drill Hall WM panel 10, column 2.**

SHARP Sam – 241343 Corporal.
Enlisted at Huddersfield.
1/5th Battalion DWR; killed in action 03 9 1916, Battle of the Somme (Thiepval).
Buried – Mill Road Cemetery, 1, F, 6.
Commemorated – Longwood WM; M Stansfield, page 379, and the **Drill Hall WM panel 10, column 2.**

SHARPE Arthur Noel – Lieutenant.
Born in Huddersfield on 30 12 1888 to Arthur Calvert and Mary. Resided in Edgerton, Huddersfield. Enlisted as a Private, 2577 West Riding Regiment, on 09 8 1914. Commissioned into the 1/5th DWR in January, 1915. Embarked for France and Flanders on 07 7 1915.
1/5th Battalion DWR; wounded in action and reported missing 03 9 1916, aged 27, Battle of the Somme (Thiepval).
Buried – Mill Road Cemetery, 1, H, 17.
Commemorated – Huddersfield Parish Church RoH; Huddersfield College School RoH; J J Fisher, page 129; M Stansfield, page 378, and the **Drill Hall WM panel 10, column 2.**
Mentioned in the Unit war Diary (promoted Lt) on 30 1 1916; (OC B Company) on 03 9 1916; (reported missing) on 30 9 1916.

Mentioned in the Huddersfield Examiner (wrote to the family of Lance Corporal S Milnes) on 11 7 1916; (reported wounded and missing in action) on 11 9 1916; (previously reported missing, now presumed killed) on 07 8 1917; (in memoriam) on 03 9 1917, 1918 and 1919.

SHAW David – 2066 Corporal.
Born in Huddersfield to Tom and Emma. Resided in Huddersfield. Enlisted into the local Territorials in 1912. Embodied at the outbreak of war and embarked for France and Flanders in April, 1915. Evacuated as sick to UK in 1915.
1/5th Battalion DWR, A Company; died of pneumonia, Royds Hall War Hospital, Huddersfield, on 20 12 1915, aged 20.
Buried – Huddersfield (Edgerton) Cemetery, 11B, 115.
Commemorated – the **Drill Hall WM panel 10, column 1.**
Mentioned in the Huddersfield Examiner (died in Huddersfield Hospital) on 18 12 1918; (in memorial) on 19 12 1919.

SHAW Edwin – 16109 (later 242797) Private.
Born in Hull to William and Mary Hannah. Resided and enlisted at Hull.
2/5th Battalion DWR; killed in action 03 5 1917, aged 22, Battle of Bullecourt.
Commemorated – Arras Memorial, France, and the **Drill Hall WM panel 10, column 2.**
Mentioned in the Goodall collection.

SHAW Ernest – 5648 Private.
Born and resided in Greenfield. Enlisted at Upper Mill.
1/5th Battalion DWR; killed in action 03 9 1916, Battle of the Somme (Thiepval).
Commemorated – Thiepval Memorial, France; Saddleworth WM and the **Drill Hall WM panel 10, column 1.**

SHAW Ernest – 5503 (later 242016) Private.
Born in Berry Brow, Huddersfield, on 07 8 1893. Resided in Berry Brow. Enlisted at Huddersfield on 11 3 1916.
2/5th Battalion DWR; reported missing, presumed killed on 03 5 1917, Battle of Bullecourt.
Commemorated – Arras Memorial, France; Armitage Bridge WM; M Stansfield, page 381, and the **Drill Hall WM panel 10, column 1.**
Mentioned in the Goodall collection; the Huddersfield Examiner (reported missing, official casualty list) on 27 6 1917; (previously reported missing now presumed dead) on 29 6 1917; (reported missing) on 01 8 1917.

SHAW Frank – 241208 Private.
Born in Almondbury on 26 12 1895 to Sam and Alice. Resided in Almondbury. Enlisted at Huddersfield on 17 5 1915.
5th Battalion DWR; killed in action 20 7 1918.
Buried – Courmas British Cemetery, 2, C, 4.
Commemorated – Almondbury WM; M Stansfield, page 381, and the **Drill Hall WM panel 10, column 2.**

SHAW John Leslie Robert – 1749 Private.
Born in Huddersfield to Sam Shaw, of Crosland Moor. Resided and enlisted at Huddersfield. Pre-war Territorial. Embodied at the outbreak of war and embarked for France and Flanders in April, 1915.
1/5th Battalion DWR; killed in action 22 12 1915, Ypres.
Commemorated – Ypres (Menin Gate) Memorial, Belgium; M Stansfield, page 387, and the **Drill Hall WM panel 10, column 1.**

SHAW Thomas Harold – 5026 (later 241615) Lance Corporal.

Born in Huddersfield on 25 1 1894 to Thomas and Hannah. Resided in Huddersfield. Enlisted at Huddersfield on 17 3 1916.
2/5th Battalion DWR; killed in action 27 11 1917, Battle of Cambrai.
Commemorated – Cambrai Memorial (Louverval), France; memorial in Almondbury Cemetery; M Stansfield, page 385, and the **Drill Hall WM panel 10, column 2.**
Mentioned in the Goodall collection.

SHAW Walter – 205371 Private.
Mother was Elizabeth. Enlisted at Bradford.
5th Battalion DWR; killed in action 22 7 1918, aged 23, Battle of Tardenois.
Commemorated – Soissons Memorial, France, and the **Drill Hall WM panel 10, column 2.**
Originally 2/5th DWR.

SHEARD Stanley – 4957 (later 241555) Private.
Born in Battyeford in October, 1891. Resided at Deighton. Enlisted at Mirfield in March, 1916.
5th Battalion DWR; died of wounds 22 7 1918.
Buried – St Imoges Churchyard Cemetery, B, 15.
Commemorated – Thiepval Memorial, France; Deighton WM; Mirfield WM; Christ Church, Woodhouse Hill RoH; United Methodist Chapel, Deighton, RoH; Nab Wood Working Men's Club Commemorative Plaque (now held in Mirfield Library, 2018); M Stansfield, page 387, and the **Drill Hall WM panel 10, column 2.**
Mentioned in the Goodall collection; the Huddersfield Examiner (died of wounds) on 07 8 1918.
Originally 2/5th DWR.

SHEARD Thomas Henry – 3428 Private.
Son of Sarah and the late Henry, of Mirfield. Enlisted at Mirfield.
1/5th Battalion DWR, C Company; killed in action 29 4 1915, aged 32, Ypres.
Buried – Rue David Military Cemetery, 1, A, 7.
Commemorated – Mirfield WM and the **Drill Hall WM panel 10, column 2.**
Mentioned in the Unit War Diary (buried near Battalion Headquarters) on 29 4 1915.

SHEARSMITH Sydney – 5048 (later 241634) Private.
Born in Bonby, Brigg, Lincs. Resided in Worlaby, Lincs. Enlisted at Barton on 10 3 1916.
2/5th Battalion DWR, D Company; killed in action 03 5 1917, Battle of Bullecourt.
Commemorated – Arras Memorial, France, and the **Drill Hall WM panel 10, column 2.**
Mentioned in the Goodall collection.
Related to Walter? qv.

SHEARSMITH Walter – 5052 (later 241638) Corporal. Military Medal and Bar.
Born in Bonby, Brigg, Lincs, to Henry and Susan. Resided in Worlaby, Lincs. Enlisted at Barton on 10 3 1916.
5th Battalion DWR, D Company Sniper section; killed in action 13 9 1918, aged 25, Advance to Victory.
Buried – Sunken Road, Boisleux, Cemetery, 2, A, 1.
Commemorated – L Magnus, page 294; the **Drill Hall WM panel 10, column 2.**
Mentioned in the Goodall collection; the Huddersfield Examiner (award of Bar to MM) on 09 10 1918; the Unit War Diary (patrol action) on 08 8 1917; (award of MM) on 22 8 1917; (Bar to MM awarded) on 30 9 1918; the London Gazette (award of MM) on 18 10 1917, page 10727; (award of bar to MM) 11 2 1919, page 2083.
Related to Sydney? qv.

SHEPHERD Edwin – 32155 Private.
Born in Bingley to William and Hannah, of Eldwick. Resided in Bingley with his wife, Ada. Enlisted at Bingley.

5th Battalion DWR; died of wounds, home, 08 4 1918, aged 31, German Spring Offensive.
Buried – Bingley Cemetery, G2, 6.
Commemorated – the **Drill Hall WM panel 10, column 2.**
Originally 2/5th DWR.
FOR GOD, KING AND COUNTRY.

SHEPHERD Walter 3047 (later 240544) Private.
Born in Ashton under Lyne. Resided in Mossley. Enlisted at Huddersfield.
2/5th Battalion DWR; killed in action 20 11 1917, Battle of Cambrai.
Commemorated – Cambrai Memorial (Louverval), France; All Saints' Church, Mossley, RoH; St John the Baptist Church, Mossley; RoH, R Vaughan, pages 103, 155, 159 & 160, and the **Drill Hall WM panel 10, column 2.**
Mentioned in the Goodall collection.

SHEPHERDSON William – 5050 (later 241636) Corporal.
Born in Saxby, Brigg, Lincs, to John. Resided in Worlaby, Lincs. Enlisted at Brigg, Lincs.
2/5th Battalion DWR, D Company; killed in action 26 5 1917, aged 22.
Buried – Mons Communal Cemetery, 4, A, 4.
Commemorated – the **Drill Hall WM panel 10, column 2.**
Mentioned in the Goodall collection.

SHEPPARD Walter (William) – 4281 Private.
Born in Mexborough on 13 7 1895 to George William and Emily, of Fartown. Resided in Fartown. Enlisted at Huddersfield on 13 7 1915.
1/5th Battalion DWR; reported missing, presumed killed, 03 9 1916, Battle of the Somme (Thiepval).
Commemorated – Thiepval Memorial, France; Fartown and Birkby WM; Christ Church, Woodhouse Hill, RoH; M Stansfield, page 387, and the **Drill Hall WM panel 10, column 2.**
Mentioned in the Huddersfield Examiner (reported missing) on 05 10 1916.

SHERBON Charles – 2597 (later 240334) Private.
Born in Huddersfield to Ann, of Fartown. Resided in Mirfield. Enlisted at Huddersfield in September, 1914.
5th Battalion DWR; died of wounds at Beckets Park War Hospital, Leeds, on 26 9 1916, Battle of the Somme.
Buried – Huddersfield (Edgerton) Cemetery, 23, 179.
Commemorated – Thiepval Memorial, France; Fartown and Birkby WM; M Stansfield, page 388, and the **Drill Hall WM panel 10, column 2.**
Mentioned in the Huddersfield Examiner (wounded in action, left arm, Guildford hospital) on 26 9 1916; (wounded in action, official casualty list) on 07 8 1916; (died of wounds) on 03 10 1918.

SHINDLER Cecil – 235095 Private.
Born and enlisted at Halifax.
2/5th Battalion DWR; killed in action 03 5 1917, Battle of Bullecourt.
Commemorated – Arras Memorial, France, and the **Drill Hall WM panel 10, column 2.**

SHINGLES George Armine – 26303 Private.
Born in Mattishall, Norfolk. Resided in East Dereham. Enlisted at Norwich on 16 3 1915.
5th Battalion DWR, D Company; died on 14 9 1918, Advance to Victory.
Buried – Denain Communal Cemetery, D, 47.
Commemorated – the **Drill Hall WM panel 10, column 2.**
Formerly T4/059473 Army Service Corps
Mentioned in the Goodall collection, initials shows as D A.

SHIRES Herbert – 307567 Private.
Born in Wennington. Resided at Barnoldswick. Enlisted at Keighley on 26 8 1916.
2/5th Battalion DWR, D Company Lewis gunner; killed in action 27 11 1917, Battle of Cambrai.
Commemorated – Cambrai Memorial (Louverval), France; P Thompson, page 171, and the **Drill Hall WM panel 10, column 2.**
Originally 1/7th DWR.

SHORE Albert – 4622 Private.
Born in Huddersfield. Resided in Moldgreen. Enlisted at Huddersfield, F Company 5 DWR.
1/5th Battalion DWR, A Company; killed in action 27 2 1917.
Commemorated – Thiepval Memorial, France; Huddersfield Parish Church RoH; Christ Church, Moldgreen, RoH; M Stansfield, page 388, and the **Drill Hall WM panel 10, column 2.**

SHORE Lewis – 198 (later 238005) Sergeant.
Born in Holmfirth to Jesse and Ruth (father served in the Volunteers and Territorial Force). Resided in Berry Brow with this wife, Emily. Enlisted at Holmfirth into F Company, 5th DWR. Transferred as 238005 9th West Yorkshire Regiment. Embarked for France and Flanders in March, 1917.
5th Battalion DWR; killed in action, shellfire, serving with 9th West Yorkshire Regiment, on 12 6 1917, Ypres.
Commemorated – Ypres (Menin Gate) Memorial, Belgium; Holmfirth WM; Armitage Bridge WM; M Stansfield, page 388, and the **Drill Hall WM panel 10, column 2.**
Mentioned in the Huddersfield Examiner (family details) on 01 9 1915.

SHUTTLEWORTH Hedley – 4003 (later 241097) Private.
Born in Abbeysteads, Lancs, to William and Isabel, of Galgate, Lancaster. Resided in Marsden with this wife, Elsie Eliza Jane. Enlisted at Huddersfield on 14 4 1915. Embarked for France and Flanders in January, 1917.
5th Battalion DWR, B Company stretcher bearer; killed in action, gun-shot wound, 27 3 1918, aged 32, German Spring Offensive.
Commemorated – Arras Memorial, France; Marsden WM; M Stansfield, page 389, and the **Drill Hall WM panel 10, column 2.**
Mentioned in the Goodall collection.
Originally 2/5th DWR.

SIDDALL Roland Woolfall – 200675 Private.
Born in Halifax to Herbert and Helen, of West End, Halifax. Enlisted at Halifax.
5th Battalion DWR; killed in action 14 4 1918, aged 23, German Spring Offensive.
Buried – Bienvillers Military Cemetery, 9, C, 19.
Commemorated – Calderdale War Dead, page 249, and the **Drill Hall WM panel 10, column 3.**
Originally 1/4th DWR.

SILVESTER William Henry – 4637 Private.
Resided in Marsden with his wife, Mary Alice. Enlisted at Huddersfield.
3/5th Battalion DWR; died, home, 29 5 1916, aged 32.
Buried – Friezland, Christ Church (Yorks), East, 29.
Commemorated – Saddleworth WM; the **Drill Hall WM panel 10, column 3.**
REST IN PEACE.

SIMPSON Frank – 2970 Private.
Resided in Southend on Sea. Enlisted at Huddersfield.
1/5th Battalion DWR; died of wounds 01 10 1915, Ypres.
Buried – Lijssenthoek Military Cemetery, 1, C, 27.
Commemorated – Thiepval Memorial, France, and the **Drill Hall WM panel 10, column 2.**

SIMPSON Henry – 26623 Private.
Born and enlisted at Mansfield.
1/5th Battalion DWR; killed in action 27 12 1917.
Commemorated – Perth (China Wall) Garter Point Memorial 33, France, and the **Drill Hall WM panel 10, column 3.**

SIMPSON J.
Possibly duplicate of Simpson J panel 10, column 2. See below:
Commemorated – the **Drill Hall WM panel 10, column 2.**

SIMPSON James – 5081 (later 241663) Private. Military Medal
Born in Skillingthorpe, Lincs, to Joseph and Martha. Resided in Skillingthorpe Fen. Enlisted at Lincoln on 13 3 1916.
5th Battalion DWR, 13 Platoon D Company; killed in action, acting as Battalion Runner, on 26 3 1918, aged 26, German Spring Offensive (at Bouquoy).
Commemorated – Arras Memorial, France; L Magnus, page 295, and the **Drill Hall WM panel 10, column 3.**
Mentioned in the Goodall collection; the London Gazette (award of MM) on 13 3 1918, page 3244; Unit War Diary (award of MM for operations 20-27 11 1917) [Battle of Cambrai] on 20 12 1917.
Originally 2/5th DWR.

SIMPSON James Henry – 241345 Private.
Enlisted at Mirfield.
1/5th Battalion DWR; killed in action 03 9 1916, aged 28, Battle of the Somme (Thiepval).
Commemorated – Thiepval Memorial, France, and the **Drill Hall WM panel 10, column 3.**

SIMPSON William 13365 Private.
Born in Otley to Benjamin and Mary. Enlisted at Otley.
5th Battalion DWR; killed in action 07 11 1918, aged 33, Advance to Victory.
Buried – Maubeuge Centre Cemetery, B, 18.
Commemorated – Little Ouseburn Church memorial and the **Drill Hall WM panel 10, column 3.**
Mentioned in the Unit War Diary (awarded General Officer Commanding's Meritorious Service certificate for actions on 14 4 1917) on 12 5 1917.
Originally 2/5th DWR.

SINGLETON John Herbert – 4872 Private.
Born in Paddock on 09 4 1889 to Henry and Mary, of Longwood, Huddersfield. Enlisted at Huddersfield on 14 2 1916.
1/5th Battalion DWR; killed in action, shellfire, 16 9 1916, Battle of the Somme.
Commemorated – Thiepval Memorial, France; St Mark's Parish Church, Longwood, RoH; J J Fisher, page 114, M Stansfield, page 392, and the **Drill Hall WM panel 10, column 3.**
Mentioned in the Huddersfield Examiner (official casualty list – attached Kings Own Yorkshire Light Infantry) on 30 10 1916.

SISSONS Frederick Harold – 235584 Private.
Enlisted at Gainsborough.
5th Battalion DWR; killed in action 15 9 1918, Advance to Victory.
Buried – Hermies Hill British Cemetery, 2, E, 25.
Commemorated – the **Drill Hall WM panel 10, column 3.**

SLACK Tom – 5968 Private.
Born in Harrogate to Thomas and Katherine, of West Bowling, Bradford. Enlisted at Bradford.
1/5th Battalion DWR; killed in action 03 9 1916, aged 20, Battle of the Somme (Thiepval).
Buried – Serre Road Cemetery No2, 29, E, 15.

Commemorated – the **Drill Hall WM panel 10, column 3.**

SLATER Harry – 235092 Lance Corporal. Military Medal.
Born in Bankfoot, Bradford, to Fred. Enlisted at Bradford.
5th Battalion DWR; killed in action 27 3 1918, aged 20, German Spring Offensive.
Buried – St Hilaire Cemetery, 5, F, 1.
Commemorated – the **Drill Hall WM panel 10, column 3.**
Mentioned in the Goodall collection (award of MM); L Magnus (medal roll), page 295; the London Gazette (award of MM) on 13 3 1918, page 3244; Unit War Diary (award of MM for operations 20-27 11 1917) [Battle of Cambrai] on 20 12 1917.
NEVER FORGOTTEN, MOTHER. VIVA BRADFORD, YORKSHIRE, ENGLAND.

SMALES Albert – 242728 Private.
Born in Langcliffe to William and Eliza Ann. Resided in Settle. Enlisted at Skipton.
1/5th Battalion DWR; killed in action 03 9 1916, aged 20, Battle of the Somme (Thiepval).
Commemorated – Thiepval Memorial, France; Langcliffe (Settle) WM; Cravens Part in the Great War, page 175, & the cpgw.org.uk website, and the **Drill Hall WM panel 10, column 4.**
Mentioned in the book Langcliffe – Glimpses of a Dales Village, edited.

SMITH Arthur – 4427 (later 241293) Private.
Son of George and Ellen, of Moldgreen, Huddersfield. Resided in Huddersfield with his wife, Clarice Lois. Enlisted at Huddersfield.
1/5th Battalion DWR; reported missing presumed killed on 03 9 1916, aged 27, Battle of the Somme (Thiepval).
Buried – Mill Road Cemetery, 1, F, 9.
Commemorated – Paddock Parish WM (currently held in Huddersfield Drill Hall); M Stansfield, page 394, and the **Drill Hall WM panel 10, column 3.**
Mentioned in the Huddersfield Examiner (confirmed as missing since 03 9 1916) on 09 10 1916.
AT REST.

SMITH Arthur Benjamin – 242216 Private.
Born in Keighley to Joseph and Amelia. Enlisted at Keighley.
1/5th Battalion DWR; killed in action 03 9 1916, aged 21, Battle of the Somme (Thiepval).
Commemorated – Thiepval Memorial, France, and the **Drill Hall WM panel 10, column 3.**

SMITH A B
Probable duplication, see above, otherwise no trace.
Commemorated – the **Drill Hall WM panel 10, column 3 (bottom).**

SMITH Douglas – 3434 Private.
Born in Liverpool. Resided in Dewsbury. Enlisted at Mirfield.
1/5th Battalion DWR; killed in action 19 12 1915, Ypres.
Buried – Talana Farm Cemetery, 4, C, 20.
Commemorated – the **Drill Hall WM panel 10, column 3.**
SDGW shows his date of death as 23 10 1915.

SMITH Edgar – 267570 Private.
Resided in Sowerby Bridge. Enlisted at Halifax.
5th Battalion DWR; killed in action 05 11 1918, aged 30, Advance to Victory.
Buried – Frasnoi Communal Cemetery, A, 27.
Commemorated – Thiepval Memorial, France, and the **Drill Hall WM panel 10, column 4.**
Originally 2/5th DWR.

SMITH Edwin – 201092 Private.

Born in Halifax to Isaac and Mary Ann. Resided in Halifax. Enlisted at Halifax.
2/5th Battalion DWR, D Company, cook; wounded in action 20 11 1917, died of wounds on 27 11 1917, aged 36, Battle of Cambrai.
Buried – Grevillers British Cemetery, 8, A, 7.
Commemorated – Thiepval Memorial, France, and the **Drill Hall WM panel 10, column 3.**
Mentioned in the Goodall collection, date of death shown as 28 11 1917.
HE DIED THAT WE MIGHT LIVE.

SMITH Ernest – 29167 Private.
Born in Huddersfield on 28 8 1895. Resided at Crosland Moor. Enlisted at Huddersfield.
5th Battalion DWR; killed in action 17 4 1918, German Spring Offensive.
Commemorated – Pozieres Memorial, France; Emmanuel Church, Lockwood, RoH; M Stansfield, page 395, and the **Drill Hall WM panel 10, column 3.**
Originally 2/5th DWR.

SMITH Ernest William – 33635 Private.
Born in Islington to William and Mary of Hitchin, Herts. Resided in Hornsey, London, with his wife, Mary Katherine. Enlisted at Wood Green, London.
1/5th Battalion DWR; died of wounds, home, 31 12 1918, aged 33.
Buried – Hitchen (Herts) Cemetery, NE 628.
Commemorated – Thiepval Memorial, France, and the **Drill Hall WM panel 10, column 4.**
Formerly 60033 Private Queens (Royal West Surrey) Regiment.

SMITH Frank Sydney – 33112 Private.
Born in Birmingham. Resided in Birmingham. Enlisted at Sheffield.
1/4th Battalion DWR; killed in action 17 4 1918, German Spring Offensive.
Commemorated – Tyne Cot Memorial, Belgium, and the **Drill Hall WM panel 10, column 3.**

SMITH Frederick Arthur – 3565 Private.
Born at Primrose Hill, Huddersfield, on 19 8 1896 to William and Martha Alice, of Taylor Hill. Resided in Lockwood. Enlisted at Huddersfield on 02 12 1914, into the 2/5th DWR. Posted to 1/5th DWR at Doncaster. Embarked for France and Flanders on 15 4 1915.
1/5th Battalion DWR, D Company; died of wounds 16 10 1915, aged 19, Ypres.
Buried – Bard Cottage Cemetery, 1, B, 30.
Commemorated – Emmanuel Church, Lockwood, RoH; St Stephen's Church, Rashcliffe, RoH; Taylor Hill Primitive Methodist Church RoH; M Stansfield, page 396, and the **Drill Hall WM panel 10, column 3.**
Mentioned in the Huddersfield Examiner (D Company in action) on 04 8 1918; (killed in action, shellfire) on 22 10 1916; J J Fisher (account of the 'flag' patrol), page 93; T Podmore (quoted letter home) pages 31 & 33. Letters held in the DWR Archives.
HE SAVED OTHERS, NOT HIMSELF.

SMITH George – 267027 Private.
Born at Bolton Abbey. Resided in Leeds. Enlisted at Skipton.
5th Battalion DWR; killed in action 29 3 1918, German Spring Offensive
Commemorated – Arras Memorial, France, and the **Drill Hall WM panel 10, column 3.**
Originally 2/5th DWR.

SMITH George Henry – 35614 Private.
Born in Dipton, Co Durham. Enlisted at Newcastle upon Tyne.
5th Battalion DWR; killed in action 16 9 1918, aged 19, Advance to Victory.
Buried – Sunken Road, Boisleux, Cemetery, 2, B, 26.
Commemorated – the **Drill Hall WM panel 10, column 4.**
Formerly 76069 Private West Yorkshire Regiment.

PEACE PERFECT PEACE.

SMITH G N – Private.
No trace.
Possibly **SMITH George Marshall** – Private 29445
Born in Yeadon to Mary Hannah and the late Grimshaw. Resided in Yeadon. Enlisted at Keighley.
2/7th Battalion DWR, killed in action 27 11 1917, Battle of Cambrai.
Commemorated – Cambrai Memorial (Louverval), France, and the **Drill Hall WM panel 10, column 3.**

SMITH George William – 1718 Private.
Born in Huddersfield on 18 3 1884 to Henry, of Crosland Moor. Served in the Volunteers and local Territorials since 1902. Embodied at the outbreak of war. Embarked for France and Flanders in April, 1915.
1/5th Battalion DWR; killed in action 28 9 1915, Ypres.
Buried – New Irish Farm Cemetery, 2, B, 19.
Commemorated – St Barnabas Church, Crosland Moor, RoH; Huddersfield Corporation RoH; M Stansfield, page 396, and the **Drill Hall WM panel 10, column 3.**

SMITH Joseph – 34469 Private.
Born in Stoke on Trent. Resided at Oak Hill, Staffs. Enlisted at Stoke on Trent.
5th Battalion DWR; killed in action 30 8 1918, Advance to Victory.
Buried – Mont Huon Military Cemetery, 7, D, 8A.
Commemorated – the **Drill Hall WM panel 10, column 3.**
Formerly 39530 Private Essex Regiment.

SMITH J – Private.
No trace. Possibly a duplicate of the above.

SMITH John Benson – 6768 Lance Corporal.
Born in Bradford to Benson and Polly, of Moldgreen. Resided in Dalton. Enlisted at Huddersfield in 1914. Embarked for France and Flanders in 1916.
1/5th Battalion DWR; died of wounds 21 9 1916, aged 20, Battle of the Somme.
Buried – Puchevillers British Cemetery, 4, D, 22.
Commemorated – Christ Church, Moldgreen, RoH; Headstone inscription in Kirkheaton Cemetery; M Stansfield, page 397, and the **Drill Hall WM panel 10, column 3.**
Mentioned in the Huddersfield Examiner (died of wounds in hospital) on 26 9 1916; (died of wounds, official casualty list) on 25 10 1916.

SMITH Michael – 17071 Private.
Born in Glasgow to Thomas. Resided in Glasgow. Enlisted at Mary Hill, Glasgow.
1/5th Battalion DWR; killed in action 09 10 1917, aged 25.
Commemorated – Tyne Cot Memorial, Belgium, and the **Drill Hall WM panel 10, column 3.**
Formerly 1617 Army Service Corps.

SMITH Richard – 267076 Lance Corporal.
Born and resided at Clapham (Settle). Enlisted at Settle.
5th Battalion DWR; killed in action 15 9 1918, Advance to Victory.
Buried – Hermies Hill British Cemetery, 4, C, 30.
Commemorated – the **Drill Hall WM panel 10, column 4.**
Originally 2/5th DWR.

SMITH Thomas – 242761 Private.
Born in Gilsland, Cumbria. Enlisted at Haltwhistle.

1/5th Battalion DWR; killed in action 07 8 1917.
Buried – Ramscappelle Road Military Cemetery, 2, A, 32.
Commemorated – the **Drill Hall WM panel 10, column 3.**
Formerly 3845 Private Northumberland Fusiliers.

SNOWDEN James William – 34552 Private. Military Medal.
Born in Stockton. Resided in Thornaby on Tees. Enlisted at Middlesbrough.
5th Battalion DWR; killed in action 20 10 1918, Advance to Victory.
Buried – Carnieres Communal Cemetery, 1, C, 2.
Commemorated – the **Drill Hall WM panel 10, column 4.**
Mentioned in the Goodall collection & L Magnus award list (award of MM); Unit War Diary (award of MM) on 31 10 1918; London Gazette (award of MM) on 14 5 1919, page 6031.

SOUTHALL William – 3704 Private.
Born in Blackheath, Staffs. Resided in Thurnscoe. Enlisted at Doncaster.
1/5th Battalion DWR; killed in action 03 7 1916, Battle of the Somme.
Buried – Connaught Cemetery, 12, J, 9.
Commemorated – the **Drill Hall WM panel 10, column 4.**

SPEIGHT George Lacy – 3661 Private.
Born in Dewsbury to Thomas William and Mary Jane. Resided in Dewsbury. Enlisted at Mirfield.
1/5th Battalion DWR; killed in action 05 7 1916, aged 22, Battle of the Somme.
Buried – Puchevillers Cemetery, 1, C, 15.
Commemorated – the **Drill Hall WM panel 10, column 4.**
Brother of Thomas Greenwood Lacy SPEIGHT, qv.
FOR ALL HE NOBLY PAID THE PRICE, HIS LIFE HE GAVE IN SACRIFICE.

SPEIGHT John William – 240967 Private.
Born in Wakefield. Resided in Batley. Enlisted at Mirfield on 06 1 1915.
1/5th Battalion DWR; killed in action 03 9 1916, Battle of the Somme (Thiepval).
Commemorated – Thiepval Memorial, France, and the **Drill Hall WM panel 10, column 4.**

SPEIGHT Thomas Greenwood Lacy – 3709 (later 240910) Private.
Born in Dewsbury to Thomas William and Mary Jane. Resided in Dewsbury. Enlisted at Mirfield.
2nd Battalion DWR D Company; killed in action 21 7 1918, aged 22.
Buried – Gonnehem British Cemetery, F, 4.
Commemorated – the **Drill Hall WM panel 10, column 4.**
Mentioned in the Goodall collection (wounded in action on 03 9 1916).
Brother of George Lacy SPEIGHT
THY WILL BE DONE.

SPENCE Frank (Frederick) – 2571 Private.
Born in Dalton, Huddersfield on 04 10 1888, to Frederick and Jane. Resided in Dalton. Enlisted at Huddersfield on 08 8 1914.
1/5th Battalion DWR; killed in action 19 9 1916, aged 28, Battle of the Somme.
Commemorated – Thiepval Memorial, France; St Thomas' Church, Longroyd Bridge, RoH; Huddersfield General post Office RoH; Christ Church, Moldgreen, RoH; J J Fisher, page 114; M Stansfield, page 400, and the **Drill Hall WM panel 10, column 4.**
Mentioned in the Huddersfield Examiner (killed in action) on 26 9 1916; (killed in action, official casualty list) on 26 9 1916.
CWGC shows his name as Frederick. Brother of Norman, qv.

SPENCE Norman – 2271 Private.

Born in Dalton, Huddersfield on 17 12 1897, to Frederick and Jane. Resided in Dalton. Enlisted at Huddersfield on 05 8 1914. Embarked for France and Flanders on 12 4 1915.
1/5th Battalion DWR, D Company; killed in action, gun-shot wound, on 09 9 1915, aged 18, Ypres.
Buried – Bard Cottage Cemetery, 1, H, 26.
Commemorated – Christ Church, Moldgreen, RoH; St Thomas' Church, Longroyd Bridge, RoH; M Stansfield, page 400, and the **Drill Hall WM panel 10, column 4.**
Mentioned in the Huddersfield Examiner (killed in action) on 14 9 1916; The Holmfirth Express (family bereavement) on 30 9 1916.
Brother of Frank (Frederick), qv.

SPIVEY Frank – 268050 Sergeant. Military Medal and Bar.
Born in Kirkburton. Resided in Kirkburton. Enlisted at Huddersfield.
5th Battalion DWR; killed in action 15 9 1918, Advance to Victory.
Buried – Ruyalcourt Military Cemetery, J, 7.
Commemorated – All Hallows Parish Church, Kirkburton, RoH; M Stansfield, page 401, and the **Drill Hall WM panel 10, column 4.**
Mentioned in Goodall collection (MM award); the Huddersfield Examiner (award of MM for 2nd battle of the Marne (Battle of Tardenois) on 09 9 1918; (award of bar to MM) on 09 10 1918; Unit War Diary (award of MM) on 30 8 1918; (award of bar to MM) on 30 9 1918; L Magnus (medal list), page 293; London Gazette (award of MM) on 11 12 1918, page 14658; (Bar to MM) on 11 2 1919, page 2086.

STAMFORD Frank – 5034 (later 241640) Lance Corporal.
Born in Winterton, Scunthorpe, to Mary and the late George. Enlisted at Brigg, Lincs.
2/5th Battalion DWR Sniper; died of wounds, shrapnel, 19 7 1917, aged 22.
Buried – Vaulx Australian Field Ambulance, A, 21.
Commemorated – the **Drill Hall WM panel 10, column 4.**
HIS MEMORY IS AS FRESH TODAY AS IN THE HOUR HE PASSED AWAY.

STANDISH Alfred – 300077 Lance Corporal. Military Medal.
Born in Milnsbridge, then adopted. Resided at Moldgreen. Enlisted at Milnsbridge in September, 1914. Embarked for France and Flanders in April, 1915.
2/5th Battalion DWR; killed in action 29 3 1918, aged 24, German Spring Offensive.
Commemorated – Arras Memorial, France; St Paul's Methodist Church, Dalton, RoH; M Stansfield, page 403, and the **Drill Hall WM panel 10, column 4.**
Mentioned in the Goodall collection (medal awards); 2/6th DWR Unit War Diary (award of General Officer Commanding's Meritorious Service Certificate) on 12 5 1917; (award of MM for operations between 20-21 11 1917 [Battle of Cambria]) December, 1917; L Magnus (medal award list), page 297.
Originally 2/6th DWR.

STANTON Leonard – 35077 Private.
Son of Eleanor, of Stafford. Enlisted at Stafford.
5th Battalion DWR; died of wounds 13 9 1919, aged 21, Advance to Victory.
Buried – Hermies Hill British Military Cemetery, 2, A, 19.
Commemorated – the **Drill Hall WM panel 10, column 4.**
REST IN PEACE.

2/5th Battalion Signals Platoon. C 1916

The cap badge of the Huddersfield Rifle Corps, 1883 to 1908.

Lapel Badge of the 5th Battalion Old Comrades Association, post WW1.

SULCH. A.	PTE.	SYKES. STANLEY.	SGT.	THORPE. E.	CPT.	TURNER. E.A.	PTE.
SUTHERN. W.	"	SYKES. E.	PTE.	THORPE. T.	PTE.	TURNER. F.	"
SUTCLIFFE. W.D.	"	SYKES. NORMAN.	"	THORPE. N.	SGT.	TURNER. J.	"
SUTCLIFFE. R.	"	SYKES. J.	"	THOMAS. J.A.	PTE.	TURNBULL. J.	"
SUTCLIFFE. E.	"	SYKES. WALTER.	"	THORNHILL. T.	"	UTTLEY. A.	"
SUTCLIFFE. G.	"	SYKES. WILLIE.	"	THEWLIS. H.	"	VARLEY. J.	"
SUDDICK. T.	L/CPL.	TAYLOR. J.R.	"	THORNTON. L.	"	VARLEY. G.	L/CPL.
SUGDEN. J.	2/LT.	TAYLOR. J.S.	SGT.	THORNTON. S.H.	"	VAUSE. A.	PTE.
SUMMERILL. J.	PTE.	TAYLOR. E.	"	THORNTON. H.	"	VICKERS. J.	"
SWANN. W.	CPL.	TAYLOR. J.	L/CPL.	THORNLEY. H.	"	VICKERS. J.E.	"
SWALLOW. A.	PTE.	TAYLOR. P.	PTE.	THOMPSON. H.	"	WALKER. L.	L/CPL.
SWALE. A. M.M.	"	TAYLOR. T.	"	TIDSWELL. W.	"	WALKER. H.	PTE.
SWALE. S.	"	TAYLOR. JOE.	"	TIFFANY. C.E. M.C.	A/R.S.M.	WALKER. B.	"
SYKES. R.	"	TAYLOR. ALBERT.	"	TINDAL. P.	PTE.	WALKER. O	LT.
SYKES. H.	"	TAYLOR. N.	"	TINDALL. J.	L/CPL.	WALKER. A.	2/LT.
SYKES. SAMUEL.	"	TAYLOR. W.	"	TINKER. P.	PTE.	WALKER. R.F.	PTE.
SYKES. NORMAN.	"	TAYLOR. ALBERT.	"	TINKER. F.	"	WALKER. W.	2/LT.
SYKES. J.H.	L/CPL	TAYLOR. JAMES.	SGT.	TOWN. W.	"	WARD. J.T.	A/SGT.
SYKES. NORMAN.	PTE.	TATE. W.	PTE.	TOWNSON. J.	"	WARD. B.	PTE.
SYKES. FRED.	"	TEARNE. F.	"	TONG. A.C.	SGT.	WARD. J.	"
SYKES. ARTHUR.	SGT.	TEALE. W.	"	TOYNE. J.	PTE.	WAKELIN. W.	"
SYKES. G.	PTE.	TETLEY. E.	"	TOWERS. M.H.	"	WALLACE. A.	"
SYKES. HAROLD.	"	TEMPEST. H.	"	TOWNEND. L.	"	WALLACE. T.	"
SYKES. A.W.	CPT.	THACKRAY. E.	"	TOWSE. A.	L/CPL.	WATERHOUSE. D.	"
SYKES. E.T.	2/LT.	THORPE. W.	L/CPL.	TRUEMAN. J.	PTE.	WATERHOUSE. W.	SGT.
SYKES. FREDDY.	L/CPL.	THORPE. G.H.	CPL.	TRENHOLME. G.L.	L/CPL.	WARDLE. M.	"

WAITE. H.	PTE.	WEBSTER. G.	PTE	WILKINSON. J.W.	PTE.	WINFIELD. P.	PTE.
WATTON. J.H.	"	WEBSTER. C.W.	"	WILKINSON. H.	L/CPL.	WOMERSLEY. W.	"
WATSON. E.	"	WEBSTER. H.	"	WILKINSON. W.	PTE.	WOMERSLEY. S.	CPL.
WATSON. J.E.	"	WEST. E.	L/CPL.	WILKINSON. J.A.	CPL.	WORSLEY. J.	PTE.
WATSON. R.	"	WEAR. F.	PTE.	WILKINSON. S.	L/CPL.	WOODCOCK. J.	"
WATSON. J.H.	"	WESTERBY. J.J.	"	WILKINSON. J.A.	PTE.	WOOD. R.F.	L/CPL.
WATSON. J.W.	"	WHEATLEY. A.N.	MJR.	WILKINSON. S.	L/CPL.	WOOD. G.W.	"
WATSON. W.	"	WHITING. F.	PTE.	WILKINSON. G. M.M.	SGT.	WOOD. T.	CPL.
WATSON. N.	"	WHITELAM. L.	2/LT.	WILLIAMS. H.	PTE.	WOOD. H.	PTE.
WATSON. N.	"	WHITEOAK. T.C.	PTE.	WILLIAMS. A.	"	WOOD. R.H.	CPL.
WARDEN. H.	"	WHARTON. P.	"	WILLIAMSON. G.	"	WOOD. J.	PTE.
WALTON. G.	"	WHITELEY. H.	"	WILD. J.	"	WOOD. W.	C.Q.M.S.
WALTON. A.	"	WHITELEY. R.	"	WILDE. J.C.	"	WOOD. J.W.	PTE.
WADESON. J.W.	"	WHITELEY. G.A.	"	WILDE. F. M.M.	A/CPL.	WOOD. W.B.	"
WALMSLEY. H.	"	WHIPP. P.S.	"	WILDS. F.	PTE.	WOOD. C.	"
WASS. G.W.	"	WHEELDON. J.	"	WILKINS. F.A.	"	WOODHEAD. F.	"
WALTER. F.W.	"	WHEELHOUSE. N.	"	WISHANT. D.M.	"	WOODWARD. H.	"
WALSHAW. R.E.	"	WHITEHOUSE. H.	"	WILSON. A.	"	WRIGHT. F.S.	"
WARHURST. J.E.	"	WHITE. H.	"	WILSON. C.	"	WRIGHT. J.W.	2/LT.
WAUGH. E.	"	WHITE. A.J.	"	WILSON. F.	"	WRIGLEY. H.	PTE.
WATMOUGH. F.	"	WHITE. A.	"	WILSON. J.S.	"	WRIGLEY. B.A.	"
WALSH. A.G.	"	WHITEHEAD. W.A.	"	WISEMAN. J.R.	"	WRIGLEY. E.	"
WALLING. J.	"	WHITAKER. J.	"	WIBBERLEY. F.	"	WRIGLEY. W.H.	"
WARDMAN. W.R.	"	WELDON. A.	"	WILCOCK. W.	"	YOUNG. N.	"
WEEDER. W.J.	"	WINDSOR. E.	"	WINTERBOTTOM. N.	L/CPL.	DOUGHTY. L.	"
WEAVER. T.W.	"	WILKINSON. H.	"	WINTERBOTTOM. H.	PTE.		

STAVELEY Frank – 205621 Private.
Born in Sheffield. Resided at Wicker, Sheffield. Enlisted at Sheffield
2/5th Battalion DWR; killed in action 20 7 1918, Battle of Tardenois.
Commemorated – Soissons Memorial, France, and the **Drill Hall WM panel 10, column 4.**

STEAD Arthur – 204878 Private.
Born in Cleckheaton to Haley and Fanny. Enlisted at Cleckheaton on 28 11 1914.
2/5th Battalion DWR D Company; wounded in action on 20 11 1917, died of wounds 21 11 1917, aged 23, Battle of Cambrai.
Buried – Rocquigney-Equancourt Road Cemetery, 2, D, 23.
Commemorated – Spenborough (Cleckheaton) WM and the **Drill Hall WM panel 10, column 4.**
AMID CHANGING SCENES WE THINK OF THEE AND CHERISH STILL THE MEMORY.

STEEL Arthur -26302 Private.
Born in Stratford on Avon. Enlisted at Birmingham.
2/5th Battalion DWR; killed in action 22 5 1918, aged 21, German Spring Offensive.
Buried – Bienvillers Military Cemetery, 20, A, 10.
Commemorated – the **Drill Hall WM panel 10, column 4.**
Formerly T4/045381 Army Service Corps.

STEVENS Edward Conway – 26245 Private.
Son of Francis Curtis and Elizabeth, of Kingsdown, Bristol. Enlisted at Bristol.
2/5th Battalion DWR; killed in action 22 7 1918, aged 25, Battle of Tardenois.
Commemorated – Soissons Memorial, France, and the **Drill Hall WM panel 10, column 4.**
Formerly 23313 Private, Wiltshire Regiment.

STEVENS Henry Cheslyn – 24238 Private.
Born and resided in King's Lynn, Norfolk. Enlisted at East Dereham.
1/5th Battalion DWR; killed in action 16 8 1917, Nieuport Sector.
Commemorated – Nieuport Memorial, Belgium, and the **Drill Hall WM panel 10, column 4.**

STEVENSON Alec – 6511 Private.
Born in Lesbury, Northumberland, to James and Susanna. Enlisted at Alnwick.
1/5th Battalion DWR; died of wounds 20 1 1917, aged 22.
Buried – Warlincourt Halte British Cemetery, 12, C, 10.
Commemorated – the **Drill Hall WM panel 10, column 4.**
Formerly 3819 Private, Northumberland Fusiliers.
CWGC show his forename as Alexander.
EVER REMEMBERED.

STIRK Henry – 235645 Private.
Born and enlisted at Kirkby Fleetham, Bedale, Yorks.
5th Battalion DWR; killed in action 27 8 1918, aged 23, Advance to Victory.
Buried – Gommecourt South Cemetery, 1, C, 8.
Commemorated – the **Drill Hall WM panel 10, column 4.**
Originally 2/5th DWR.
PEACE PERFECT PEACE.

STOCKDALE Joseph – 3770 (later 240952) Private.
Born in Batley, to Henry and Elizabeth Ann. Resided in Batley. Enlisted at Mirfield in 1915.
2/5th Battalion DWR, 14 Platoon, D Company bomber; killed in action 03 5 1917, aged 21, Battle of Bullecourt.
Commemorated – Arras Memorial, France, and the **Drill Hall WM panel 10, column 4.**
Mentioned in the Goodall collection.

STOKES John Henry – 240230 Private.
Born in Hull. Resided in Meltham. Enlisted at Huddersfield.
1/5th Battalion DWR; killed in action 03 9 1916, Battle of the Somme (Thiepval).
Commemorated – Thiepval Memorial, France; Helme WM; St Bartholomew's Church, Meltham, RoH; Helme Parish Church RoH; M Stansfield, page 407, and the **Drill Hall WM panel 10, column 4.**
Brother of William, qv.

STOKES William – 240892 Private.
Born in Sheffield to the late F W and Rosa, of Meltham. Resided Meltham. Enlisted at Huddersfield.
1/5th Battalion DWR; killed in action 03 9 1916, aged 21, Battle of the Somme (Thiepval).
Buried – Mill Road Cemetery, 1, D, 6.
Commemorated – St Bartholomew's Church, Meltham, RoH; Helme Parish Church RoH; M Stansfield, page 407, and the **Drill Hall WM panel 10, column 4.**
Brother of John Henry, qv.
ALSO IN THE MEMORY OF HIS BROTHER, JACK, AGED 23, KILLED IN ACTION THE SAME DAY – THY WILL BE DONE.

SUDDICK Tom – 242541 Lance Corporal.
Son of Joseph and Jane. Resided in Claremount, Halifax, with his wife, Frances. Enlisted at Halifax.
1/5th Battalion DWR; killed in action 10 10 1917, Ypres.
Commemorated – Tyne Cot Memorial, Belgium, and the **Drill Hall WM panel 11, column 1.**

SUGDEN John – 2nd Lieutenant.
Born on 17 7 1895 in Liverpool to William Harry and Annie. Later moved to Huddersfield. Enlisted into the local Territorials in 1910. Embodied on the outbreak of war. Embarked for France and Flanders on 13 4 1915. Commissioned on 26 6 1917.
5th Battalion DWR; killed in action, shellfire, 29 3 1918, aged 22, German Spring Offensive.
Buried – Gommecourt British No2, 5, D, 2.
Commemorated – 62nd Division History, page 197; C D Bruce History, page 214; B Heywood, page 238; M Stansfield, page 409, and the **Drill Hall WM panel 11, column 1**.
Mentioned in the Unit War Diary (killed in action) on 31 3 1918.
Formerly 1950 Private, later 240097 WO2, commissioned 1917. From 1st DWR to 2nd DWR, attached 5th DWR.

SULCH Arthur – 2963 Private.
Born in Huddersfield on 21 3 1894 to John and Alice, of Fartown. Resided in Fartown. Enlisted at Huddersfield on 05 9 1914. Embarked for France and Flanders in April, 1915.
1/5th Battalion DWR, C Company; killed in action, shellfire, 18 9 1915, aged 21, Ypres.
Commemorated – Ypres (Menin Gate) Memorial, France; Fartown and Birkby WM; Christ Church, Woodhouse Hill, RoH; M Stansfield, page 409, and the **Drill Hall WM panel 11, column 1.**
Mentioned in the Huddersfield Examiner (kiiled by shellfire) on 24 9 1915.

SUMMERILL John – 34502 Private.
Born in New Lampton, Co Durham. Resided in Fence Houses. Enlisted at Houghton le Spring.
5th Battalion DWR; killed in action 28 9 1918, Advance to Victory.
Buried – Grand Ravine British Cemetery, A, 7.
Commemorated – the **Drill Hall WM panel 11, column 1.**
Formerly 18181 Private, Yorkshire Regiment.

SUTCLIFFE Ellis – 29351 Private.

Born in Halifax. Enlisted at Halifax on 15 9 1916.
2/5th Battalion DWR, D Company; died as Prisoner of War on 30 8 1918.
Buried – Caudrey British Cemetery, 4, A, 7.
Commemorated – Calderdale War Dead, page 264, and the **Drill Hall WM panel 11, column 1.**

SUTCLIFFE Greenwood – 235436 Private.
Born Cross Stones, Todmorden, to John William and Hannah. Enlisted at Todmorden.
5th Battalion DWR; killed in action 20 7 1918, aged 38, Battle of Tardenois.
Commemorated – Soissons Memorial, France, and the **Drill Hall WM panel 11, column 1.**
Originally 2/5th DWR.

SUTCLIFFE Robert – 11808 Private.
Resided Meltham. Enlisted Huddersfield. Did not serve overseas, died in training.
3/5th Battalion DWR; died, home, 31 3 1916, aged 22.
Buried – Meltham Mills (Old Church) Cemetery, E, M, 8.
Commemorated – St Bartholomew's Church, Meltham, RoH; M Stansfield, page 411, and the
Drill Hall WM panel 11, column 1.

SUTCLIFFE William Denton – 242432 Private.
Born in Farsley to Lemuel and Emma Jane, of Farsley. Enlisted at Farsley.
1/5th Battalion DWR, A Company, killed in action 07 8 1917, aged 20.
Buried – Coxyde Military Cemetery, 2, E, 27, Nieuport Sector.
Commemorated –the **Drill Hall WM panel 11, column 1.**
A LOVED ONE CALLED TO REST.

SUTHERN William – 3192 Private.
Son of John and Barbara Jane, of Ancroft, Berwick on Tweed. Enlisted at Alnwick.
1/5th Battalion DWR; killed in action 03 9 1916, Battle of the Somme (Thiepval).
Commemorated – **Thiepval Memorial, France, and the Drill Hall WM panel 11, column 1.**
Formerly 1/7th Northumberland Fusiliers, via 2/7th Northumberland Fusiliers, attached 1/5th DWR.

SWALE A –
No trace, not on CWGC, possibly duplicated as below.
Commemorated – the **Drill Hall WM panel 11, column 1.**

SWALE Soloman – 4165 (later 241184) Private. Military Medal.
Son of Jonas and Martha Elizabeth. Resided in Scammonden, Huddersfield. Enlisted at
Huddersfield in May 1915. Embarked for France and Flanders on 02 12 1916.
5th Battalion DWR, Transport Section; died of wounds at 29 Casualty Clearing Station, at Delsaux
Farm, on 21 10 1918, aged 21, Advance to Victory.
Buried – Delsaux Farm Cemetery, 1, H, 7.
Commemorated – M Stansfield, page 411, and the **Drill Hall WM panel 11, column 1.**
Mentioned in the Goodall collection; L Magnus (medal list), page 296; the London Gazette, 14 5
1919, page 6013.
IN LOVING MEMORY.

SWALLOW Arthur – 3220 Private.
Born in Huddersfield to John William and Jane, of Kirkheaton. Resided in Kirkheaton. Enlisted at
Huddersfield in 1914. Embarked for France and Flanders in April, 1915.
1/5th Battalion DWR; killed in action 04 11 1916, aged 20, Battle of the Somme.
Buried – Foncquevillers Military Cemetery, 1, J, 7.
Commemorated – St John's Church, Kirkheaton, RoH; Lepton Parish Church RoH; J J Fisher,
page 114; M Stansfield, page 411, and the **Drill Hall WM panel 11, column 1.**
Mentioned in the Huddersfield Examiner (killed in action) on 30 11 1916.

EVER REMEMBERED.

SWANN Willie – 2959 Corporal.
Born in Lindley to Albert William and Mary Hannah. Resided in Lindley. Enlisted at Huddersfield.
1/5th Battalion DWR; died of wounds 02 7 1916, Battle of the Somme.
Commemorated – J J Fisher, page 110, and the **Drill Hall WM panel 11, column 1.**
Mentioned in the Huddersfield examiner (died of wounds) on 17 7 1916.

SYKES Arnold Walker – Captain.
Born in Huddersfield on 26 6 1875. Baptised 12 8 1875, the son of John Henry and Emmeline. Resided in Huddersfield with his wife, Mary. Pre war Territorial. Embarked for France and Flanders on 25 6 1917. Attached as Adjutant to the York and Lancaster Regiment at their barracks in Pontefract. Passed fit for general service and joined a front line unit in July, 1917.
9th Battalion York and Lancaster Regiment; killed in action 30 9 1917, aged 42, Ypres.
Buried – Bedford House Cemetery, 21, E, 12.
Commemorated – Holy Trinity Church, Huddersfield, RoH; St Mary Magdalene Church, Outlane, RoH; St Andrew's Church, Stainland, RoH; M Stansfield, page 413, and the **Drill Hall WM panel 11, column 1.**
Link to 5 DWR is not recorded but he was previously in the local Volunteer Battalion, 1900/1902.
THE DEARLY LOVED HUSBAND OF MARY SYKES, NETHERLEIGH, HUDDERSFIELD.

SYKES Arthur – 2449 Sergeant.
Born in Upperthong to Company Sergeant Major Henry James DCM and Ann, of Holmfirth. A pre war Territorial, F Company (Holmfirth) and embodied in August, 1914. Embarked for France and Flanders in January, 1917.
2/5th Battalion DWR, C Company; killed in action 14 2 1917, aged 20.
Buried – Auchonvillers Military Cemetery, 2, K, 9.
Commemorated – Upperthong WM; M Stansfield, page 414, and the **Drill Hall WM panel 11, column 1.**
Territorial Force War Medal posthumously awarded on 28 6 1923.
Mentioned in the Huddersfield Examiner (serving in the UK) on 01 9 1915; (killed in action) on 27 2 1917; (killed in action, official casualty list) on 16 3 1917.
WAITING IN A HOLY STILLNESS WRAPT IN SLEEP.

SYKES Eric Turner – Captain.
Born in Honley to James and Emma Amelia. Commissioned into DWR from Cambridge OTC on 19 11 1914. Embarked for France and Flanders in December 1915, posted to 1/5th DWR.
2/5th Battalion DWR; killed in action 03 5 1917, aged 22, Battle of Bullecourt.
Buried – Bailleul Road East Cemetery, 2, D, 22.
Commemorated – Honley WM; Moorbottom Chapel Brass Plaque; Fixby Golf Club RoH; Almondbury Grammar School RoH; J J Fisher, page 129; C Ford, pages 26-29; M Stansfield, page 415; D Tattersfield, page 201, and the **Drill Hall WM panel 11, column 1.**
Mentioned in the Huddersfield Examiner (wounded in action) on 13 9 1916; (killed in action) on 23 8 1917; (will published) on 22 5 1918; in the 1/5th DWR War Diary (joined Bn) on 30 1 1916; (A Company, in action) on 03 9 1916; (promoted Lt & Capt and wounded in action – to UK) on 30 9 1916; in 2/5th DWR War Diary (reported missing, Bullecourt) on 03 5 1917.

SYKES Ernest – 240730 Private.
Born in Fenay Grange, Almondbury, on 17 10 1896 to George. Resided in Marsh. Enlisted at Huddersfield in October, 1914.
2/5th Battalion DWR; reported missing (killed in action) 03 5 1917, Battle of Bullecourt.
Commemorated – Arras Memorial, France; Almondbury WM; Holy Trinity Church, Huddersfield, RoH; M Stansfield, page 416, and the **Drill Hall WM panel 11, column 2.**

Mentioned in the Huddersfield Examiner (reported missing, official casualty list) on 27 6 1917.

SYKES Fred – 242408 Private. Military Medal.
Born in Huddersfield on 16 2 1896. Resided in Paddock. Enlisted at Huddersfield on 27 1 1916.
1/5th Battalion DWR; killed in action 06 10 1917, 3rd Battle of Ypres (Passchendaele).
Commemorated – Tyne Cot Memorial, Belgium; Paddock Parish WM (currently in Huddersfield Drill Hall); All Saints Church, Paddock, RoH; The Shared Church, Paddock, RoH; L Magnus, page 251; M Stansfield, page 416, and the **Drill Hall WM panel 11, column 1.**
Mentioned in the Goodall collection (medal awards); the Unit War Diary (award of MM) on 31 8 1917; the London Gazette (award of MM) on 28 9 1917, page 10035.

SYKES Freddy – 3639 (later 240870) Lance Corporal.
Resided in Dewsbury. Enlisted at Mirfield.
2/5th Battalion DWR; killed in action 03 5 1917, aged 22, Battle of Bullecourt.
Buried – Achiet le Grand Communal Cemetery Extension, 1, E, 6.
Commemorated – D Tattersfield, pages 284 & 385, and the **Drill Hall WM panel 11, column 1.**
Mentioned in the Goodall collection.
REST IN PEACE.

SYKES George – 4999 Private.
Born in Keighley. Enlisted at Bradford.
2/5th Battalion DWR; died of wounds 28 2 1917.
Buried – Dernancourt Communal Cemetery Extension, 5, D, 22.
Commemorated – the **Drill Hall WM panel 11, column 1.**

SYKES Harold – 3932 Private.
Born in Longwood, Huddersfield, on 08 5 1897 to Ely and Hannah Maria. Resided in Paddock. Pre War Territorial. Embodied at the outbreak of war and embarked for France and Flanders in April, 1915.
1/5th Battalion DWR; killed in action (sniper) 22 12 1915, aged 28, Ypres.
Buried – Talana Farm Cemetery, 3, 11.
Commemorated – All Saints Church, Paddock, RoH; M Stansfield, page 417, and the **Drill Hall WM panel 11, column 1.**
THY WILL BE DONE.

SYKES Harold – 241581 Private.
Born in Huddersfield. Resided in Slaithwaite. Enlisted at Huddersfield in 1916. Embarked for France and Flanders in January, 1917.
2/5th Battalion DWR; killed in action 17 3 1917.
Commemorated – Thiepval Memorial, France; Slaithwaite WM; St James's Church, Slaithwaite, RoH; M Stansfield, page 418, and the **Drill Hall WM panel 11, column 1.**

SYKES James Henry – 240663 Lance Corporal.
Born in Almondbury to Joe. Resided in Almondbury. Enlisted at Huddersfield in November, 1914. Embarked for France and Flanders in April, 1915.
1/5th Battalion DWR; killed in action 27 8 1917, aged 22.
Buried – Coxyde Military Cemetery, 3, C, 21.
Commemorated – Almondbury WM; M Stanfield, page 420, and the **Drill Hall WM panel 11, column 1.**
Mentioned in the Huddersfield Examiner (wounded in action, official casualty list) on 07 8 1916; (killed in action, shellfire) on 03 9 1917.

SYKES John – 2966 Private.

Born in Saddleworth on 05 4 1893 to Percival Pointon and Emma T. Resided in Almondbury. Enlisted at Huddersfield into the local Territorial unit in September, 1914. Embarked for France and Flanders in April, 1915.
1/5th Battalion DWR; died (disease) at Huddersfield Royal Infirmary on 11 5 1916, aged 23.
Buried – Huddersfield (Almondbury) Cemetery, C, A, C.
Commemorated – Almondbury WM; Saddleworth WM; M Stansfield, page 421, and the **Drill Hall WM panel 11, column 2.**
Mentioned in the Huddersfield Examiner (died) on 11 5 1916; (funeral at Almondbury) on 16 5 1916.

SYKES Norman – 242409 Private.
Born in Huddersfield on 14 11 1889 to George W and Alice. Resided in Fartown, Huddersfield. Enlisted at Huddersfield in January, 1916.
1/5th Battalion DWR; killed in action 27 8 1917, aged 22.
Buried – Coxyde Military Cemetery, 3, C, 20.
Commemorated – Fartown and Birkby WM; M Stansfield, page 422, and the **Drill Hall WM panel 11, column 1.**
Brother of 240672 Sergeant Stanley Sykes, qv.
Mentioned in the Huddersfield Examiner (killed in action) on 03 9 1917; (in memoriam) on 27 8 1918, 1919 and 1920.
HE TRUSTED IN GOD, GOD CALLED HIM, HIS WILL DONE.

SYKES Norman – 242528 Private.
Born in Bradford. Resided in Greengates, Bradford. Enlisted at Bradford.
1/5th Battalion DWR; killed in action 07 8 1917, Nieuport Sector.
Buried – Ramscappelle Road Military Cemetery, 2, A, 31.
Commemorated – the **Drill Hall WM panel 11, column 1.**

SYKES Norman.
Possible duplication of one of the two Norman Sykes, on column 1. Otherwise, no trace.
Commemorated – the **Drill Hall WM panel 11, column 2.**

SYKES Ronald – 2417 Private.
Born in Lindley on 27 6 1896 to William and Isaac and Ada Ann. Resided in Lindley. Enlisted at Huddersfield on the outbreak of war. Embarked for France and Flanders in April, 1915.
1/5th Battalion DWR; killed in action 09 12 1915, aged 19, Ypres.
Buried – Artillery Wood Cemetery, 2, C, 9.
Commemorated – St Stephen's Church, Lindley, RoH; M Stansfield, page 423, and the **Drill Hall WM panel 11, column 1.**
RONALD, AU REVOIR.

SYKES Samuel – 6728 Private.
Born in Halifax to Edwin and Alice. Resided in Siddal, Halifax. Enlisted at Halifax.
1/5th Battalion DWR; died of wounds 04 11 1916, aged 20, Battle of the Somme.
Buried – Foncquevillers Military Cemetery, 1, J, 26.
Commemorated – Calderdale War Dead, page 266, and the **Drill Hall WM panel 11, column 1.**
GONE BUT NOT FORGOTTEN.

SYKES Stanley – 240672 Sergeant.
Born in Birkby, Huddersfield on 10 11 1899 to George W and Alice. Resided in Fartown. Enlisted at Huddersfield in October, 1914.
2/5th Battalion DWR, B Company; reported missing (killed in action) 03 5 1917, aged 27, Battle of Bullecourt.

Commemorated – Arras Memorial, France; Fartown and Birkby WM; M Stansfield, page 423, and the **Drill Hall WM panel 11, column 2.**
Mentioned in the Huddersfield Examiner (killed in action) on 17 5 1917; (reported missing, official casualty list) on 27 6 1917; (previously reported missing, now killed in action, official casualty list) on 19 9 1917.
Brother of 242409 Norman Sykes, qv.

SYKES Walter – 241919 Private.
Born and resided in Upper Hopton. Enlisted at Dewsbury.
2/5th Battalion DWR; killed in action 03 5 1917, Battle of Bullecourt.
Commemorated – Arras Memorial, France; Upper Hopton WM; R Leedham, page 89, and the **Drill Hall WM panel 11, column 2.**

SYKES Willie – 265338 Private.
Born in Linthwaite to Ned. Resided in Linthwaite. Enlisted at Milnsbridge.
2/5th Battalion DWR; reported missing (killed in action) 27 7 1918, aged 21, Battle of Tardenois.
Commemorated – Soissons Memorial, France; Linthwaite WM; M Stansfield, page 424, and the **Drill Hall WM panel 11, column 2.**

TATE Wilfred – 5023 (later 241613) Private.
Born in Golcar to John William and Sarah. Resided in Golcar. Enlisted at Huddersfield in March, 1916. Embarked for France and Flanders in January, 1917.
2/5th Battalion DWR; reported missing (killed in action) 03 5 1917, aged 22, Battle of Bullecourt.
Commemorated – Arras Memorial, France; St John's Church, Golcar, RoH; Golcar Baptist Church, RoH; M Stansfield, page 425, and the **Drill Hall WM panel 11, column 2.**
Mentioned in the Goodall collection; the Huddersfield Examiner (reported missing, news requested by relatives) on 12 6 1917; (reported missing, official casualty list) on 27 6 1917.

TAYLOR Albert – 5407 (later 241987) Private.
Born in Hogley Green, Holmfirth. Resided in Holmfirth. Enlisted at Holmfirth in March 1916.
2/5th Battalion DWR; reported missing (killed in action) 03 5 1917, Battle of Bullecourt.
Commemorated – Arras Memorial, France; Holme Valley Memorial Hospital WM (plaques 1 & 2, Holme and Holmbridge); M Stansfield, page 425, and the **Drill Hall WM panel 11, column 2.**
Mentioned in the Huddersfield Examiner (reported missing, official casualty list) on 27 6 1917.

TAYLOR Albert – 34909 Private.
Born in Lofthouse to Dalton and Emily. Resided in Middlesbrough with his wife, Johanna. Enlisted at Aldershot.
5th Battalion DWR; killed in action 13 9 1918, aged 24, Advance to Victory.
Buried – Hermies Hill British Cemetery, 2, A, 15.
Commemorated – the **Drill Hall WM panel 11, column 2.**
Formerly 11593 Private Yorkshire Regiment.
GREATER LOVE HATH NO MAN, SWEET JESUS HAVE MERCY.

TAYLOR Edward – 2546 Sergeant.
Born in Marsh on 18 2 1892 to George Washington Taylor. Resided in Huddersfield. Pre war Territorial, embodied on the outbreak of war.
1/5th Battalion DWR; died of wounds at 35 Casualty Clearing Station, Doullens, on 08 7 1916, aged 24, Battle of the Somme.
Buried – Doullens Communal Cemetery Extension, 3, B, 17.
Commemorated – Huddersfield Parish Church RoH; M Stansfield, page 427, and the **Drill Hall WM panel 11, column 2.**
DEARLY LOVED SON OF THE LATE G. W. TAYLOR AND M. A. TAYLOR, HUDDERSFIELD.

TAYLOR James Robert – 2105 Private.
Born in Bexley Heath, Kent. Resided in Blackheath, London. Enlisted at Mirfield.
1/5th Battalion DWR, D Company; killed in action 09 5 1915, aged 22, Fleurbaix Sector
Buried – Rue David Military Cemetery, 1, H, 25.
Commemorated – Upper Hopton WM; R Leedham, page 24, and the **Drill Hall WM panel 11, column 2.**
Mentioned in the Goodall collection.
Originally 2/5th DWR, volunteered for foreign service in 1915.
EVER IN OUR THOUGHTS, FATHER, SISTERS AND BROTHERS.

TAYLOR Joe – 4925 Private.
Born in Huddersfield to William Henry and Eleanor. Resided in Milnsbridge. Enlisted at Huddersfield on 08 3 1916. Embarked for France and Flanders on 10 1 1917.
2/5th Battalion DWR, A Company; killed in action, shellfire, aged 30, 27 2 1917.
Commemorated – Thiepval Memorial, France; Milnsbridge WM; Colne Valley Almanac; M Stansfield, page 430, and the **Drill Hall WM panel 11, column 2.**

TAYLOR John Samson – 1088 Sergeant.
Born in Netherton, Huddersfield, on 16 8 1872 to James and Hannah. Resided in Berry Brow with his wife, Selina. Enlisted at Huddersfield on 04 8 1914.
1/5th Battalion DWR; killed in action, shot through the head by a sniper, 16 8 1915, aged 43, Ypres.
Commemorated – Ypres (Menin Gate) Memorial, France; Armitage Bridge WM; Lockwood Baptist Church RoH; Armitage Bridge National School RoH; Armitage Bridge Mills RoH; M Stansfield, page 430, and the **Drill Hall WM panel 11, column 2.**

TAYLOR James – 35914 Sergeant.
Born in Werneth, Lancs. Enlisted at Oldham.
5th Battalion DWR; killed in action 20 10 1918, Advance to Victory.
Buried – Quievy Communal Cemetery Extension, C, 66.
Commemorated – the **Drill Hall WM panel 11, column 2.**
Formerly 59586 Private, Liverpool Regiment.

TAYOR James – 240074 Lance Corporal.
Born in Barrow in Furness. Resided in Northowram, Halifax. Enlisted at Huddersfield.
1/5th Battalion DWR; killed in action 03 9 1916, Battle of the Somme (Thiepval).
Commemorated – Thiepval Memorial, France, and the **Drill Hall WM panel 11, column 2.**

TAYLOR Norman – 4947 (later 241546) Private.
Born in Almondbury. Resided with Aunt and Uncle, George Roebuck, at Berry Brow. Enlisted at Huddersfield. Embarked for France and Flanders in January, 1917.
2/5th Battalion DWR; reported missing 11 6 1917, later accepted as killed in action on that day.
Buried – Flesquieres Hill British Cemetery, 4, D, 7.
Commemorated – Almondbury WM; Huddersfield Corporation RoH; M Stansfield, page 431, and the **Drill Hall WM panel 11, column 2.**
Mentioned in the Goodall collection; the Huddersfield Examiner (reported missing, official casualty list) on 27 6 1917; (reported missing) on 07 8 1917; (previously reported missing, now killed in action) on 21 9 1917.

TAYLOR Percy – 204164 Private.
Born in Golcar. Resided in Golcar. Enlisted at Huddersfield in September, 1916. Embarked for France and Flanders on 28 12 1916.
1/5th Battalion DWR; killed in action 07 8 1917, Nieuport Sector.
Buried – Coxyde Military Cemetery, 2, E, 28.

Commemorated – St John's Church, Golcar RoH; Colne Valley Almanac; M Stansfield, page 432, and the **Drill Hall WM panel 11, column 2.**
Mentioned in the Huddersfield Examiner (killed in action) 07 8 1917 and 21 8 1917.

TAYLOR Tom – 242435 Private.
Born in Bradford to William and Mary. Resided in Bradford. Enlisted at Bradford.
1/5th Battalion DWR; killed in action 07 8 1917, aged 20, Nieuport Sector.
Commemorated – Nieuport Memorial, Belgium, and the **Drill Hall WM panel 11, column 2.**

TAYLOR Wilfred – 202924 Private.
Enlisted at Halifax.
5th Battalion DWR; killed in action 27 3 1918, German Spring Offensive.
Buried – Gommecourt British Cemetery No2, 5, D, 3.
Commemorated – the **Drill Hall WM panel 11, column 2.**

TEAL Wilfred – 241529 Private.
Born in Huddersfield on 10 7 1896 to Sarah Ellen. Resided in Paddock Foot, Huddersfield. Enlisted at Huddersfield on 06 3 1916.
2/5th Battalion DWR; killed in action 17 3 1917, aged 20, Advance to the Hindenburg Line.
Buried – Adanac Military Cemetery, 4, H, 34.
Commemorated – New North Road Baptist Church RoH; All Saints Church, Paddock, RoH, M Stansfield, page 432, and the **Drill Hall WM panel 11, column 2.**
Mentioned in the Huddersfield Examiner (training at Henham Park) on 17 7 1916; (in memoriam) on 17 3 1919.
PEACE PERFECT PEACE.

TEARNE Frederick – 242226 Private.
Born in Bradford. Resided at Allerton, Bradford. Enlisted at Bradford.
1/5th Battalion DWR; killed in action 03 9 1916, Battle of the Somme (Thiepval).
Buried – Mill Road Cemetery, 2, A, 9.
Commemorated – the **Drill Hall WM panel 11, column 2.**

TEMPEST Horace – 242370 Private.
Born in Leeds to Mary Eliza of Armley. Enlisted at Leeds.
1/5th Battalion DWR, D Company; died of wounds 29 3 1918, aged 21, German Spring Offensive.
Buried – St Sever Cemetery Extension, P. 7, N, 1B.
Commemorated – the **Drill Hall WM panel 11, column 2.**

TETLEY Ernest – 306653 Private.
Born in Manningham, Bradford, to Alfred Ernest and Sarah Ann. Enlisted at Bradford.
5th Battalion DWR; killed in action 13 9 1918, aged 21, Advance to Victory.
Commemorated – Vis en Artois Memorial, France, and the **Drill Hall WM panel 11, column 2.**
Originally 2/5th DWR.

THACKRAY E – Private.
No trace under this spelling but probably Thackra Ernest – see below:
Commemorated – the **Drill Hall WM panel 11, column 2.**

THACKRA Ernest - 2439 (later 204478) Private.
Born in Denby Dale to George and Ann. Employed in Scissett. Pre war Territorial, F Company, Holmfirth, embodied on the outbreak of war. Embarked for France and Flanders in 1916.
9th Battalion, A Company; died of wounds 21 10 1918, aged 24, Advance to Victory (Canal du Nord).
Buried – Rocquigny-Equancourt Road British Cemetery, 14, D, 35.

Commemorated – Denby Dale and Cumberworth WM; GH Norton (Nortonthorpe Mills), Scissett RoH; M Stansfield, page 433, and the **Drill Hall WM panel 11, column 2.**
Mentioned in the Huddersfield Examiner (wounded in action, hospital London) on 15 9 1916.
FOR HONOUR, LIBERTY AND TRUTH, HE SACRIFICED HIS GLORIOUS YOUTH.

THEWLIS (TREWLIS?) Herbert – 2211 Private.
Born in Kirkheaton on 07 11 1893 to Levi and Annie E. Resided in Huddersfield with his wife, Daisy. Enlisted at Huddersfield on 04 8 1914.
1/5th Battalion DWR; died of wounds at No 13 General Hospital, Boulogne, 11 9 1916, aged 23, Battle of the Somme.
Buried – Boulogne Eastern Cemetery, 8, C, 136.
Commemorated – J J Fisher, page 113; M Stansfield, page 434, and the **Drill Hall WM panel 11, column 3.**
Mentioned in the Huddersfield Examiner (died of wounds, hospital Boulogne) on 15 9 1916; (in memoriam) on 13 9 1918 & 13 9 1920.
CWGC and M Stansfield shows Thewliss, SDGW shows Trewlis.
MEMORY STILL HOLDS DEAR, FROM HIS WIFE.

THOMAS James Arthur – 2990 Private.
Born in Lockwood on 02 10 1888 to Sam. Resided in Lockwood with his wife, Nellie. Pre war Volunteer and Territorial, embodied on the outbreak of war.
1/5th Battalion DWR; killed in action 04 7 1916, aged 27, Battle of the Somme.
Buried – Connaught Cemetery, 4, M, 8.
Commemorated – St Stephen's Church, Rashcliffe, RoH; J J Fisher, page 110; M Stansfield, page 434, the **Drill Hall WM panel 11, column 3.**
Mentioned in the Huddersfield Examiner (killed in action) on 11 7 1916.
M Stansfield shows James Albert.

THOMPSON Harry – 204737 Private.
Born in Fartown, Huddersfield, on 18 9 1892 to John and Ellen. Resided in Fartown. Enlisted at Huddersfield on 10 2 1916.
2/5th Battalion DWR, D Company; died of wounds on 19 7 1917, aged 25.
Buried – Vaulx Australian Field Ambulance Cemetery, A, 20
Commemorated – Fartown and Birkby WM; Christ Church, Woodhouse Hill, RoH; M Stansfield, page 435, and the **Drill Hall WM panel 11, column 3.**
Mentioned in the Goodall collection (also served with 1/5th DWR).
EVER REMEMBERED.

THORNHILL Thomas – 4410 Private.
Resided in Waterfoot, Lancs. Enlisted at Huddersfield.
1/5th Battalion DWR; killed in action 28 7 1916, Battle of the Somme.
Buried – Connaught Cemetery, 3, M, 3.
Commemorated – the **Drill Hall WM panel 11, column 3.**

THORNLEY Henry – 26642 Private.
Born in Mexborough to Ralph and Grace, of Sheffield. Enlisted at Sheffield.
1/5th Battalion DWR; killed in action 05 1 1918, aged 19.
Buried – Lijssenthoek Military Cemetery, 27, DD, 3A.
Commemorated – the **Drill Hall WM panel 11, column 3.**

THORNTON Herbert – 241533 Private.
Born in Fartown on 26 6 1891 to Sam and Clara. Resided in Fartown. Enlisted at Huddersfield on 09 3 1915.

2/5th Battalion DWR, A Company; reported missing (killed in action) 03 5 1917, aged 25, Battle of Bullecourt.
Commemorated – Arras Memorial, France; Fartown and Birkby WM; Netheroyd Hill Methodist Church RoH; Christ Church, Woodhouse Hill, RoH; M Stansfield, page 439, and the **Drill Hall WM panel 11, column 3.**
Mentioned in the Huddersfield Examiner (reported missing, official casualty list) on 27 6 1917.

THORNTON Leslie – 29209 Private.
Born in Bradford to Mark T, of West Bowling. Resided in West Bowling. Enlisted at Bradford.
1/5th Battalion DWR; killed in action 25 11 1917, aged 19, Battle of Passchendaele.
Buried – Dochy Farm New British Cemetery, 7, E, 16.
Commemorated – the **Drill Hall WM panel 11, column 3.**

THORNTON Samuel Hopkinson – 235100 Private.
Born and resided in Idle, Bradford. Enlisted at Bradford on 25 9 1916.
2/5th Battalion DWR, D Company; killed in action 03 5 1917, Battle of Bullecourt.
Commemorated – Arras Memorial, France, and the **Drill Hall WM panel 11, column 3.**
Mentioned in the Goodall collection.

THORPE E – Cpt on the board, probably:
THORPE Ernest – 3576 Private.
Born in Birkby on 31 12 1895 to Joe and Florence., of Huddersfield. Resided in New Zealand (NZ Army). Enlisted on return to UK in 1914.
1/5th Battalion DWR, D Company; died of wounds 30 11 1915, Ypres.
Buried – Talana Farm Cemetery, 4, F, 1.
Commemorated – Fartown and Birkby WM; Christ Church, Woodhouse Hill, RoH; M Stansfield, page 439, and the **Drill Hall WM panel 11, column 3.**

THORPE George Herbert – 2787 Corporal.
Born Walton, Liverpool, on 16 5 1893 to Thomas Henry and Jane Middlebrook, of Edgerton. Enlisted at Huddersfield on 04 9 1914.
1/5th Battalion DWR, A Company Bombing Corporal; killed in action 17 11 1915, aged 22, Ypres.
Buried – Talana Farm Cemetery, 3, E, 1.
Commemorated – Gledholt Wesleyan Church RoH; St Stephen's Church, Lindley, RoH; M Stansfield, page 440, and the **Drill Hall WM panel 11, column 2.**
Mentioned in the Huddersfield Examiner (award of Distinguished Conduct Certificate for bombing a sap in 1915); (killed in action) on 22 11 1915.

THORPE Ned – 240330 Sergeant.
Born in Underbank, Holmfirth, to Sam. Resided in Holmfirth. Enlisted at Huddersfield on the outbreak of war. Embarked for France and Flanders in January, 1917.
2/5th Battalion DWR; killed in action 27 11 1917, Battle of Cambrai.
Commemorated – Cambrai Memorial (Louverval), France; Underbank WM; M Stansfield, page 440, and the **Drill Hall WM panel 11, column 3.**

THORPE Turner – 24793 Private.
Born in Holmfirth to Edith. Resided in Holmbridge and Holmfirth with his wife, Edith. Enlisted at the outbreak of war at Holmfirth.
1/7th Battalion DWR; died as Prisoner of War, of illness, on 16 7 1918, aged 29.
Buried – Conde sur L'Escaut Communal Cemetery, A, 72.
Commemorated – Holme Valley Memorial Hospital WM (plaques 1 & 2, Holme and Holmbridge); M Stansfield, page 441, and the **Drill Hall WM panel 11, column 3.**
Probably pre war Territorial, 1036 Private, F (Holmfirth) Company.

Mentioned in the Huddersfield Examiner (wounded in action, official casualty list) on 13 9 1916; (reported missing 13 4 1918, since reported as POW, not returned) on 20 1 1919.

THORPE (THORP?) William – 2985 Lance Corporal.
Born in Huddersfield on 20 4 1891 to John and Clara, of Marsh. Resided in Marsh. Enlisted at Huddersfield on 06 9 1914.
1/5th Battalion DWR; died of wounds in 14 General Hospital, Wimereux, 19 5 1915, aged 23, Fleurbaix Sector.
Buried – Wimereux Communal Cemetery, 1, H, 8.
Commemorated – Huddersfield Parish Church, RoH; M Stansfield, page 441, and the **Drill Hall WM panel 11, column 2.**
CWGC and SDGW show name as THORP.
Brother, 2Lt J E Thorp, is commemorated on 7 DWR War Memorial Tablets, panel 3, column 3, in Huddersfield Drill Hall.

TIDSWELL Willie – 5980 Private.
Born and enlisted at Bradford.
1/5th Battalion DWR; killed in action 03 9 1916, Battle of the Somme.
Commemorated – Divion Wood No2 Cemetery, Memorial 4, and the **Drill Hall WM panel 11, column 3.**

TIFFANY Charles Edward – 3433 (Vol); 4 (later 240002) Regimental Sergeant Major. Military Cross.
Born in Almondbury on 08 7 1873 to Ernest. Resided in Paddock with his wife, Clementine. Pre war Volunteer and Territorial, G Company, Kirkburton. Embodied on outbreak of war. Embarked for France and Flanders in April, 1915.
1/5th Battalion DWR; killed in action 07 8 1917, aged 45, Nieuport Sector.
Buried – Ramscappelle Road Military Cemetery, 2, A, 33.
Commemorated – All Hallows, Kirkburton, Church (G Company) RoH; All Saints Church, Paddock, RoH; M Stansfield, page 441, and the **Drill Hall WM panel 11, column 3.**
Mentioned in the Goodall collection (award of MC); L Magnus (award of MC), page 250; the Huddersfield Examiner (serving with local unit) on 14 10 1914; (father of Private E Tiffany and wounded in action, official casualty list) on 07 8 1916; (killed in action) on 15 8 1917; (killed in action, official casualty list) on 14 9 1917; (in memoriam) on 07 8 1918 & 1919; Unit War Diary (award of GOC's Gallantry Card) on 31 7 1916; (appointed RSM wef 05 9 1916) on 30 9 1916. The London Gazette (award of MC) on 27 7 1916, page 7445; citation published on 19 8 1916, page 8239.
His Military Cross and Volunteer Long Service Medals are held in the Regimental Museum, Halifax.
FAITHFUL UNTO DEATH.

TINDAL Peter – 242311 Private.
Born in Duns, Berwickshire. Resided in Amble, Northumberland. Enlisted at Alnwick.
1/5th Battalion DWR; killed in action 14 8 1917, aged 21.
Buried – Coxyde Military Cemetery, 2, H, 31.
Commemorated – the **Drill Hall WM panel 11, column 3.**
SAFE IN THE ARMS OF JESUS, SAFE ON HIS GENTLE BREAST.

TINDALL James – 241621 Lance Corporal.
Born and resided in Messingham, Lincs. Enlisted at Scunthorpe.
2/5th Battalion DWR; killed in action 03 5 1917, Battle of Bullecourt.
Commemorated – Arras Memorial, France, and the **Drill Hall WM panel 11, column 3.**

TINKER Fred – 32104 Private.

Born in Upperthong to Alfred. Resided in Holmbridge. Enlisted at Holmfirth in 1915. Embarked for France and Flanders in August, 1917.
2/5th Battalion DWR, D Company; killed in action, shellfire, 22 7 1918, Battle of Tardenois.
Commemorated – Soissons Memorial, France; Holme Valley Memorial Hospital WM (plaques 1 & 2, Holme and Holmbridge); M Stansfield, page 442, and the **Drill Hall WM panel 11, column 3.**

TINKER Percy – 5495 (later 242008) Private.
Born in Hepworth, Holmfirth, to Fred of Scholes. Resided in Holmfirth. Enlisted at Holmfirth.
2/5th Battalion DWR; reported missing (killed in action) 03 5 1917, Battle of Bullecourt.
Commemorated – Arras Memorial, France; Holme Valley Memorial Hospital WM (plaque 6, Hepworth, Scholes and Hade Edge); Hepworth Church RoH; M Stansfield, page 442, and the **Drill Hall WM panel 11, column 3.**
Mentioned in the Goodall collection; the Huddersfield Examiner (request for information by relatives) on 15 6 1917; (reported missing, official casualty list) on 27 6 1917.

TONG Arthur Clifford – 2613 (later 240345) Sergeant.
Born in Berry Brow, Huddersfield, on 21 1 1891 to John William and Sarah Elizabeth. Resided in Berry Brow. Pre war Territorial, rejoined in August, 1914.
1/5th Battalion DWR, Bombing Sergeant; reported missing (killed in action) 03 9 1916, aged 25, Battle of the Somme (Thiepval).
Commemorated – Thiepval Memorial, France; Armitage Bridge WM; M Stansfield, page 444, and the **Drill Hall WM panel 11, column 3.**
Mentioned in the Huddersfield Examiner (reported missing) on 23 8 1916; (reported missing, official casualty list) on 13 12 1916; (bombing Sergeant previously reported missing, now killed in action) on 21 9 1917.

TOWERS Matthew Horsman – 241471 Private.
Born in Otley. Resided in Barhead, Lanarkshire. Enlisted at Keighley.
1/5th Battalion DWR; killed in action 03 9 1916, Battle of the Somme (Thiepval).
Commemorated – Thiepval Memorial, France, and the **Drill Hall WM panel 11, column 3.**

TOWN West – 4316 Private.
Resided in Hipperholme, Halifax. Enlisted at Huddersfield.
1/5th Battalion DWR; killed in action 03 7 1916, Battle of the Somme.
Buried – Connaught Cemetery, 12, J, 3.
Commemorated – Coley Church RoH; Calderdale War Dead, page 454; J J Fisher, page 104, and the **Drill Hall WM panel 11, column 3.**

TOWNEND Lewis – 5496 (later 242009) Private.
Born in Paddock, Huddersfield on 11 8 1892 to Benjamin and Annie of Crosland Moor. Resided in Huddersfield. Enlisted at Huddersfield on 28 3 1916.
2/5th Battalion DWR; reported missing (killed in action) 03 5 1917, aged 24, Battle of Bullecourt.
Commemorated – Arras Memorial, France; All Saints Church, Paddock, RoH; St Barnabas Church, Crosland Moor, RoH; Colne Valley Almanac; M Stansfield, page 446, and the **Drill Hall WM panel 11, column 3.**
Mentioned in the Goodall collection; the Huddersfield examiner (reported missing) on 04 6 1917; (reported missing, official casualty list) on 27 6 1917; (previously reported missing, now killed in action) on 27 6 1917.

TOWNSON James – 5982 Private.
Born and resided in Addingham. Enlisted at Keighley.
1/5th Battalion DWR; killed in action 03 7 1916, Battle of thee Somme.
Buried – Aveluy Wood Cemetery, 1, C, 7.
Commemorated – Addingham WM and the **Drill Hall WM panel 11, column 3.**

TOWSE Alfred – 34474 Lance Corporal.
Born and enlisted at Middlesbrough.
5th Battalion DWR; killed in action 26 8 1918, Advance to Victory.
Buried – Douchy les Ayette Cemetery, 4, J, 13.
Commemorated – the **Drill Hall WM panel 11, column 3.**

TOYNE J – Private
No trace of military service.
Commemorated – the **Drill Hall WM panel 11, column 3.**

TRENHOLME George Leonard – 49713 Lance Corporal.
Born in Egton, N Yorks. Resided in Roxby, N Yorks. Enlisted at Staithes.
5th Battalion DWR; killed in action 13 9 1918, Advance to Victory.
Buried – Sunken Road (Boisleux) Cemetery, 2, A, 9.
Commemorated – the **Drill Hall WM panel 11, column 3.**
Formerly 22687 Private Yorkshire Regiment.

TRUEMAN John – 240725 Private.
Born in Huddersfield to William and Myra, of Milnsbridge. Resided in Milnsbridge. Enlisted at Huddersfield.
1/5th Battalion DWR; killed in action 16 9 1916, aged 21, Battle of the Somme (Leipsig Salient).
Commemorated – Thiepval Memorial, France; Milnsbridge WM; M Stansfield, page 447, and the **Drill Hall WM panel 11, column 3.**

TURNBULL Jack – 4282 Private.
Born in Oughtershaw, Skipton, to John and Elizabeth. Resided in Skipton. Enlisted at Skipton.
1/6th Battalion DWR, A Company; killed in action 03 9 1916, aged 23, Battle of the Somme (Thiepval).
Buried – Connaught Cemetery, 12, D, 9.
Commemorated – Cravens' Part in the Great War, page 175, & the cpgw.org.uk website; Taylor, page 161, and the **Drill Hall WM panel 11, column 4.**
Mentioned in the Unit War Diary (A Company, killed in action, shellfire) on 03 9 1916.
Mentioned in S Barber (killed in action, shellfire on dug-out, 03 9 1916) page 84.
CWGC shows name as John. SDGW records him on pages 40 (2/5th DWR) and 46 (1/6th DWR).
LORD ALL PITYING, JESU BLEST, GRANT HIM THINE ETERNAL REST.

TURNER Ernest Arthur – 5055 (later 241641) Private.
Born in Boston, Lincs. Resided in Market Deeping, Lincs. Enlisted in Lincoln.
2/5th Battalion DWR, D Coy; killed in action 03 5 1917, Battle of Bullecourt.
Commemorated – Arras Memorial, France, and the **Drill Hall WM panel 11, column 4.**
Mentioned in the Goodall collection (Battalion Routine Order award of Commanding Officer's Commendation for actions during 20-28 2 1917, Battle of Cambrai) on 06 3 1917.

TURNER Frank – 13529 Private.
Born in Huddersfield in May 1890. Resided at Aspley, Huddersfield, with his wife, Beatrice. Enlisted in September, 1914.
5th Battalion DWR; killed in action 29 3 1918, German Spring Offensive.
Commemorated – Arras Memorial, France; M Stansfield, page 448, and the **Drill Hall WM panel 11, column 4.**
Mentioned in the Huddersfield Examiner (reported missing) on 12 6 1916; (wounded in action, casualty list) on 31 7 1916; (previously reported missing, now killed in action) on 14 10 1918.
Originally 2/5th DWR.

TURNER James William – 260026 Private.

Born in Halifax to Fred and Ellen. Resided in Halifax. Enlisted at Halifax.
5th Battalion DWR; killed in action 22 7 1918, aged 26, Battle of Tardenois.
Commemorated – Soissons Memorial, France, and the **Drill Hall WM panel 11, column 4.**
Originally 2/5th DWR.

UTTLEY Arthur – 5/6088 Private.
Born in Haworth to Miles and Eliza, of Haworth. Resided Haworth. Enlisted at Haworth.
1/5th Battalion DWR; killed in action 30 8 1916, aged 19, Battle of the Somme.
Buried – Faubourg d'Amiens Cemetery, 1, F, 50.
Commemorated – the **Drill Hall WM panel 11, column 4.**
Attached to 10th Battalion King's Own Yorkshire Light Infantry.
EVER REMEMBERED.

VARLEY Gerald – 267957 Lance Corporal.
Born in Marsh, Huddersfield, on 27 3 1897 to Joseph and Sarah. Resided in Marsh. Enlisted at Huddersfield in February, 1916. Embarked for France and Flanders on 25 12 1916.
2/5th Battalion DWR, C Company, killed in action 27 11 1917, aged 26, Battle of Cambrai.
Commemorated – Cambrai Memorial (Louverval), France; Huddersfield Parish Church RoH; His parents' headstone, Edgerton Cemetery; M Stansfield, page 451, and the **Drill Hall WM panel 11, column 4.**

VARLEY Joe – 1174 Lance Sergeant.
Born in Marsden to Luke and Agnes. Resided in Marsden. Enlisted at Slaithwaite at the outbreak of war. Embarked for France and Flanders in April, 1915.
1/7th Battalion DWR; killed in action 20 9 1915, aged 20, Ypres.
Buried – Bard Cottage Cemetery, 1, H, 22.
Commemorated – Marsden WM; 7 DWR WM, Huddersfield Drill Hall; M Stansfield, page 451, and the **Drill Hall WM panel 11, column 4.**
Mentioned in the Huddersfield Examiner (shot, in Belgium) on 28 9 1915.
GOD MOVES IN A MYSTERIOUS WAY.

VAUSE Arthur – 4773 (later 241455) Private.
Born in Selby to John A and Mary, of Selby. Resided in Selby and Thurstonland. Enlisted at Huddersfield.
1/5th Battalion DWR; killed in action 03 9 1916, aged 23, Battle of the Somme.
Commemorated – Thiepval Memorial, France; Thurstonland WM; M Stansfield, page 452, and the **Drill Hall WM panel 11, column 4.**

VICKERS James Edwin – 5165 (later 241734) Private.
Born in Louth, Lincs, to Henry and Eliza. Resided in Louth. Enlisted at Gainsborough.
2/5th Battalion DWR; killed in action 03 5 1917, aged 37, Battle of Bullecourt.
Commemorated – Arras Memorial, France, and the **Drill Hall WM panel 11, column 4.**
Mentioned in the Goodall collection.

VICKERS John – 307337 Private.
Born in Campsall, Doncaster, to John and Mary. Resided in Campsall. Enlisted at Doncaster.
5th Battalion DWR; died of wounds 27 3 1918, aged 23, German Spring Offensive.
Buried – Humbercamps Communal Cemetery Extension, 1, F, 6.
Commemorated – the **Drill Hall WM panel 11, column 4.**
Originally 2/5th DWR.
HE DID THAT WHICH WAS RIGHT IN THE SIGHT OF THE LORD.

WADESON James Wright – 242643 Private.
Born in Barbon, Lancs, to James Henry, of Pontefract. Enlisted at Ingleton.

1/5th Battalion DWR; killed in action 08 10 1917, aged 22, 3rd Battle of Ypres (Passchendaele).
Commemorated – Tyne Cot Memorial, Belgium; Ingleton WM and the **Drill Hall WM panel 12, column 1.**

WAITE Henry – 241476 Private.
Born in Lindley, Huddersfield on 29 4 1890, to Mary of Marsh. Resided in Marsh. Enlisted at Huddersfield on 17 2 1916.
1/5th Battalion DWR; reported missing (killed in action) 03 9 1916, Battle of the Somme (Thiepval).
Commemorated – Thiepval Memorial, France; Marsh WM; All Saints Church, Paddock, RoH; M Stansfield, page 456, and the **Drill Hall WM panel 12, column 1.**
Mentioned in the Huddersfield Examiner (reported missing) on 04 10 1916; (previously reported missing, now killed in action) on 03 7 1917; (reported missing 03 9 1916, now officially presumed dead on that date) on 03 9 1919.

WAKELIN Walter – 3491 Private.
Born to Timothy and Emelia. Resided in Clay Cross, Derbyshire. Enlisted at Doncaster.
1/5th Battalion DWR; killed in action 24 5 1915, aged 36, Fleurbaix Sector.
Buried – Rue David Military Cemetery, 1, B, 16.
Commemorated – the **Drill Hall WM panel 11, column 4.**

WALKER Adolphus – 2nd Lieutenant.
Son of Thomas, of Wakefield, possibly resided in Leeds, his next of kin, sister, lived in Rothwell Haigh, Leeds. Embarked for France and Flanders on 21 5 1916. Commissioned into 2/5th DWR in August, 1917.
5th Battalion DWR; killed in action 15 4 1918, aged 21, German Spring Offensive.
Buried - Gezaincourt Communal Cemetery, 2, L, 20.
Commemorated – Arras Memorial, France; C D Bruce RoH, page 215, and the **Drill Hall WM panel 11, column 4.**
Mentioned in 62nd Division History (wounded) page 198; Unit War Diary (to hospital 14 2 1918 to 22 2 1918) on 28 2 1918; (wounded in action 09 4 1918, died of wounds 15 4 1918) on 30 4 1918. Formerly 15/1818 Sergeant West Yorkshire Regiment (1st Leeds Pals). Originally 2/5th DWR.
IN MEMORY OF OUR DEAR AND DEVOTED BROTHER, LOVED BY ALL. WAR'S BITTER COST.

WALKER B – 3210 (later 240619) Private.
Resided in Mirfield. Enlisted into D Company, 2/5th DWR, Mirfield, on 25 10 1914.
2/5th Battalion DWR, D Company, 15 Platoon; died, Rugeley Camp, 11 10 1917.
Buried – not known.
Commemorated – the **Drill Hall WM panel 11, column 4.**
Mentioned in the Goodall collection (15 Platoon D Company and Battalion Transport Section, returned to UK on 11 10 1917, died Rugeley Camp).
Not listed in either CWGC or SDGW records.

WALKER Harry – 241372 Private.
Born in Slaithwaite to Lister G. Enlisted at Huddersfield in October, 1915.
1/5th Battalion DWR; reported missing (killed in action) 03 9 1916, Battle of the Somme (Thiepval).
Commemorated – Thiepval Memorial, France; Slaithwaite WM; St James's Church, Slaithwaite, RoH; M Stansfield, page 458, and the **Drill Hall WM panel 11, column 4.**

WALKER Lewis – 3006 Lance Corporal.
Born in Armitage Bridge, Huddersfield, on 13 3 1892 to James and Katherine Mary, of Armitage Bridge. Resided in Armitage Bridge. Enlisted at Huddersfield on 04 9 1914. Embarked for France and Flanders in April, 1915.
1/5th Battalion DWR, A Company; killed in action, shrapnel, 15 5 1915, aged 23, Fleurbaix Sector.

Buried – Rue David Military Cemetery, 1, B, 20.
Commemorated – Armitage Bridge WM; Huddersfield Parish Church RoH; B Heywood, page 46; M Stansfield, page 459, and the **Drill Hall WM panel 11, column 4.**
Mentioned in the Huddersfield Examiner (announcement of death) on 19 5 1915.
GREATER LOVE HATH NO MAN THAN THIS.

WALKER Oscar – Lieutenant.
Born in Lindley on 15 5 1889 to Arthur Edward and Kate, of Edgerton. Enlisted as 2641 Private on 06 8 1914. Commissioned February 1915. Embarked for France and Flanders on 11 1 1917.
2/5th Battalion DWR, B Company; killed in action 03 5 1917, aged 27, Battle of Bullecourt.
Commemorated – Arras Memorial, France; Oakes Baptist Church RoH; St Stephen's Church, Lindley, RoH; T Ashworth, page 76; J J Fisher, page 129; L Magnus, page 134; T Podmore, page 58; M Stansfield, page 459; D Tattersfield, page 201, and the **Drill Hall WM panel 11, column 4.**
Mentioned in the Goodall collection; the Unit War Diary (Roll of Officers) on 10 1 1917; (killed in action) on 03 5 1917; the Huddersfield Examiner (killed in action, official casualty list) on 17 5 1917; (killed in action on the Hindenburg Line) on 24 9 1919; (B Company, killed alongside 35 men between 03 and 06 5 1917, in memoriam) on 03 5 1921.

WALKER Richard Frederick – 25413 Private.
Born in Brixton. Resided in Merton. Enlisted at Wimbledon.
5th Battalion DWR; killed in action 23 7 1918, Battle of Tardenois.
Commemorated – Soissons Memorial, France, and the **Drill Hall WM panel 11, column 4.**
Formerly 45725 Private, Suffolk Regiment. Originally 2/5th DWR.

WALKER Walter – 2nd Lieutenant.
Son of George and Rebecca Ann, of Manchester. Enlisted as Private soldier, 840, into RAMC. Transferred to 252539 Lancashire Fusiliers. Embarked for Egypt on 21 5 1916. Commissioned into the 6th Battalion Lancashire Fusiliers on 27 3 1918 and attached to the 5th DWR on 06 8 1918.
5th Battalion DWR; died of wounds 25 8 1918, Advance to Victory.
Buried – Douchy les Ayette British, 4, A, 9.
Commemorated – 62nd Divisional History, page 204; the **Drill Hall WM panel 11, column 4.**
Mentioned in the Unit War Diary (joined the Battalion & wounded in action) on 30 8 1918; the Huddersfield Examiner (from 6 Lancs Fus, buried with a cross) on 08 8 1919.

WALLACE Arthur – 5997 Private.
Born in Bradford to John William and Mary Ann. Enlisted at Bradford.
1/5th Battalion DWR; killed in action 20 9 1916, aged 21, Battle of the Somme.
Commemorated – Thiepval Memorial, France, and the **Drill Hall WM panel 11, column 4.**

WALLACE Thomas – 240765 Private.
Born in Aberfeldy, Perthshire. Enlisted at Mirfield.
1/5th Battalion DWR; killed in action 03 9 1916, Battle of the Somme (Thiepval).
Commemorated – Thiepval Memorial, France, and the **Drill Hall WM panel 11, column 4.**

WALLING James – 29963 Private.
Born in Barnoldswick to Francis and Hannah. Enlisted at Barnoldswick.
5th Battalion DWR; died, as POW, 17 11 1918, aged 21.
Buried – Berlin South Western Cemetery, 2, G, 1.
Commemorated – Barnoldswick WM; Cravens Part in the Great War, page 374, & the cpgw.org.uk website; P Thompson, pages 239 & 244, and the **Drill Hall WM panel 12, column 1.**
Mentioned in the Unit War Diary (A Company, wounded in action, shellfire, leg) on 02 8 1917.
TO LIVE IN HEARTS WE LEAVE BEHIND IS NOT TO DIE.

WALMSLEY Harry – 5992 Private.

Born Farnhill, Kildwick, to Seth and Ida. Enlisted at Keighely.
1/5th Battalion DWR; died, home, 14 12 1916, aged 23, Battle of the Somme.
Buried – Kildwick (St Andrew's) Cemetery, South East part.
Commemorated – Farnhill WM; Cravens Part in the Great War, page 198, & the cpgw.org.uk website; Farnhill Volunteers Project website; and the **Drill Hall WM panel 12, column 1.**

WALSH Arthur Garfield – 242923 Private.
Born in Greetland, Halifax, to William and Emma Jane. Resided in Greetland. Enlisted at Halifax.
5th Battalion DWR; killed in action 08 4 1918, aged 36, German Spring Offensive.
Buried – Bienvillers Military Cemetery, 9, A, 10.
Commemorated – Greetland WM and the **Drill Hall WM panel 12, column 1.**
HE DIED THAT WE MIGHT LIVE.

WALSHAW Robert Ernest – 2053 (later 240132) Private.
Born in Sheepridge, Huddersfield, on 17 2 1893 to Alfred and Mary Ann. Resided in Sheepridge.
Pre war Territorial from 21 5 1912.
2/5th Battalion DWR, B Company; wounded in action on 21 11 1917, died of wounds at 21 Casualty Clearing Station, Ytres, on 22 11 1917, aged 24, Battle of Cambrai.
Buried – Rocquigney-Equancourt Road Cemetery, 2, B, 23.
Commemorated – Providence United Methodist Church, Sheepridge, RoH; Christ Church, Woodhouse Hill, RoH; M Stansfield, page 461, and the **Drill Hall WM panel 12, column 1.**
Mentioned in the Goodall collection.
GREATER LOVE HATH NO MAN.

WALTER Fred William – 5104 (later 241684) Private.
Born in Grimsby. Resided in New Clee, Lincs. Enlisted at Grimsby.
2/5th Battalion DWR; killed in action 03 5 1917, Battle of Bullecourt.
Commemorated – Arras Memorial, France, and the **Drill Hall WM panel 12, column 1.**
Mentioned in the Goodall collection.

WALTON Arthur – 6716 (later 267711) Private.
Born in Lothersdale. Resided in Earby. Enlisted at Keighley on 26 8 1916.
2/5th Battalion DWR, D Company; reported missing (killed in action) 27 11 1917, Battle of Cambrai.
Commemorated – Cambrai Memorial (Louverval), France; Earby WM; Cravens Part in the Great War, page 336, & the cpgw.org.uk website, and the **Drill Hall WM panel 12, column 1.**
Mentioned in the Goodall collection; the 1/6th DWR Part 2 Routine Orders (change of Regimental Number) on 20 4 1917.
CWGC shows number as 26771, incorrectly.

WALTON Garnet – 4801 Private.
Born in Oxenhope. Enlisted at Haworth.
1/5th Battalion DWR; killed in action 20 11 1916, Battle of the Somme.
Commemorated – Thiepval Memorial, France, and the **Drill Hall WM panel 12, column 1.**

WARD Bernard – 579 Private.
Born and enlisted at Mossley.
1/5th Battalion DWR; died of wounds 06 9 1916, Battle of the Somme.
Buried – St Sever Cemetery, B, 23, 14.
Commemorated – the **Drill Hall WM panel 11, column 4.**

WARD Joseph – 4342 (later 241253) Private.
Born in Huddersfield on 25 6 1894 to William. Enlisted at Huddersfield in May 1915.
1/5th Battalion DWR; reported missing (killed in action) 03 9 1916, Battle of the Somme (Thiepval).

Buried – Mill Road Cemetery, 3, F, 1.
Commemorated – M Stansfield, page 463, and the **Drill Hall WM panel 11, column 4.**

WARD John Thomas – 3004 Sergeant.
Born in Thornbury, Bradford, on 20 8 1891 to Sarah. Resided in Bradford and Cowcliffe, Huddersfield. Enlisted at Huddersfield on 03 9 1914.
1/5th Battalion DWR; killed in action 02 7 1916, aged 24, Battle of the Somme.
Commemorated – Thiepval Memorial, France; M Stansfield, page 463, and the **Drill Hall WM panel 11, column 4.**

WARDEN Henry (Harry?) – 7062 Private.
Born and resided in Roberttown. Enlisted at Heckmondwike.
1/6th Battalion DWR; killed in action 03 9 1916, Battle of the Somme (Thiepval).
Commemorated – Thiepval Memorial, France; Hartshead WM and the **Drill Hall WM panel 12, column 1.**
Mentioned in S Barber (reported missing 03 9 1916).

WARDLE Marcus – 240427 Sergeant.
Born Leytonstone, Essex, on 06 12 1891 to Gilbert and Emma. Resided in Dalton. Enlisted at Huddersfield on 03 9 1914.
1/5th Battalion DWR; reported missing (killed in action) 03 9 1916, aged 24, Battle of the Somme (Thiepval).
Buried – Mill Road Cemetery, 9, C, 9.
Commemorated – Christ Church, Moldgreen, RoH; Learoyd Brothers RoH; M Stansfield, page 463, and the **Drill Hall WM panel 11, column 4.**
Mentioned in the Huddersfield Examiner (wounded in hospital, France) on 14 9 1916; (previously reported missing, now killed in action) on 31 8 1917); (in memoriam) on 03 9 1919 & 07 10 1919.

WARDMAN William Raper – 32505 Private.
Born in Baildon to Robert and Elizabeth. Resided in Baildon. Enlisted at keighely.
5th Battalion DWR; killed in action 31 8 1918, aged 19, Advance to Victory.
Buried – Bac du Sud British Cemetery, 1, F, 6..
Commemorated – the **Drill Hall WM panel 12, column 1.**
TODAY RECALLS SAD MEMORIES OF OUR LOVED ON GONE TO REST.

WARHURST James Ewart – 241817 Private.
Born in Slaithwaite to John William and Sarah Ann. Resided in Slaithwaite. Enlisted at Huddersfield in March, 1916. Embarked for France and Flanders on 10 1 1917.
2/5th Battalion DWR; reported missing (killed in action) 27 11 1917, aged 24, Battle of Cambrai.
Commemorated – Cambrai Memorial (Louverval), France; Slaithwaite WM; St James's Church, Slaithwaite RoH; M Stansfield, page 464, and the **Drill Hall WM panel 12, column 1.**

WASS George William – 242784 Private
Enlisted at Hull.
2/5th Battalion DWR; killed in action 16 3 1917.
Buried – Queens Cemetery, 3, E, 7.
Commemorated – the **Drill Hall WM panel 12, column 1.**

WATERHOUSE William – 240011 Sergeant
Born in Leeds on 10 11 1882, to Charles Edward and Mary Ann. Resided in Birkby with his wife, Ada. Ex Volunteer and re-enlisted at the outbreak of war.
2/5th Battalion DWR; died of wounds at 2nd Canadian General Hospital, Le Treport, on 06 4 1918, aged 36.
Buried – Etaples Military Cemetery, 33, D, 6A.

Commemorated – Fartown and Birkby WM; M Stansfield, page 465, and the **Drill Hall WM panel 11, column 4.**
UNTIL THE DAWN, ADA.

WATMOUGH Frank – 17653 Private.
Enlisted at Bradford.
5th Battalion DWR; killed in action 20 7 1918, Battle of Tardenois.
Buried – Courmas British Cemetery, 2, C, 8.
Commemorated – the **Drill Hall WM panel 12, column 1.**

WATSON Ernest – 242055 Private.
Born in Hillsborough, Sheffield, to Mary Jane. Resided in Sheffield. Enlisted at Halifax.
1/5th Battalion DWR; killed in action 03 9 1916, aged 26, Battle of the Somme (Thiepval).
Buried – Serre Road No2 Cemetery, 10, C, 16.
Commemorated – the **Drill Hall WM panel 12, column 1.**

WATSON John Ernest – 242754 Private
Enlisted at Newcastle upon Tyne.
1/5th Battalion DWR; killed in action 07 8 1917.
Buried – Ramscappelle Road Military Cemetery, 2, A, 36.
Commemorated – the **Drill Hall WM panel 12, column 1.**

WATSON J H – Private.
No trace.
Commemorated – the **Drill Hall WM panel 12, column 1.**

WATSON James William – 235104 Private.
Born in Scarborough. Resided in Stainland, Halifax. Enlisted at Halifax on 08 9 1916.
2/5th Battalion DWR, D Company; killed in action 03 5 1917, Battle of Bullecourt.
Commemorated – Arras Memorial, France, and the **Drill Hall WM panel 12, column 1.**
Mentioned in the Goodall collection.

WATSON Norman – 241574 Private.
Born, resided and enlisted at Bradford.
2/5th Battalion DWR; killed in action 03 5 1917, Battle of Bullecourt.
Commemorated – Arras Memorial, France, and the **Drill Hall WM panel 12, column 1.**

WATSON Norman – 269248 Private.
Born at Steeton to Fred and Jane Edith. Resided in Steeton. Enlisted at Keighley.
2/5th Battalion DWR; died of wounds at 30 Casualty Clearing Station, near Arras, on 05 2 1918, aged 20.
Buried – Anzin St Aubin British Cemetery, 4, A, 6.
Commemorated – Cravens Part in the Great War, page 335, & the cpgw.org.uk website, and the **Drill Hall WM panel 12, column 1.**

WATSON Robert Burton – 268587 Private.
Born in Yeadon to Siddal and Mary. Resided in Yeadon Enlisted at Yeadon.
1/5th Battalion DWR; killed in action 09 8 1917, aged 23, Nieuport Sector.
Buried – Adinkerke Military Cemetery, A, 22.
Commemorated – the **Drill Hall WM panel 12, column 1.**

WATSON Walter – 4566 (later 241362) Private.
Resided in Eye, Suffolk, with his wife, Harriet Hepzibah. Enlisted at Gainsborough.
2/5th Battalion DWR; killed in action 03 5 1917, aged 40, Battle of Bullecourt.

Commemorated – Arras Memorial, France, and the **Drill Hall WM panel 12, column 1.**

WATTON John Hubert 240161 Private.
Born in Bedale. Resided in Burslam, Staffs. Enlisted at Bradford.
1/5th Battalion DWR; killed in action 24 11 1917.
Buried – Dochy Farm New British Cemetery, 3, D, 9.
Commemorated – K Taylor, page 296, and the **Drill Hall WM panel 12, column 1.**

WAUGH Ernest – 235102 Private.
Born in Horsforth. Resided in Ilkley Enlisted at Ilkley on 04 8 1916.
5th Battalion DWR, 14 Platoon, D Company, Lewis gunner; killed in action 26 3 1918, German Spring Offensive.
Commemorated – Arras Memorial, France; Ilkley WM and the **Drill Hall WM panel 12, column 1.**
Mentioned in the Goodall collection.
Originally 2/5th DWR.

WEAR Frank – 5112 (later 241690) Private.
Born in Moldgreen, Huddersfield, on 01 4 1896 to Frederick. Resided in Huddersfield. Enlisted at Huddersfield on 15 3 1916.
2/5th Battalion DWR, 13 Platoon, D Company; reported missing (killed in action) 03 5 1917, aged 21, Battle of Bullecourt.
Commemorated – Arras Memorial, France, and the **Drill Hall WM panel 12, column 2.**
Mentioned in the Goodall collection; the Huddersfield Examiner (reported missing) on 20 8 1917.

WEAVER Thomas William – 242480 Private.
Born in Finsbury, London. Resided in Bethnal Green. Enlisted at Hackney.
1/5th Battalion DWR; killed in action 10 10 1917, Ypres.
Commemorated – Tyne Cot Memorial, Belgium, and the **Drill Hall WM panel 12, column 1.**

WEBSTER Charles William – 5175 (later 241743) Private.
Born in Steeton to Alfred and Annie Maria. Resided in Beelby, Grimsby, with his wife, Annie Ann. Enlisted at Grimsby.
2/5th Battalion DWR; killed in action 03 5 1917, aged 30, Battle of Bullecourt.
Commemorated – Arras Memorial, France, Memorial, and the **Drill Hall WM panel 12, column 2.**
Mentioned in the Goodall collection.

WEBSTER George – 242645 Private.
Born in Clapham. Resided Middleton Mont with his wife, Lily (also of Blackpool). Enlisted at Keighley.
1/5th Battalion DWR; killed in action 07 8 1917, aged 27, Nieuport Sector.
Buried – Ramscappelle Road Military Cemetery, 2, A, 35.
Commemorated – Cravens part in the Great War, page 274, & the cpgw.org.uk website, and the **Drill Hall WM panel 12, column 2.**
AT REST.

WEBSTER Harry – 2019 (later 240142) Private.
Mother Hannah. Resided in Ravensthorpe. Pre war Territorial, enlisted at Mirfield on 22 2 1912.
2/5th Battalion DWR, 13 Platoon, H, later D, Company Pioneer; reported missing (killed in action) 03 5 1917, aged 29, Battle of Bullecourt.
Commemorated – Arras Memorial, France, D Tattersfield, pages 204 & 387, and the **Drill Hall WM panel 12, column 2.**
Mentioned in the Huddersfield Examiner (reported missing, official casualty list) on 27 6 1917.

WEEDER William James – 242231 Private.
Born in Boulton, Derbyshire. Resided in Crouton, Derbyshire. Enlisted at Keighley.
1/5th Battalion DWR; killed in action 03 9 1916, Battle of the Somme (Thiespval).
Commemorated – Thiepval Memorial, France, and the **Drill Hall WM panel 12, column 1.**

WELDON (WHELDON?) Albert – 7114 Private.
Born in Burton on Trent to Jane (remarried to Alfred Hall). Enlisted at Burton on Trent.
1/5th Battalion DWR; died of wounds at 8 Stationary Hospital, Wimereux, on 27 9 1916, aged 33, Battle of the Somme.
Buried – Wimereux Communal Cemetery, 1, Q, 21.
Commemorated – the **Drill Hall WM panel 12, column 2.**
Formerly 3833 Private Northumberland Fusiliers.
CWGC, Medal Index Card and Medal Roll shows spelling as Wheldon.
HIS DUTY NOBLY DONE.

WEST Edwin – 4923 (later 241526) Lance Corporal.
Born in Newsome, Huddersfield, on 13 10 1896 to Arthur. Resided in Newsome. Enlisted at Huddersfield on 06 3 1916.
2/5th Battalion DWR; wounded and taken prisoner; died as POW 12 6 1917, aged 20.
Buried – Mons Communal Cemetery, 7, E, 7.
Commemorated – United Methodist Church, Newsome, RoH; M Stansfield, page 467, and the **Drill Hall WM panel 12, column 2.**
Mentioned in the Goodall collection; the Huddersfield Examiner (information requested by the family) on 05 6 1917; (reported missing, official casualty list) on 27 6 1917; (died as POW) on 28 8 1917.
GONE BUT NOT FORGOTTEN, FROM HIS SORROWING MOTHER AND FATHER.

WESTERBY Joseph John – 5136 (later 241711) Private.
Born in Ashby cum Fenby, Lincs, to George and Rachel of Donington on Bain, Louth, Lincs, Resided in Louth. Enlisted at Louth.
2/5th Battalion DWR; killed in action 03 5 1917, aged 25, Battle of Bullecourt.
Commemorated – Arras Memorial, France, Memorial, and the **Drill Hall WM panel 12, column 2.**

WHARTON Percy – 7070 Private.
Born in Earby to Michael and Elizabeth. Resided in Earby. Enlisted at Keighley.
1/6th Battalion DWR; killed in action 03 9 1916, aged 22, Battle of the Somme.
Commemorated – Thiepval Memorial, France; Earby WM; Cravens part in the Great War, page 179, & the cpgw.org.uk website, and the **Drill Hall WM panel 12, column 2.**

WHEATLEY Arthur Nevin – Major. Mention in Despatches.
Born in Mirfield in 1888 to Joseph and Elizabeth. Resided in Mirfield with his wife, Mabel. Pre-war Territorial, promoted Lt on 26 11 1908. H Company (Mirfield) 2/5th DWR from August 1914. Volunteered for active service and posted to 1/5th DWR, 1915. Embarked for France and Flanders 14 4 1915.
1/5th Battalion DWR; died of wounds 05 7 1916, aged 28, Battle of the Somme.
Buried – Etaples Military Cemetery, 1, A, 32.
Commemorated – Mirfield WM; Upper Hopton Church WM; Shrewsbury (Salop) School WM; J J Fisher, page 107, 108 & 127; B Heywood, page 134; R Leedham, page 28, and the **Drill Hall WM panel 12, column 2.**
Mentioned in the Goodall collection; the Huddersfield Examiner (died of wounds) on 6 7 1916; (died of wounds, one of 250 casualties in July 1916) on 29 7 1919; Unit War Diary (OC D Coy) on 29 4 1915; (returned from leave) on 28 11 1915; (promoted Major) on 30 1 1916; (Commanded the

Battalion) on 31 5 1916; (wounded in action) on 03 7 1916; (died of wounds & to be Major) on 31 7 1916. Award of Mention in Despatches announced in the London Gazette of 15 6 1916, page 5943.
GREATER LOVE HATH NO MAN THAN THIS, TO LAY DOWN HIS LIFE FOR HIS FRIEND.

WHEELDON James – 26647 Private.
Born in Burton on Trent to Thomas and Sarah Ann. Enlisted at Burton on Trent.
5th Battalion DWR; killed in action 04 1 1918, aged 19.
Buried – Ypres Reservoir Cemetery, 4, A, 17.
Commemorated – the **Drill Hall WM panel 12, column 2.**
SLEEP ON DEAR SON, THY WARFARE'S O'ER, THY HANDS SHALL BATTLE NO MORE.

WHEELHOUSE Norman – 2133 (later 240160) Private. Territorial Force War Medal.
Born in Huddersfield on 16 8 1896 to Fred. Resided in Birkby. Pre war Territorial enlisted at Huddersfield in 1912.
2/5th Battalion DWR; reported missing (killed in action) 03 5 1917, Battle of Bullecourt.
Commemorated – Arras Memorial, France; Fartown and Birkby WM; Great Northern Street Congregational Church RoH; M Stansfield, page 467, and the **Drill Hall WM panel 12, column 2.**
Mentioned in the Goodall collection; the Huddersfield Examiner (reported missing, official casualty list) on 27 6 1917; (previously reported missing, now presumed killed in action) on 17 9 1917; (previously reported missing now killed in action) on 04 10 1917.
Awarded the Territorial Force War Medal, posthumously, on 20 4 1922

WHIPP Phillip Stuart – 6867 Private.
Born in Hornsea, Yorks. Resided in Brentwood, Essex. Enlisted at London.
1/5th Battalion DWR; killed in action 13 10 1916, Battle of the Somme.
Buried – Foncquevillers Military Cemetery, 1, J, 4.
Commemorated – the **Drill Hall WM panel 12, column 2.**

WHITAKER Joseph – 235101 Private.
Born in Bradford to William Henry and Catherine. Resided in Bradford. Enlisted at Bradford.
2/5th Battalion DWR, B Company; died of wounds 28 5 1917, aged 21.
Buried – Etaples Military Cemetery, 25, E, 7.
Commemorated – the **Drill Hall WM panel 12, column 2.**
REST IN PEACE, FROM FATHER, MOTHER, BROTHER AND SISTERS.

WHITE Arthur – 24153 Private.
Born in Ingrow to John and Lavinia. Resided in Ingrow, Keighley. Enlisted at Skipton.
5th Battalion DWR; killed in action 31 8 1918, aged 27, Advance to Victory.
Buried – Bagneux British Cemetery, 6, B, 31.
Commemorated – the **Drill Hall WM panel 12, column 2.**
THY WILL BE DONE.

WHITE Albert James – 16630 Private.
Born Horley, Surrey, to James. Resided in Horley. Enlisted at Redhill.
5th Battalion DWR; killed in action 25 8 1918, aged 25, Advance to Victory.
Buried – Gommecourt South Cemetery, 1, D, 2.
Commemorated – the **Drill Hall WM panel 12, column 2.**
Formerly 8090 Tpr, Dragoons.

WHITE Harry – 241686 Private.
Born in Croft, Lincs. Resided and enlisted at Wainfleet.
2/5th Battalion DWR; killed in action 03 5 1917, Battle of Bullecourt.
Commemorated – Arras Memorial, France, and the **Drill Hall WM panel 12, column 2.**

WHITEHEAD William Arthur – 26461 Private.
Born in Hinckley, Leics. Resided in South Wigston. Enlisted at Leicester.
2/5th Battalion DWR; killed in action 22 7 1918, Battle of Tardenois.
Commemorated – Soissons Memorial, France; Wigston WM and the **Drill Hall WM panel 12, column 2.**
Formerly 30938 Private, Leicestershire regiment.

WHITEHOUSE Henry – 22504 Private.
Born in Wolverhampton. Resided in Willenhall, Staffs. Enlisted at Willenhall.
1/6th Battalion DWR; killed in action 11 10 1918, aged 19, Battle of Iwuy.
Buried – Wellington Cemetery, 3, D, 4.
Commemorated – the **Drill Hall WM panel 12, column 2.**
Mentioned in S Barber (killed in action 11 10 1918) page 209.

WHITELAM Lewis – 2nd Lieutenant.
Born in Wootton, Lincs, in 1897 to Christopher George and Georgina. Resided in Hull. Served as 4437 Private in the OTC. Commissioned on 15 11 1915 into the 5th DWR. Served in UK with 3/5th DWR.
1/5th Battalion DWR; killed in action 03 9 1916, aged 19, Battle of the Somme (Thiepval).
Commemorated – Thiepval Memorial, France, and the **Drill Hall WM panel 12, column 2.**

WHITELEY George (Albert?) – 306847 Private.
Born in Ripponden to Joe and Sarah Ann. Resided Ripponden. Enlisted at Halifax.
5th Battalion DWR; killed in action 07 9 1918, aged 27, Advance to Victory.
Buried – Mont Huon Military Cemetery, 8, E, 11A.
Commemorated – Ripponden WM and the **Drill Hall WM panel 12, column 2.**
THERE IS A LINK DEATH CANNOT SEVER, LOVE AND REMEMBRANCE LIVE FOREVER.

WHITELEY Herbert – 4691 Private.
Born in Halifax to John. Resided in Linthwaite. Enlisted at Huddersfield in February, 1916. Embarked for France on 24 6 1916.
1/5th Battalion DWR; killed in action, shellfire, 16 9 1916, Battle of the Somme (Leipsig Salient).
Commemorated – Thiepval Memorial, France; Linthwaite WM; Fartown and Birkby WM; M Stansfield, page 470, and the **Drill Hall WM panel 12, column 2.**

WHITELEY R
No trace. Probably Whitley R, below:
Commemorated – the **DRILL HALL WM panel 12, column 2**

WHITEOAK Thomas Clifford – 242230 Private.
Born in Lothersdale to Alfred and Margaret Ellen. Resided at Connonley. Enlisted at Skipton.
1/5th Battalion DWR; killed in action 03 9 1916, aged 22, Battle of the Somme (Thiepval).
Commemorated – Thiepval Memorial, France; Cravens Part in the Great War, page 179, & the cpgw.org.uk website, and the **Drill Hall WM panel 12, column 2.**

WHITING Frank – 3830 Private.
Resided at Hartshead. Enlisted at Mirfield.
1/5th Battalion DWR; killed in action 04 7 1916, Battle of the Somme.
Buried – Connaught Cemetery, 3, M, 9.
Commemorated – the **Drill Hall WM panel 12, column 2.**

WHITLEY Richard – 242382 Private.
Born and enlisted at Shipley.
1/5th Battalion DWR; killed in action 08 8 1917.

Buried – Ramscappelle Road Military Cemetery, 2, B, 14.
Commemorated – the **Drill Hall WM panel 12, column 2.**

WIBBERLEY Fred – 5533 Private.
Born in Austenley, Holmfirth on 29 3 1897 to George. Resided in Holmbridge. Enlisted at Holmfirth on 29 3 1916. Embarked for France and Flanders in August, 1916.
1/5th Battalion DWR; wounded in action, shellfire on 11 3 1917, aged 19, died of wounds at 33 Casualty Clearing Station, Bethune, 13 3 1917.
Buried – Bethune Town Cemetery, 6, C, 7.
Commemorated – Holme Valley Memorial Hospital WM (plaque 1 & 2, Holme & Holmbridge); M Stansfield, page 475, and the **Drill Hall WM panel 12, column 3.**
Mentioned in the Huddersfield Examiner, (died of wounds, shellfire) on 21 3 1917.
CHERISHED MEMORIES OF ONE SO DEAR ARE OFT RECALLED BY A SILENT TEAR.

WILCOCK Willie – 3835 (later 240989) Private.
Resided in Denby Dale. Enlisted at Huddersfield.
2/5th Battalion DWR; reported missing (killed in action) 03 5 1917, Battle of Bullecourt.
Commemorated – Arras Memorial, France; Denby Dale and Cumberworth WM; M Stansfield, page 476, and the **Drill Hall WM panel 12, column 3.**
Mentioned in the Goodall collection; the Huddersfield Examiner (reported missing, official casualty list) on 27 6 1917.
SDGW shows Wilcox.

WILD James – 3692 Private.
Born and Resided in Dewsbury.
1/5th Battalion DWR; killed in action 03 9 1916, Battle of the Somme (Thiepval).
Commemorated – Thiepval Memorial, France, and the **Drill Hall WM panel 12, column 3.**

WILDE Fred Benjamin – 34510 Corporal. Military Medal.
Born in Hillsborough, Sheffield, to Harry Gordon and Alice. Resided in Hillsborough. Enlisted at Sheffield in August 1914
5th Battalion DWR; killed in action 28 9 1918, aged 23, Advance to Victory.
Buried – Grand Ravine British Cemetery, A, 6.
Commemorated – the **Drill Hall WM panel 12, column 3.**
Mentioned in the Goodall collection (medal award); L Magnus (medal award, page 294; the London Gazette (award of MM) on 13 3 1919, page 3429.
Formerly 11281 Private, Yorkshire Regiment.
A LOVING BROTHER TRUE AND KIND, A BEAUTIFUL MEMORY LEFT BEHIND. R.I.P.

WILDE John Clarke – 1119 (later 205585) Private.
Born in Windhill, Shipley, to William and Lavinia. Resided in Shipley with his wife, Gerlinde. Enlisted at Shipley in 1914.
5th Battalion DWR; killed in action 29 3 1918, German Spring Offensive.
Commemorated – Arras Memorial, France, and the Drill Hall WM panel 12, column 3.
Originally 2/5th DWR.
SDGW shows John Clark.

WILDS Frank – 3011 (later 240522) Private.
Born Hampshire. Resided in Lindley and Oakes, Huddersfield. Enlisted at Huddersfield.
2/5th Battalion DWR; reported missing (killed in action) 03 5 1917, Battle of Bullecourt.
Commemorated – Arras Memorial, France; St Stephen's Church, Lindley, RoH; Huddersfield Corporation RoH; M Stansfield, page 477, and the **Drill Hall WM panel 12, column 3.**

Mentioned in the Goodall collection; the Huddersfield Examiner (reported missing) on 04 6 1917; (reported missing, official casualty list) on 27 6 1917; (previously reported missing, now killed in action) on 17 9 1917 & 04 10 1917.

WILKINS F A – Private.
No trace.
Commemorated – the **Drill Hall WM panel 12, column 3.**

WILKINSON George Emsley – 240112 Sergeant. Military Medal.
Born in Skipton area (Littondale) to R A and Jane of Cote Farm, Kilnsey, later Lane Head Farm, Kirkburton. Resided in Kirkburton. Pre war Territorial in G Company at Kirkburton and mobilised on the outbreak of war. Embarked for France and Flanders in April, 1915.
5th Battalion DWR; died of wounds 26 7 1918, aged 23.
Buried – Vertus Communal Cemetery, 79.
Commemorated – Kirkburton Church (G Company) RoH; headstone commemoration in Kirkburton Church yard; Coniston Church, Wharfedale, plaque; J J Fisher, page 87, K Taylor, page 263; M Stansfield, page 478, and the **Drill Hall WM panel 12, column 3.**
Mentioned in the Goodall collection (gallantry award list); L Magnus (medal roll) page 250; the Huddersfield Examiner (award of MM) on 27 9 1917; the Unit War Diary (award of MM, 29 8 1917) on 31 8 1917; (MM presented by Corps Commander) on 01 9 1917; the London Gazette (award of MM) on 18 10 1917, page 10730.
THY WILL BE DONE.

WILKINSON Herbert – 3747 Private.
Born in Dewsbury to Leonard and Alice. Resided in Dewsbury. Enlisted at Mirfield.
1/5th Battalion DWR; killed in action 03 12 1915, aged 27, Ypres.
Buried – Duhallows ADS [*Advanced Dressing Station*] Cemetery, 7, F, 6.
Commemorated – the **Drill Hall WM panel 12, column 2.**
SAFE IN THE ARMS OF JESUS, A BRITISH HERO RESTS.

WILKINSON H
Unable to positively identify. Probably a duplicate of above entry.
Commemorated – the **Drill Hall WM panel 12, column 3.**

WILKINSON John William – 6003 Private.
Born in Bradford to Elizabeth of Wyke. Enlisted at Bradford.
1/5th Battalion DWR; killed in action 03 9 1916, aged 23, Battle of the Somme (Thiepval).
Commemorated – Thiepval Memorial, France, and the **Drill Hall WM panel 12, column 3.**

WILKINSON Jonas Archie – 205647 Private.
Born in Denholme to William and Ann. Resided in Bawtry. Enlisted at Bradford.
5th Battalion DWR; killed in action 27 3 1918, aged 30, German Spring Offensive.
Commemorated – Arras Memorial, France, and the **Drill Hall WM panel 12, column 3.**
Originally 2/5th DWR.

WILKINSON Joseph Auckland – 241673 Corporal.
Born in Thorp Tinley, Lincs, to John of Branston, Lincs. Resided in Greetwell, Lincs, with his wife, Clarice. Enlisted at Lincoln on 13 3 1916.
2/5th Battalion DWR, 13 Platoon D Company; killed in action 03 5 1917, aged 29, Battle of Bullecourt.
Commemorated – Arras Memorial, France, and the **Drill Hall WM panel 12, column 3.**
Mentioned in the Goodall collection (Commanding Officer's Commendation for action between 20 and 28 2 1917) on Battalion Routine Order dated 06 3 1917.

WILKINSON Stanley – 2551 Lance Corporal.
Born in Lockwood to Fred and Frances. Enlisted at Huddersfield.
2/5th Battalion DWR; accidentally shot, died at Selby Cottage Hospital, on 18 4 1915, aged 17.
Buried – Huddersfield (Lockwood) Cemetery, A, U, 314.
Commemorated – Armitage Bridge WM; Emmanuel Church, Lockwood, RoH; M Stansfield, page 480, and the **Drill Hall WM panel 12, column 3.**
SDGW shows date of death as 20 4 1915.

WILKINSON Stanley – 241103 Lance Corporal.
Born in Linthwaite in 1888 to Charles William and Ruth of Outlane. Enlisted in April, 1915, at Huddersfield.
5th Battalion DWR; wounded in action on 20 7 1918, died of wounds 21 7 1918, aged 29.
Buried – Terlincthun British Cemetery, 17, A, 25.
Commemorated – Outlane Trinity Methodist Church RoH; Memorial in Salendine Nook Churchyard; M Stansfield, page 480, and the **Drill Hall WM panel 12, column 3.**
Originally 2/5th DWR.
Mentioned in the Huddersfield Examiner (died of wounds) on 14 8 1918

WILKINSON William – 5029 (later 241618) Private.
Born and resided in Caister, Norfolk. Enlisted at Grimsby.
2/5th Battalion DWR; killed in action 03 5 1917, Battle of Bullecourt.
Commemorated – Arras Memorial, France, and the **Drill Hall WM panel 12, column 3.**
Mentioned in the Goodall collection.

WILLIAMS Allan – 5990 Private.
Born in Barnoldswick to Lavinia (later Mrs Lister). Resided in Barnoldswick. Enlisted at Barnoldswick.
1/5th Battalion DWR; killed in action 03 9 1916, aged 22, Battle of the Somme (Thiepval).
Commemorated –Thiepval Memorial, France; CPGW, page 178, & the cpgw.org.uk website; P Thompson, pages 82 & 87, and the **Drill Hall WM panel 12, column 3.**
Mentioned in S Barber (from 3rd Bn DWR, killed in action 28 7 1916).
CPGW page 178 shows entry as Harold Williams.

WILLIAMS Herbert – 5701 Private.
Born in Yeadon to Joshua and Annie of Guiseley. Resided at Guiseley. Enlisted at Guiseley.
1/6th Battalion DWR; killed in action 28 7 1916, aged 20, Battle of the Somme.
Buried – Connaught Cemetery, 2, J, 7.
Commemorated – the **Drill Hall WM panel 12, column 3.**
This is the only name with the initial H that can be found.
HE DIED THAT WE MIGHT LIVE.

WILLIAMSON George – 6001 (later 242238) Private.
Born in Skipton to Sarah Jane, later of Tyersal, Bradford. Enlisted at Bradford.
1/5th Battalion DWR; killed in action 03 9 1916, aged 20, Battle of the Somme (Thiepval).
Buried – Mill Road Cemetery, 1, H ,18.
Commemorated – the cpgw.org.uk website, and the **Drill Hall WM panel 12, column 3.**
SDGW shows number as 6001.
SLEEPING WITH ENGLAND'S HEROES IN THE WATCHFUL CARE OF GOD.

WILSON Albert – 204590 Private.
Resided in Bradford. Enlisted at Wyke.
5th Battalion DWR; killed in action 28 4 1918, German Spring Offensive.
Commemorated – Lijssenthoek Military Cemetery, Special Memorial 5, Belgium, and the **Drill Hall WM panel 12, column 3.**

Originally 2/5th DWR.
SDGW shows date of death as 23 4 1918.
THEIR GLORY SHALL NOT BE BLOTTED OUT.

WILSON Carrol – 242235 Private.
Born in Barnoldswick to Thomas and Mary. Enlisted at Barnoldswick.
1/5th Battalion DWR; killed in action 09 10 1917, aged 20.
Commemorated – Tyne Cot Memorial, Belgium; CPGW, page 307 & the cpgw.org.uk website; P Thompson, pages 155 & 157, and the **Drill Hall WM panel 12, column 3.**

WILSON Freeman – 235103 Private.
Resided in Birstall, son of David. Enlisted at Bradford on 25 9 1916.
2/5th Battalion DWR, D Company; killed in action 03 5 1917, aged 19, Battle of Bullecourt.
Commemorated – Arras Memorial, France, Memorial, and the **Drill Hall WM panel 12, column 3.**
Mentioned in the Goodall collection.

WILSON James Schofield – 3885 (later 241025) Private.
Born in Dalton, Huddersfield, on 21 10 1891 to Wright and Mary. Resided in Kirkheaton with his wife, May. Enlisted at Huddersfield on 14 1 1915.
2/5th Battalion DWR, A Company; died of wounds 18 7 1917, aged 25.
Buried – Fevreuil British Cemetery, 1, A, 18.
Commemorated – St John's Church, Kirkheaton, RoH; All Hallows Parish Church, Kirkburton, RoH; M Stansfield, page 483, and the **Drill Hall WM panel 12, column 3.**
Mentioned in the Goodall collection; the Huddersfield Examiner (died of wounds) on 08 8 1917.
His brother, 14900 Frank Haydn, serving with 2 DWR was killed on 03 5 1917.
EVER REMEMBERED.

WINDSOR Ernest – 3848 Private.
Born in Knaresborough. Resided in Bradford. Enlisted at Huddersfield.
1/5th Battalion DWR; killed in action 12 11 1915, Ypres.
Buried – Longuenesse Souvenir Cemetery, 3, A, 10.
Commemorated – the **Drill Hall WM panel 12, column 2.**

WINFIELD Percival – 26308 Private.
Born in South Cerney, Glos, to Jessie and Annie E. Resided in South Cerney. Enlisted at Cirencester, Glos.
5th Battalion DWR; killed in action 17 4 1918, aged 24, German Spring Offensive.
Commemorated – Pozieres Memorial, France, and the **Drill Hall WM panel 12, column 4.**
Originally 2/5th DWR.
Formerly T/4/055926 Army Service Corps.

WINTERBOTTOM Hugh – 10464 Private.
Born and resided in Oldham. Enlisted at Halifax.
5th Battalion DWR; killed in action 29 3 1918, German Spring Offensive.
Commemorated – Arras Memorial, France, and the **Drill Hall WM panel 12, column 3.**
Originally 2/5th DWR.

WINTERBOTTOM Nelson – 3868 (later 241012) Lance Corporal.
Born in Huddersfield on 22 8 1886. Resided in Lockwood Huddersfield with his wife. Enlisted at Huddersfield on 11 2 1915.
2/5th Battalion DWR; killed in action 27 11 1917, Battle of Cambrai (Bourlon Wood).

Commemorated – Cambrai Memorial (Louverval), France; St John's Church, Newsome, RoH; Emmanuel Church, Lockwood, RoH; M Stansfield, page 485, and the **Drill Hall WM panel 12, column 3.**
Mentioned in the Goodall collection.

WISEMAN John Rushton – 26651 Private.
Born in Barnoldswick to Fred and Sarah Ellen. Resided in Barnoldswick. Enlisted at Keighley.
5th Battalion DWR; died of wounds 22 11 1918, aged 19, Advance to Victory.
Buried – Aeroplane Cemetery, 2, A, 22.
Commemorated – Barnoldswick WM; CPGW, page 320, & the cpgw.org.uk website; P Thompson, pages 169 & 174, and the **Drill Hall WM panel 12, column 3.**
Originally 1/5th DWR.
REST IN PEACE TILL WE MEET AGAIN.

WISHANT (WISHART?) Donald Mackenzie – 3723 Private.
Born in Manchester. Enlisted at Bradford.
1/7th Battalion DWR; killed in action 03 9 1916, Battle of the Somme (Thiepval).
Commemorated – Thiepval Memorial, France; 7 DWR WM, Huddersfield Drill Hall, and the **Drill Hall WM panel 12, column 3.**
All other sources use the spelling Wishart.

WOMERSLEY Shaderick – 3945 (later 241065) Corporal.
Born in Heckmondwike. Resided in Roberttown, Liversedge, with his wife, Mary Elizabeth. Enlisted at Mirfield on 02 3 1915.
5th Battalion DWR, 15 Platoon, D Company; died of wounds 06 3 1918, aged 36, Advance to Victory.
Buried – St Sever Cemetery Extension, Q, 3, M, 16.
Commemorated – Battyeford WM; Spenborough (Cleckheaton) WM (name added 01 7 2000); C Turpin, page 21, and the **Drill Hall WM panel 12, column 4.**
Mentioned in the Goodall collection.
Originally 2/5th DWR.

WOMERSLEY William – 3194 Private.
Born in Turnbridge, Huddersfield. Resided in Huddersfield with his wife, Mary. Enlisted at Huddersfield on 21 10 1914.
1/5th Battalion DWR; killed in action 17 7 1915, Ypres.
Commemorated – Ypres (Menin Gate) Memorial, Belgium; M Stansfield, page 487, and the **Drill Hall WM panel 12, column 4.**
Mentioned in the Huddersfield Examiner (killed in action) on 23 7 1915.

WOOD Charlie – 34381 Private.
Born in Grassington to Hubert and Jane. Resided in Grassington. Enlisted in July, 1917. Embarked for France and Flanders at Easter, 1918. Took part in the British Army of Occupation of Germany with 62nd Division.
5th Battalion DWR; died of disease and the effects of gas in hospital at Boulogne, 02 4 1919, aged 19.
Buried – Terlincthun British Cemetery, 15 B, 45.
Commemorated – K Taylor, page 294, and the **Drill Hall WM panel 12, column 4.**
HIS SPIRIT EVER LIVETH IN A VILLAGE HOME ACROSS THE SEA.

WOOD George William – 242570 Lance Corporal.
Born in Doncaster. Resided in Sheffield with his wife, Alice. Enlisted at Doncaster.
1/5th Battalion DWR; killed in action 03 8 1917, aged 24, Nieuport Sector.
Buried – Coxyde Military Cemetery, 2, D, 7.

Commemorated – the **Drill Hall WM panel 12, column 4.**
FAITHFUL UNTO DEATH.

WOOD Harry – 241580 Private.
Born in Kirkburton. Resided in Linthwaite. Enlisted at Huddersfield in March, 1916. Embarked for France and Flanders on 11 1 1917.
2/5th Battalion DWR, A Company; wounded in action on 22 11 1917; died of wounds at 48 Casualty Clearing Station, at Ytres, on 23 11 1917, aged 26, Battle of Cambrai.
Buried – Rocquigny – Equancourt Road Cemetery, 1, E, 29.
Commemorated – Linthwaite WM; St James' Church, Slaithwaite, RoH; M Stansfield, page 492, and the **Drill Hall WM panel 12, column 4.**
Mentioned in the Huddersfield Examiner (medals found during house clearance) on 04 3 2018.
THY WILL BE DONE.

WOOD John – 2419 (later 240257) Private.
Born in Mirfield to Emma and the late James, of Mirfield. Resided in Mirfield. Enlisted at Mirfield on 10 7 1914.
2/5th Battalion DWR, 13 Platoon, D Company; wounded in action 03 5 1917, died of wounds 26 5 1917, aged 19.
Buried – St Sever Cemetery Extension, P, 1, G, 7A.
Commemorated – Mirfield WM and the **Drill Hall WM panel 12, column 4.**
Mentioned in the Goodall collection.
CWGC shows his date of death as 20 5 1917.
GOD'S WILL BE DONE.

WOOD Joseph Walker – 299 Private (served under the name of J W Sanderson).
Born in Holmfirth. Resided in Holmfirth with his wife, Edith. Pre war Territorial, F Company 5 DWR, and was embodied in August, 1914.
1/5th Battalion DWR; died of wounds, severe head wound, at 13 General Hospital, Boulogne, 19 7 1915, aged 27, Ypres.
Buried – Boulogne Eastern Cemetery, 8, B, 64.
Commemorated – Holme Valley Memorial Hospital WM (plaque 1 & 2, Holme and Holmbridge); M Stansfield, page 493, and the **Drill Hall WM panel 12, column 4.**
IN THE MIDST OF LIFE WE ARE IN DEATH, REST IN PEACE.

OR (either of these two men could be the one listed on the Roll of Honour Board, it is impossible to ascertain the correct one):

WOOD John Worthington – 306358 Private.
Resided in Oldham. Enlisted at Milnsbridge.
5th Battalion DWR; died 19 10 1918, Advance to Victory.
Buried – Quievy Communal Cemetery Extension, B, 3.
Commemorated – the **Drill Hall WM panel 12, column 4.**

WOOD Robert Frederick – 2762 Lance Corporal.
Born in Kirkby, Yorks, to Fred and Annie, of Kirkby in Ashfield, Notts. Resided in Kirkby. Enlisted at Huddersfield in September, 1914. Embarked for France and Flanders in April, 1915.
1/5th Battalion DWR; killed in action 04 7 1916, aged 21, Battle of the Somme.
Commemorated – Thiepval Memorial, France; M Stansfield, page 494, and the **Drill Hall WM panel 12, column 4.**

WOOD Richard Hammond – 5154 (later 241727) Corporal.
Born in Barton on Humber to Jane and the late George. Resided and enlisted at Barton on Humber.
2/5th Battalion DWR; died of wounds, 27 11 1917, aged 34, Battle of Cambrai.

Buried – Etaples Military Cemetery, 30, N, 4A.
Commemorated – the **Drill Hall WM panel 12, column 4.**
Mentioned in the Goodall collection.
FEAR NOT FOR I HAVE REDEEMED THEE, I HAVE CALLED THEE BY THY NAME.

WOOD Tom – 242571 Corporal.
Born in Golcar to Samson and Miriam. Resided in Golcar. Enlisted at Milnsbridge on 03 4 1916. Embarked for France and Flanders on 25 12 1916.
1/5th Battalion DWR, C Company; killed in action, sniper, 10 10 1917, aged 20, Ypres,
Commemorated – Tyne Cot Memorial, Belgium; St John's Church, Golcar, RoH; Golcar Baptist Church RoH; the Colne Valley Almanac; M Stansfield, page 494, and the **Drill Hall WM panel 12, column 4.**

WOOD Willie – 240129 Company Quartermaster Sergeant.
Born in Rochdale to Walter and Emily, later of Mirfield. Resided in Mirfield. Enlisted at Mirfield.
5th Battalion DWR; died of wounds 19 10 1918, aged 23, Advance to Victory.
Buried – Delsaux Farm Cemetery, 2, B, 27.
Commemorated – Mirfield WM and the **Drill Hall WM panel 12, column 4.**
THE END OF THE ROAD.

WOOD William Benjamin – 34750 Private.
Born in Longton, Staffs, to Annie and the late David. Resided in Longton. Enlisted at Stoke on Trent.
5th Battalion DWR, D Company; killed in action 20 10 1918, Advance to Victory.
Buried – Quievy Communal Cemetery Extension, C, 63.
Commemorated – and the **Drill Hall WM panel 12, column 4.**
Formerly 46822 Private, Yorkshire Regiment.
HE GAVE HIS LIFE IN HONOUR OF HIS COUNTRY.

WOODCOCK Jack – 3613 Private.
Born in Collingham, Yorks, to John and Kate of Bedford. Enlisted at Mirfield.
1/5th Battalion DWR; killed in action 09 11 1915, aged 16, Ypres.
Commemorated – Ypres (Menin Gate) Memorial, Belgium, and the **Drill Hall WM panel 12, column 4.**

WOODHEAD Frank – 4916 (later 241520) Private.
Born in Warrington to John and Julia. Resided in Ovenden, Halifax. Enlisted at Halifax.
2/5th Battalion DWR; killed in action 03 5 1917, aged 31, Battle of Bullecourt.
Commemorated – Arras Memorial, France, and the **Drill Hall WM panel 12, column 4.**
Mentioned in the Goodall collection.

WOODWARD Harry – 240617 Private.
Born in Leeds to Harry and Mary A. Resided in Leeds. Enlisted at Huddersfield.
5th Battalion DWR; killed in action 16 4 1918, aged 23, German Spring Offensive.
Buried – Gezaincourt Communal Cemetery, 2, L, 8.
Commemorated – the **Drill Hall WM panel 12, column 4.**
IN EVER DEAR MEMORY OF MY DARLING BOY, THE BLOOD OF JESUS CHRIST CLEANSETH FROM ALL SIN.

WORSLEY Joseph – 1854 Private.
Born in Holmfirth. Resided in Thongsbridge, with his aunt and uncle, Albert Downes. Enlisted at Holmfirth in August, 1914. Embarked for France and Flanders in April, 1915.
1/5th Battalion DWR; killed in action 28 9 1915, Ypres.

Commemorated – Ypres (Menin Gate) Memorial, Belgium; Holme Valley Memorial Hospital WM (plaque 5 Netherthong & Thongsbridge); St Andrew's Church, Netherthong, RoH; Netherthong Methodist Church RoH; M Stansfield, page 498, and the **Drill Hall WM panel 12, column 4.**

WRIGHT Fred Stanley – 4581 Private.
Born in Huddersfield on 18 11 1889 to William Henry and Pamela, of Grimescar, Huddersfield. Enlisted at Huddersfield in October, 1915.
1/5th Battalion DWR; killed in action, shellfire, 12 8 1916, Battle of the Somme.
Buried – Connaught Cemetery, 3, J, 6.
Commemorated – Fartown and Birkby WM; All Saints Church, Paddock, RoH; J J Fisher, page 113; M Stansfield, page 499, and the **Drill Hall WM panel 12, column 4.**

WRIGHT James William – Lieutenant.
Parents were James William and Sarah Elizabeth. Commissioned in October, 1915. Served in the UK with 3/5th DWR. Embarked for France and Flanders on 02 8 1916. Joined the 1/5th DWR on 07 8 1916.
1/5th Battalion DWR; killed in action 10 11 1917, aged 20, Battle of Passchendaele.
Commemorated – Tyne Cot Memorial, Belgium, and the **Drill Hall WM panel 12, column 4.**
Mentioned in the Unit war Diary (joined the Battalion) on 31 8 1916.
SDGW shows his date of death as 10 10 1917.

WRIGLEY Ben Allen – 203925 Private.
Born in Slaithwaite. Resided in Slaithwaite. Enlisted in Slaithwaite in July, 1916. Embarked for France and Flanders in November, 1916.
1/5th Battalion DWR; killed in action, 07 8 1917, Nieuport Sector.
Buried – Ramscappelle Road Military Cemetery, 2, A, 26.
Commemorated – Slaithwaite WM; St James' Church, Slaithwaite, RoH; Carr Lane United Methodist Church, Slaithwaite, RoH; Colne Valley Almanac; J J Fisher, page 115; M Stansfield, page 500, and the **Drill Hall WM panel 12, column 4.**
Mentioned in the Huddersfield Examiner (killed in action, official casualty list) on 04 9 1917.

WRIGLEY Ernest – 241872 Private.
Born in Greenfield. Resided in Oldham. Enlisted at Uppermill.
25th Battalion DWR; died of wounds 05 5 1917, Battle of Bullecourt.
Buried – Achiet le Grand Communal Cemetery Extension, 1, E, 26.
Commemorated – Arras Memorial, France, Memorial; Saddleworth WM; and the **Drill Hall WM panel 12, column 4.**
Mentioned in the Huddersfield examiner (died of wounds, official casualty list) on 01 6 1917.

WRIGLEY Harry – 242649 Private.
Born in Waterhead, Oldham. Resided in Waterhead. Enlisted at Milnsbridge.
1/5th Battalion DWR; killed in action, 08 8 1917, aged 21, Nieuport Sector.
Commemorated – Nieuport Memorial, Belgium; Saddleworth WM, and the **Drill Hall WM panel 12, column 4.**

WRIGLEY William Henry – 5022 (later 241612) Private.
Born in Crosland Hill, Huddersfield, to Joe and Elizabeth. Resided in Crosland Moor. Enlisted at Huddersfield on 13 3 1916.
2/5th Battalion DWR; killed in action, 25 11 1917, Battle of Cambrai.
Commemorated – Cambrai Memorial (Louverval), France; Crosland Moor Wesleyan Church RoH; St Barnabas Church, Crosland Moor, RoH; The Rising Sun Public House RoH; M Stansfield, page 500, and the **Drill Hall WM panel 12, column 4.**
Mentioned in the Goodall collection.

YOUNG Norman – 240669 Private.
Born in Marsden to Edwin and Sarah. Resided in Marsden. Enlisted at Huddersfield in November, 1914. Embarked for France and Flanders in June, 1915.
1/5th Battalion DWR; killed in action 12 8 1917, aged 22.
Buried – Coxyde Military Cemetery, 2, G, 9.
Commemorated – Marsden WM, Colne Valley Almanac; J J Fisher, page 115, : M Stansfield, page 501, and the **Drill Hall WM panel 12, column 4.**
Mentioned in the Huddersfield Examiner (killed in action) on 23 8 1917; (killed in action, official casualty list) on 14 9 1917.
THE LORD IS THY KEEPER.

Capt Keith Sykes, seated centre, Adjutant 1/5th and 5th Battalions, 1916-1918, with his Company Officers, D Company, Mirfield, post war.

ADDENDA

In addition to the names above, the following officers and soldiers are eligible for inclusion, but do not appear on the War Memorial Boards for various reasons. 2Lt Anson, for example, was posted to the 1/5th Battalion but was sent to 2 DWR whilst on his journey to the front line. He was killed with the 2nd Battalion just a few days later and, therefore, not commemorated by either of the Battalions.

It is impossible to know why so many of these men were left off the rolls, but the ease of modern research has given our generation greatly improved capabilities to collect the information required. At the time, it was largely left to the relatives, the local newspapers and the veterans returning from the conflict to produce the lists for the many war memorials being erected in all the cities, towns and villages throughout the country, in all but the 53 'blessed' villages (five of which are in Yorkshire) which did not lose any inhabitants during the war.

The national centenary commemorations of the war years has resulted in a nationwide updating of memorials, with missing names being added in many instances, or moved from one memorial to another (such as the CWGC memorials in France where the names of two 'Dukes' soldiers have been taken from the Arras Memorial and added to the Soissons Memorial, when proof of their place of death was sent to the CWGC) and, indeed, the creation of new War Memorials, as at Farnley Tyas, where five soldiers from that community were discovered not to be commemorated in the village – although Percival Dodson, qv, would also appear to have a claim on being on that memorial.

Our research shows that the men, listed below, did serve with the 1/5th, 2/5th 3/5th or 5th Battalions of the Regiment and should now be commemorated in the Huddersfield Drill Hall, if only in the pages of this book:

AKED Thomas Henry - 34592 Private.
Born in Mirfield, to Thomas Henry and Elizabeth. Enlisted at Cleckheaton.
1/4th Battalion, killed in action, 02 9 1918, aged 32, Advance to Victory.
Buried – Vaulx Hill Cemetery, 3, K, 16.
Commemorated – Spenborough (Cleckheaton) WM; C Turpin, page 3.
REST IN PEACE.

ANSON Harris Hartis - 2nd Lieutenant.
Son of Harris Anson, of Hambleton, Selby.
Commissioned into 5 DWR with effect 31 12 1917. Posted to 2rd Battalion 22 4 1918.
5th Battalion, attached 2nd Battalion, killed in action, 30 8 1918, aged 28.
Buried – Vis en Artois British Cemetery, 1, A, 13.
Commemorated – C D Bruce History, page 179.
Mentioned in C D Bruce History (joined Battalion on 22 4 1918), page 174; the Unit War Diary (joined Battalion) on 27 4 1918; (killed in action) on 31 8 1918.

BEARDSELL Albert – 240351 Private.
Born in Lockwood, Huddersfield, on 12 4 1893 to Sophia and the late John. Resided in Huddersfield. Enlisted 07 8 1914. Embarked for France and Flanders in April 1915.
1/5th Battalion DWR; reported wounded and missing in action 03 9 1916, aged 23, Battle of the Somme (Thiepval).
Commemorated – Thiepval Memorial, France; St Matthews Church, Primrose Hill, RoH; St John's Church, Newsome, RoH; M Stansfield page 30.
Mentioned in the Huddersfield Examiner (reported missing since 03 9 1916) on 04 10 1916.

BOOTHROYD Thomas Raymond – 241865 Private.
Born in Almondbury on 24 12 1896 to Wright. Resided in Almondbury. Enlisted at Huddersfield on 16 2 1916.
2/5th Battalion DWR; wounded in action on 04 12 1917, evacuated to England, died at home, pneumonia, on 19 1 1920.
Buried – Almondbury Cemetery, L, C, 222.
Commemorated – Almondbury WM; M Stansfield page 53.

CARTWRIGHT Ernest – 2nd Lieutenant.

Born in Wooldale, Holmfirth to Herbert and Minnie. Enlisted on 23 8 1914.
5th Battalion DWR; killed in action, near Famars, on 01 11 1918, aged 26.
Buried – Maing Communal Cemetery Extension, C 5.
Commemorated – Wooldale WM; M Stansfield page 84.
Mentioned in the Huddersfield Examiner (wrote to family of Private A E Williamson) on 10 3 1916; (commissioned from the ranks; killed in action) on 11 11 1918.
ENLISTED AUG 23rd 1914 HE SLEEPS WITH ENGLAND'S HEROES IN THE WATCHFUL CARE OF GOD.

COLLINS J – 1797 Private.
5th Battalion DWR; died, home, 19 5 1915.
Buried – Almondbury Cemetery, 3, U, 30.
Commemorated – M Stansfield page 101.

COOPER Willie – Lieutenant Colonel Order of the British Empire, Victoria Decoration..
Son of James of Huddersfield. Resided in Huddersfield with his wife Amy Louisa.
2/5th Battalion DWR; died at home 18 12 1920, aged 58.
Buried – Edgerton Cemetery, Huddersfield, 53, C, 7.
Commemorated – J J Fisher, pages 127-8; M Stanfield, page 103.
Mentioned in the Goodall collection (left the Battalion to command a Home Service unit, 17 8 1915); the Huddersfield Examiner (led a recruiting march through Huddersfield) on 10 5 1915 & 11 5 1917; (raised 2./5th DWR, November, 1914; relinquished command of the unit 17 8 1915) on 30 7 1918, 24 9 1919 & 27 9 1919.
Joined the 3rd Volunteer Battalion and transferred to the Territorial Force in 1908. He was an architect in civilian life and designed the Huddersfield Drill Hall, which was constructed between 1899 and 1902.

CRINES H – 4604481 Private.
5th Battalion DWR; died, home, 31 7 1921.
Buried – Edgerton Cemetery, Huddersfield, 11B, 177.
Commemorated – M Stansfield, page 108.

CROCKER Joseph – Lieutenant.
Born on 02 10 1881 in Blackheath, London. Resided in Blackheath. Enlisted at Blackheath. Commissioned from the Artists Rifles into the 5th DWR on 14 7 1916. Later transferred to the 10th DWR.
10th Battalion DWR; killed in action, shellfire, 19 9 1917.
Commemorated – Tyne Cot Memorial, Belgium.
Formerly 5168 Private, Artists Rifles.
Mentioned in the 5th DWR War Diary (joined the Battalion) on 30 9 1916; (transferred to 10 DWR) on 31 10 1916; the 10th DWR War Diary (wounded in action) on 30 4 1917; (killed in action) on 30 9 1917; the Isles History, page 69; the Tunstill's Men Internet Blog – tunstillsmen.blogspot.com.

DEMITRIADI Louis Petro – Lieutenant Colonel RAMC. Mention in Despatches, Territorial Decoration.
Born in Manchester in 1862.
2nd Volunteer Battalion, appointed Medical Officer on 19 12 1909, later 1/5th DWR (served 18 years as MO), then promoted as CO 58th Casualty Clearing Station, died home, Southport, 26 10 1918.
Buried – St Stephens Churchyard, Lindley, Huddersfield, 5, J.
Commemorated –St Stephen's Church, Lindley, RoH and dedicated chair; Leeds University Roll of Honour, pages 63 (MID) & 194; M Stansfield, page 121.
Mentioned in the Army List (Surgeon Lieutenant Demetriadi, Medical Officer of the 2nd Volunteer Battalion of DWR) 1900. He deployed to France and Flanders with 1/5th DWR in April, 1915, and was then promoted to command the West Riding (58th) Casualty Clearing Station at Lillers, from

October, 1915 to April 1918, then Longeunesse to October, Roisel, briefly, and Tincourt from late October to December, 1918. The Matron in Chief of the British Expeditionary Force wrote,
> "W Riding CCS quite splendid, under canvas in a beautiful park and every possible thing has been well thought out. More like a miniature General Hospital and an entirely Territorial Unit, with a Territorial Nursing Staff, Miss Todd Sister in Charge. The whole unit reflects great credit upon everyone concerned." (18 9 1915, Maude McCarthy, Matron-in-Chief, BEF, 12 Aug 1914 to 05 Aug 1919).

Mentioned in the Huddersfield Examiner (wrote letter of thanks to Mayor of Huddersfield) on 28 9 1916; (award of Mention if Despatches) on 05 1 1917; (died, home, obituary) on 28 10 1918; (details of funeral) on 29 10 1918; B Heywood (medical examinations) pages 6; (German letter re gas attack) page 46; (account of life in CCS) pages 188-9; (died, home) page 190.
Originally 1/5th DWR.

HIRST Henry (Harry) – 4495 Private.
Born in Marsden. Resided in Marsden with his wife and one child.
3/5th Battalion DWR; died at Clipstone Camp, pneumonia, on 03 1 1916.
Buried – St Bartholomew's Parish Church, Marsden, South, 29, 5.
Commemorated – Marsden WM; M Stansfield page 217.

HUNT Albert – 240609 Private.
Born in Manningham, Bradford in 1893 to Martin and Esther Ann. Resided in Halifax (1911). Enlisted at Huddersfield.
2/5th DWR; died of wounds 03 4 1917.
Buried – Pozieres British Cemetery, 11, J. 6.
Commemorated – No known commemoration.

MCCLUSKY J – 241167 Sergeant.
5th Battalion DWR; died, home, 06 7 1918.
Buried – Edgerton Cemetery, Huddersfield, 60, 126G.
Commemorated – M Stansfield, page 295.
Possibly mentioned in the Unit War Diary (awarded gallantry card by the General Officer Commanding, 147th Infantry Brigade) on 31 7 1916.

PROBYN John William – 2nd Lieutenant.
Born in Huddersfield On 12 2 1893 to John and Harriet, of Birkby. Enlisted at Huddersfield on 28 8 1914 as a Trooper in the Dragoon Guards. Later served in the Kings Own Yorkshire Light Infantry. Gazetted as 2Lt in August, 1917, to the 1/5th DWR.
1/5th Battalion DWR; killed in action at Bailleul on 12 4 1918, aged 25.
Commemorated – Tyne Cot Memorial, Belgium; Fartown and Birkby WM; M Stansfield, page 344.
Mentioned in the Unit War Diary (joined the Battalion, 13 10 1917) on 31 10 1917; S Barker (killed in action with 1/6th DWR), page 175.

STANCLIFFE Oliver – 23967 Private.
Born in Huddersfield on 01 12 1897 to Charles Frederick. Resided in Huddersfield. Pre war Territorial from February, 1914. Embarked for France and Flanders in October, 1916.
1/5th Battalion DWR; killed in Action 05 1 1917, aged 19, Ypres.
Buried – Menin Road, South, Military Cemetery, 1 Q, 9.
Commemorated – South Street Primitive Methodist Chapel RoH; St Thomas's Church, Longroyd Bridge, RoH; M Stansfield page 403.

WATERHOUSE Daniel – 4857 Private.
Born in Marsden to Alice and the late James. Resided in Marsden. Enlisted at Marsden on 17 2 1916. Embarked for France and Flanders in July, 1916.

1/5th Battalion DWR; wounded in action in early September, 1916, to 14 General Hospital, Wimereux, died of wounds on 21 9 1916, aged 27.
Buried – Wimereux Communal Cemetery, 1, Q 15A.
Commemorated – Marsden WM; Marsden Churchyard memorial; Marsden Conservative Club RoH and M Stansfield, page 465.
REST IN PEACE.

The Trustees of the Huddersfield Drill Hall are committed to investigate the production of a special memorial to these men for display in the Drill Hall.

Restored trench, Thiepval Wood, Somme Sector, France, 2018.

The following synopsis was originally published in the pages of the Huddersfield Examiner in 1919 and reproduced with kind permission of the Huddersfield Examiner, 2019:

LOCAL TERRITORIAL BATTALION

[1/5th Battalion – April 1915 to January 1918
2/5th Battalion – January 1917 to January 1918
5th Battalion – January 1918 – February 1919]

Extracts from the Huddersfield Examiner, 1919:
29th & 30th July 1919 – Effort and cost
6th Aug, 24th & 25th Sep 1919 – 2/5th War record

Transcribed by Scott Flaving, Dec 2014.

Tue 29 Jul 1919

A UNIQUE DISTINCTION. WAR RECORD OF THE 5th BATTALION WRR.

THE EFFORT AND THE COST.

It is with mixed feelings that one approaches the task of placing on record the doings of our own Battalions of Territorials during the Great War. The supreme emotion one experiences is a feeling of intense pride that our lads joined in so nobly in the great task of stemming the tide which had almost over-whelmed the Old Contemptibles and holding back a grim and determined enemy, not only until the Kitchener Battalions could be raised, but also throughout the remainder of the war period until final victory crowned our arms.

The circumstances of the time called for men and they responded readily and achieved real distinction in the field. So far as one could ascertain the 5th Battalion the Duke of Wellington's (West Riding) Regiment was the only Battalion to be singled out for special reference as a Battalion in the whole of the hundreds of communiqués issued from General Headquarters throughout the whole period of the war. This is a unique honour and it marks out the Battalion as worthy of special commendation. The individual gallantry displayed by the Officers and Men was no less notable than their collective achievements. No fewer than 429 honours, including one Victoria Cross, were won by members of the combined 1/5th, 2/5th and 5th Battalions. And there is the other side. The appalling sacrifice of life and limb which the operations in which the Battalions took part entailed on our men.

During the period that elapsed from that sunny April morning in 195 when the Battalion marched to the Station at Doncaster and entrained for the front in such high spirits to the dismal evening in May, 1919, when the Cadre returned, 1,116 of our men had crossed the Bar. 17 are still missing, nearly 3,000 were so seriously wounded or sick as to be sent to England, and thousands of others were treated in hospital in France and Belgium. No one can perhaps realise the suffering and sadness which these figures mean better than those whose mournful duty was to record the casualties, day after day, month after month, year after year. Sometimes in one single week to the number of 150 or more. In this painful duty one learnt scraps of family history and details of personal sacrifice which were deeply and genuinely moving. In honouring our gallant dead and recording the operations in which they fell let us not forget the desolation of the widow and the fatherless or the ache of parents bereaved. With them we long for the touch of vanished hand and the sound of a voice that is still. Let us pay our debts to those who have fallen and be worthy of the men who have died.

MOBILISATION

On July 25th, 1914, the Battalion went to its yearly training on the East Coast. But, owing to the lowering of the war clouds, the Battalion was, on August 2nd, sent back to Huddersfield. Mobilisation was effected after 8pm on August 3rd and the next day, about noon, the Battalion entrained for their war stations at Grimsby where they took over the defences there and on the coast southwards. After a week or 10 days on coast defence the Battalion went into training, first at Laceby, near Grimsby, then at Ribey Camp, Lincolnshire, later at Warmsworth, Doncaster, and drafts from Huddersfield at once joined up. The Battalion volunteered for foreign service. Whilst at Ribey, to the regret of all ranks, Lieutenant Colonel W Cooper relinquished command of the Battalion and went to Huddersfield with a nucleus of Officers and Men to command and raise a new 2/5th Battalion. On joining the British Expeditionary Force, a 3rd Battalion was formed and became 3/5th WRR, which provided drafts for the 1/5th and 2/5th Battalions. This Battalion was afterwards merged into the 4th (Reserve) battalion WRR. The 1/5th Battalion, on April 14th, 1915, under the command of Lieutenant Colonel H Wilson, joined the BEF as part of the 49th West Riding Division [*sic – 1st West Riding Division until May 1915*]. After leaving Folkestone for Boulogne the Battalion went into billets at Estaires, near Merville, and six days later they began to go into the trenches, for instructional purposes, attached to units of the 7th Division. On the evening of April 26th the Battalion went into a line of their own at Le Boutillerie, Fleurbaix. The trenches consisted mainly of a very thin breastwork with no communication trench to the Front Line. After a comparatively quiet line for 10 days the battalion was in reserve for the Battle of Aubers Ridge on May 9th, 1915. Had the attack of the Division on the right been successful in breaking the enemy's line, the Battalion was to have advanced and occupied the line, but this did not take place. Remaining in the Fleurbaix area until June 26th, the Battalion then moved to St Jean ter Biezen, near Poperinghe in Belgium, on transfer to the 6th Corps, 2nd Army. Before leaving 1st Army the Army Commander (Sir Douglas Haig) sent to the Division an expression of his great satisfaction at the state of discipline in the 49th West Riding Division and also congratulated the Division on its soldier like bearing and efficiency.

6 MONTHS IN YPRES SALIENT

After preliminary reconnaissance the Battalion went into the line on June 8th, just north of Ypres and south of Boesinghe and east of the Yser Canal. The Battalion went into this line just after a British attack and the shelling was very heavy. On July 16th Major General T S Baldock was severely wounded and was succeeded by Major General E M Perceval. On August 8th, the Battalion took part in a demonstration with the object of diverting the enemy's attention from the preparations of an attack to be made by the 6th Division on the right of Hooge Chateau. It was at this time that the Battalion had their first real taste of gas. On August 31st Lieutenant Colonel H R Headlam (York and Lancaster Regiment) assumed the command of the Battalion in place of Lieutenant Colonel H Wilson, who had been evacuated sick. During the next few months the Battalion underwent, along with the remainder of the Division, almost continuous duty in the worst trenches of the Allied line in the Ypres salient. When out of the line the officers and men had no huts, but made use of their groundsheets as bivouacs. Every night they had to go up into the line on working parties. During the whole of this long period (25 weeks in all) the Battalion unflinchingly sustained an unrelaxing bombardment and defeated with the utmost steadiness some serious attacks by the Germans. In addition to this the men bore with unfailing cheerfulness the most trying conditions of weather and climate, in permanently flooded trenches and elicited from Higher Commanders several messages of sympathy and praise. The Battalion was in support during the great German gas attack on the 19th December, 1915, and had a most trying time. On October 27th Captain and Adjutant H S Rendall left the Battalion to take command of the 5th Battalion York and Lancaster Regiment. The Battalion was relieved in the Ypres Salient on December 30th, 1915, much diminished in numbers, but holding a proud record. During all this time the Battalion did not lose a single man as a prisoner or an inch of trench and the enemy got no identification from them whatsoever.

From the Ypres Salient the Battalion moved back into rest quarters at or near Wormhoudt where they stayed until February 2nd, 1916. From there they went to Camps en Amienois and, on February 13th, over to Bouzencourt, where they were happy to meet some of their Huddersfield friends in the 168th Brigade RFA. After living for a period in the line at Authuille, just north of Albert, in March, they marched back to Naours on March 29th and 30th, where they remained until the end of May, with the exception of small periods of a few, doing working parties near the line north of Albert. During all this period since the beginning of the year the Battalion, like all the other Territorial units had not received any reinforcements owing to the difficulty of recruiting in England and had become very low in numbers. Much to their sorrow, Lieutenant Colonel H R Headlam left the Battalion on June 4th to command the 2nd Battalion York and Lancaster Regiment and, a few days later, a Brigade in the 21st Division. His period of command had been most beneficial to the Battalion and his ideas and training left their mark in all their subsequent history during the war. He was succeeded in command by Lieutenant Colonel H S Stanton. Throughout June the Battalion was very busy making assembly trenches in Aveluy Wood, north of Albert, and marking out cross-country routes in readiness for the Somme Battle.

HARD TIMES ON THE SOMME

On July 1st the Somme Battle commenced and the Battalion were in reserve to the 36th and 32nd Divisions. The advance on their front between Thiepval and Albert did well at first but, by the end of the day, the line remained substantially the same, with the fighting troops utterly worn out. Parts of 49th Division were involved in the day's fighting, but not until the next day did the 5th Battalion go into the line. Towards evening the Battalion took over the line in Thiepval Wood and, from that day until the middle of August, the Battalion had a very hard and harassing time in Thiepval Wood all the while. The trench system merely consisted of battered fragments of trenches with but little cover and all the while the Battalion was overlooked from Thiepval Ridge and subjected to heavy bombardments with high explosive and gas shells. During July alone, in merely holding the line, the Battalion sustained 250 casualties and, amongst them, was that famous and intrepid Officer and friend of all, Major Wheatley, who died of wounds sustained on July 2nd. During this period the Battalion lost many valuable Officers and men and the continual strain on all was very severe. Thiepval was the pivot of the Somme fighting in the north and none who were there are likely to forget such places as Belfast City, Gordon Castle, Elgin Avenue, Speyside, Blighty Valley and many others. The Battalion was relieved on August 19th and went into billets at Raincheval, very tired and dirty, but still with that wonderful spirit which the Battalion ever maintained in good days and bad. The men had 10 days of intensive training and recreation with a few motor trips to Amiens and then marched up to the line again on September 2nd and assembled in the old line in front of Thiepval Wood. On the morning of September 3rd, in conjunction with the 1/4th Battalion (Halifax) on the right and the West Yorkshire Brigade on the left, the Battalion took a leading part in the great battle for Thiepval which met with but little real success. Leaving the front trenches at 5.10am in semi-darkness the three assaulting Companies quickly reached their objectives in the German front and second line trenches, round about what was called "The Pope's Nose", between Thiepval and St Pierre Divion. In spite of enormous difficulties in getting through the German wire, which was not sufficiently cut, the men of the 5th and 4th Battalions, splendidly left by their Officers, fought like demons. Unfortunately both flanks were 'in the air' and the troops from the left had not got into the German line. Counter-attacks from St Pierre Divion and the Schwaben redoubt (Thiepval) drew the remnants of both Battalions back to their lines. The Battalion lost in casualties that day: 12 Officers and 355 Other Ranks. No troops could have fought better. Only 11 men of the Battalion were captured by the enemy alive and effectiveness of the day's work was seen later when the German Official account of the battle was captured. It showed that the casualties affected on the enemy must have been as great, if not greater, than those of the Battalion. After 10 days withdrawal from the line in order to reorganise and to be reinforced, the Battalion was thrust back into the battle line in the Leipzig Salient on the south side of Thiepval. There they had some very difficult fighting to do, chiefly of a bombing nature which severely tested the grit and endurance of the new drafts. We were finally relieved on the 24th September, after having won more ground in the Leipzig Salient, in conjunction with other troops. After about 10 days rest, on October 9th, the Battalion went into the line opposite the German trenches at Gommecourt, just north of Hebuterne, which was a very much quieter sector. October and November were comparatively uneventful, except for a very successful raid executed by A Company, under Captain J B Cockhill DSO MC, on November 20th. The enemy's trenches in front of Gommecourt were entered and the raiding party stayed there for 20 minutes. Many Germans were killed and our casualties were very small. On December 4th the Battalion moved back to rest billets at Halloy and spent a very good Christmas there.

TEACHING THE PORTUGUESE

On January 6th, 1917, the Battalion went into the line again, this time to trenches near Berles-au-Bois. The weather was very cold and severe during January 1917 and the men's feet were a constant care. Early in February the Battalion side-slipped and went to Bellacourt, near Arras. It was in this neighbourhood that Lieutenant Colonel H A S Stanton was severely wounded by a vane bomb whilst going round the Battalion sector. He was succeeded in the command by Lieutenant Colonel H S Tew CMG, East Surrey Regiment. Early in March the Battalion moved to the Rue au Bois sector, just north-east of Festubert and south of Richebourg l'Avoue. The line was all breastworks and the front line was held very thinly. The remainder of the Battalion being distributed in depth behind. In this sector there was a great deal of patrol work and many encounters took place. Beyond a moderate amount of trench mortaring the days were fairly quiet. During April the Battalion had many of the Portuguese Division attached to them in the line for instruction. Generally speaking, they were very willing to learn and were very good imitators when workin g alongside our men. The Battalion finally handed over the line to the Portuguese towards the end of May and, for a while, were in close support to them. During the first part of June the Battalion (and 1/4th Battalion) was lent to the 57th Division and went into the line in the Cordonniere sector, near Fleurbaix. The line was a very long one, held by isolated posts. On June 5th, Corporal B Siswick and three men in one post very cleverly and with a coolness beyond all praise repulsed a large enemy raiding party – 60 or 70 strong, and gained for the Battalion a good deal of kudos. About this time Lieutenant Colonel G P Norton (2nd in Command) left the Battalion to command the 2/10th Battalion Manchester Regiment. For the latter half of June the two Battalions were lent to the 6th Division in the St Elie sector at Hulloch. This was a mining district and quite new to the Battalion, with its deep shafts and subterranean passages with small posts at the shaft heads. The Battalion experienced a good deal of gas shelling in this neighbourhood and the enemy seemed very anxious to get an identification from the Battalion, but his wish was not gratified. During the first fortnight in July the Battalion was in rest billets at Paradis, near Merville. On the 18th July the Battalions entrained from Merville for Dunkirk and, after a few days there, moved on to Bray Dunes and then on to Ghyvelde where preparations were made for a big offensive action at Lombartzyde, which was destined never to take place. On August 3rd the Battalion took over the line in the left sub-sector of the Lombartzyde sector and, from then until the 17th August, the Battalion had a very rough time. Shelling was always most intense and there was a profuse amount of gas shelling, chiefly of the deadly mustard variety. The line was a precarious one and there was a wide canal behind us and the men themselves, in a narrow salient, were shelled from all sides. It was here that a disaster occurred to the bulk of the Headquarters Staff who were entombed in a large dugout by and ammunition dump being blown up close by. On relief, on August 17th, the Battalion went back to La Panne on the coast and had an enjoyable month's rest. On September 11th, Lieutenant Colonel H S Tew relinquished command of the Battalion and Lieutenant Colonel J Walker DSO was appointed to the command. Lieutenant Colonel Tew was an expert in training and in this direction he left the Battalion far more efficient than he found it. He was always most patient and thorough on parade. After spending a few days at Bray Dunes, on September 23rd the Battalion moved from the Belgian coast and marched in very hot weather, finally arriving, on October 4th, at Vlamertinghe, near Ypres. On October 5th the Battalion marched through Ypres and, at night, relieved the Wellington and Otago Battalions of the New Zealand Division on Abraham's Heights which they had captured the day before. The Battalion had a miserable three days in the battle line, with no recognised trenches and the only shelters were a few broken down pill-boxes. The weather was consistently bad as it knows how to be in the Ypres Salient and, on account of the mud, it was extraordinarily difficult to get rations and supplies up to the front line. On the afternoon of October 8th the enemy were seen to be massing for a counter-attack on the line, but this was successfully repulsed by the quick and ready action of D Company who wer holding the front posts.

BATTLE ON ABRAHAM'S HEIGHTS

The Battalion was relieved on the night of October 8th and then went into assembly positions on Abraham's Heights, ready for battle on October 9th. The attack, which was on a big scale, was launched at 5.20am, the Brigade being in Divisional Reserve. The shelling all morning was most intense, but the barrage was excellent. The Division had two objectives for the day, the furthermost one being the Bellevue Spur overlooking Passchendaele. At 1.30pm the Battalion was sent up into the battle and, after negotiating the enemy's counter barrage of artillery and machine gun fire on Abraham's heights, supported the attack of the 148th Infantry Brigade. By the end of the day a new line was established on the Bellevue Spur approximating to the first objective or a little more. The enemy's machine gunners and snipers were particularly aggressive and very clever in concealment. The ground was an absolute morass and very difficult to advance over. Next day (October 10th) the Battalion was relieved and went to a very comfortable camp at St Jean where everyone had to sleep in shell holes and it was a favourite hunting ground fro enemy bombing planes. All ranks were thoroughly tired out and exhausted – the Battalion had been in a swampy line for four days under appalling conditions of weather and ground and then had had to take part in offensive operations. The men's cheerfulness however was most remarkable and they had done their job in a manner worthy of the best traditions of the service. The losses of the Battalion during the fighting were: 8 Officers and 200 Other Ranks.

Messages of congratulation were sent to the Battalion from the Army, Corps and Brigade Commanders.

On October 12th the New Zealand Division attacked again, through the Battalion's line, and met with little success and with enormous casualties. In spite of the tight satte of the Battalion three Officers and 100 men at once volunteered as Stretcher Bearers for the New Zealand Division to go and reclaim their wounded from the Battlefield.

Wed 30 Jul 1919

SECOND PART OF THE 5th BATTALION WRR

A UNIQUE DISTINCTION

The following is a continuation of the article which was published yesterday on the same subject.

On October 16th the Battalion moved back to Vlamertinghe where it stayed a few days and then moved back to rest billets at Steenvorde. On November 9th the men were sent forward again in buses to camps at Dickebusch near Ypres. After being in close support for a few days they went into the line at Broodseinde Ridge, just east of Zonnebeke, on November 19th where they remained until the end of the year. It was a difficult battle line with much shelling (both high explosive and gas) and the difficulties in getting rations and stores over the boggy ground were still enormous. Casualties were above normal, but the men were always keen and cheerful. A vast amount of new work on trenches, etc, was accomplished by the Battalion. Early in January, 1918, the Battalion was given the task of putting out a continuous apron fence of barbed wire entanglement along the whole Divisional front in the Mocrsede and Broodseinde sectors – a distance of over 4,000 yards. This was completed in record time of about eight hours and the Corps and Divisional Commanders inspected it and expressed their keen admiration and satisfaction. During the later part of January the Battalion was billeted at Winnipeg Camp, near Ouderdom, and went from there each day by train to the forward area on working parties. On January 27th, the Battalion moved back to Hondeghem, near Hazebrouck, and spent two days on the melancholy task of dismembering the Battalion. All except a nucleus of 12 Officers and 200 Other Ranks were compulsorily transferred to the other West Riding Regiments and a Brigade. After the Divisional Commander and Brigade Commander had said goodbye, the Battalion nucleus left the 49th Division on January 30th, entrained at Ebbingham and finally reached the 62nd West Riding Division at St Aubin, near Arras. There the Battalion joined onto the 2/5th Battalion and became one Battalion, named the 5th Battalion Duke of Wellington's Regiment. Lieutenant Colonel Walker (1/5th Battalion) remained in command of the amalgamated Battalion and Lieutenant Colonel F Brook (2/5th Battalion) as second in command. The Adjutant of the 1/5th remained in that capacity with the newly constituted Battalion. The men of the 2/5th formed the new A and B Companies and the men of the 1/5th Battalion went to C and D Companies. At the same time the two 8th Battalions West Yorkshire Regiment and the 5th Battalion KOYLI were amalgamated. It was on this reorganisation that all Infantry Brigades were reduced to three Battalions.

THE GREAT GERMAN OFFENSIVE

On February 1st the Battalion went into the line in front of Gavrelle, just north of Arras, and after a period of further training the Battalion again, on March 9th, went into the line in the Acheville sector, quite close to the Vimy Ridge. Throughout this month the air was full of rumours of an impending enemy offensive and very strict precautionary measures were taken. On March 22nd the Battalion was moved back to Mont St Eloi and became General Headquarters Reserve. News of the enemy offensive then reached the Battalion whilst concentrated at Bucquoy on March 24th and was most ominous. The Brigade was ordered, at 4pm, to advance and take up a position in front of Achiet le Petit which they did. Large numbers of retiring troops, utterly worn out, from five different Divisions, passed through the Brigade as they advanced and no definite information could be obtained except that the enemy was advancing steadily in large numbers. At dusk the Battalion themselves saw large numbers of the enemy on the high ground above Irles. They had no artillery behind except one gun which they persuaded to remain until it had fired all its ammunition. All seemed chaos behind the lines. After a thrilling night in which the Battalion got some prisoners, the men were ordered to retire at 4pm to the high ground between Bucquoy and Puiseaux as their flanks were exposed and there were no troops at all on their right. The orders were received late and the Battalion had to go back in daylight which resulted in some losses and many unpleasant surprises. On March 26th/27th repeated onslaughts by the enemy were repulsed many times. The Battalion was well supported by tanks and the line did not break. By degrees supporting artillery came to the assistance and the Battalion successfully consolidated a line. On March 28th, at 10.30am, after a heavy bombardment the enemy attacked heavily on the Battalion's whole front. The supporting artillery put down a splendid counter barrage and a stiff fight ensued and, in no single case, did any enemy reach the British line, except as a prisoner. Time after time the enemy (German 2nd Guards Reserve Division) massed to make fresh attacks, but were decimated by the rifle and Lewis gun fire to our glorious men. Towards evening the attack waned and finally collapsed. March 29th and 30th were very trying days and the enemy attemted to attack many more times, but was always frustrated by the accurate fire of our splendid men. On April 1st the Battalion went back to Henu for a few days rest and recuperation. The casualties in these few days fighting numbered: 9 Officers and 206 Other Ranks.

Many congratulatory messages were received during the fighting. One, from the Divisional Commander on March 28th, ran, "Congratulate 5th DWR on their fine fight. The fight put up by the isolated platoon is worthy of the best traditions of the Regiment to which it belongs."

Until the end of June the Battalion remained in this sector at Bucquoy and Ablainzeville and had a very exciting and difficult period. The enemy was most aggressive and the men were continually 'on the quiver', but on no single occasion did the Battalion give ground and minor offensive operations went in their favour.

10 DAYS BATTLE

After three weeks rest at Thievres the battalion entrained at Mondecourt and were taken through Paris to the French area around Rheims and there joined the 5th French Army. Besides the 62nd Division the 51st British Division was also attached to the French. After being billeted in various places near Chalon the Battalion concentrated at Germaine in the Forest of Rheims on July 19th. Next day the fighting began and the two British Divisions, for the next ten days, took a leading part in the Second Battle of the Marne. The fighting was in most difficult and densely wooded country but, little by little, the enemy were driven back and many casualties were inflicted on them. Courmas, Bois de Petit Champs and Cuitron will ever have proud association for the Battalion. On July 22nd the Battalion captured the Bois de Petit Champs, under a creeping barrage, held by two German machine gun battalions. The attack was excellently conceived and carried out and the Battalion secured more than 200 prisoners and 45 machine guns. On July 29th the whole Division was withdrawn from the line after a most strenuous and nerve wracking battle lasting 10 days. The morale of the Battalion was still very high in spite of heavy casualties amounting to 13 Officers and 400 Other Ranks. After marching past General Bertholet (5th French Army Commander) and receiving many congratulatory messages on August 4th they were moved back to the old area to Authie, east of Doullens. There they received large new drafts and did some training. Further rest was cut short by the successful British advance north of Albert and the Battalion was moved up to the line again on August 24th. After concentrating at Courcelles the Battalion attacked due east through Behagnies and Sapignies. Enemy opposition was very severe and after the first objective and well on to the second had been secured it was found that the troops on either side of us had not got so far forward, so the new line was consolidated. Towards the evening the enemy made a big counter-attack which utterly failed and the line was further improved. On August 29th, A and D Companies, under Captain G H Ellis DSO, carried out a further attack. They killed many of the enemy and took 90 prisoners, two trench mortars and 15 machine guns with a loss to themselves of only 30 casualties. Next day, B and C Companies did a good show in continuing the advance and, with a loss of 22 casualties, secured more than a hundred prisoners. On September 2nd the Battalion was relieved.

A UNIQUE DISTINCTION

After a week's rest the Battalion again moved up to the line and concentrated in the south west corner of Havrincourt Wood on September 10th. Two days later, two Companies, B and D, attacked on the right of the Brigade front, just south of Havrincourt, and A and C Companies were left in Brigade Reserve. In face of heavy opposition the north east fork of Havringcourt Wood was captured, but it cost more than 100 casualties. On September 13th A and C Companies were brought up and made a bombing attack up the Hindenburg Line next day in conjunction with the 2/20th London Regiment. The attack was continued and the Battalion secured 57 prisoners in the Hindenburg Line with but one casualty to themselves. After rest and re-organisation the Battalion, on September 28th, attacked with 2/4th Hampshire Regiment at Marcoing. Leap frogging through the Hampshires in Marcoing the Battalion, in face of great opposition attained the almost impossible and seized the crossings of the River Escaut, in spite of this the bridge-head was formed, thereby gaining for the Battalion the rare distinction of being specially mentioned in the Commander in Chief's daily communiqué. Later the same evening a strong enemy counter-attack was completely repulsed and we secured 450 prisoners and 23 machine guns. It was in this engagement that Private H Tandy earned his Victoria Cross.

The British night Official message issued on that day (Saturday) stated that during the morning the 62nd Division captured Marcoing and made progress to the south east of it. Before midday the 5th Battalion WRR forced the crossing of the Canal du l'Escaut at Marcoing and established itself in German defences on the east bank. Describing this attack, Mr Perceval Phillips, the War Correspondent, wrote, "The fighting, south and south west of Cambrai, where various English, Scottish and other battalions had been engaged, has resulted in a further advance round the town on that side. One of the finest exploits has been the storming of the German salient east of Marcoing by men of the WRR."

On October 1st the Battalion was relieved and went into bivouacs near Havringcourt. Whilst there, other troops continued the victorious advance and the Battalion had to begin marching on October 8th to keep in touch with them. Marching via Marcoing and Serenvilliers the Battalion was billeted at Carnieres on October 11th and, six days later, relieved the 2nd Battalion Coldstream Guards just west of St Python. At 2am on October 29th the Battalion crossed La Selle river under a barrage and attacked the village of St Python and the high ground beyond, securing all objectives. The Battalion casualties were only 34 altogether and they captured 300 prisoners, 15 machine guns and one trench mortar, whilst over 100 German dead were left in St Python.

After a rest at Bevillers the Battalion moved to Solemnes on October 31st and, on November 2nd, concentrated at Escermaim. Early on November 4th the Battalion moved forward, leap-frogging through the 2/4th Battalion Hampshire Regiment and the 2/4th Battalion WRR as they obtained their objective and advanced 7,000 yards to a line facing east, due south of Fresnoy. The advance was in the nature of an exploitation as artillery could not support the Battalion until later in the day. Notwithstanding this circumstance, 18 guns, 200 prisoners and many machine guns were secured by the Battalion. On November 5th the 185th Infantry Brigade advanced through the 186th Brigade encountering little opposition. On November 7th the Battalion concentrated at Obies and, next day, made an advance of over 3,500 yards in face of little opposition as far as Vieux-Mesnil and obtained three prisoners and three machine guns. Supporting the 187th Infantry Brigade the Battalion moved on November 9th via Neuf Mesnil to Louvroil (a suburb of Maubeuge). All bridges across the River Sambre were blown up and the Battalion crossed over into the town by means of a temporary plank bridge amid the great enthusiasm of the civilian population. The Cavalry were now on the left and entered Maubeuge at the same time as the 62nd Division. In these last five days the Battalion had covered 30 kilometres of new ground in drenching wet weather. On November 11th at 11am hostilities finally ceased. After a week's halt they marched out of Maubeuge en route for Germany. The whole journey was traversed by route march and, on December 17th, the Battalion marched to attention and the Band played the Regimental March. The march in Germany was continued via Hamel, Mooringen, Blumenthal and Schaben until the Battalion finally reached their destination at Mechernich on Christmas Day. The Colour Party, which was sent to Huddersfield for the Colours, reached the Battalion at Blumenthal on December 23rd. The Battalion remained in the Mechernich area as part of the Army of Occupation until March 29th, 1919, when it was reduced to cadre establishment (five Officers and 46 Other Ranks). The remainder of the Battalion was either disembodied or, those who were retainable in the Army were transferred to the 2/4th Battalion WRR. After being attached to the 5th Division at Fleurus, near Charleroi, for a few weeks the Battalion Cadre finally reached Huddersfield with the Colours on May 9th, 1919.

THE COST

Of those who originally went out with the 1/5th Battalion in April, 1915, one Officer and five Other Ranks returned with the Cadre and there were One Officer and 11 Other Ranks of the 2/5th Battalion who went out to France in January, 1917. The casualties of the Battalions are as follows:

1/5th Battalion – for period 14 4 15 to 31 1 18

Killed or died	506
Taken prisoner	22
Still missing	2
Wounded or sick sent home to England	1,633

2/5th Battalion – for period 17 1 1917 to 31 1 18

Killed or died	305
Taken prisoner	111
Still missing	3
Wounded or sick sent home to England	458

Combined 5th Battalion for period 01 12 18 to date

Killed or died	306
Taken prisoner	56
Still missing	12
Wounded or sick sent home to England	874

TOTALS

Killed or died	1,117
Taken prisoner	189
Still missing	17
Wounded or sick sent home to England	2,965

Wed 6 Aug 1919

THE DUKE OF WELLINGTON'S REGIMENT

Our article last week on the War Record of this Regiment was incomplete. This, however, was not indicated owing to the inadvertent omission of the intimation that we hope shortly to publish the record of the 2/5th Battalion for the period January 1917 to January 1918 during which time they fought as a separate unit in France.

Wed 24 Sep 1919

The following is a continuation of the articles on the record of the 5th Battalion of the Duke of Wellington's West Riding Regiment.

There were many high spirited lads who, in its early days, looked upon the 2/5th Battalion with some little disfavour. They wanted to get to the front and they saw no possible chance of doing so through what was then a Reserve Battalion, particularly as the 1st Battalion was not then being utilised in actual fighting operations. The 2/5th Battalion had not, therefore, a promising start but, as time went on, it attracted a large number of spirited young men who got their chance and won a very proud reputation for themselves whilst still a separate Battalion. Their capture of Orchard Alley, Puiseux, Achiet-le-Petit and Gommecourt, their heroic valour at Bullecourt and the magnificent work they did in the operations at Cambrai will be written in the records of the deeds of men who performed worthily the very difficult tasks imposed upon them. The 2/5th Battalion was formed by Lieutenant Colonel W Cooper VD, Commanding Officer, with Captain J L Robinson as Adjutant in November, 1914. These Officers were cordially assisted in the recruiting part of their work by the Huddersfield Recruiting Committee of which Sir William Raynor was Chairman, by the late Captain Harold Hanson and by Lieutenant T P Crosland, who had charge of the recruiting at Mirfield where a very large number of recruits joined the Battalion. During the months of November and December, 1914, and January/February, 1915, the Battalion was in training at the Drill Hall and Greenhead Park, Huddersfield, and did much route marching in the Huddersfield area and, in this period, it provided drafts for the 1/5th Battalion which was then stationed at Doncaster. Early in March the Battalion moved from Huddersfield to Derby and, later, to Doncaster. On the

14th April the Battalion lined the road and gave a hearty send-off to the 1/5th Battalion as they marched to Doncaster railway station to entrain for France. Subsequent camps were made at Thoresby Park; Babworth, near Retford; Gainsborough; Newcastle upon Tyne; Larkhill; Salisbury Plain (where intensive training commenced); Henham Park, near Southwold, and Bedford.

On the 17th August, 1915, Colonel W Cooper, much to the regret of the whole Battalion, left to take command of a Home Service unit on the Lincolnshire coast. He was succeeded by Colonel W O M Mosse, late of the Indian Army, who was an excellent trainer and organiser and did good work for the Battalion. Colonel Mosse left the Battalion in April, 1916, on his appointment as Officer in Command of the Tyne Garrison. He was succeeded by Lieutenant Colonel T A D Best DSO, a capable and popular Commanding Officer whose loss (he was killed in the Cambrai fighting) was mourned by all. Major Frank Brook, second in command of the Battalion, succeeded Colonel Best and remained in command until the amalgamation of the 1/5th and 2/5th Battalions in January, 1918. During the months July to October, 1916, the Battalion had a very exciting time during the German air raids. Many of the Zeppelins came inland over the bay at Southwold and the work of the anti aircraft guns could be seen from the camp. On one occasion, a gondola, which had been shot off one of the Zeppelins was found a few miles from the camp. The conduct of the men in billets and during their home training was exemplary and their behaviour was excellent. On many occasions they were complimented on their behaviour and, while billeted on the civilian population at Derby, Gainsborough and Bedford, they made many friends.

IN THE TRENCHES

On the 21st January, 1917, the Battalion was stationed at Bedford, whence they departed on the 10th and embarked at Southampton on the following day. They arrived at Le Havre in the early morning of 12th January. Later they proceeded to Auxi le Chateau and afterwards marched through Ampliere, Orville, Thievres, Authie to Bus les Artois. About this time the weather was so cold that the oil in the Lewis guns and the ink in the fountain pens was frozen. The Battalion underwent instruction duty with the 9th Battalion Welsh Regiment in the trenches east of Hebuterne. Preparations for going into the line were made en march through Bertancourt, Bousart, Mailly Maillet and Auchonvillers. The Battalion entered the trenches at Bermwork, near Beaumont Hamel, relieving the 1st Battalion Dorsetshire Regiment in trenches before Serre, which place the Germans held. The trenches in this part did not exist as such as, in most places, they had been blown in and work in deepening and widening them occupied the Battalion for some days. The Battalion was relieved on February 17th by the 2/6th Battalion WRR. On the 24th February, Major Negus (second in command) left the Battalion to take command of the 2/8th Battalion West Yorkshire Regiment. The first recorded attack took place on February 27th when two fighting patrols, of D Company, and a third, of A Company, attacked Orchard Alley, about 800 yards away. The trench was only lightly held by the enemy and it was captured. The attacking parties killed one of the enemy and took another prisoner but the remainder of the garrison escaped, while they themselves had three men slightly wounded. Later D Company followed up and consolidated the newly won trench. The capture of Orchard Alley compelled the enemy to withdraw from the village of Puiseux. D Company's patrols entered the village at dawn and it was occupied and the position consolidated by D and C Companies later in the day. For the attack Lieutenant Ridley, D Company, who was in command of the attacking parties, was awarded the Military Cross and Lance Corporal Hubert Priestley, of A Company, was awarded the Military Medal. These were the first awards of honours to be made in the Battalion.

About the middle of March the Battalion held the line south of Achiet le Petit and B Company was detailed to hold Resurrection Trench and capture the village. They were very heavily bombarded for three days and nights and suffered severe casualties. An hour before dawn on the 17th March, two battle patrols were despatched to the flanks of the town followed by the rest of the Company. Some opposition from machine guns was encountered but the village was quickly occupied and passed through. The Company immediately consolidated, digging in on the north side. An outflanking movement was attemted by the enemy but it was frustrated. A terrific barrage was also put over the village by the enemy but the Company was already pressing on to the north. In the evening orders were received for the whole of the line to move forward. A Company was detailed to clear Logeast Wood of the enemy which, after many exciting incidents, they did. B and C Companies had to cut the German wire and assist the Cavalry. The wire was nearly 100 yards in depth in three broad belts and so thick that it had to be dug up in parts. The task of cutting the wire was completed before daylight by B and C Companies and these Companies then advanced to their objective and captured the enemy positions north-west of Achiet le Grand. At 4.30am on the 18th March D Company completed the capture of Gommecourt and large bodies of our Cavalry and Royal Horse Artillery went through the village in pursuit of the retreating enemy during the day. The only buildings left standing in the village were the Chateau which had been mined and a billet with 50 wire beds in it, in which, amongst other things, a German whip with 6 lashes was found.

CUT OFF FOR THREE DAYS

The remainder of March and early April were occupied in training and working parties and, towards the end of the month, preparations were made for the attack on Bullecourt. At Zero Hour on 3rd May, 1917, the barrage opened promptly and the tanks went forward to do their part in the attack. The Battalion steadily advanced to the attack, crossed a sunken road and fought their way up a slope to the ridge to the left of Bullecourt. The Battalion was subjected to decimating machine gun fire from hidden concrete emplacements and to a terrific barrage of high explosives and shrapnel. Those who were left rallied and continued to press forward to the Hindenburg Line through a tornado of bullets. At this point Lieutenant O Walker, of Lindley, was killed as he was charging, rifle in hand, with his platoon through the German wire. Two enemy machine guns were captured and their crews killed by the bombers. With a handful of men the commander of B Company pressed on and succeeded in forcing the way into a boche strongpoint which was defended by more hidden emplacements. In these emplacements the party held cut, according to arrangements, for three days and nights without water and with only their iron rations to subsist upon. They were bombed and shelled all the time. On the 2nd day the enemy made an effort to take the little party prisoners but he was driven back. The shortening of the range of the British Batteries on the third day caused the position to be badly blown in and, in consequence of the untenable nature of the position, the Company Commander, with a few other wounded men, succeeded in forcing his way back to the British lines through the German outpost line. The return journey was made in broad daylight and the members of this gallant party were fired upon from every side. Their difficulties were increased by reason of the fact that the enemy were wearing British steel helmets and tunics but, after an nine hour struggle, they got back, as by a miracle, to their own lines. The troops, who should have rendered support were unable to reach the small party owing to the fire of German machine guns from hidden emplacements, approached by subterranean passages from the Hindenburg Tunnel trench. Posts were established and held during the night and the following day machine gun firing and shelling were continuous. On May 5th the Battalion was relieved by the 2/7th Battalion and marched back to Mory Copse. 24 of the Stretcher bearers went over with the Battalion in the attack and only six returned.

During the remainder of May the Battalion provided garrisons at various places, notably at the Sunken Road, a strongpoint on the Bullecourt – Croissilles road, north-west of Bullecourt. Early in the following month the Battalion was again at Achiet le Petit, in rest, where, in the Coliseum, 'The Pelicans', the Divisional Concert Party, and the Divisional Band gave concerts. The Coliseum was a large hole in the ground made by the blowing up of a German ammunition dump. It had been converted into an open air theatre with sitting accommodation, a stage and boxing ring. Another noteworthy event was the Brigade Gymkhana, in which the Battalion won four events out of five. The latter part of June and the early part of July were chiefly occupied in training and the usual trench duties. On the 2nd July a remarkable trench digging feat is recorded. In three hours, during darkness of the night, the Battalion dug 600 yards of front line trench, three feet wide and three feet deep. Towards the end of the month the Battalion was specially mentioned in Divisional Orders for the amount of work done in the trenches during the last tour. Part of the line occupied early in the

August, before Riencourt (The Apex) was a very tricky piece of line to hold. The enemy Advanced Post and that held by our men being only 30 yards apart. In consequence, much bombing, on both sides, took place; sniping and trench mortaring were very common during the next few days. On August 10th, it is recorded two Officers took the honey from a beehive in a part of our billet and got from 30 to 40 pounds of honey. It was very good! They put gas helmets on to avoid being stung, discovered a mushroom bed from which we gathered several pounds so we did rather well here; went round the village of Vraucourt in the morning trying to find more beehives.

CALLING THE CUCKOOS

Near the end of August the Battalion relieved the West Yorkshire Regiment at Bullecourt on ground which had been fought over so very often during the previous month of May. The Battalion collected so much salvage that it went to the head of the Divisional Slavage List and was specially congratulated by the Divisional General. During a tour of duty towards the end of the month propaganda work was carried on by the British, leaflets being sent over into the enemy lines. If one of the enemy, on reading the leaflet, wished to give himself up he had to approach our line at dawn and call out "Cuckoo". There were no Cuckoos collected during the Battalion's tour in the line!
The month of September was taken up by the usual round of trench duties and there was not much of importance to record, though some excellent reconnaissance and lying in wait patrols were carried out by the platoon commanders and NCOs. Early in October The Apex was again held for the third time and the place got worse every time for enemy shelling and trench mortars. Later in the month intensive training for an attack took place. No 14 Platoon took the lead in the Battalion Platoon competitions. One man in the Platoon got a possible and another 43 out of 45. TO BE CONCLUDED TOMORROW.

Thur 25 Sep 1919

THE TERRITORIALS CAMPAIGN. HEROIC WORK OF THE 2/5th BATTALION AT CAMBRAI.

DESPERATE ATTACKS.

The following is a continuation of the article published yesterday on the record of the local Territorial Battalions. It carries the record of the 2/5th Battalion up to the time when the 1st and 2/5th Battalions were amalgamated in January, 1918.

The Battalion experienced some very severe fighting in the Cambrai operations from November 20th to December 3rd, 1917. They left billets at Bertincourt early on the ……….[*gap in copy*] Wood and moved forward towards Havrinvcourt. When approaching the Chateau Wood beyond the British front line, heavy machine gun and rifle fire was encountered from a strongpoint situated in the wood. The Battalion deployed and endeavoured to get through gaps in the wire. At this point the Commanding Officer, Lieutenant Colonel T D Best DSO, was killed and three other Officers and a considerable number of men became casualties. Captain and Adjutant H S Jackson took command of the Battalion and endeavoured to re-organise. Captain T Goodall, Officer Commanding D Company, in the most gallant manner, entered the wood to locate the point from which the casualties were being sustained and, having done this, signalled to Lieutenant D Black to advance with his other Platoon. The strongpoint was rushed and one Officer, 58 Other Ranks and two machine guns were captured and a British Officer and NCO were rescued. A considerable number of the enemy were killed at this point. Meanwhile, the Battalion had re-organised, continued its advance in lines of sections and passed beyond the second Objective. Very heavy machine gun and rifle fire was encountered. Captain C S Moxon, with the aid of a tank, went forward and later, with the assistance of No 14 Platoon, took the post, killing five and capturing three of the enemy.

CAMBRAI ADVANCE

The remainder of the garrison ran away towards Graincourt, but were annihilated by Lewis gun fire. After re-organising on the forming up line, the Battalion moved to the final Objective. Kangaroo Alley was captured and occupied by D Company. A strongpoint near Lock 6 on the Canal du Nord was taken by C Company, under Lieutenant E W Harris and two Officers and 64 Other Ranks were taken prisoner. The remainder of the garrison would not leave the dug-out, which was set on fire and the garrison were killed. As the Battalion, by this time, was in advance of the Battalion operating on its right and casualties were being caused, No 14 Platoon, under Lieutenant D Black, attacked another enemy strongpoint and captured two Officers, 59 Other Ranks and two machine guns. A, B and C Companies then passed through D Company, which was occupying Kangaroo Alley, advanced beyond the Bapaume-Cambrai Road and B Company, then commanded by Lieutenant G V Bernays, captured a trench and another strongpoint with two Officers, 12 Other Ranks and two machine guns. During this day (November 20th, 1917) the Battalion captured 353 prisoners, 15 machine guns and one trench mortar. Their total casualties were three Officers killed, one wounded; 10 Other Ranks killed, 55 wounded and four Other Ranks missing. This attack was, at that time, a record for penetrating the enemy trench system in depth in one day. The 2/5th Battalion, with the 2/7th and 2/4th Battalions on their right, having advanced 7,000 yards from the original British front line.

The night of the 20th passed quietly and Major Frank Booth took command of the Battalion. It was expected that early next morning two tanks would assist the Battalions in taking the Hindenburg Support Line. As the tanks had not arrived by Zero Hour and endeavour was made to work up the Hindenburg Support line and clear it with the object of moving forward. A, B and C Companies attemted to bomb their way along the trench, but very strong resistance was encountered. In some parts the trenches were only partly dug and the shallow parts were subjected to by the enemy to continuous machine gun fire. A most determined effort was made by A Company to drive the enemy along the trench. Lieutenant J E Ridgeway led a rush for a strongpoint. It was captured and 40 prisoners were taken but Lieutenant Ridgeway was killed and Captain Moxon was wounded. About the middle of the afternoon it was found impossible to advance and, in this impasse, the services of a tank which had lost direction was obtained. Captain Jackson directed the tank to the spot and the Battalion made a further effort to clear this sector of the Hindenburg Support Trench. At length the enemy resistance was completely broken down and they fled in disorder. Large numbers of the enemy were killed and by darkness the Battalion was in possession of the whole of the Hindenburg Support Line in this sector, being the Objective for the day. The tank proceeded on its way and encountered a large force of the enemy, advancing in waves to counter-attack. The tank was attacked furiously but managed to get away and very heavy casualties were inflicted on the disorganised enemy. Towards evening an enemy patrol was captured and from one of the prisoners it was learned that a counter-attack in force was to be made. This counter-attack was attemted half an hour later but it was broken up by Lewis gun and rifle fire and the enemy did not reach the Battalion's line. At midnight the Battalion was relieved by the 2/6th West Yorkshire Regiment and moved into support in the Hindenburg Line. The prisoners captured during the day numbered 70 with two machine guns. The Battalion's casualties were one Officer killed, one wounded, six Other Ranks killed and eight wounded After remaining in support until the night of the 22nd, the Battalion marched to Havringcourt Wood and then to Bertincourt on the following day.

AN EARLY MORNING ATTACK.

Shortly after midday on the 25th November the Battalion marched in support again, near Anneux Chapel, after being subjected to very heavy shellfire on the way up. Heavy shelling was continuous in the same position on the 26th November. In the evening the Battalion took over a line on Bourlon Wood. The night passed quietly but a heavy fall of snow and sleet caused much hardship. Early next morning the attack was recommenced in the darkness, the Objectives being the railway line east of Bourlon Village. It was difficult to ascertain the exact position of the barrage and immediately terrific machine gun fire was encountered on the right of the Battalion sector. Heavy casualties were sustained, especially among the Officers and A, B and D Companies were held up for some time. Supplies of ammunition were very short and the Brigade Trench Mortars were brought into action until all their ammunition was expended. About an hour after the attack had commenced the enemy put down an intense barrage and heavy casualties were sustained. When the enemy shelling slackened, three hours later, the Battalion was re-organised and a further attempt was made to advance. A small enemy counter-attack made from the direction f the north east corner of the wood was broken and most of the enemy were killed without reaching the Battalion position. Early in the afternoon some ammunition was obtained and a change of position was commenced. Strong enemy counter-attacks were started from Bourlon, but they did not develop. The Battalion was relieved in this position by dismounted Cavalry and went into support at Bourlon Wood. During the day 12 prisoners were taken and the casualties incurred were two Officers killed, one Officer missing, six Officers wounded; 18 Other Ranks killed, 14 missing and 144 wounded. During the night of the 27th and the day of the 28th the Battalion remained in position ready to repel counter-attacks. Heavy shelling by the enemy incessantly maintained and the Battalion was relieved on the evening of the 28th November. The next two days were spent in Reserve in the Hindenburg Support Line and although the Battalion was subjected to heavy artillery fire no casualties were incurred. During this period the weather was intensely cold and, as most of the men were occupying trenches with dug-out accommodation, great hardship was endured. The Battalion was relieved on the night of 2nd December and marched back to Lebuquiere, later going into billets at Bellecourt.

The decorations for the Cambrai fighting, which were announced shortly before Christmas, were three DSOs and six Military Crosses for Officers; one bar to the Military Medal and 24 Military Medals for NCOs and men. The ribbons for these decorations were presented by the GOC Division (General Sir Walter Braithwaite) on January 4th at a Battalion Parade at Bailleul aux Cornailles. The honours and awards to the Battalion in the New Year's Honours List (1918) were as follows:

Officers:

Lieutenant Colonel T D Best (killed in action) - Bar to his DSO.

1 Military Cross; 1 Mention in Despatches.

NCOs

Company Sergeant Major W S Wilkinson and Sergeant Harold Hirst (then serving with 186th Brigade Trench Mortar Battery) – DCM.

Sergeants H Schofield and Norman Haigh – Mention in Despatches.

Those to whom the Divisional Commander had not presented ribbons on January 4th received from the Army Commander on January 13th, 1918.

The usual trench warfare took place early in the New Year and until the 1/5th and 2/5th Battalions WRR amalgamated at the end of January. The record from this point of the combined Battalion has already been published.

HARD EARNED HONOURS.

The honours won by members of the Battalion during the 13 months spent in France before its amalgamation with the 1/5th were as follows:

DSO – 3
Bar to DSO – 1
Military Cross – 8
DCM – 1
Military Medal – 28
Bar to Military Medal – 1
Mentioned in Despatches – 5
Croix de Guerre (French) – 1
Croix de Guerre (Belgian) – 2
Making a total of 50.

No record of the Battalion would be complete without reference to the Stretcher Bearers and Transport sections. Much was expected of the Stretcher Bearers and the trust was amply fulfilled. When the call "Stretcher Bearers" was heard in the night or in the day the stretcher bearers 'jumped to it' and many are the tales that could be told of their gallantry. Nothing could be finer than the conduct of the stretcher bearers of the Battalion. There was an urgent need at times for improvised tourniquets and the Stretcher Bearer section had invented a method of making their own which proved very useful and successful in saving pain to wounded men. During the period in which the Battalion was in France the Transport section was under the command of Captain T P Crosland and it was always the section's proud boast that, whatever the conditions, bad weather, the state of the roads or enemy shelling, they would 'get there' and they always did so. As may be imagined, whenever the rations were being dealt with, this determination on the part of the Transport section was always appreciated by the Officers and men of the Battalion. It is also worthy of special note in any reference to the work of the Battalion that the Adjutant of the 5th, Captain Keith Sykes MC, served with his Unit from the outbreak of war until the return of the Cadre in 1919, continuously as Adjutant from 1915 onwards and never missed one engagement in which his Unit was concerned.

THE BATTLES

Wherever possible we have listed the battle in which the men fell. Extraordinarily, the majority of the men commemorated did appear to fall in battle, rather than the smaller number who fell in the daily grind and attrition of trench warfare, and still fewer men who succumbed to disease and sickness. Disease had been the major killer in previous wars, far more soldiers died of enteric fever during the South African War than were killed by Boer bullets or shells. By April, 1914, inoculations had been introduced into the British Army and the incidence of deaths from disease dropped dramatically. Only three of the men who are named on the War Memorial died of disease.

A total of 104 Battle Honours were awarded for the whole of the Western Front during the war, 72 of which were awarded to the various battalions of the Regiment, ten of these are emblazoned on the Regulation Colours. There were nine major battles in which the first and second line battalions of the 5th DWR were involved:

The Battles for Ypres.

There were three officially accepted Battles for Ypres, although some historians consider the second German Spring Offensive, Operation *Georgette*, in Flanders, as being the Fourth Battle of Ypres:

1st Ypres: 19th October – 22nd November, 1914;
2nd Ypres: 22nd April – 25th May, 1915;
3rd Ypres: 31st July – 10th November, 1917 (commonly known as the Battle of Passchendaele).

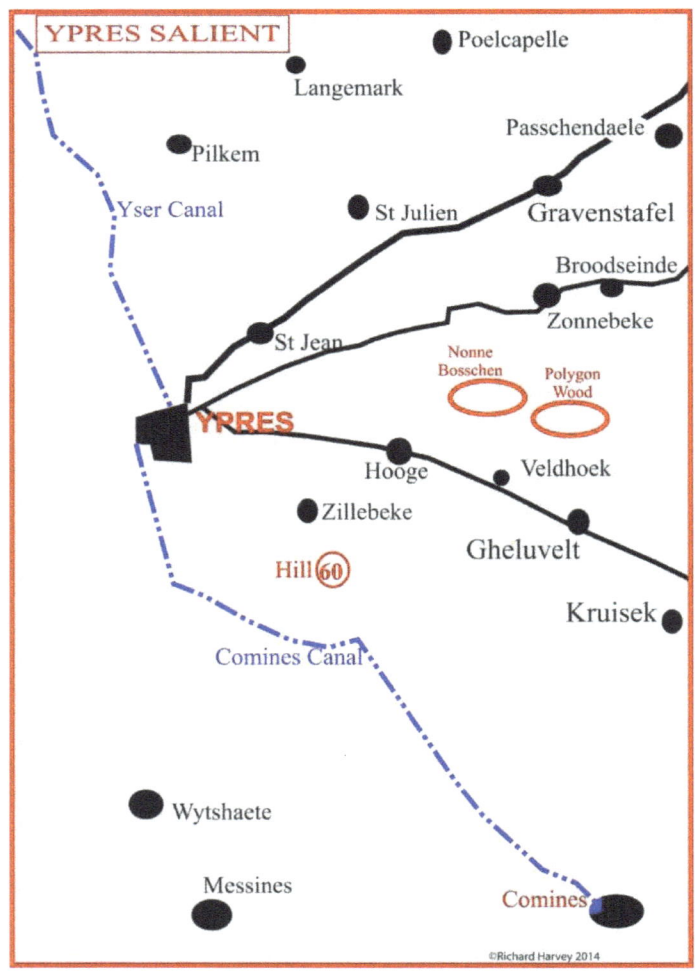

The First Battle of Ypres was fought in 1914 and none of the DWR Territorial Force battalions were in France and Flanders at that time. The Second Battle of Ypres, between April and May, 1915, was at a time when the 1/5th Battalion was under instruction for trench warfare in the Fleurbaix Sector, and a number of men were killed or died of wounds during this period, before moving to the Ypres Sector in early July, 1915. There were many casualties in this sector during the time that the 49th Division was holding the line until December, 1915.

See also Battle of Passchendaele, below:

The Battle of the Somme.
1st July – 18th November, 1916.

The Battle of the Somme was actually a series of forty two separate battles or actions, for which thirteen Battle Honours were awarded to Regiments after the war for their involvement in these major attacks.

The 1/5th DWR was involved mainly in the Battle for Thiepval in 2nd Corps (2nd – 28th September, 1916) and went 'over the top' on 3rd September as part of a much larger operation, the Battle of Pozieres, with 14th Corps attacking Guillemont and 15th Corps attacking Delville Wood, further to the south, on the same day.

The Battalion was further involved in the Somme battle until moving to the Nieuport Sector, see below, in July 1917.

The Battle of Bullecourt.
3rd May, 1917.

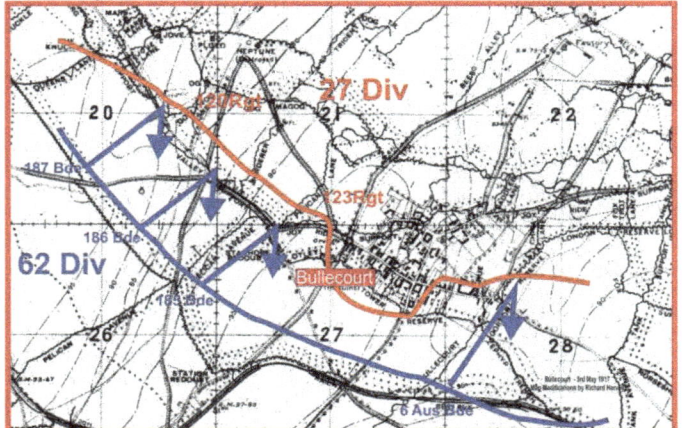

Battle of Bullecourt.

R Harvey

By February, 1917, the second line Territorial Force Battalions in 62nd Division had completed their trench warfare instruction and were ready to take their place in the line, moving into the trenches at Beaumont Hamel on 13th February, 1917. On 27th February, the 2/5th DWR successfully attacked and captured a German trench, Orchard Alley, which raised their morale. On 11th April, 1917, the Canadians attemted to breach the German Hindenburg line at Bullecourt but had been repulsed and a major German counter-attack had taken ground from the Allies. In May, reinforced with the 62nd (TF) Division, they were to have another go. The second Battle for Bullecourt was one of the worst days in the war for the 2/5th Battalion, 145 men listed on the War Memorial were reported as missing, killed or died of wounds as a result of a few hour's fighting (with another man who is not on the Memorial but is commemorated in this book).

The Nieuport Sector.
13th July – 24th September, 1917.

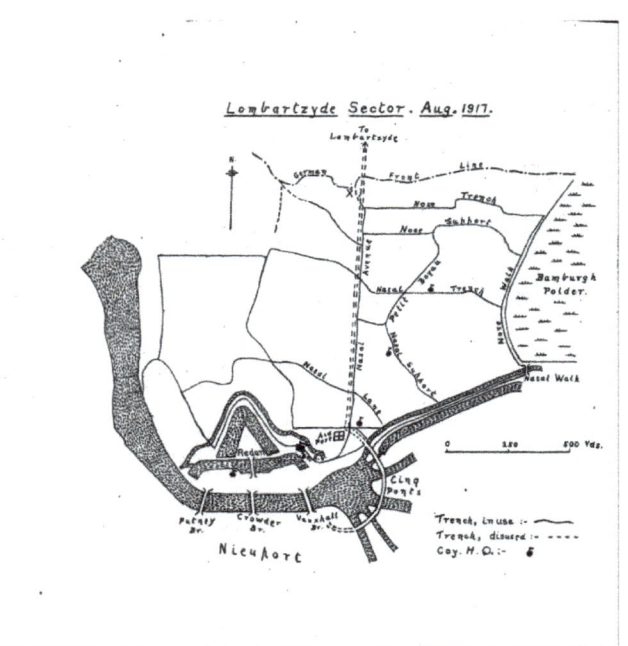

Nieuport Sector.

Capt P G Bales.

This Sector, on the Belgian coast, was scheduled to be the start line for a major attack eastwards in support of an amphibious landing further along the coast by the British 1st Division. This was due to be a major part of what was to become the 3rd Battle of Ypres, commonly called the Battle of Passchendaele. Unfortunately, the Germans launched a spoiling attack in this area and pushed the Allied forces back from the proposed start line on the right bank of the canal, overwhelming the two battalions occupying the bridgehead. The 49th Division arrived in Dunkirk by rail on 13th July, 1917, as this attack took place. Following some training on the beaches and in the dunes for an attack, 147 Brigade took their place in the front lines on 3rd August, 1917, and heavy casualties were suffered by the Division from heavy German artillery fire and gas during the next fifty two days. The Brigade started to move out of the area on 23rd September and 49th Division left 15 Corps, Fourth Army. Twelve men are recorded on the War Memorial who were killed here, however, the Archives Volunteers Team has recorded 5 Officers and 107 ORs who died in this sector between 25th July and 6th October, 1917, in all four DWR Battalions in 147 Brigade.

The Battle of Passchendaele (3rd Battle of Ypres).
31st July – 10th November, 1917.

This Battle was one of the largest battles fought on the Western Front, certainly in terms of casualties. As with the Battle of the Somme, it, too, consisted of many battles and actions, with a total of eight Battle Honours being awarded for this period.

The 49th Division reached this battle area again in mid November, 1917, being in action until relieved on 3rd April, 1918. Their rest period was to be short lived, by 10th April the Division was helping to stem the German Spring Offensive, Operation *Georgette*, in the Erquinghem Lys/Nieppe area, although the 1/5th Battalion had, by then, moved to 62nd Division.

The Battle of Cambrai.
20th November – 3rd December, 1917.

The Germans were not expecting an assault of this size, supported by tanks in force and they fled in disarray initially. However, mechanical failure and the German realisation that tanks were not proof against artillery brought the attack to a halt, along with the winter weather. The German counter attack regained most of the ground lost but the scope and daring of the attack had shattered their 'impregnable' defences and was another crack in their belief of invincibility, leading to eventual victory.

The German Spring Offensive.

Actually a number of German assaults at different times and in different areas designed to break through to the Chanel Ports and force Britain out of the war, by cutting off the supply lines, (Operation *Michael*, 21st March – 4th April and Operation *Georgette*, 9th – 25th April) and then to seize Paris (Operation *Blucher-York*, 27th May – 4th June; Operation *Gneisnau*, 9th – 11th June, and Operation *Friedensturm*, 15th – 17th July, 1918). A final assault to take Ypres and the Channel Ports (Operation *Hagen*) was cancelled when the German High Command realised that the Allied counter-attack in the Soissons region (18th July) was much greater than they believed to be possible at that stage of the war and that they were facing defeat. Their forces for Operation Hagen were redirected to the Rheims area in July, 1918.

87 men are recorded as having died in this period who are also commemorated on the War Memorial, which is an indication of how desperate a time it was.

Battle of Tardenois.
20th – 30th July, 1918

Sunday 28 and Monday 29 July 1918

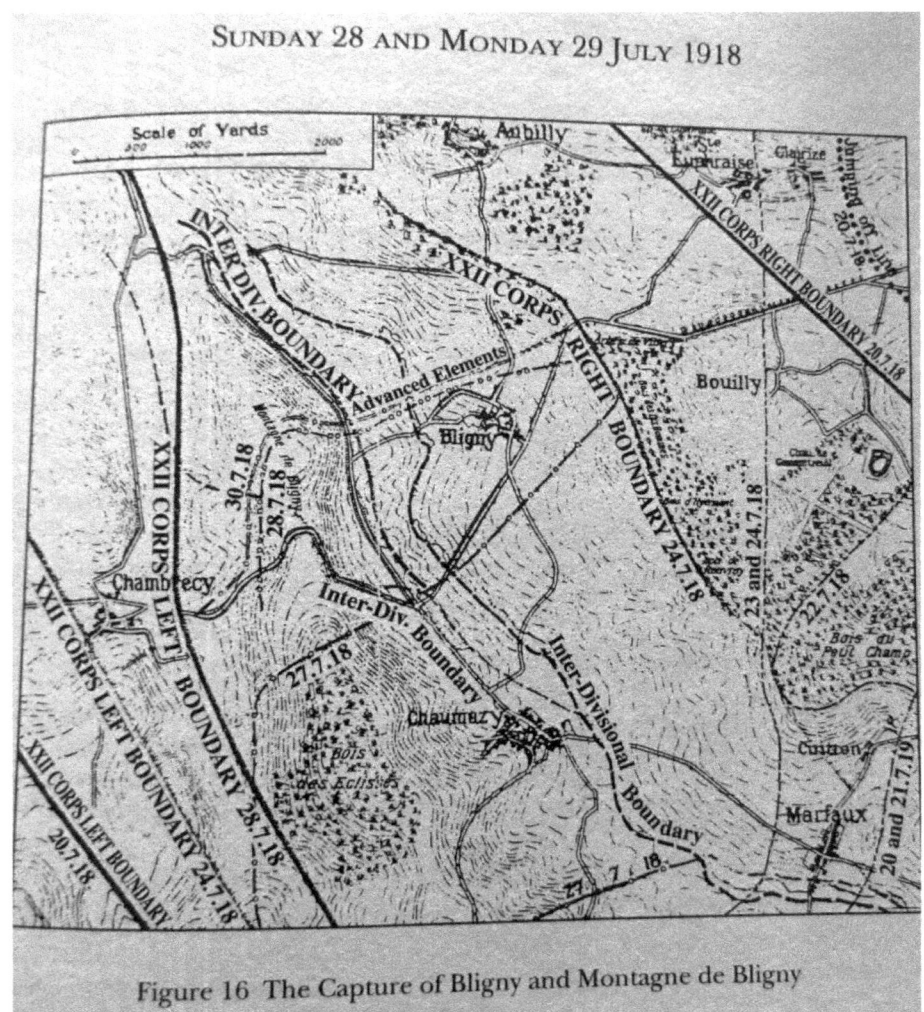

Figure 16 The Capture of Bligny and Montagne de Bligny

Extract from the Official History of the War

The French were aware of a large German build up of troops released from the Russian Front after the collapse of the Russian Army and the Treaty of Brest Litovsk. The German objective of Operation *Blucher-York* was Paris. The French requested assistance from the British and the 9th British Corps was soon in action in the Ardre Valley in May, 1918, helping to stem the German assault. Another request for British support, as a result of intelligence of another major German offensive, resulted in the 22nd Corps, with 62nd Division, being entrained to join General Berthelot's French 10th Army. The Germans launched Operation *Friedensturm* in the Rheims Sector on 15th July and the 62nd, alongside the 51st Highland Division, arrived to take over from the exhausted Italians fighting with the French in time to stem the German advance and then counter-attack, retaking the village of Bligny before being relieved and returning to the British area. By this time the 1/5th and 2/5th Battalions had been amalgamated and were fighting as the 5th Battalion in 62nd Division. Forty seven men are recorded as having been killed during this battle who are commemorated on the War Memorial. Research shows that the two DWR Battalions engaged, the 2/4th and 5th DWR, suffered between 100 and 140 (CWGC and SDGW, respectively) deaths overall in this ten day battle. The Battle Honours 'Marne 1918' and 'Tardenois' were awarded for this action.

The Advance to Victory.
8th August – 11 November, 1918.

Once more, this was a series of battles and actions, for which twenty Battle Honours were awarded, post war. The Germans dubbed the 8th August as the Black Day for the German Army and saw the beginning of the collapse of their fighting force and its morale, which had been sapped from the end of the Battle of the Somme in November, 1916, and through a series of Allied victories in 1917, culminating in the Battle of Cambrai in November of that year. Their early collapse was only prevented by the arrival of approximately a million battle hardened reinforcements from the Eastern Front, who brought new ideas and tactics and higher morale with them. However, after the blunting of each of their major Operations, due to the tenacity of the troops fighting against them and the arrival of fresh American troops who proved to be just as tough, if not as experienced, in the final actions during the German Spring Offensive, German morale began to crumble. This was hastened by the unrest, food riots and strikes in the Fatherland, since 1915 and which were growing in tempo and becoming more widespread in 1917, laying the seeds of their complete collapse and the Armistice of 1918. The Germans had been outfought, outgunned and blockaded to a standstill both on the Western Front and at home. The Germans were pushed back to a line close to where the British and German armies had clashed on August 23rd, 1914. The 2nd Battalion DWR ended up about 11 kilometres from Mons, where they had started, a mere sixty six of the original 992 men remained with that Battalion on the 11th November, 279 of these 'original soldiers' had been killed and 247 had been taken prisoner. It is worth remembering that, by this stage of the war, the majority of soldiers were conscripts rather than the eager volunteers of the first sixteen months of the war.

156 men commemorated on the War Memorial Boards died during this period. The Germans may have been withdrawing and even surrendering in large numbers, but they were still resisting strongly in defence of the Fatherland, leaving much destruction and many booby traps behind them, in the same way as they had done in early 1917 during their withdrawal to the Hindenburg Line, after the Battle of the Somme.

The only disturbing element was the fact that after the Armistice the German Army marched back into Germany, carrying their weapons and with banners flying. Very little damage had been done inside Germany, compared to the devastated area astride the trench lines in Belgium and France, as well as naval shelling and the aerial bombing of Britain between 1915 and 1918, leaving scope for German nationalists to claim that the Army had not been defeated in the Great War but had been betrayed by politicians and communist factions involved in six general strikes, mutinies in ten German Naval bases, along with workers' takeovers in seven major cities and the declaration of the Bolshevik Free State of Bavaria in 1918.

Battle Honours

For these and other battles the 5th DWR battalions were involved in, the following Battle Honours were awarded:

1/5th DWR	2/5th DWR	5th DWR
Ypres 1917	Arras 1917	Somme 1918
Aubers	Bullecourt	Ancre 1918
Somme 1916	Cambrai 1917	Marne 1918
Albert 1916	France and Flanders 1914-18	Tardenoise
Poelcappelle		Bapaume 1918
France and Flanders 1914-18		Hindenberg Line
		Havringcourt
		Canal du Nord
		Selle
		Sambre
		France and Flanders 1914-18

Note that the 1/5th and 2/5th Battalions were amalgamated in January, 1918; the 1/5th Battalion leaving 49th Division and joining the 2/5th Battalion in 62nd Division, subsequently being heavily involved in the German Spring Offensive and the Allied Advance to Victory between March and November, 1918.

WEAPONS

The causes of death of many of the men commemorated on the War Memorial have been recorded where possible.

The weapons and terminology of the First World War differed from later conflicts and the major differences are set out, below:

WW1	WW2
Aerial torpedo.	Bomb.
Bomb.	Hand Grenade.
Gas: Chlorine Lachrymatory – White, Black or Green. Sneezing – Blue Cross. Phosgene – White C, White D. Mustard – Yellow Cross. (German colour codes, as used on the shell casings).	Not used, officially. CS Tear Gas.
Mine – subterranean, using Tunnelling Companies to dig under the enemy front line. Extensively used.	Land mine – normally surface laid or shallowly concealed. Very extensively used.
Shellfire – high explosive, gas.	Shellfire – high explosive, illuminating, smoke.
Shrapnel – air burst munitions scattering numerous 'ball bearings'; extensively used.	Shrapnel – rarely used.
Trench Mortar.	Mortar.
Stokes Mortar.	3" Mortar.
Livens Projector.	Nebelwerfer (copied by the Germans for WW2 after they eventually captured some in 1918).
Large Gallery Flame Projector – dug in underground near Mametz for the first day of the Battle of the Somme.	Tank flame thrower.

HERITAGE AND LEGACY

The Volunteer Movement soon recovered from the trauma of the war years and the Territorials were reconstituted, as the Territorial Army, in 1921. The 5th Battalion, with its Headquarters again in St Pauls Street Drill Hall, Huddersfield, had Companies at both Huddersfield and Mirfield, with detachments at Holmfirth and Kirkburton.

The first camp of the 5th Battalion was held in the summer of 1920 at Scarborough. The great number of the decorated soldiers who had once again volunteered, after what they had gone through, including some whose camp had been so rudely interrupted by German dreams of empire and conquest seven years previously, enjoyed another period of soldiering and, undoubtedly, tale telling which the newer recruits would listen to in awe.

The Territorials were also invited to furnish recruits for the Defence Corps for the National Emergency of April, 1921, before heading for camp in Whitby that July.

Numbers and recruiting fluctuated during the inter war period but, by 1939, the 'Terriers' were once again prepared to defend King and Country, and once more in the numbers to furnish the first and second lines of Territorial Divisions – but that is another story.

1938 UK Huddersfield, 5DWR (43 AA Bn RE TA) Sound Ranging Equipment at St Pauls St Drill Hall

5 DWR was mobilised for World War 2 as a Searchlight Regiment RE, seeing action again, as infantry once more, despite its title of 600 Regiment RA, at the siege of Dunkirk in 1945.

The current unit occupying the Drill Hall, now termed Reserve Army Centre, is Corunna Company of the 4th Battalion The Yorkshire Regiment.

ACKNOWLEDGEMENTS

The compilers would like to thank all those who have helped and supported this book from its inception; the Trustees of the Huddersfield Drill Hall, for their encouragement and support; Jean Hancock, who helped with the original set up and layout; Richard Harvey for his invaluable help with the images and maps; Alan Stansfield, for allowing us to use the information painstakingly gathered by his late wife, Margaret, for her book 'Huddersfield's Roll of Honour 1914 - 1922', as well as his kind offer to proof read the draft for us; Graham Sargeant for his painstaking research; The staff of the Huddersfield Examiner for allowing us to publish the transcription of the 5th Battalion's exploits in WW1 from their pages in 1919; Dr Bill Smith, for allowing us to use information from his internet blog – tunstillsmen.blogspot.com; Derek Alexander for his time, patience and expertise in publishing this book; as well as the late Major Tom Goodall, for creating, and his family, for safekeeping and making available, his detailed records on H (later D) Company (Mirfield) of the 2/5th Battalion.

Finally, I would like to thank the relatives of those who are commemorated on the Drill Hall War Memorial Boards for making arrangements to visit the Drill Hall to pay their respects and, thereby, giving us the idea that these names should be remembered with pride. This led to the project for the refurbishment of the memorial boards in 2018, and the inspiration for this book - to make available more information concerning the men whose names are recorded.

Mr Derek Alexander, Valence House Museum Volunteer, visiting the Drill Hall in 2017, prior to the plans for refurbishment.

SELECT BIBLIOGRAPHY

Anon – *4th Bn DWR Casualty Record, Army Book 316* (France & Flanders, 1914-1918).

Ashworth, Tom – *Photos on the Wall*, (Huddersfield, 2015) ISBN 978-0-9569814-2-4.

Baker, Anthony – *Battle Honours of the British and Commonwealth Armies* (Ian Allen, 1986).

Bales, P G – *History of The 1/4th Battn Duke of Wellington's (WR) Regiment*, (Halifax, 1928).

Barker, Stephen – *Guiseley Terriers a small part in the Great War* (Pen and Sword, 2018) ISBN 978-1-52670-352-1.

Brooks, Andrew – *The Ingleton War Memorial 1914-1918 & 1939-1945*.

Bruce, C N, Brigadier – *History of The Duke of Wellington's Regiment [1st & 2nd Battalions 1881-1923]*. (The Medici Society, 1927).

Hornshaw, C R & Fowler, M W – *Calderdale War Dead a Biographical Index of the War Memorials of Calderdale*, (Privately published, 1995).
- *Calderdale War Dead*, Addendum.

Commonwealth War Graves Commission – publications (1986) and website (accessed May 2019).

Clayton, J T – *Craven's Part in the Great War* (Craven Pioneer and Chronicle, 1919).
and CPGW website – cpgw.org.uk (accessed May, 2019).

Ed – *Colne Valley Almanac*.

Ed – *The Huddersfield Examiner*.

Ed – *Officers Died in the Great War 1914-1919* – (War Office, September, 1921). Also available in CD Rom format, Naval and Military Press (Uckfield).

Ed – *Soldiers Died in the Great War 1914-1919 – Part 38*, (War Office, September, 1921). Reprinted by J B Hayward & Son, (1989), ISBN 1-871505-38-0. Also available in CD Rom format, Naval and Military Press (Uckfield).

Duke of Wellington's Regiment – *Regimental Rolls and Index Lists*.

Fisher, J J – *History of The Duke of Wellington's Regiment, August 1914 to December 1917*. (1917).

Ford, Cyril & Honley Civic Society – *Honley in the Great War* (Tempus, Honley, 2014) ISBN 13/928-0-957-2638-5-7.

Goodall collection – Major Tom Goodall: *diary, papers, documents, photographs and maps*. Copy held in the Royal Armouries, Leeds.

Green, Michael – *Nominal Roll of Territorial Force War Medal awards* (unpublished papers).
- *Nominal Roll of Silver War Badge awards* (unpublished papers).

Heywood, Brian – *Huddersfield in World War 1* (Upper Calder Valley Publications, 2014) ISBN 978-0-9547146-7-3.

Isles, Donald E, Maj Gen – *History of the Service Battalions in World War One*, (DWR/Reuben Holroyd Print, Halifax, 2007)

Leedham, Roger – *WW1 and Upper Hopton*, (Huddersfield, 2018).

Magnus, Laurie – *West Riding Territorials in The Great War*, (Keegan Paul, Trench, Trubner & Co, 1920).

Sargeant, G, et al, - *Death of the 'Dukes'*, (Valence House Publications 2017) ISBN 978-1-911391-99-9.

Stansfield, Margaret J – *Huddersfield's Roll of Honour 1914-1922*, J Margaret Stansfield, edited by Rev Paul Wilcock; (University of Huddersfield Press, 2014), ISBN 978-1-86218-126-7.

Tattersall, David – *A Village goes to War a History of the Men of Ravensthorpe who Fell in the Great War*, Barkers Trident Publications (2001) ISBN 978-0953468935.

Taylor, Keith – *Swaledale and Wharfedale Remembered*, (Ashridge Press Country Books, 2006) ISBN 1-901214-66-4

Thompson, Peter – *Barnoldswick, a small town's history 1800 to 2014*, (Barnoldswick Town Council, 2014).

Turpin, C – *Cleckheaton's Finest - First World War, Duke of Wellington's Regiment*, Unpublished booklet, (undated).

Vaughan, Rita – *Remember all the Boys, The Men of Mossley, Carrbrook and Luzley In The Great War (including 63 men born in Saddleworth)*. Unpublished booklet – mossley@btinternet.com, (2011).

Westlake, Ray – *Kitchener's Armies,* (Spellmount, 1998), ISBN 10-1873376987.

Wyrall, Everard – *The History of the 62nd (West Riding) Division 1914-1919*, (John Lane The Bodley Head Ltd, 1924-5). Reprinted by the Naval and Military Press (2003) ISBN 978-1843425823.

THE STATISTICS

The following chart and statistics illustrates the casualties suffered by the two front line battalions from Huddersfield and district during the war. The war weariness that set in during 1916 was accentuated by the even larger casualty list of 1917. However, the authorities stopped the publication of large casualty lists in the Press and were producing weekly HMSO booklets available, at a cost, to the public, as announced in the Huddersfield Examiner:

Mon 30 Jul 1917

CASUALTY LIST TO BE OBTAINED BY PUBLIC THROUGH BOOKSELLERS.

The Secretary of the War Office states that, as it has become impossible owing to the limitation of space imposed by the shortage of paper for newspapers to publish the full casualty list which is supplied to them, daily arrangements have been made for the issue of these lists by the Stationery Office in a weekly edition. Copies will be obtainable through any bookseller or from branches of the Stationery Office. The first issue will appear on Tuesday August 7th and this will be sold at the price of 3d per copy to cover cost of production or post free at 4d. Subscriptions will be received by the Stationery Office at the rate of 4 shillings per quarter including postage.

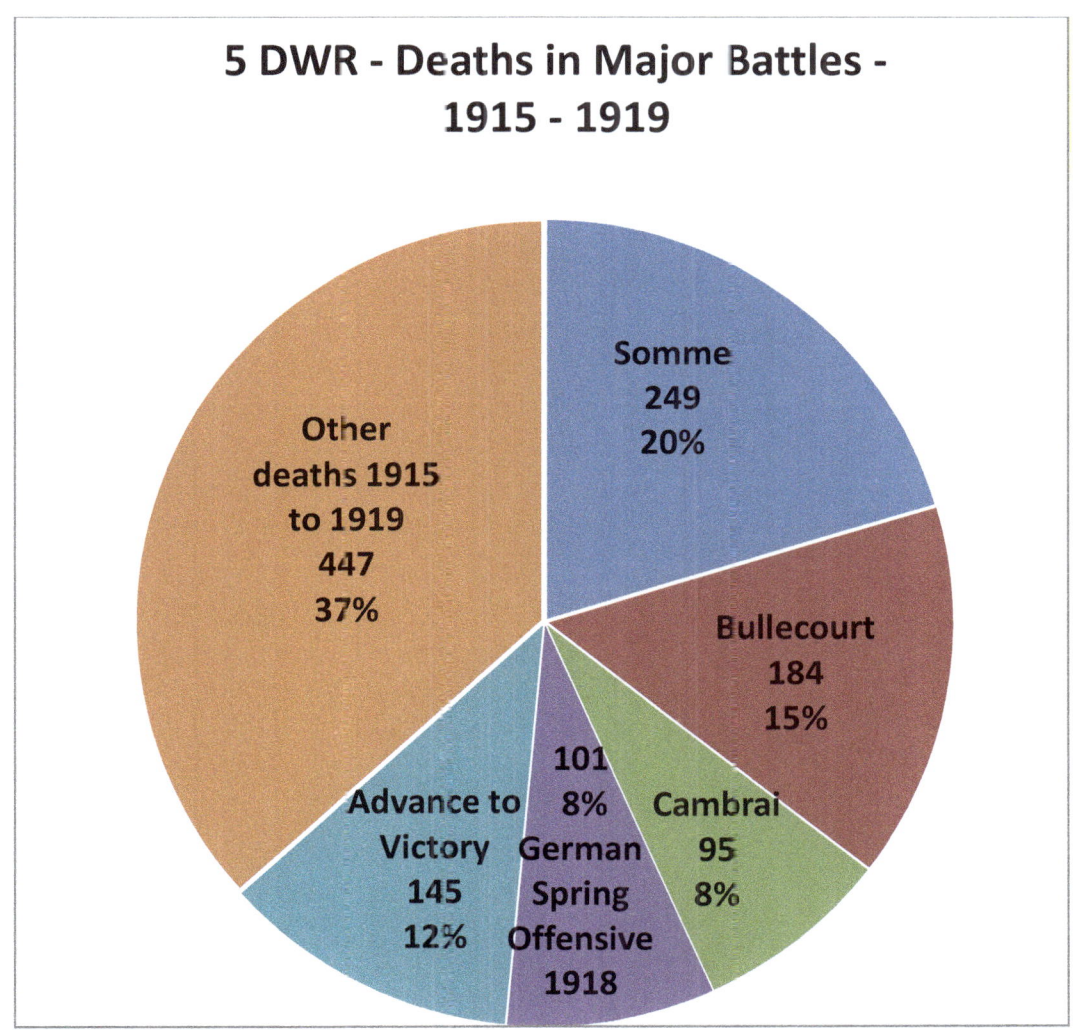

The Battle of the Somme was by far the greatest battle fought by the British Army, in scale if nothing else. It received great publicity, with picture houses screening films of the combat, which were very popular, found its way into the national psyche and is still remembered by school children today, by name if not for any great detail.

Year	Deaths
1915	108
1916	261
1917	463
1918	337
1919	5

Battles	Deaths
Somme	249
Bullecourt	184
Cambrai	95
German Spring Offensive	101
Advance to Victory	145
Other deaths 1915 to 1919	447

Statistics compiled by Graham Sargeant.

Soldiers were still dying in 1919, and beyond, of their wounds and there were approximately 578,000 soldiers in hospital at the signing of the Armistice, according to the Director General of Army Medical Services, as reported in the Huddersfield Examiner on Friday, 3rd October, 1919.

www.ingramcontent.com/pod-product-compliance
Lightning Source LLC
Chambersburg PA
CBHW042016090526
44588CB00023B/2877